SCHAUM'S OUTLINE OF

THEORY AND PROBLEMS

OF

COMPUTERS AND BUSINESS

•

by

LAWRENCE S. ORILIA, Ph.D.
Professor of Data Processing and Computer Science
Nassau Community College

•

SCHAUM'S OUTLINE SERIES
McGRAW-HILL BOOK COMPANY

New York   St. Louis   San Francisco   Auckland   Bogotá   Guatemala   Hamburg   Johannesburg
Lisbon   London   Madrid   Mexico   Montreal   New Delhi   Panama   Paris
San Juan   São Paulo   Singapore   Sydney   Tokyo   Toronto

LAWRENCE S. ORILIA is a full professor at Nassau Community College and has been teaching computer courses since 1969. He specializes in introductory data processing and programming courses and has been instrumental in developing them. Dr. Orilia has taught as an adjunct in the City University of New York system and has worked as an analyst in the CUNY Research Foundation. He has written *Introduction to Business Data Processing* (McGraw-Hill textbook, 1982), as well as books in the areas of business systems and computer operations. A current project relates to the integration of flowcharts, BASIC, and structured programming. Professor Orilia has also served as a consultant, applying his skills in the evaluation of computer manuscripts and the analysis of systems employed by various business organizations.

Schaum's Outline of Theory and Problems of
COMPUTERS AND BUSINESS

Copyright © 1984 by McGraw-Hill, Inc. All rights reserved. Printed in the United States of America. Except as permitted under the Copyright Act of 1976, no part of this publication may be reproduced or distributed in any form or by any means, or stored in a data base or retrieval system, without the prior written permission of the publisher.

1 2 3 4 5 6 7 8 9 10 11 12 13 14 15 16 17 18 19 20 SHP SHP 8 9 8 7 6 5 4

ISBN 0-07-047834-1

Sponsoring Editor, Elizabeth Zayatz
Editing Supervisor, Marthe Grice
Production Manager, Nick Monti

Library of Congress Cataloging in Publication Data

Orilia, Lawrence.
  Schaum's outline of theory and problems of computers
and business.

  (Schaum's outline series)
  Includes index.
  1. Business--Data processing--Outlines, syllabi, etc.
2. Business--Data processing--Problems, exercises, etc.
I. Title. II. Series.
HF5548.2.O689 1984   658'.054   83-16187
ISBN 0-07-047834-1

In memory of

Marie E. Orilia
Evelina E. Emmi, M.D.
Venera Emmi

Their commitment to education and the happiness they brought helped shape a family's character.

Preface

My aim in writing *Schaum's Outline of Computers and Business* was to provide business people embarking on a study of computerized data processing with a broad range of introductory topics. The content of this book ranges from fundamental computer codes to computerized networks supporting multinational corporations. *Schaum's Outline of Computers and Business* thereby provides its readers with a sound basis from which to continue their studies.

In presenting the material, I avoided the temptation to gloss over any information or to cover only currently popular topics. Concepts are developed from fundamental principles to their current forms, as is evident in the discussion of computer codes, where coding concepts are developed from the Hollerith code. By learning how and why computer codes were evolved, readers can apply that knowledge when working with computerized data.

Each chapter provides readers with an outline of the requisite theory and historical background of the topic. Solved problems then expand and illuminate the topic under discussion and are followed by review questions and supplementary problems, which reinforce the concepts presented and permit readers to test their comprehension. For easy reference, each chapter ends with a glossary.

In *Schaum's Outline of Computers and Business*, I attempted to write a book that was both informative and easy to read, despite the technical nature of computer-related topics. I hope that its readers will enjoy learning about one of the most fascinating and exciting fields in business, one that affects students, business people, and, in fact, all of society.

LAWRENCE S. ORILIA

Contents

Chapter 1   INTRODUCTION TO DATA PROCESSING CONCEPTS   1
- 1.1 Computer Factors   1
- 1.2 The EDP Cycle   1
- 1.3 Inventory Application   1

Chapter 2   COMPUTER SYSTEM COMPONENTS   12
- 2.1 A Computer System Overview   12
- 2.2 The Central Processing Unit (CPU)   13
- 2.3 Secondary Storage   13
- 2.4 Operational Software   13
- 2.5 Overlapped Processing   13
- 2.6 Virtual Storage (VS)   14

Chapter 3   COMPUTER CODES   30
- 3.1 The Hollerith Card   30
- 3.2 The Hollerith Code   30
- 3.3 Card Fields   30
- 3.4 Binary-Coded Decimal (BCD)   30
- 3.5 Extended Binary-Coded Decimal Interchangeable Code (EBCDIC)   31
- 3.6 American Standard Code for Information Interchange (ASCII)   31

Chapter 4   INPUT AND OUTPUT DEVICES   53
- 4.1 Card-Related Devices   53
- 4.2 Printing Devices   53
- 4.3 Terminals   53
- 4.4 Intelligent Devices   54
- 4.5 Word Processing (WP)   54
- 4.6 Data Processing Techniques for Business   54

Chapter 5   INFORMATION PROCESSING SYSTEMS   84
- 5.1 Online Processing Systems   84
- 5.2 Data Communications Facilities   84
- 5.3 Multiprogramming and Multiprocessing   84
- 5.4 Distributed Data Processing Systems (DDPS)   84
- 5.5 Distributed Word Processing Systems (DWPS)   85

CONTENTS

Chapter 6 INTRODUCTION TO PROGRAM LANGUAGES 100
- 6.1 Early Programming Languages 100
- 6.2 High-Level Languages 100
- 6.3 Modern Programming Languages 100
- 6.4 Program Execution 101
- 6.5 Program Specifications 101

Chapter 7 FLOWCHARTING 122
- 7.1 Flowcharting Documentation 122
- 7.2 Program Flowchart Loops 122
- 7.3 Looping Sequences 123
- 7.4 Accumulators 123
- 7.5 Additional Flowcharting Concepts 124

Chapter 8 STRUCTURED DESIGNS 154
- 8.1 Top-Down Design Concepts 154
- 8.2 HIPO Documentation 154
- 8.3 Control Block Structures 155
- 8.4 Structured Design Techniques 155
- 8.5 Pseudocode 155
- 8.6 The Personnel Involved 155

Chapter 9 SYSTEMS ANALYSIS AND DESIGN 185
- 9.1 The Systems Group and Its Analysts 185
- 9.2 Business Systems 185
- 9.3 Systems Analysis 186
- 9.4 Collecting Data 186
- 9.5 Systems Flowcharts 186
- 9.6 Design of the New System 187
- 9.7 The Feasibility Committee 187

Chapter 10 THE ROLE OF SECONDARY STORAGE 214
- 10.1 Introduction 214
- 10.2 Magnetic Disk 214
- 10.3 Magnetic Tape 214
- 10.4 Hardware Considerations 214
- 10.5 File Types 215
- 10.6 Related File Software 215

Chapter 11 MANAGEMENT INFORMATION SYSTEMS (MIS) 240
- 11.1 Introduction 240
- 11.2 Reporting Information to Management 240
- 11.3 MIS Configurations 240

CONTENTS

11.4 Database Structures	241
11.5 Administration of the Database	241
11.6 Information Management Systems (IMS)	241

Chapter 12 A SURVEY OF COMPUTER SYSTEMS **262**

12.1 Types of Computers	262
12.2 Microcomputers	262
12.3 Minicomputers	262
12.4 Four Computer Categories	263
12.5 Managerial Considerations in Purchasing New Computer Hardware	263

INDEX **287**

Chapter 1

Introduction to Data Processing Concepts

1.1 COMPUTER FACTORS

Three factors to consider when deciding whether to install a computer system are accuracy, reliability, and speed. *Accuracy* refers to a computer's ability to perform complex data manipulations and computations without error, for example, to carry out computations to six decimal points.

Reliability defines a computer's ability to accurately perform difficult tasks under all types of operating conditions. Maintenance requirements are considered along with reliability. Computers serviced on a regular basis are said to undergo *scheduled maintenance*. Emergency services, referred to as *unscheduled maintenance*, are performed whenever a computer malfunctions. The period of time that a computer is nonoperational is called *downtime*.

Speed describes a computer's ability to perform millions of computations each second. Two factors associated with a computer's speed are volume and frequency. *Volume* defines the total number of data items processed, whereas *frequency* notes the number of times a specific data item was processed.

1.2 THE EDP CYCLE

The three fundamental operations that make up the electronic data processing (*EDP*) *cycle* are input, processing, and output. *Input* is the entry of data into the computer, *processing* is the manipulation of data, and *output* is the retrieval of information in a predetermined format.

Data processing applications comprise a series of distinct, well-planned tasks. The *collection of data* represents the gathering of input data slated for processing. Input data are generally verified prior to entry into the computer. Input may take a variety of forms depending on the computer equipment available. Processing can include the manipulation of input data and the updating of a file. The output of printed reports can commence with the completion of processing. Manual operations instituted to check the accuracy of processing are referred to as *controls*.

Online devices have direct communication links to the computer, whereas *offline devices* do not and cannot interact with computers. In many applications, *raw data* drawn from *source documents* may be keyed directly to the computer via online terminal devices.

1.3 INVENTORY APPLICATION

The computerized handling of inventory data involves a series of well-planned activities. Inventory data are collected by manually gathering inventory logs. Each inventory usage log is scanned for accuracy, which is a validation operation. Data drawn from the inventory logs are keyed into the computer via online terminal devices. The data are then processed against existing inventory records to *update* the contents of the inventory file.

Reports are produced from data held in the updated inventory file and distributed to management for verification. This procedure is a good example of a control instituted to ensure the accuracy of processing. Reports provided to management are also used for decision-making purposes.

Solved Problems

COMPUTER FACTORS

1.1 Considering the expense involved in the installation of a computer system, the decision to convert to the computerized handling of data must be made on sound factors. What three factors should a business manager consider in this evaluation?

Accuracy, *reliability*, and *speed* are the three factors considered when a decision is made to computerize.

1.2 Why is accuracy an important factor?

Accuracy is a primary consideration because all computations undertaken by a computer must be performed without error. A computer will handle both routine and complex computations, and it must handle them properly.

1.3 Generally, when computer-related errors are detected, to whom should the errors be attributed?

In the majority of cases, mistakes attributed to computers are really the result of human error. Most mistakes are traced to the preparation and entry of faulty data by humans. The probability of computer error is quite small.

1.4 Are computers tested before installation?

Yes. Computer manufacturers spend literally hundreds of hours testing their equipment before installation. An equal amount of time and energy are expended testing the procedures used with computerized data handling activities.

1.5 Will good equipment alone ensure successful data processing operations?

No. For data processing activities to function smoothly, both the procedures used and equipment involved must properly interface. Good computer equipment cannot compensate for poorly prepared data. Conversely, error-free input data are useless on inoperable or malfunctioning equipment.

1.6 Why is reliability a vital factor?

Computers must operate for extended periods of time under adverse conditions without error.

1.7 Isn't it possible for computer equipment to break down?

Yes. Computers do malfunction and require servicing by trained technicians. When a computer is inoperable, the computer is said to be "down."

1.8 What does the term *downtime* mean?

Downtime refers to the amount of time a computer remains in a nonoperating, or down, state.

1.9 When are computers serviced?

Computer systems undergo two types of service—scheduled and unscheduled maintenance. *Scheduled maintenance* is performed on a regular basis (e.g., weekly) to ensure that the computer is operating up to standard. *Unscheduled maintenance* is performed whenever the computer malfunctions between scheduled maintenance sessions.

CHAP. 1] INTRODUCTION TO DATA PROCESSING CONCEPTS 3

1.10 About what percent of the time are most computers down?

Most computer systems are down well under 1 percent of the time.

1.11 Why is the factor of speed important when evaluating computers?

It is the speed of computers that makes it possible for them to perform the many tasks they undertake.

1.12 How fast do computers operate?

Modern computers are capable of performing, on the average, 3 million computations per second. Future computer systems are expected to execute more than 100 million computations per second. It is these extremely high processing speeds that enable computers to complete the most complex tasks in minutes.

1.13 How are computer speeds evaluated and compared?

The yardstick used to measure computer speeds is a rating of *millions of instructions per second*, or *MIPS*. The higher the MIPS rating, the greater the number of instructions executed in one second and the faster the computer. Computer speeds are compared in MIPS in much the same manner as car speeds are compared in miles per hour.

1.14 Two terms associated with the speed of computers are *volume* and *frequency*. How are these terms used?

Volume and frequency are used to describe the amounts of data handled by computers since the speed of computers will affect the quantity of data processed. *Volume* is defined as the total quantity of data handled by a computer. *Frequency* is defined as the number of times a specific data item was used in processing.

1.15 What are examples of volume and frequency, respectively?

An example of volume is the total number of telephone calls handled by a computerized message-switching system in one day. In contrast, an example of frequency is the number of times one specific telephone number is dialed.

1.16 Is it true that the EDP cycle may be used to generally describe a data processing operation?

Yes. Activities composing a data processing operation may be individually identified as either input, processing, or output. These are the three fundamental operations of the EDP cycle (Fig. 1-1).

Input → Processing → Output

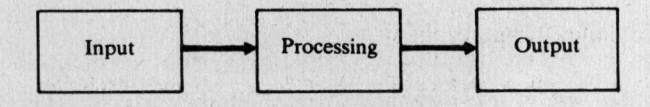

Fig. 1-1 The EDP cycle.

1.17 Define the three operations composing the EDP cycle.

(1) *Input*: the entry of data into the computer system
(2) *Processing*: the manipulation of data
(3) *Output*: the retrieval of information in a predetermined format

1.18 Why is the term *input* broadly defined as "the entry of data into a computer"?

This definition recognizes that many methods are available for entering data into a computer, including computer cards and a variety of other devices (as discussed in later chapters).

1.19 What is the operational significance of the input operation?

The operational importance of input lies in the fact that it is one of the first tasks undertaken to begin processing.

1.20 Why is the definition of *processing* equally broad?

Processing represents a wide range of activities and is not restricted solely to arithmetic operations.

1.21 What arithmetic operations can the computer perform?

The computer can perform the basic operations of addition, subtraction, multiplication, and division. Other operations such as exponentiation, that is, raising a number to a power (for example, X^2), are also possible. In fact, any arithmetic operation could be used to develop the answer to a problem.

1.22 In addition to arithmetic manipulations, what other types of activities could processing represent?

The processing operation could, for example, represent the comparison of two data items, the sorting of a group of data into numerical order, or the movement of data between two storage locations within a computer system.

1.23 What is a common misconception related to processing operations?

Many people believe that processing is restricted to performing only arithmetic operations, and they overlook the varied processing activities that do not involve numeric manipulations.

1.24 The definition of *output* notes specifically the retrieval of information, not data. Why?

The term *information* refers to the results of processing, whereas the term *data* refers to input.

1.25 What type of data is used in processing?

It is *raw data* that is input to the computer and used in processing to develop the useful facts and figures called *information*.

1.26 How does raw data differ from information?

Raw data is provided to the computer as an input, whereas information is the product of processing and presented to users via output operations.

1.27 In the definition of *output*, why is the word *retrieval* used?

Retrieval denotes some form of selectivity and planning as to what information is desired from all the data stored within a computer.

1.28 Why must the information output appear in a predetermined format?

Information cannot be retrieved haphazardly from a computer. Prior to any processing activities, the operator must carefully detail how the outputs should appear. Thus the operator predetermines the output format desired and then instructs the computer to provide it in exactly that manner.

1.29 How are these instructions given to the computer?

All instructions are supplied to the computer in the form of a computer *program*. The program will direct the computer via carefully written instructions, in all the activities it undertakes.

INVENTORY APPLICATION

1.30 Are all the EDP cycle operations directed from a computer program?

Yes. All input, processing, and output operations are initiated from the carefully prepared instructions in a computer program. Each instruction may be considered a statement that directs the computer to perform an input, processing, or output operation.

INVENTORY APPLICATION

1.31 Does the ordering of tasks within a data processing application require much planning?

Computerized processing always represents a methodical, well-thought-out series of events. Many hours of planning are expended to ensure the efficient processing of data.

1.32 Using the framework of an inventory application, what are the major steps likely to be encountered in handling such data?

The major steps taken in the handling of inventory data are illustrated in Fig. 1-2. The individual steps denote major operational tasks within this procedure.

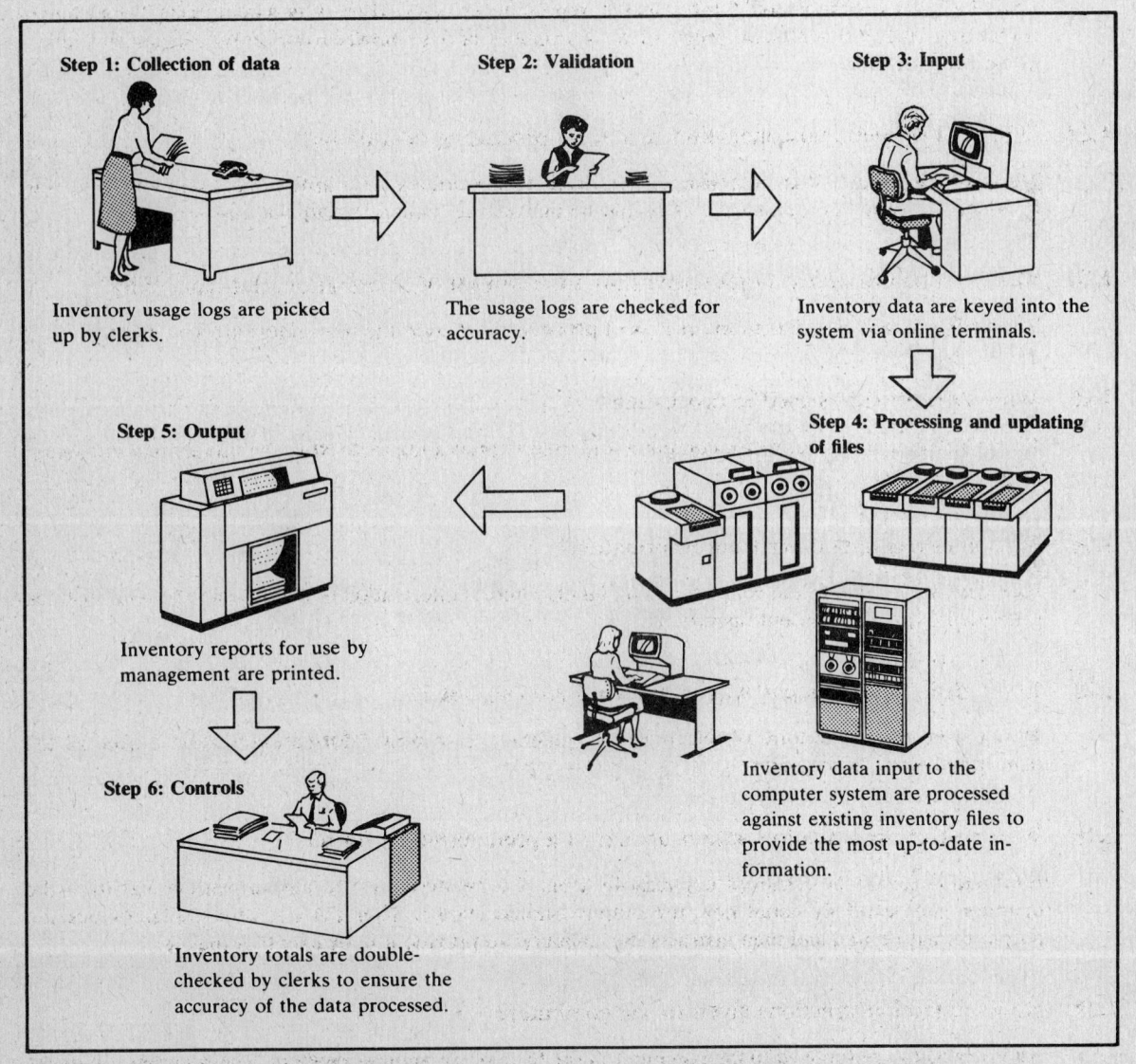

Step 1: Collection of data
Inventory usage logs are picked up by clerks.

Step 2: Validation
The usage logs are checked for accuracy.

Step 3: Input
Inventory data are keyed into the system via online terminals.

Step 4: Processing and updating of files
Inventory data input to the computer system are processed against existing inventory files to provide the most up-to-date information.

Step 5: Output
Inventory reports for use by management are printed.

Step 6: Controls
Inventory totals are double-checked by clerks to ensure the accuracy of the data processed.

Fig. 1-2 The six major steps employed in the computerized handling of inventory data.

1.33 What purpose does step 1 in Fig. 1-2 serve?

Step 1 represents the collection of data, where data designated for processing are collected at one central point.

1.34 In the preceding example, data are collected manually. Is that always the case?

No. Data may be collected either manually or via some automated means. The mode of collection reflects the resources made available by the organization for that purpose. In many organizations, computer-related devices are used to collect data and speed it to the computer for processing.

1.35 Why is the proper collection of data important?

Disorganized, erratic data collection procedures often result in input errors, which are then carried through the entire EDP cycle. Thus the positional importance of sound data collection procedures cannot be overlooked.

1.36 Why are the inventory logs called *source documents*?

The term *source document* refers to documents from which data is removed and used in a data processing sequence. For example, inventory logs are a source of data which can be used to process inventory information.

1.37 Why are the inventory logs checked in step 2 of Fig. 1-2?

The data in the inventory logs are verified to ensure completeness and correctness. This procedure permits the clerk to correct any erroneous data before they are input to the computer.

1.38 What examples might illustrate the verification of a data item?

The verification effort might focus on the correction of an inventory part number that was incorrectly recorded in the log or on the insertion of digits missing from a partially entered data entry (that is, only four of six required digits were recorded).

1.39 Once the inventory logs are checked, how are the data entered into the computer system?

Data are input to the computer via an online device called a *terminal*, part of which is a keyboard. Thus as inventory data are being typed, or "keyed," they are also being transmitted to the system.

1.40 What does the word *online* signify?

The term *online* denotes that a direct communication link exists between the terminal and the computer such that both devices are capable of interacting directly. With an online device, data keyed via a terminal are directly input to the computer.

1.41 What term is applied to devices that are not directly tied to a computer system?

The term *offline* is assigned to devices that do not have a direct communication link to the computer and cannot interact with it. Data keyed into an offline terminal will not be directly transmitted to a computer. (A terminal is offline until the common link is activated.)

1.42 What operations follow the input of the inventory data?

As step 4 of Fig. 1-2 depicts, the inventory data are processed within the computer system.

CHAP. 1]   INTRODUCTION TO DATA PROCESSING CONCEPTS   7

1.43 Within the processing cycle, what tasks are undertaken?

The new inventory data are compared to the existing file of inventory information. The data input is used to update the inventory file. This processing might involve adding some items to or removing other items from the existing inventory.

1.44 What will be the net effect of these processing activities?

All data held within the inventory file will be current information; thus the reports produced on the basis of this will be up to date.

1.45 Why was the term *file* used to describe a group of inventory data?

In computer terminology a *file* denotes a classified grouping of data. All data to be stored within a computer must be categorized into files. Without this form of organization it is impossible to process data efficiently.

1.46 Would part numbers be sufficient to organize a file of inventory data?

Yes. The inventory file would be sequenced in ascending numerical order by part number. Any data item within the inventory file could be readily accessed by using a specific part number.

1.47 What is the general term applied to modification of data within a computerized file?

The term *updating* applies to the general range of data processing activities.

1.48 With the updating of the inventory file complete, may the output of inventory reports commence?

Yes. Because the updated files reflect the most current inventory status, the output of printed reports is appropriate. It has already been determined what format these reports will assume; thus they can be quickly generated and distributed. Step 5 of Fig. 1-2 represents this activity.

1.49 How will these reports be used?

Generally these reports will be used to monitor the use of inventory materials and provide information concerning the status of parts held within that inventory; for example, how many units of a specific part are on hand? when were new parts ordered? how many parts are used per week?

1.50 More specifically, how might an inventory clerk use this information?

An inventory clerk might cross-reference data printed in the report against actual invoices. For example, the report may indicate that ten units of a part were placed into inventory, whereas an actual invoice might note that a total of fifteen units were received by the company. The discrepancy of five units would have to be checked.

1.51 What could cause a difference in totals?

Frequently items received are examined by inspectors, rejected as being damaged, and returned to the issuing company. Thus the quantity of units accepted into inventory may differ from the total amount ordered and received.

1.52 Is there a special name normally assigned to this checking activity performed by the clerk?

Yes. The comparison of reported and actual totals is generally referred to as a *control*. Controls are applied to minimize errors and check the results of processing.

1.53 Is the use of controls restricted to outputs?

No. Controls may be applied to any aspect of the computerized processing of data. They are especially important when financial or politically sensitive data items are processed.

Review Questions

1.54 Considerations related to the installation of a computer system include accuracy, reliability, processing potential, and speed. (*a*) True, (*b*) false.

1.55 Reliability is a factor identified with the computer's ability to function under adverse conditions and provide consistently accurate results. (*a*) True, (*b*) false.

1.56 Downtime is the period of time a computer remains idle between processing different jobs. (*a*) True, (*b*) false.

1.57 *Frequency* relates to the number of times a specific data item is accessed during processing. (*a*) True, (*b*) false.

1.58 A computer that is currently nonoperational is said to be "down." (*a*) True, (*b*) false.

1.59 The three fundamental operations used to describe a data processing operation are referred to as the EDP cycle. (*a*) True, (*b*) false.

1.60 The term *input* refers to the entry of data into a computer system. (*a*) True, (*b*) false.

1.61 Output operations are primarily designed to present data in its raw, unprocessed state. (*a*) True, (*b*) false.

1.62 Outputs need not be defined prior to a computer's preparation of them. (*a*) True, (*b*) false.

1.63 The positional importance of the collection of data in the overall processing cycle is minimal. (*a*) True, (*b*) false.

1.64 Data collection activities are always manually performed. (*a*) True, (*b*) false.

1.65 The verification of input data ensures the completeness and correctness of that data, prior to its input for processing. (*a*) True, (*b*) false.

1.66 Input data keyed via an offline terminal will be directly communicated to the computer for immediate processing. (*a*) True, (*b*) false.

1.67 A *file* is a grouping of data with no organizational scheme required. (*a*) True, (*b*) false.

1.68 The results of processing data against a file should produce the most up-to-date status of that information. (*a*) True, (*b*) false.

1.69 The information in printed outputs should be in a format that is appropriate for presentation to management. (*a*) True, (*b*) false.

1.70 A computer's capacity to perform complex computations without error is called (*a*) accuracy, (*b*) reliability, (*c*) speed, (*d*) efficiency.

1.71 Service activities performed on an as-needed basis are normally referred to as (*a*) scheduled maintenance, (*b*) contract maintenance, (*c*) unscheduled maintenance, (*d*) service engineering.

1.72 The total number of daily charge sales handled by a computer is an example of (*a*) quantity, (*b*) frequency, (*c*) volume, (*d*) speed.

1.73 Current computer systems are capable of performing an average of (*a*) 3 MIPS, (*b*) 30 MIPS, (*c*) 300 MIPS, (*d*) 3000 MIPS.

1.74 An example of a processing operation is (*a*) computations related to a formula, (*b*) the comparison of two data items, (*c*) the ordering of data into a desired sequence, (*d*) all of the above.

1.75 Facts made available in their unprocessed state are generally referred to as (*a*) collected data, (*b*) raw data, (*c*) statistics, (*d*) information.

1.76 Instructions related to the processing of data are input to the computer in the form of a(n) (*a*) output statement, (*b*) typed message, (*c*) program, (*d*) raw data item.

1.77 The gathering of data to be processed is called (*a*) data investigation, (*b*) data collection, (*c*) data input, (*d*) all of the above.

1.78 A document from which data to be used in processing are drawn is called a(n) (*a*) source document, (*b*) input document, (*c*) original document, (*d*) manual document.

1.79 A direct communication link to a computer is denoted by the term (*a*) offline, (*b*) online, (*c*) interact, (*d*) terminal.

1.80 The term used to denote activities relating to the modification of data within a file, to produce the most current data status, is (*a*) maintenance, (*b*) file processing, (*c*) updating, (*d*) report/file generation.

1.81 Operations performed to ensure the accuracy of processing are referred to as (*a*) controls, (*b*) updating, (*c*) validation, (*d*) verification activities.

1.82 A computer's accuracy relates to its ability to properly perform both routine and complex _____.

1.83 Most computer-related errors are the result of _____ mistakes made within data handling procedures.

1.84 When a computer is nonoperational, it is said to be _____.

1.85 The term _____ identifies a rating that may be used to compare the operating speeds of various computer systems.

1.86 The total number of shares handled by the New York Stock Exchange's computerized brokerage system is an example of _____.

1.87 The total number of times the price of a specific stock is quoted is an example of _____.

1.88 The three operations composing the EDP cycle are _____, _____, and _____.

1.89 The manipulation of data is a broad definition applied to _____.

1.90 In the definition of an output, the term *information* is used to differentiate between facts that have been processed and _____ data.

1.91 Instructions to the computer regarding the EDP cycle appear in the form of a computer _____.

1.92 In a computer program, each statement represents a specific _____ to the computer to undertake an input, processing, or output operation.

1.93 The _____ of raw data, prior to processing, ensures its completeness and correctness.

1.94 The term *online* denotes that a(n) _____ communication link exists between a device and the computer with which it interacts.

1.95 A terminal not directly linked to a computer is referred to as a(n) _____ device.

1.96 After processing, the _____ file should contain the most current data available.

1.97 Controls are utilized to minimize costly _____ and should be applied when critical data items are processed.

Answers: 1.54 (b); 1.55 (a); 1.56 (b); 1.57 (a); 1.58 (a); 1.59 (a); 1.60 (a); 1.61 (b); 1.62 (b); 1.63 (b); 1.64 (b); 1.65 (a); 1.66 (b); 1.67 (b); 1.68 (a); 1.69 (a); 1.70 (a); 1.71 (c); 1.72 (c); 1.73 (a); 1.74 (d); 1.75 (b); 1.76 (c); 1.77 (b); 1.78 (a); 1.79 (b); 1.80 (c); 1.81 (a); 1.82 computations; 1.83 human; 1.84 down; 1.85 MIPS; 1.86 volume; 1.87 frequency; 1.88 input, processing, output; 1.89 processing; 1.90 raw; 1.91 program; 1.92 instruction; 1.93 verification; 1.94 direct; 1.95 offline; 1.96 updated; 1.97 errors.

Supplementary Problems

1.98 In your own words, define the following terms:

        Controls   Reliability
        File   Speed
        Frequency   Updating
        Online   Volume

1.99 Explain the EDP cycle and the three operations that comprise it. Why is it possible to describe any data processing application using these three operations?

1.100 Examine Fig. 1-3 and answer the following questions.
    (*a*) Controls are applied in step _____?
    (*b*) Input operations are performed in step _____?
    (*c*) The collection of data occurs in step _____?

1.101 Prepare a list of computer applications. Describe how you believe the computer is used in each case.

Glossary

Accuracy. The computer's capability to perform complex computations without error.

Collection of data. An initial task in a data processing application involving the gathering of input data to be used in processing.

Controls. Checks applied to the results of processing to minimize errors and ensure the accuracy of processing.

Downtime. The period of time that a computer spends in a nonoperative state.

EDP cycle. The three fundamental operations of input, processing, and output that make up a data processing operation.

File. An organized grouping of data.

Frequency. The number of times a particular data item is accessed during processing.

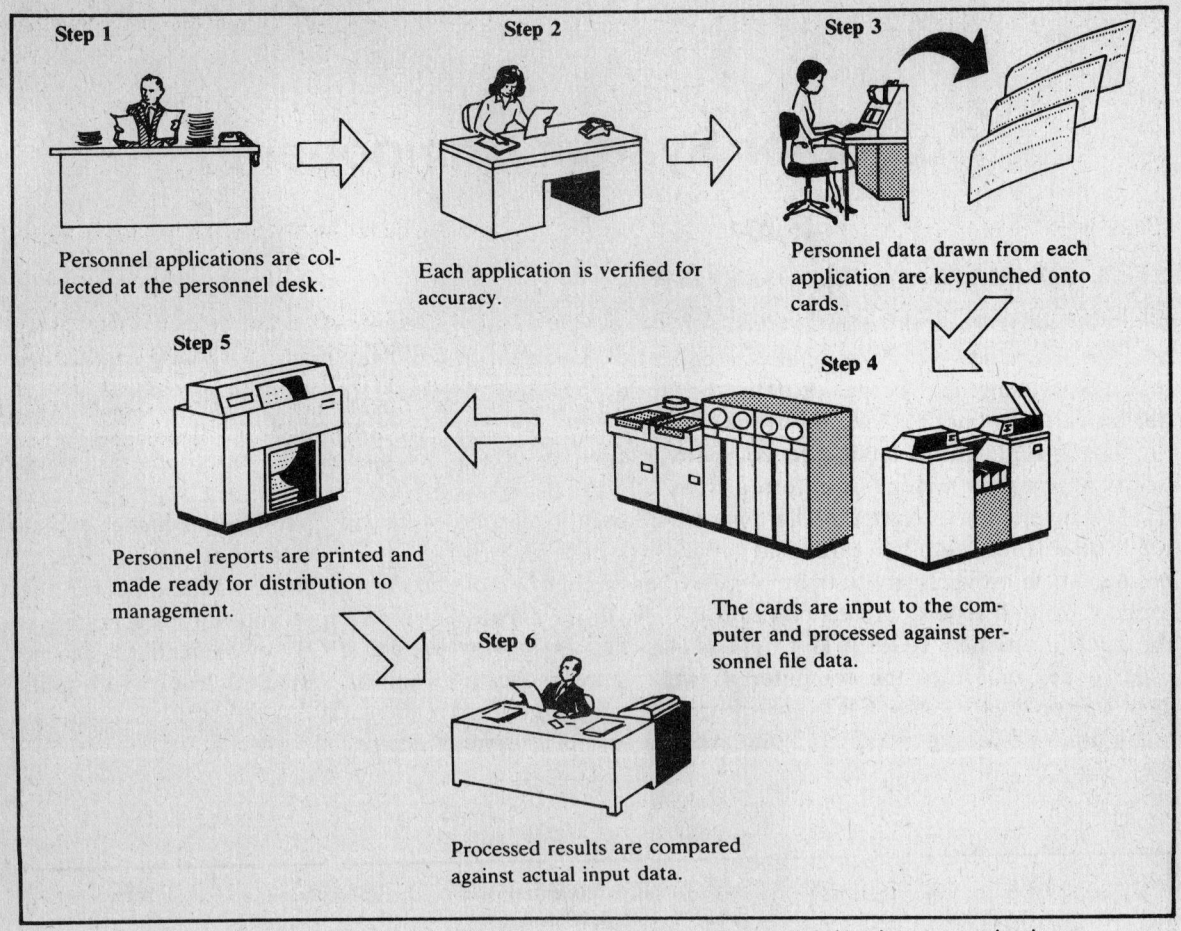

Fig. 1-3 The major steps involved in the processing of personnel data in an organization.

Input. The entry of data into a computer system.

Millions of instructions per second (MIPS). A measure of computer speed based on the number of instructions that are executed in one second.

Offline. The condition in which direct communication with a computer is not possible.

Online. A direct communication link exists to the computer, and interaction with the computer is possible.

Output. The retrieval of information in a predetermined format.

Processing. The manipulation of data.

Program. The detailed list of instructions provided to the computer to direct all phases of processing.

Raw data. Input data in its preprocessed state.

Reliability. The computer's ability to repeatedly perform processing tasks under all types of operating conditions.

Scheduled maintenance. Regular maintenance performed on computer systems.

Source document. A document from which input data are drawn and used in processing.

Speed. The computer's ability to amass, process, and present data in millionths of a second.

Unscheduled maintenance. Special maintenance activities performed when a computer enters a down, nonoperative state.

Updating. Modifications processed against an existing file to provide the most current information on file.

Volume. The total quantity of data processed.

Chapter 2

Computer System Components

2.1 A COMPUTER SYSTEM OVERVIEW

A computer system is composed of many devices that make possible the computerized processing of data. These devices are generally categorized in terms of the specific functions they perform: the input, processing, and output of data, the three functions composing the EDP cycle. Some devices perform only an input or an output function, whereas other units can accomplish both.

The general term applied to computer-related devices is *hardware*. The programs processed within a computer system are referred to as *software*.

A representative computer hardware configuration is shown in Fig. 2-1. A *card reader*, which reads data from computer cards and inputs that data for processing, is one form of *input device*. A *printer*, which provides printed outputs, is an example of an *output device*. Outputs that appear in the form of printed reports are called *hardcopy*. A device capable of both input and output activities is the *cathode ray tube* (*CRT*). The CRT is classified as an *input-output* (*I/O*) *device* in that it can be used to key data into the computer as well as to display information retrieved from it. Outputs displayed on the screens of CRTs are referred to as *softcopy*. Card readers, CRTs, and printers, as well as many other devices, generally fall into the category of *peripheral devices*.

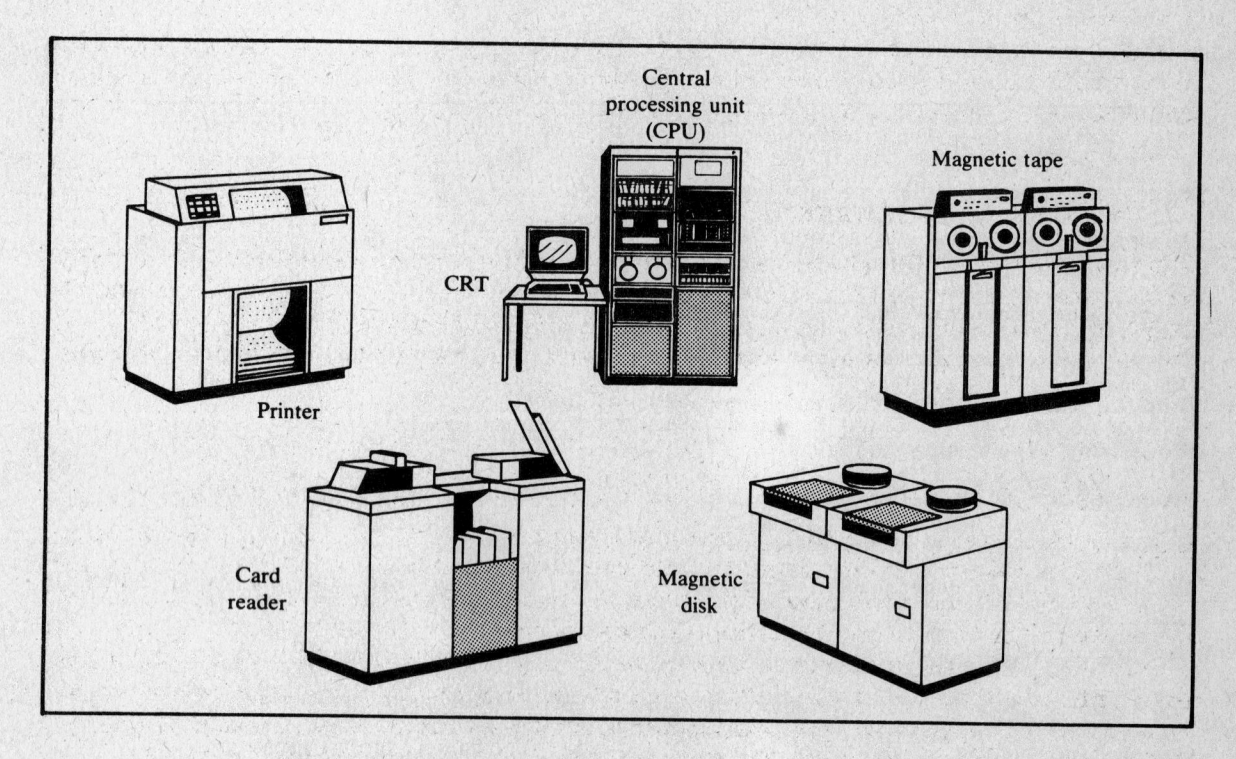

Fig. 2-1 A computer system is composed of many devices. The computer hardware shown in this system includes a card reader, line printer, cathode ray tube (CRT), central processing unit (CPU), and magnetic tape and magnetic disk units.

All processing within a computer system is performed within, and under the control of, the *central processing unit* (*CPU*). No processing is undertaken without the support of the CPU. *Secondary storage* units, such as *magnetic tapes* and *magnetic disks*, retain data that have been or will be used in processing. Data held in secondary storage are directly accessible for processing by the CPU.

2.2 THE CENTRAL PROCESSING UNIT (CPU)

The central processing unit is the hub of all processing activities in the computer system. Programs being processed are held in the CPU during their execution. The three major CPU components are the control unit, arithmetic-logic unit, and primary storage unit. The *control unit* oversees the execution of all programs processed by a computer. The *arithmetic-logic unit* is responsible for arithmetic and logical comparisons between two items of data. The *primary storage unit* is the main storage area of the computer system. All data and programs being processed are stored in primary storage during their execution.

The storage capacity of a system's CPU is directly related to the size of its primary storage unit. These storage capacities vary among different computers. The symbol K is a shorthand convention adopted to denote the storage of 1,024 bytes of data. Generally 1 *byte* is said to be equal to one character of data. A CPU of 4K, for example, has primary storage capacity of 4,096 bytes of storage.

2.3 SECONDARY STORAGE

Data that are essential to processing but that cannot be retained in primary storage are assigned to secondary storage. Data held in secondary storage must be immediately accessible to the CPU in a format that is directly usable by it.

Two principal means of secondary storage in current computer systems are magnetic tape and disk. Magnetic tape is used for sequential storage, whereas magnetic disk is used for direct access of storage. Sequential access to data is considerably slower than direct access.

2.4 OPERATIONAL SOFTWARE

Though the control unit plays a critical part in the supervision of programs executed within a computer system, it does not perform these activities alone. It is aided by the *operational software* incorporated into a computer system. Because the processing capabilities of a system are defined by its operational software, two equivalent computer systems with comparable hardware may possess radically different processing capabilities.

2.5 OVERLAPPED PROCESSING

Early computers were referred to as *dedicated systems* because of their inability to handle two or more activities concurrently. These systems proceeded to a second task only when the first one was finished. A disadvantage of this kind of system was the minimal usage of the CPU since the CPU was constrained by the speed of its I/O devices—a condition known as *I/O bound*.

A technique called *overlapped processing* overcomes the I/O-bound problem, enabling the computer to output one program's results, process another program's data, and input data relating to a third program all at one time. This is accomplished through the use of *channels*, devices attached to the CPU that assume control over I/O operations once they have been initiated by the CPU. The CPU commences the I/O activity, directs the channel to assume control over that task, and turns its attention to processing. Overlapped processing techniques may also make use of *buffers*, which are storage areas that temporarily retain data for I/O operations. Channels supervise the storage of I/O data in buffers in preparation for their use.

2.6 VIRTUAL STORAGE (VS)

Virtual storage (*VS*) techniques were developed to overcome problems that arose when a limited amount of primary storage was available in a CPU. In many of the smaller computer systems, this limitation restricted the processing of large programs. Virtual storage takes a large program and divides it into modules of equal size called *pages*. Each page is processed as needed, swapping its position on disk with the page undergoing processing in the CPU. Though initially developed for smaller systems, most current computers possess some type of VS supporting software.

Solved Problems

A COMPUTER SYSTEM OVERVIEW

2.1 Can the three functions—input, processing, and output—of the EDP cycle be associated with a computer system?

Yes. Just as it is possible to define the elements of the EDP cycle, components of a computer system may be identified as input, processing, and output devices.

Note: Problems 2.2–2.12 relate to Fig. 2-1.

2.2 What classification is assigned to the card reader in Fig. 2-1?

The card reader is considered an input device because it can read data punched onto computer cards and input that data into the computer.

2.3 Why is the card reader solely an input device?

The card reader can only input data to the computer; it does not possess any processing or output capabilities.

2.4 Is the card reader the only input device available within the computer system shown in Fig. 2-1?

No. Another input device shown is the *visual display terminal*, or CRT. The initials *CRT* stand for cathode ray tube, the television-like picture tube on which data keyed into the CRT are displayed.

2.5 Does the CRT also display data transmitted from the computer?

Yes. Data issued by the computer are also displayed on the CRT screen. Thus, the CRT has an output capability.

2.6 What term is applied to devices, such as the CRT, that can be used for both input and output operations?

Generally devices capable of performing both input and output operations are referred to as *input/output devices* or simply *I/O devices*.

2.7 Is the printer shown in Fig. 2-1 also considered an I/O device?

No. The printer (sometimes called a *line printer*) is only an output device.

CHAP. 2] COMPUTER SYSTEM COMPONENTS 15

2.8 What does the printer do?

The printer receives data processed by the computer and outputs it as information in a format predetermined by the computer program. The printer operates at high speeds when outputting printed report materials.

2.9 What are the differences between the outputs provided by the CRT and those provided by the printer?

The CRT displays information on its screen in a nonpermanent form, whereas the printer displays information on paper in a tangible form. Printed documents are permanent records of the data that have been processed.

2.10 What terms are applied to the outputs described in Prob. 2.9 to distinguish between them?

The term *softcopy* is applied to nonpermanent outputs, such as those of CRTs. Printed outputs that assume a more permanent form are called *hardcopy*.

2.11 What are examples of hardcopy and softcopy outputs?

A monthly report on all personnel employed by a company is an example of hardcopy. The same report displayed on a CRT screen is an example of softcopy. Figure 2-2 compares these two types of output.

```
SSN:  099-38-7752

EMPLOYEE NAME:  BARLETT, CHRIS G.

TITLE:  MANAGER, NORTH AM DIVISION

CODE:  GRADE-27

LAST PROMOTION:  6/13/79, FROM GRADE-23

SALARY:  $26,540       FROM:  $23,500

REVIEW DATE:  11/3/82   BY:  C. SMITH, VP-NAD
```

(*a*) An excerpt of a printed report.

CUST NUMBER	RUN CODE	CUSTOMER NAME	ADDRESS 1	CITY	ZIP CODE
105	5	E J ELECTRIC	39 E.21 ST.	NY,NY	10010
116	16	P&A CONSTRUCTION	22 W. MAIN	MERRICK	11582
125	24	YY CONCRETE	649 HEMP TPKE	FRANKLIN SQ	11010
1003	243	CAJUN-CRAWLER	71B MARSHALL	FARMINGDALE	11735
1004	31	BOMACK FLEET INC	39-04 WALL ST	LIC, NY	11106
1009	55	I E V CORP	66-53 BRIDGE	NY,NY	10004
1029	237	PETES PLUMBING	3 BRONX EXPWY	BRONX, NY	10457
10045	87	JACKSON LIGHTS INC	224 CONEY AVE	BROOKLYN, NY	12236
10266	6	BRONCO MOTORS	35 N. BLVD.	BAYSIDE, NY	11364
13390	201	DWYER SCAFFOLDS	552 MARTINWAY	CHAPPAQUA, NY	12408

(*b*) An excerpt of a visual display of data.

Fig. 2-2 Computer outputs can appear as printed documents, called hardcopy, or as visual displays, called softcopy.

2.12 Are card readers, CRTs, and printers the only input and output devices available?

No. A variety of other I/O devices exists to satisfy a wide range of user needs. Many more of these devices will be discussed in later chapters.

2.13 What is the general term applied to I/O devices incorporated into computer systems?

I/O devices are generally referred to as *peripheral devices*. Card readers, CRTs, and printers are some examples of peripheral devices.

2.14 What general terms are used to distinguish between the equipment that makes up a computer system and the programs that are used to process data within it?

The term *hardware* applies to the mechanical equipment and devices that make up a computer system. The term *software* refers to the computer programs that are used to direct the hardware in its handling and processing of data. Peripheral devices, for example, fall into the category of hardware.

2.15 If I/O devices support the handling of input and output operations, where does the actual processing of data occur?

All processing activities occur within the central processing unit (CPU). Without the CPU, no processing takes place.

2.16 What does the CPU do?

The central processing unit oversees all processing activities undertaken by the computer and ensures that they are properly handled. (The components and specific responsibilities of the CPU are covered in Probs. 2.20–2.36.)

2.17 If processing is undertaken within the CPU, what function do the magnetic tape and disk units play?

These units, which are secondary storage units, retain data that cannot be held in the CPU. Magnetic tapes and magnetic disks greatly increase the computer's storage capacity.

2.18 What is the operational impact of secondary storage?

Computerized data files are stored on secondary storage devices. Data within these files can be obtained by the CPU in thousandths of a second, making possible the speedy processing of a vast amount of data. (For an in-depth discussion of secondary storage, see Probs. 2.37–2.44.)

2.19 What is an illustration of the use of secondary storage files?

Consider the case of a company's charge account file retained in secondary storage. Changes to customer accounts (such as payments or new charges) may be entered via a CRT to the computer. Because these files are retained in secondary storage, the processing of this new charge data is readily accomplished.

THE CENTRAL PROCESSING UNIT (CPU)

2.20 Why is the CPU the focal point of all processing activities within a computer system?

All processing must occur within the CPU, under the direction of a program that is also there. Data are brought to the CPU, processed, and then stored elsewhere in the computer system (e.g., in secondary storage), or they are issued in the form of output (e.g., printed reports).

2.21 During processing operations, must all data utilized in any form of processing and all supporting programs occupy the CPU for a period of time?

Yes. The time these materials remain in the CPU is related to the nature of the processing being performed. Complex processing tasks will generally utilize the resources of the CPU to a greater extent and for longer periods of time.

2.22 What specific units comprise the CPU?

As shown in Fig. 2-3, the CPU comprises three units:
(1) The control unit
(2) The arithmetic-logic unit (ALU)
(3) The primary storage unit

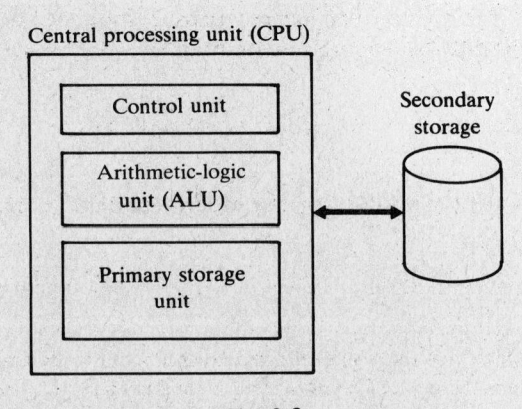

Fig. 2-3

2.23 Does each unit have a specific function?

Yes. Each CPU component has a unique function for which it is solely responsible. Thus, for example, the control unit and arithmetic-logic unit will not overlap in their responsibilities.

2.24 What is the function of the control unit?

As its name implies, the control unit oversees the processing being performed. The control unit is responsible for

(1) Monitoring the execution of all jobs processed by the system
(2) Facilitating the execution of I/O operations
(3) Coordinating the transfer of data between storage areas and secondary storage

In effect, the control unit is responsible for monitoring the use of the computer system's resources.

2.25 What role does the arithmetic-logic unit play, and how is its function related to the main function of the control unit?

The control unit can perform many supervisory functions, but it cannot perform any arithmetic or logical operations. These tasks are assigned to the arithmetic-logic unit (ALU).

2.26 What is considered an arithmetic operation?

Any of the basic operations of addition, subtraction, multiplication, and division qualify as arithmetic operations—all of which the arithmetic-logic unit can handle.

2.27 Is it true that each of these operations is handled as an addition operation in the ALU?

Yes. Due to the internal construction of the ALU, all arithmetic manipulations are handled as addition.

2.28 What is a logical operation?

A *logical operation* is merely a comparison of two values. Using a logical operation, it is possible to compare two numbers or two sets of alphabetic characters. Thus in a payroll application, we could determine whether an employee has worked the regular 40-hour week (HOURS = 40?) and his or her managerial level (MANAGEMENT LEVEL = 'A'?).

2.29 What CPU component is involved in handling arithmetic and logical operations of the ALU?

The CPU unit supporting ALU activities is the *register*. Registers are temporary storage areas that hold data during the completion of logical and arithmetic operations. The number of registers available in a CPU varies, depending on the computer model and manufacturer.

2.30 Where are the data stored that are being processed?

The principal storage area of a computer system is the CPU's primary storage unit. Each data item being processed must stay in primary storage prior to its processing.

2.31 Must data drawn from the system's secondary storage units also go to the CPU for processing?

Yes. Data drawn from these storage units will enter the CPU and be stored in primary storage before being processed. Once processing is complete, that data will stay in primary storage before being returned to secondary storage.

2.32 How is the capacity of primary storage measured?

Storage capacities of primary storage are assessed in terms of *bytes* of storage. Generally, 1 byte of storage is capable of holding the equivalent of one character of data. Thus it would require 5 bytes of storage to store the word *party*. A CPU is said to have a capacity of so many thousands or millions of bytes of storage.

2.33 What shorthand notation is used in references to CPU storage capacity?

The letter K, which is equal to 1024 bytes of storage, is used in simplified estimates of primary storage. Thus a CPU is said to have a capacity of approximately 64K, which is equal to 65,536 bytes of storage (64×1024).

2.34 What does the term *megabyte* denote?

The term *megabyte* represents 1 million characters of storage, and it is generally used in describing large storage areas.

2.35 What is really meant when it is said that a CPU has a capacity of 128K?

This statement implies that a CPU possesses a primary storage unit with a capacity in excess of 128,000 bytes of storage. Note the distinction: The CPU itself does not have 128K; rather, the *primary* storage has a capacity of approximately 128K.

2.36 What other terms are used to refer to the primary storage unit?

The terms *memory*, *core*, and *main storage* are sometimes used to identify the primary storage unit.

CHAP. 2]   COMPUTER SYSTEM COMPONENTS   19

SECONDARY STORAGE

2.37 What role does secondary storage play in the processing cycle?

Referring to Fig. 2-3, we note that secondary storage is attached to the CPU and can interact with it. The principal purpose of secondary storage is to retain data that cannot be held within the primary storage unit.

2.38 How did the concept of secondary storage evolve?

Early computers had very limited primary storage capacities, which were quickly filled with data related to processing. It was not possible to retain large amounts of data in the primary storage unit and at the same time process large programs. Secondary storage simplified this problem by storing data currently undergoing processing in a device that was directly accessible by the CPU. Thus data not in the primary storage unit were readily accessible in fractions of a second.

2.39 What are the operational constraints on data held in secondary storage?

Data in secondary storage units must be directly accessible, that is, they must be stored in a format that is ready for immediate use in processing.

2.40 In current computer systems, what are two primary means of secondary storage?

Two current modes of secondary storage are magnetic tape and magnetic disk, shown in Figs. 2-4a and 2-4b, respectively.

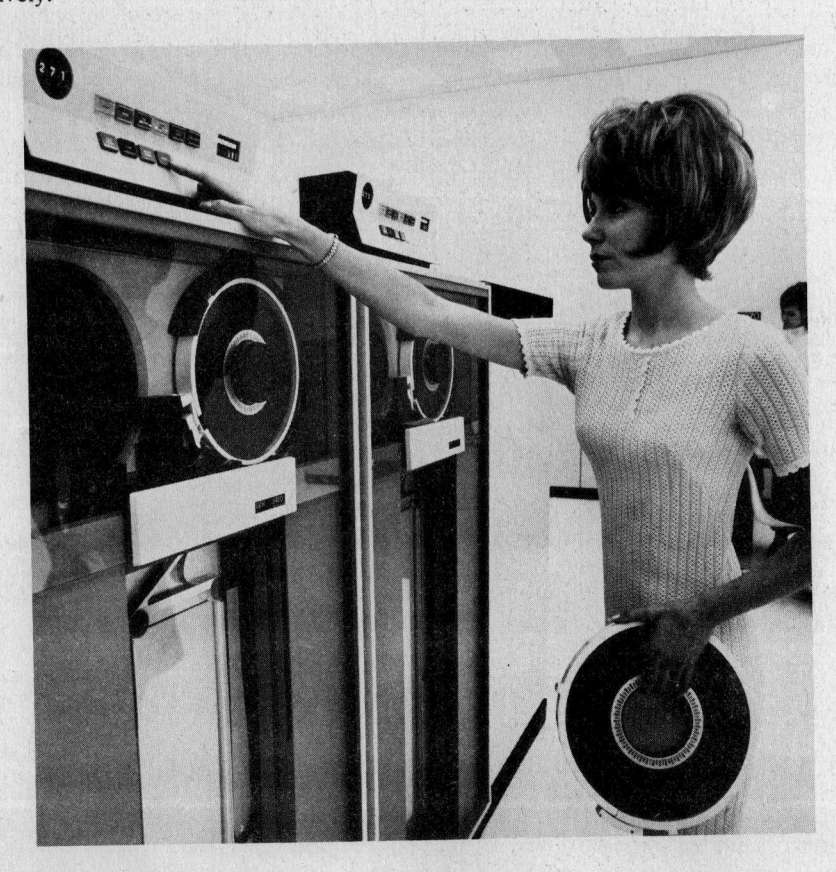

(a) Magnetic tape. (*IBM*)

Fig. 2-4 Two primary means of secondary storage.

Fig. 2-4 (*cont.*)

2.41 How do magnetic tape and disk differ in their storage modes?

Magnetic tape is a sequential storage medium in that it accesses data one record at a time until the desired data item is found. Magnetic disk is a *direct access medium* in that an individual data item may be accessed without first going through all the rest of the data.

2.42 Name one application in which magnetic tape could be used advantageously and another application in which magnetic disk would be preferable.

In a payroll application, in which a series of records is read sequentially according to social security number (in order to ensure that everyone is paid), magnetic tape could prove a successful secondary storage medium. Accessing data relating to a passenger reservation system would require the support of magnetic disk since the computer would be jumping from one reservation to another (the order in which customers will call cannot be predicted).

2.43 Generally, how do the capacities of secondary storage compare with the capacities of primary storage units?

Under existing technology, the storage capacities found in secondary storage units far exceed those of primary storage. Whereas larger primary storage units may range into 3–5 megabytes of storage, secondary storage units may exhibit storage capacities as high as 2000 megabytes. Secondary storage offers the CPU access to a vast amount of data.

OPERATIONAL SOFTWARE

2.44 Is the control unit the sole controlling feature of a computer, or are there other elements in a computer system that contribute to the supervision of data processing?

As important as the CPU's control unit is, it is not the sole supervisory feature of a computer system. The control unit primarily focuses on the efficient use of hardware within the system, responding to conditions or instructions resulting from the processing of programs. It assumes a major share of monitoring the use of the computer's resources, but it must interact with and rely on other forms of supervisory software.

2.45 What are these other supervisory programs called?

The supervisory programs that interact with the control unit to govern all aspects of processing are referred to as the *operational software* of the computer. Frequently the term *operating system* is applied to the groups of programs that make up a system's operational software. Note that the operational software needed to control a system's processing potential may comprise one or more programs, depending on the scope and complexity of the computer system.

2.46 Is there a relationship between the complexity and size of a system's operational software and the level of processing performed in that system?

Generally, the more complex the processing to be performed, the more complex the operating system used. It must control more tasks and therefore needs a higher level of controlling software.

2.47 Are all operating systems the same?

No. Operating systems are purchased from individual computer manufacturers and vary in size, complexity, and ability to support processing activities. The same manufacturer may offer many types of operational software, often making recommendations on which software is suited to a particular user's needs.

2.48 How can the relationship of the CPU and the operating system be illustrated?

Consider three computer systems consisting of exactly the same hardware. The systems are identical in terms of their CPUs and peripheral devices, yet each computer supports markedly different forms of processing. Since their hardware is identical, the obvious differences in their processing potential must arise in the operational software used. The CPUs available are ready to support any processing required by the computer's operating system.

2.49 Then is it the operational software, when coupled with the CPU, that defines the operational characteristics of a computer system?

Yes. The capabilities of a specific computer for handling a given processing workload relate directly to both factors.

2.50 During the computer's execution of jobs, where is the operational software stored?

A system's operational software generally stays within primary storage during the execution of programs. Its position there enables it to rapidly interact with any program undergoing execution and respond immediately to programmed instructions.

2.51 What are some of the names assigned to the operational software used in computer systems?

The names associated with operational software vary among manufacturers. However, some of the more commonly encountered titles are *supervisor control program*, *master control program*, and *systems software package*.

OVERLAPPED PROCESSING

2.52 Were computers always capable of concurrently performing the many tasks associated with running multiple jobs?

No. This operational capability was developed a few years ago, and it greatly enhanced the computer's processing potential.

2.53 Why were early computing systems called *dedicated systems*?

Early computers earned this title because they were "dedicated" to the program they were running. In other words, while processing one job, they completely ignored all other processing activities. Thus dedicated computers would not start program 2 until program 1 was done, program 3 until program 2 was done, and so on. Figure 2-5 illustrates the relationship between jobs in a dedicated system.

	Units of Processing					
	1	2	3	4	5	6
Program 1	I	P	O			
Program 2				I	P	O

I = Input   P = Processing   O = Output

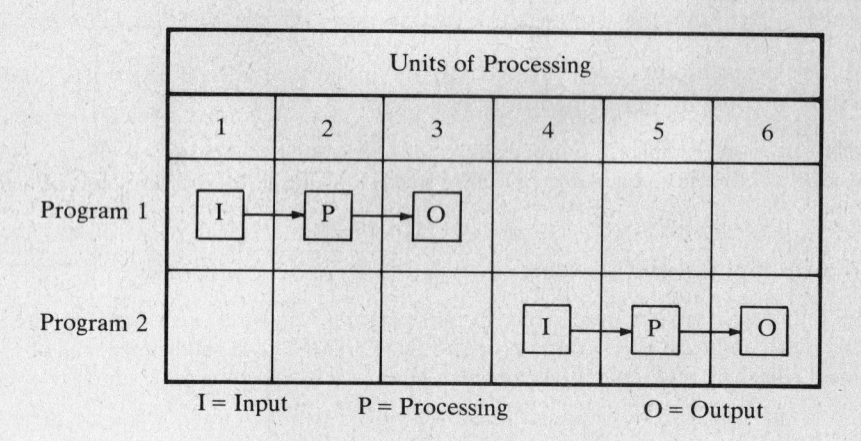

Fig. 2-5 Six units of processing are required to process only two programs.

2.54 Was the dedicated system an efficient data processing system?

The dedicated system was inefficient because it utilized the CPU, its most vital component, the least. The CPU of any computer system offers the maximum processing potential because of its speed.

2.55 In comparison to its peripheral devices, how does the CPU rate?

The CPU works faster than any hardware, attaining speeds in billionths of a second, or *nanoseconds*. Card readers, printers, and other peripheral devices cannot approach that speed, lagging well behind. In fact, the CPU generally must wait for its peripherals during I/O operation because of their relative slowness.

2.56 Is the condition defined in which the CPU is restrained by the slower speed of its I/O devices?

Yes. A system is said to be *I/O bound* when the processing potential of its CPU is restrained by the speed of its I/O devices. This condition always existed in dedicated systems.

2.57 Is there a parallel situation in industry?

Yes. A practical example illustrating an I/O-bound state occurs in a production-line setup where one person on the line is a very slow worker. Even if the next person down the line is a faster worker, he or she cannot proceed until receiving the assembly from the slower worker. If, for example, a fast worker can handle twelve units per hour but the person ahead of him or her hands over only six units per hour, the faster worker's ability to produce twelve units per hour is negated. In a dedicated I/O-bound system a CPU capable of handling 1 million characters per second is forced to wait for the card reader that handles only 500 characters per second.

2.58 What device was developed to overcome an I/O-bound condition?

The creation of overlapped processing greatly minimized the inefficiency of I/O-bound systems.

2.59 What was the operational rationale of overlapped processing?

Overlapped processing was conceived to free the CPU of controlling I/O operations so that it could concentrate on processing programs. Figure 2-6 illustrates the interaction of programs in an overlapped system.

2.60 Explain overlapped processing in terms of Fig. 2-6.

The input of program 1 precedes all processing activities. Once completed, the input of program 2 commences while the CPU begins processing program 1. In cycle 3, three tasks occur concurrently—namely, the output of program 1, the processing of program 2, and the input of program 3. This overlapping of tasks can continue indefinitely.

2.61 By comparing Figs. 2-5 and 2-6, is it possible to gauge the overall efficiency of overlapped processing?

Yes. In Fig. 2-5 only two programs were processed in six units of time. In the overlapped system, Fig. 2-6, four programs were processed in the same time frame. A 100 percent increase in productivity was achieved.

	Units of Processing					
	1	2	3	4	5	6
Program 1	I	P	O			
Program 2		I	P	O		
Program 3			I	P	O	
Program 4				I	P	O

I = Input   P = Processing   O = Output

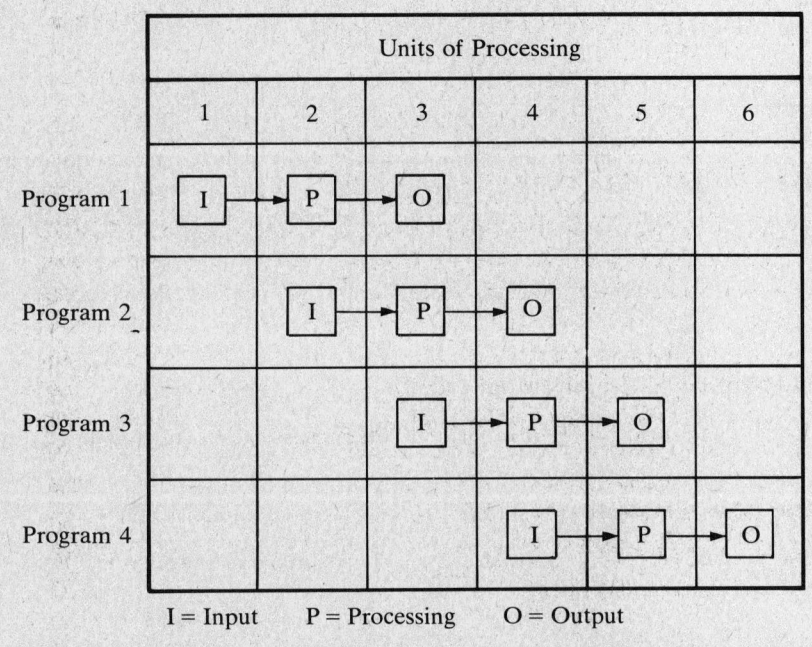

Fig. 2-6 In an overlapped system, parts of many programs are handled concurrently. It is possible to process four programs in the six units of processing shown here.

2.62 Was any special technology used in the development of the overlapped system?

Yes. The key to a successful overlapped system is the use of channels. *Channels* are specialized units that are attached to the CPU and that assume control over I/O operations once instructed to do so by the CPU.

2.63 How do the CPU and channels interact in overlapped activities?

The CPU initiates the I/O operations, assigns a channel to monitor its completion, and then turns its attention to other processing activities. With the channel overseeing the I/O operation, the CPU is free to process. The CPU does not have to wait for the I/O devices since the responsibility for controlling the I/O operation is assumed by a channel.

2.64 How are buffers incorporated into overlapped processing?

Buffers are temporary storage areas used to retain data read from input devices or information slated for output. They are online storage units that hold data immediately prior to or after processing. The operational positioning of buffers is illustrated in Fig. 2-7.

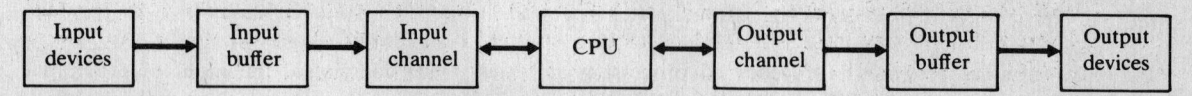

```
┌────────┐   ┌────────┐   ┌────────┐   ┌─────┐   ┌────────┐   ┌────────┐   ┌────────┐
│ Input  │→ │ Input  │→ │ Input  │↔ │ CPU │↔ │ Output │→ │ Output │→ │ Output │
│devices │   │ buffer │   │channel │   │     │   │channel │   │ buffer │   │devices │
└────────┘   └────────┘   └────────┘   └─────┘   └────────┘   └────────┘   └────────┘
```

Fig. 2-7 In an overlapped system, buffers and channels interact to facilitate the continuous input and output of data, thereby freeing the CPU to concentrate on processing.

2.65 How do buffers and channels interact?

Recall the purpose of overlapped processing, which was to increase CPU usage. Data input under control of the input channel are stored in the input buffer and made available for processing on demand of the CPU. Data removed from the input buffer and processed are replaced by other items awaiting processing. Similarly, processed data are sent to the output buffer where the output channel will monitor the output. Once the processed information is placed in the output buffer, the CPU accesses the next program to be processed.

2.66 Are computer systems restricted to one input and one output channel?

No. Computer systems may have many channels. Some channels may handle only input tasks or output tasks, respectively, while others may assume I/O activities for a particular device. The number of channels used will depend on the hardware, operating systems, and informational needs of the user's system.

VIRTUAL STORAGE (VS)

2.67 What is the purpose of virtual storage (VS)?

The purpose of *virtual storage* (VS) is to facilitate the processing of extremely large programs.

2.68 Does virtual storage increase a system's primary storage capacity?

No. Virtual storage has no effect on the size of a system's primary storage unit. It is a software technique incorporated into a computer's operating system.

2.69 How does VS handle the processing of large programs?

Virtual storage divides large programs into units that fit comfortably within primary storage for processing. One unit is held within primary storage, with the remaining units retained in an online, secondary storage device (i.e., magnetic disk).

2.70 What are these subdivided units called?

The units resulting from the application of virtual storage are referred to as *pages*. The initial program page is held in primary storage, with all subsequent pages retained on disk.

2.71 How are pages processed?

The initial program page is processed first. As subsequent pages become involved in processing, the page remaining on disk is swapped with the page held in primary storage. This swapping process is repeated, as often as necessary, until the program is completely processed.

2.72 Does processing via virtual storage assume any unusual form?

No. There is no difference apparent to the user in the processing of VS-related programs.

2.73 Why was VS developed?

Computer designers recognized that limitations in the capacities of primary storage units might preclude the processing of very large programs in some computer systems. Virtual storage was an attempt to overcome this problem.

2.74 Do most computers possess a VS capability?

Yes. The majority of today's computers incorporate some form of VS software.

Review Questions

2.75 The card reader is defined as an I/O device because of its ability to read and punch cards. (a) True, (b) false.

2.76 Hardcopy outputs are the primary output of a CRT. (a) True, (b) false.

2.77 The display of customer credit data on a CRT is an example of a softcopy output. (a) True, (b) false.

2.78 Programs being processed must stay in the primary storage unit during their execution. (a) True, (b) false.

2.79 Program data that cannot be retained in primary storage may be stored in secondary storage. (a) True, (b) false.

2.80 The sequential storage of file data can be accomplished on magnetic tape. (a) True, (b) false.

2.81 Using DP conventions, a CPU may be said to have a storage capacity of 64,000 K. (a) True, (b) false.

2.82 Generally, 1 byte of storage may contain exactly one character's worth of data. (a) True, (b) false.

2.83 The control unit is solely responsible for directing the processing activities of a computer system. (a) True, (b) false.

2.84 Computer systems composed of equivalent hardware may have different operational capacities based on their operational software. (a) True, (b) false.

2.85 Registers are temporary storage areas of the CPU that hold data involved in arithmetic and logical operations. (a) True, (b) false.

2.86 A dedicated system represents the most efficient form of computerized data processing systems. (a) True, (b) false.

2.87 A *buffer* is a temporary storage area used to hold I/O data undergoing processing. (a) True, (b) false.

2.88 In a VS system, program pages not involved in processing are stored on disk until they are required for use. (a) True, (b) false.

2.89 Virtual storage technology is used solely in small computer systems. (a) True; (b) false.

2.90 The CRT is properly identified as a(n) (a) input device; (b) output device; (c) I/O device; (d) processing device.

2.91 The outputs generated by a printer are referred to as (a) I/O outputs; (b) hardcopy outputs; (c) softcopy outputs; (d) pages.

2.92 The term applied to the mechanical equipment comprising a computer system is (a) hardware; (b) peripheral devices; (c) software; (d) all of the above.

2.93 The CPU component responsible for performing logical operations is the (a) control unit; (b) arithmetic-logic unit; (c) primary storage unit; (d) secondary storage unit.

2.94 A secondary storage unit is a (a) card reader; (b) line printer; (c) CRT; (d) none of these.

2.95 A responsibility assigned to the control unit is the (a) supervision of all programs being processed; (b) coordination of I/O operations; (c) movement of data between storage locations; (d) all of the above.

2.96 In DP shorthand, the letter K is equivalent to (a) 1000 bytes of storage; (b) 1024 bytes of storage; (c) 1 million bytes of storage; (d) none of these.

2.97 A characteristic of secondary storage is that (a) data must be held in an offline device; (b) data are not directly available; (c) data are retained in a readily accessible form; (d) all of the above.

2.98 Which of the following applications is best suited to the use of magnetic disk as secondary storage? (a) the weekly processing of card inventory data; (b) the offline processing of savings bank data; (c) the acceptance of car rental reservations on a nationwide basis; (d) all of the above.

2.99 The condition in which a CPU is constrained by the speed of its I/O devices is referred to by the term (a) dedicated system; (b) I/O bound; (c) defined system; (d) peripheral defined.

2.100 In overlapped processing, the device that assumes control over I/O operations, once initiated by the CPU, is a (a) buffer; (b) control unit; (c) channel; (d) disk.

2.101 The program units resulting from the application of virtual storage are called (a) defined units; (b) program components; (c) modules; (d) pages.

2.102 The card reader is classified as a(n) _____ device.

2.103 A CRT may also be called a _____ terminal.

2.104 A computer-prepared monthly report of inventory costs would be generated by a _____.

2.105 The general term applied to the I/O devices that may be incorporated into a computer system is _____.

2.106 All processing undertaken by a computer system must occur with its _____.

2.107 A logical operation is a _____ of two data items.

2.108 The secondary storage device that permits the random access of data is _____.

2.109 Arithmetic operations are accomplished in the CPU's _____.

2.110 One million bytes of storage is referred to as a _____.

CHAP. 2]   COMPUTER SYSTEM COMPONENTS   27

2.111 The sequential processing of data relating to personal characteristics by a computerized dating service is readily supported by magnetic _____.

2.112 The group of supervisory programs of a computer system is referred to as a(n) _____ system.

2.113 A computer system that handles only one program at a time is referred to as a(n) _____ system.

2.114 In computer terms a(n) _____ is equivalent to one-billionth of a second.

2.115 Overlapped processing is designed to _____ the CPU for more processing activities.

2.116 The technology developed to overcome the restriction of processing large programs in a limited CPU size is called _____.

Answers: 2.75 (*b*); 2.76 (*b*); 2.77 (*a*); 2.78 (*a*); 2.79 (*a*); 2.80 (*a*); 2.81 (*a*); 2.82 (*a*); 2.83 (*b*); 2.84 (*a*); 2.85 (*a*); 2.86 (*b*); 2.87 (*a*); 2.88 (*a*); 2.89 (*b*); 2.90 (*c*); 2.91 (*b*); 2.92 (*a*); 2.93 (*b*); 2.94 (*d*); 2.95 (*d*); 2.96 (*b*); 2.97 (*c*); 2.98 (*c*); 2.99 (*b*); 2.100 (*c*); 2.101 (*d*); 2.102 input; 2.103 visual display; 2.104 printer; 2.105 peripheral devices; 2.106 central processing unit (CPU); 2.107 comparison; 2.108 magnetic disk; 2.109 arithmetic-logic unit (ALU); 2.110 megabyte; 2.111 tape; 2.112 operating; 2.113 dedicated; 2.114 nanosecond; 2.115 free; 2.116 virtual storage (VS).

Supplementary Problems

2.117 Why is the CPU important to a computer system?

2.118 What are the specific responsibilities of the control unit, the arithmetic-logic unit, and primary storage unit?

2.119 How does secondary storage function in a computer system? What were the reasons for its development? Cite two examples of secondary storage media.

2.120 How does an operating system assist in the processing of programs? Define the characteristics of a computer system.

2.121 How has overlapped processing improved usage of the CPU's resources? Explain the execution of I/O operations in an overlapped system; use illustrations where necessary.

2.122 Explain how buffers and channels are used in an overlapped processing system. How do they assist in alleviating the condition referred to as "I/O bound"?

2.123 Describe the application of virtual storage to the processing of large programs.

2.124 Define the following terms.

        Byte   Nanosecond
        Channel   Operational software
        Hardware   Page
        I/O bound   Peripheral device
        K   Software
        Megabyte   Visual display terminal

2.125 Examine the following list of activities and identify each as either a hardcopy or softcopy output or input operation.
    (a) Keying employee data via a CRT
    (b) Customer account data displayed on bank CRT
    (c) Printed student programming results
    (d) Motor vehicle bureau data viewed on a visual display terminal
    (e) Inventory data read by card reader
    (f) Printed payroll checks and statements
    (g) Credit data displayed on a point-of-sale terminal in retail sales
    (h) A monthly statement from a credit card company

2.126 For each of the following, identify the device that could perform the task or operation.
    (a) The keying of control data into the computer to effect the processing of a particular program
    (b) The printing of personnel reports for management
    (c) The retention of payroll data on a sequential storage medium
    (d) The CPU component where all data are retained during processing
    (e) The storage of airline reservation information which must be accessible on an independent basis
    (f) The display of medical data for physicians
    (g) The reading of telephone charges contained on punched cards

Glossary

Arithmetic-logic unit (ALU). The CPU component that performs all arithmetic operations and logical comparisons.

Buffer. A temporary storage area, used in overlapped processing, that retains data for I/O operations.

Byte. A measure of computer storage that represents one character's worth of primary storage.

Card reader. An input device that reads data from computer cards and enters that data into the system.

Cathode ray tube (CRT). An I/O device that provides for the entry of data via its keyboard and displays data on a television-like screen.

Central processing unit (CPU). The computer component in which all processing occurs, which is composed of the control, the arithmetic-logic, and the primary storage units.

Channel. A special unit attached to the CPU that assumes control of I/O operations after initiated by the CPU.

Control unit. The CPU component that oversees the execution of all programs processed by a computer.

Dedicated system. A computer that can process only one program at a time.

Hardcopy. An output that appears in a permanent, printed form.

Hardware. The term applied to all mechanical equipment in a computer system.

Input device. A device used solely to enter data into the computer (e.g., a card reader).

I/O bound. The condition in which a computer system's CPU is constrained by the speed of its I/O devices.

Input-output (I/O) device. A device capable of performing both input and output operations.

K. Computer notation for 1024 bytes of storage.

Magnetic disk. A random-access storage medium, one of the principal examples of secondary storage.

Magnetic tape. A primary means of secondary storage in which data are filed sequentially.

Megabyte. A term representing 1 million bytes of storage.

Nanosecond. One-billionth of a second.

Operating system. Another term for *operational software*.

Operational software. The group of supervisory programs that controls all processing activities and that defines the operational characteristics of a computer system.

Output device. A device capable of performing only output operations (e.g., a printer).

Overlapped processing. The concurrent performance of I/O and processing operations from multiple programs, permitting the resources of the CPU to be used more efficiently and overcome an I/O-bound state.

Pages. The modules of a program divided by virtual storage.

Peripheral devices. The general term applied to all devices composing a computer system, utilized for I/O operations and/or the storage of data.

Printer. An output device that generates printed reports and documents (sometimes called a *line printer*).

Register. A temporary storage area of the CPU that holds data involved in arithmetic and logical operations.

Secondary storage. Storage media, directly attached to the CPU, which retain data necessary for processing that cannot remain permanently in primary storage.

Softcopy. Output in a visual, nonpermanent form (e.g., data displayed on the screen of a CRT).

Software. The term applied to all programs used within a computer system.

Virtual storage (VS). A data processing (DP) technique in which large programs are divided into modules (pages) for processing.

Visual display terminal. A general term applied to the many forms of CRTs.

Chapter 3

Computer Codes

3.1 THE HOLLERITH CARD

In the 1880s Dr. Herman Hollerith originated the *80-column card*. Since that time the card has remained physically the same size although the codes used with it have been expanded. The *Hollerith*, or standard, punch card consists of 80 columns and 12 *rows*. Each row is identified by its own number. The topmost row is the 12 row, followed by the 11 row, 0 row, and rows 1–9. Each *card column* is capable of retaining exactly one character's code.

3.2 THE HOLLERITH CODE

The *Hollerith code*, used with the 80-column card, provides code configurations for numeric, alphabetic, and special characters—the three types of characters used with the standard punch card. The *numeric* characters are the digits 0 to 9, and the *alphabetic* characters are the letters A to Z. All other characters are treated as *special* characters.

Numeric character codes utilize exactly one punch per card column. By definition, alphabetic characters consist of two punches per card column—a zone punch and a digit punch. *Zone punches* appear in the 12, 11, and 0 rows since these rows are defined as the *zone rows*; *digit punches* appear in rows 1–9. Special-character codes may require one, two or three punches per card column. One character code is punched per card column, and the number of columns used depends on the size of the data item.

3.3 CARD FIELDS

Data are collectively organized into *card fields*. Three types of card fields into which data may be recorded are *numeric*, *alphabetic*, and *alphameric*. Whereas numeric and alphabetic fields are restricted to number or letter characters, respectively, alphameric fields may contain both types of characters and/or special characters. Generally, numeric fields are *right-justified*, that is, they occupy the rightmost columns of a field, whereas alphabetic and alphameric fields are *left-justified*, that is, they occupy the leftmost columns of a field.

3.4 BINARY-CODED DECIMAL (BCD)

Binary-Coded Decimal (*BCD*) was reintroduced for use with the IBM System/3 computer series. The BCD code is used with the *96-column card*, a physically smaller version of the standard (Hollerith) card. Six bits are used to code BCD, namely, the B, A, 8, 4, 2, and 1 bits. The B and A bits represent the equivalent of the Hollerith code's zone punches. Hollerith's digit punches are defined using BCD's 8, 4, 2, and 1 bits. A simple three-step procedure is available to compose the BCD codes for alphabetic and numeric characters.

3.5 EXTENDED BINARY-CODED DECIMAL INTERCHANGEABLE CODE (EBCDIC)

The *Extended Binary-Coded Decimal Interchangeable Code* (*EBCDIC*) scheme was developed as an expansion of BCD. It consists of 8 bits, whereas BCD uses only 6 bits. The 8 EBCDIC bits are divided into two 4 bit groupings. The first grouping represents zone bits, and the second 4 bit grouping represents the equivalent of Hollerith's digit punches. Again, a three-step procedure is followed to compose EBCDIC character codes.

A unique aspect to EBCDIC is its usage of 0s and 1s to represent data. The use of 0s and 1s represents a *binary notation* (based on the number 2), which closely relates to the electric impulses actually used to store data in the CPU's primary storage unit.

3.6 AMERICAN STANDARD CODE FOR INFORMATION INTERCHANGE (ASCII)

A consortium of computer manufacturers created the *American Standard Code for Information Interchange* (*ASCII*) to standardize the codes used on terminal devices. Like EBCDIC, ASCII is made up of 8 bits. ASCII is not related to the Hollerith code, defining its character codes on the chronological order of alphabetic and numeric characters. Composing ASCII character codes means literally counting to the desired code.

Tables throughout this chapter provide a guide to not only the ASCII code but also to the BCD, EBCDIC, and Hollerith codes previously discussed.

Solved Problems

THE HOLLERITH CARD

3.1 Who developed the concept of the computer card?

The computer (or punch) card was invented by Dr. Herman Hollerith in the 1880s.

3.2 Has the card been refined since its inception?

Yes. The card has remained the same in size, but the original code used with it has been expanded.

3.3 What are the operational capacities of the standard punch card?

The standard punch card consists of 80 columns and 12 rows. Each card column may contain one character of data. The 12 rows are an integral part of the Hollerith code.

3.4 Why is the 80-column card referred to as the *standard punch card*?

Because of its widespread acceptance, the 80-column card is employed in the vast majority of data processing operations. It has become the standard card form used within most computer systems.

3.5 What are the physical characteristics of the 80-column card?

The card is approximately 7 inches wide, 3 inches high, and 0.007 inch thick. All devices equipped to handle the 80-column card are constructed to those specific measurements. Devices that do not meet those measurements will not support usage of the standard punch card.

3.6 Where do the 12 rows appear on the card?

The 12 rows run horizontally across the card, as shown in Fig. 3-1.

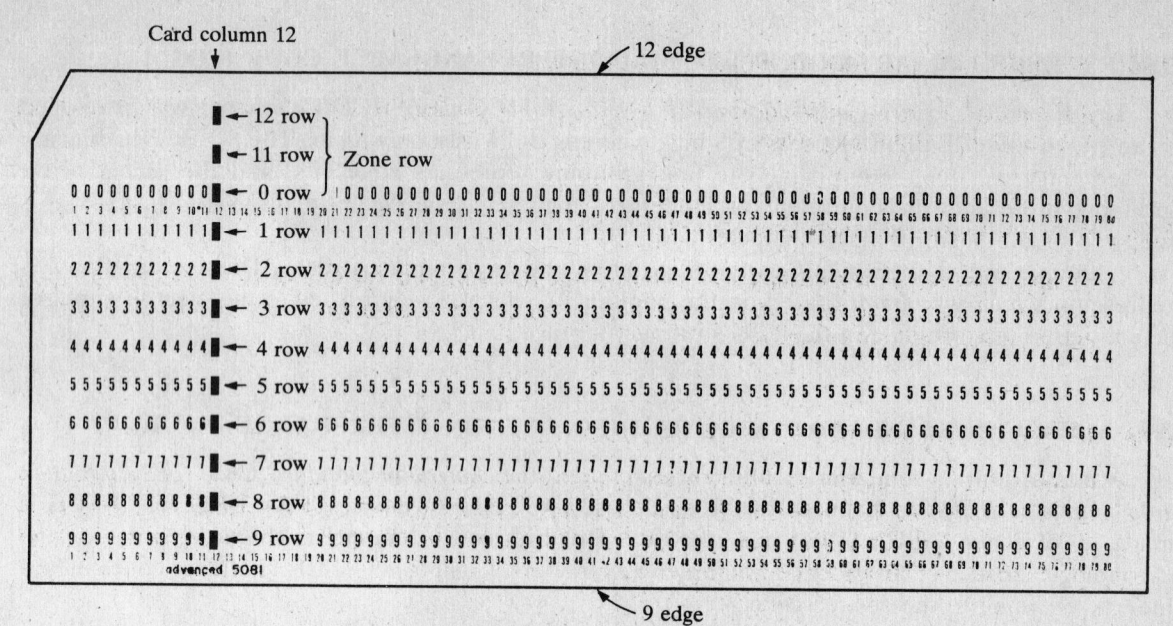

Fig. 3-1 The standard punch card.

3.7 How are the individual rows referenced?

Each row is identified by its own number. For example, down the card the 0 row, the 1 row, the 2 row, and the 3 row can be read up to the 9 row, which is at the card's bottom. Each of these 10 rows is identified by a series of numbers, equivalent to the number of the row, that are printed across the face of the card. Note that the two rows above the 0 row are not identified by printed numbers. The topmost row is the 12 row, and the row beneath it is the 11 row.

3.8 Reading down the card, how are the rows ordered?

The topmost row is the 12 row, followed by the 11, 0, 1, 2, 3, 4, 5, 6, 7, 8, and 9 rows. Each of these rows carries its own number. Note that a rectangular punch appears in every row, as shown in Fig. 3-1.

3.9 Are all punches on the 80-column card rectangular?

Yes. This physical feature is one of the characteristics of the 80-column card.

3.10 How are the individual card columns defined on the standard punch card?

The position of the 80 columns is identified by a series of numbers located between the 0 row and 1 row. These numbers range from 1 to 80 and identify each of the 80 columns into which data may be punched. A second series of column numbers appears below the 9 row.

3.11 Is there a specific title assigned to these numbers?

The numbers appearing between the rows 0 and 1 (and also beneath the 9 row) are referred to as *card column numbers* because they help define the location of each card column.

3.12 What is unusual about card column 12, as shown in Fig. 3-1?

In card column 12 a punch is placed within each of the 12 rows of the card to highlight their position.

3.13 Does a reference exist for the top and bottom of the 80-column card?

Yes. The top edge of the 80-column card is referred to as the *12 edge* because of its proximity to the 12 row. Similarly, the bottom edge of the card is the *9 edge*.

CHAP. 3] COMPUTER CODES

3.14 What do the terms *face up* and *face down* mean?

If the numbers on the surface of the card face the reader, the card is said to be *face up*. If the numbers face away, the card is *face down*.

3.15 Why are these references important?

Computer personnel are instructed to handle cards in a particular manner when feeding them into a computer device. If the cards are not fed properly into the device, data will not be read by the computer and processing will not commence.

3.16 Is there an example of card handling?

In many computer systems card readers are used to input data for processing. Cards must be positioned properly within the card reader to be accurately read. Thus a computer operator might be instructed to place the cards in the card reader, "9 edge first, face down." Inserting all cards in exactly this manner will ensure that they are properly read.

THE HOLLERITH CODE

3.17 What code is used with the 80-column card?

The code used with the standard punch card is the Hollerith code. It provides the basis for punching all types of characters onto the 80-column card.

3.18 What types of characters may be punched onto an 80-column card using this code?

The Hollerith code provides configurations for numeric characters, alphabetic characters, and special characters.

3.19 Is it possible to code any type of data onto an 80-column card?

Yes. The data may consist of numeric characters (that is, 0 to 9); alphabetic characters (that is, A to Z); and special characters (for example, *, /, ?, #, :).

3.20 Should any character that is not numeric or alphabetic be considered a special character?

Yes. Only the numbers 0 to 9 and the letters A to Z are specifically assigned as numeric and alphabetic characters, respectively. All other characters are assumed to be special characters.

3.21 How does the Hollerith code protect its users?

The Hollerith code ensures that only one unique code configuration exists for any one character. Thus no duplicate codes can be used when punching data onto cards.

3.22 When using the Hollerith code, how many characters may be punched into any one card column?

The coding rule is simple—one character code is punched into one card column. Any character's code may be punched into any of the 80 columns, but only one character's code is permitted in a specific card column.

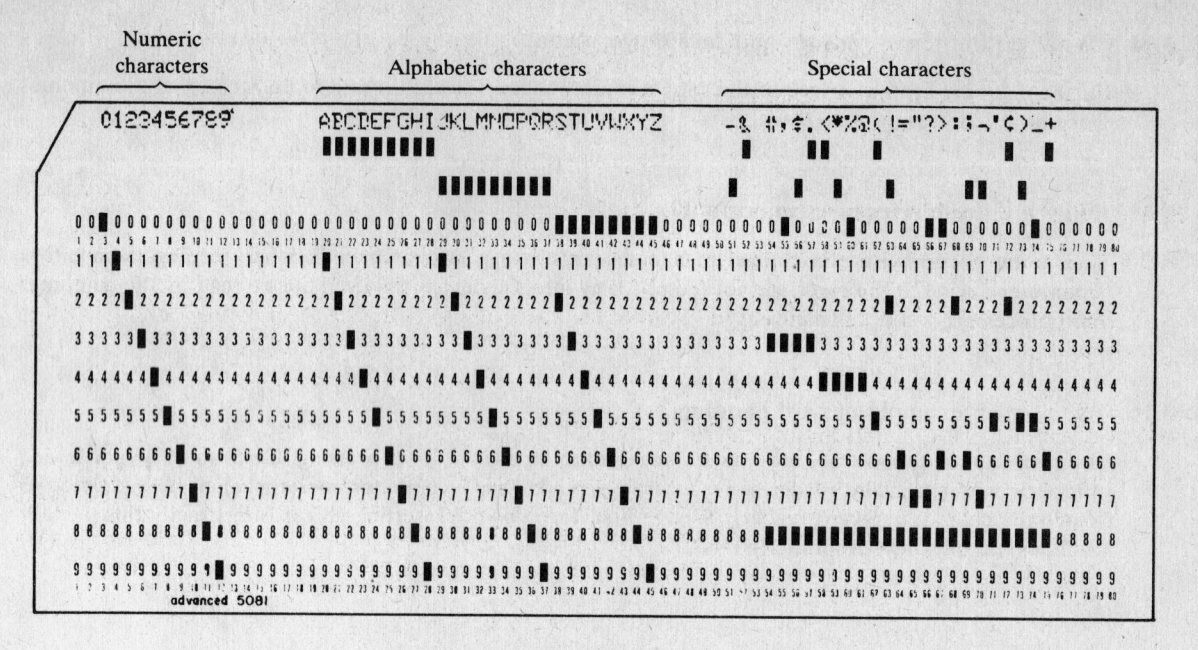

Fig. 3-2 An 80-column card containing numeric, alphabetic, and special characters.

3.23 How many punches are necessary for numeric characters?

Exactly one punch per card column is needed to represent numeric characters in the Hollerith code.

3.24 How can that be illustrated?

As shown in Fig. 3-2, the numeric characters 0 to 9 are punched into card columns 3 to 12, respectively. Note that in each case only *one* punch appears in each card column. A 0 punch is used to represent the number 0 (column 3); a 1 punch represents the numeric character 1 (column 4); a 2 punch for the number 2 (column 5); and so on. Column 12 contains a 9 punch representing the Hollerith code for the number 9.

3.25 Carrying that concept further, what are the Hollerith codes for the numbers 3 and 7?

In the Hollerith code a 3 punch represents the number 3 and a 7 punch represents the number 7. In Fig. 3-2 the individual codes for 3 and 7 appear in card columns 6 and 10, respectively.

3.26 In effect, then, one number is punched into a single card column. How many card columns would be necessary to code the number 742?

A total of three card columns would be needed to represent the numeric data 742 in the Hollerith code. The first card column would contain a 7 punch; the second column, a 4 punch; and the third column, a 2 punch.

3.27 Are alphabetic characters coded differently from numeric characters?

Yes. Whereas numeric characters require only one punch per card column, alphabetic characters require two.

3.28 What are the two types of punches used for alphabetic characters?

By definition an alphabetic character is composed of a zone punch and a digit punch.

3.29 What rows make up the zone and digit rows?

The zone rows are represented by the 12, 11, and 0 rows. The digit rows are the rows 1 to 9. Punches placed within these rows are called *zone punches* and *digit punches*, accordingly.

CHAP. 3] COMPUTER CODES 35

3.30 Applying these definitions, what is the Hollerith code for the character A?

The Hollerith code for the character A consists of a 12-zone punch and a 1-digit punch, as shown in column 20 of Fig. 3-2.

3.31 What is the code configuration for the character B?

The Hollerith code for the character B is a 12-zone and 2-digit punch. Similarly, the code for the character C is a 12-zone and 3-digit punch. This progression continues in the Hollerith code through the character I, a 12-zone and 9-digit punch. Note that the character codes for A to I all possess a 12-zone punch.

3.32 What code is assigned the character J?

The character J begins the next series of characters, all of which use an 11-zone punch. Thus the character J uses an 11-zone and 1-digit punch. The character K uses an 11-zone and 2-digit punch combination; the character L an 11-zone and 3-digit punch configuration; and so on through the character R, which uses an 11-zone and 9-digit punch configuration. In Fig. 3-2 columns 29–37 represent these codes.

3.33 What zone punch do the characters S to Z share?

The alphabetic characters S to Z all share the 0-zone punch. The character S uses a 0-zone and 2-digit punch code; the letter T uses a 0-zone and 3-digit punch code; and the character U uses a 0-zone and 4-digit punch configuration. The character Z completes this sequence of characters by using a 0-zone and 9-digit punch configuration. In Fig. 3-2, codes for S to Z appear in columns 38 to 45.

3.34 Why does the character S use a 2-digit punch instead of the 1 punch used for A and J?

The designer of the Hollerith code chose to end the code with a 0-zone and 9-digit punch for Z rather than begin with a 0-zone and 1-digit configuration for S. A choice had to be made since twenty-six character codes existed (A to Z), and twenty-seven codes were possible.

3.35 Does the use of the 0 row as a zone punch conflict with its use with numeric data?

The 0 row has two functions. When used alone, the 0 row represents the number 0. However, when used in conjunction with the digit punches 2 to 9, it acts as a zone row and is an active part of the Hollerith code for the characters S to Z.

3.36 Are alphabetic characters also assigned on an individual-character basis?

Yes. Alphabetic characters occupy one card column each. Thus eight card columns would be set aside to contain the characters composing the word *dolphins*.

3.37 How many punches per card column are necessary to code special characters?

Special characters may require one, two, or three punches per card, depending on the character being punched.

3.38 What are some examples of special characters that use one, two, or three punches per column?

Examples of special characters that require one punch per card column are the ampersand (&) and minus (−), a 12 punch and an 11 punch, respectively. Special characters using two punches per column are the slash (/) and equal sign (=), and special characters using three punches per column are the dollar sign ($) and plus sign (+).

3.39 Is there any visible pattern to the coding of special characters?

No. Unlike numeric and alphabetic characters, there is no predictable pattern to the codes developed for special characters. Thus it is not easy to construct special-character codes. Generally, most operational personnel memorize the Hollerith codes for numbers and alphabetic characters, but they possess a limited knowledge of special-character codes. Table 3-1 provides the Hollerith codes for numeric, alphabetic, and selected special characters.

Table 3-1 Hollerith Code Configurations

Character	Hollerith Code, Punch	Character	Hollerith Code, Punches	Character	Hollerith Code, Punches	Character	Hollerith Code, Punches	Character	Hollerith Code, Punches
Ø	Ø	A	12 & 1	J	11 & 1	/	Ø & 1	&	12
1	1	B	12 & 2	K	11 & 2	S	Ø & 2	−	11
2	2	C	12 & 3	L	11 & 3	T	Ø & 3	=	6 & 8
3	3	D	12 & 4	M	11 & 4	U	Ø & 4	$	11, 3, & 8
4	4	E	12 & 5	N	11 & 5	V	Ø & 5	*	11, 4, & 8
5	5	F	12 & 6	O	11 & 6	W	Ø & 6	.	12, 3, & 8
6	6	G	12 & 7	P	11 & 7	X	Ø & 7	+	12, 6, & 8
7	7	H	12 & 8	Q	11 & 8	Y	Ø & 8	(	12, 5, & 8
8	8	I	12 & 9	R	11 & 9	Z	Ø & 9	>	Ø, 6, & 8
9	9							?	Ø, 7, & 8

CARD FIELDS

3.40 How are data organized when punched onto a card?

Data are entered onto cards in groups called *card fields*. A card field is defined as a consecutive number of card columns set aside for specific data.

3.41 How much data does a card field hold?

Card fields are designed to hold one complete item of data. The card field should be large enough to accommodate the largest item of data to be entered into it.

3.42 How many card columns should be set aside to make up a card field?

The size of a card field is generally established by the size of the data items to be entered into that field.

3.43 How many card columns should be set aside for a ZIP code field?

A total of five card columns would be reserved for a ZIP code field. That field size is sufficient to handle any currently existing ZIP code. When the planned expansion of ZIP codes to nine digits occurs, the size of the ZIP code field will need to be expanded from five to nine card columns.

3.44 What classification would be assigned to a ZIP code field?

The ZIP code field is classified as a numeric field since it contains only numeric data. The ZIP code field would be referred to as a "five-digit numeric field."

CHAP. 3] COMPUTER CODES 37

3.45 What other classifications apply to card fields?

In addition to the numeric field designation, card fields may be also classified as alphabetic or alphameric fields. Alphabetic fields consist solely of alphabetic character data. Alphameric fields may contain any combination of special, alphabetic, or numeric data items. Alphameric fields are sometimes also referred to as "alphanumeric fields."

3.46 How might a two-digit field for state names be defined?

Using the two-character abbreviations of the U.S. Postal Service, the state name field would be defined as a two-digit alphabetic field. This designation would be correct because the postal abbreviations consist solely of alphabetic characters.

3.47 Why might an address field be classified as an alphameric character field?

A total of 40 characters would be sufficient for most addresses in their entirety. The alphameric classification results from the fact that an address could contain a combination of special, numeric, and alphabetic characters (for example, 21-68 High Market St.).

3.48 Although these designations were developed for the medium of cards, are the concepts transferable to other storage media?

Yes. The concepts of card fields and the types of data they can hold apply to other storage media. Instead of being called "card fields," they are referred to simply as "fields." The designations of numeric, alphabetic, and alphameric fields are equally valid.

3.49 How might a nine-digit numeric card field be referred to if those same data are stored on magnetic tape?

As the data making up that field do not change, the numeric designation remains valid. The new tape field is referred to as a "nine-digit numeric field." The card field designation must be dropped since the data will be stored on tape.

3.50 Are there any conventions that must be considered when entering data into the different types of data fields?

Yes. Two conventions applied to data placement are left-justification and right-justification.

3.51 What is right-justification, and where is it applied?

Right-justification refers to the positioning of data in the rightmost columns of a card field. Normally fields containing numeric data are right-justified.

3.52 Why is right-justification important, and how is it used as a control?

Right-justification is a vital control feature for input data because it ensures that numeric data amounts are not altered. Figure 3-3a shows a number that is properly right-justified within a five-digit field, with leading zeros added. In many systems the computer is directed to fill unused columns of data (within a field) with zeros, thus potentially changing the original number. In Fig. 3-3b, the number 28 is not right justified and incorrectly becomes 28,000. The three zeros were automatically entered after the number.

| Ø | Ø | Ø | 2 | 8 |

| 2 | 8 | Ø | Ø | Ø |

(a)   (b)

Fig. 3-3

3.53 Is the lack of the right-justification a common error?

Yes. Many computer-related errors result from the lack of right-justification of data since original data items are incorrectly altered. This type of error occurs and is noted in newspaper articles about people receiving checks for millions of dollars, when in fact they should have received only a few dollars.

3.54 When is left-justification used?

Left-justification is applied to alphabetic and alphameric fields and causes that data to be moved to the leftmost columns or positions of that field. For example, if a part's name were to be entered into card columns 10 to 27, the first character of that name would appear in column 10 and continue toward column 27, using as many columns as needed.

3.55 With the data Arizona and 4278 in fields that are 10 characters and 6 characters wide, respectively, show how left- and right-justification are used.

The word *Arizona* is left-justified in the 10-character alphabetic field, whereas the digits 4278 are right-justified in the 6-character numeric field. Figure 3-4 illustrates the justification of these data items.

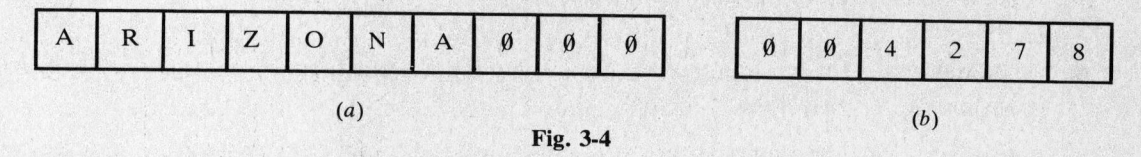

A	R	I	Z	O	N	A	Ø	Ø	Ø

(a)

Ø	Ø	4	2	7	8

(b)

Fig. 3-4

BINARY-CODED DECIMAL (BCD)

3.56 Other than the standard 80-column punch card, what other form of computer card is currently being used in some computer systems?

A smaller type of computer card, called a *96-column card*, is currently used in some computer systems manufactured by IBM. Approximately half the size of the standard card, the 96-column card is used with the IBM System 32, 34, and 38 Series computers.

3.57 Is the Hollerith code used with the 96-column card?

No. The 96-column card utilizes a coding scheme referred to as *Binary-Coded Decimal*, or simply *BCD*. Though totally different in appearance from the Hollerith code, BCD is related to the Hollerith code in its formulation. Certain aspects of BCD are derived directly from the Hollerith code.

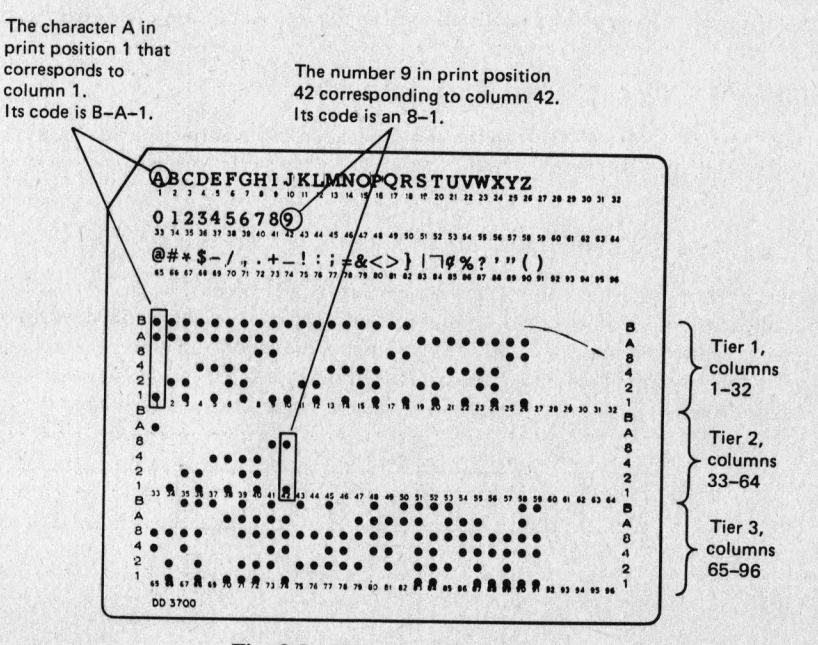

Fig. 3-5 The 96-column card.

3.58 What does the 96-column card look like, and how does it support the use of BCD?

The 96-column card is illustrated in Fig. 3-5. Physically it is about 3 inches square, about half the size of the 80-column card. The 96-column card is divided into three tiers consisting of 32 columns each, which total 96 columns of data. Note that the punches on the 96-column card are circular, not rectangular.

3.59 What role do the characters B, A, 8, 4, 2, and 1 play in BCD?

The characters B, A, 8, 4, 2, and 1 may be considered the equivalent of the rows on the standard punch card. They are defined as bits and are individually referred to as the B bit, A bit, 8 bit, 4 bit, 2 bit, and 1 bit. These 6 bits are an integral part of the BCD code.

3.60 How are these 6 bits used in BCD?

The 6 bits of the BCD are divided into two groups. The B and A bits are combined to represent the equivalent of the Hollerith code's zone punches. The 8, 4, 2, and 1 bits are grouped as the equivalent of the Hollerith code's digit punches.

3.61 How are the B and A bits configured to represent zone punches?

The B and A bits are combined to represent the 12-, 11-, and 0-zone punches, as shown in Table 3-2. A fourth zone format, the equivalent of a No Zone punch, is included for use with BCD codes for numbers.

Table 3-2 BCD Equivalents for Hollerith Zone Punches

BCD Zone Bits	Zone Punch			
	12 Punch	11 Punch	Ø Punch	No Zone
B	•	•		
A	•		•	

3.62 What are the BCD equivalents to Hollerith's 12-, 11-, and 0-zone punches?

The BCD equivalent of the 12-zone punch requires use of both the B bit and the A bit. The BCD equivalent of an 11-zone punch is a B bit alone, and the BCD equivalent of a 0-zone punch is an A bit alone. The No Zone equivalent uses neither a B nor an A bit.

Table 3-3 BCD Equivalents of the Hollerith Digit Punches

BCD Digit Bits	Hollerith Digit Punches									
	1	2	3	4	5	6	7	8	9	Ø
8								•	•	
4				•	•	•	•			
2		•	•			•	•			
1	•		•		•		•		•	

Note: A large dot placed next to any bit indicates it is used in the code. A blank space in a bit position indicates that that bit is not required in the code.

40 COMPUTER CODES [CHAP. 3

3.63 How are the 8, 4, 2, and 1 bits used to represent Hollerith's digit punches?

The 4 BCD bits are configured to represent any of the 10 digit punches 0 to 9. Table 3-3 illustrates the use of the 8, 4, 2, and 1 bits to replace the ten Hollerith digit punches.

3.64 How are the 8, 4, 2, and 1 bits combined to represent digit punches?

A single 1 bit and a single 2 bit are used to represent a 1-digit punch and a 2-digit punch, respectively. A 2 and a 1 bit are combined for a 3 punch. A lone 4 bit identifies a 4 punch. The combinations of a 4 and 1 bit, 4 and 2 bit, and 4, 2, and 1 bits are used for the 5-, 6-, and 7-digit punches. An 8 punch is an 8 bit alone. A 9 punch is a combination of an 8 and a 1 bit. No bits are used for the 0 punch.

3.65 What are the BCD equivalents for the 3-, 5-, and 9-digit punches?

The BCD equivalent of a 3 punch is a 2- and 1-bit combination. The BCD equivalent of a 5 punch uses the 4 and 1 bits, whereas a 9 punch requires an 8- and 1-bit grouping.

3.66 Why is it necessary to equate the use of BCD bits to Hollerith punches?

The establishment of a relationship between BCD and the Hollerith code is deliberate since this understanding is essential to developing a working knowledge of BCD.

3.67 What relationship exists between the Hollerith code and BCD?

The BCD code was derived from the Hollerith code. To illustrate this relationship, a simple three-step procedure will be used to develop BCD codes from Hollerith, as follows:
Step 1. Identify the character in terms of its Hollerith code.
Step 2. Convert the Hollerith zone and digit punches to their BCD equivalents; in terms of their B and A and 8-, 4-, 2-, and 1-bit groupings.
Step 3. Combine these BCD equivalents to form one BCD character.

3.68 Can any Hollerith code for a desired character be converted to its BCD configuration with this three-step procedure?

Yes. Without the conversion from Hollerith to BCD, there is no simple method of deriving the desired BCD codes.

3.69 Using the preceding three-step procedure, what is the BCD for the character F?

The BCD for F is constructed as follows:
Step 1. In the Hollerith code the character F consists of a 12-zone and 6-digit punch.
Step 2. The BCD equivalent of a 12-zone punch is a B- and A-bit configuration. The BCD equivalent of a 6-digit punch is a combination of the 4 and 2 bits.
Step 3. Combining these BCD equivalents, the BCD code for the character F consists of the B, A, 4, and 2 bits.

3.70 What is the BCD for the character P?

Using the three-step procedure, the conversion is made as follows:
Step 1. The Hollerith code for the character P is an 11-zone punch and a 7-digit punch.
Step 2. The BCD equivalent of the 11-zone punch is a B bit, and the BCD equivalent for a 7-digit punch is the 4, 2, and 1 bits.
Step 3. Combining these equivalents, the BCD code for P is the B, 4, 2, and 1 bits.

3.71 What is the BCD code for the character W?

The BCD code for the character W consists of bits A and 4.

3.72 Using the three-step procedure, what is the BCD code for the number 9?

The BCD code for 9 is constructed as follows:
Step 1. The Hollerith code for 9 consists of a No Zone punch and a 9 punch.
Step 2. The BCD equivalent of the No Zone uses neither an A nor a B bit.
Step 3. The BCD code for the number 9 consists only of an 8 bit and a 1 bit.

3.73 Where may readers verify their conversions of numeric and alphabetic characters?

Table 3-4 The BCD and Hollerith Codes

Character	Hollerith Code Punches		BCD B A 8 4 2 1
	Zone	Digit	
A	12	1	B A 1
B	12	2	B A 2
C	12	3	B A 2 1
D	12	4	B A 4
E	12	5	B A 4 1
F	12	6	B A 4 2
G	12	7	B A 4 2 1
H	12	8	B A 8
I	12	9	B A 8 1
J	11	1	B 1
K	11	2	B 2
L	11	3	B 2 1
M	11	4	B 4
N	11	5	B 4 1
O	11	6	B 4 2
P	11	7	B 4 2 1
Q	11	8	B 8
R	11	9	B 8 1
S	0	2	A 2
T	0	3	A 2 1
U	0	4	A 4
V	0	5	A 4 1
W	0	6	A 4 2
X	0	7	A 4 2 1
Y	0	8	A 8
Z	0	9	A 8 1
0	No Zone	0	A
1	No Zone	1	1
2	No Zone	2	2
3	No Zone	3	2 1
4	No Zone	4	4
5	No Zone	5	4 1
6	No Zone	6	4 2
7	No Zone	7	4 2 1
8	No Zone	8	8
9	No Zone	9	8 1

Table 3-4 provides a complete development of the Hollerith and BCD codes for all alphabetic and numeric characters. Using Table 3-4, the reader may check codes developed for BCD.

THE EBCDIC CODE

3.74 What do the letters EBCDIC stand for?

The letters EBCDIC identify the computer code Extended Binary-Coded Decimal Interchangeable Code.

3.75 Why was EBCDIC developed?

EBCDIC was introduced in the early 1960s as an expansion of the then-existing BCD code. Computer designers believed that BCD was too restrictive in terms of the numbers of character codes it could represent. The EBCDIC code provides 256 code configurations that can be used to represent data.

3.76 How does EBCDIC relate to the Hollerith code?

EBCDIC is an internal storage code that is used within the CPU's primary storage unit, whereas the Hollerith code is used solely to transfer data onto cards. When these data are input, the computer accepts the Hollerith-coded data and converts it into EBCDIC for retention in the primary storage unit. In effect, Hollerith is used outside the computer, and EBCDIC is used within the computer.

3.77 Essentially, then, input data are converted to EBCDIC for storage in a CPU?

Yes. Computers that use EBCDIC will efficiently convert input data to the EBCDIC format for placement in their primary storage units.

3.78 What format does EBCDIC assume?

Unlike BCD, EBCDIC uses a total of 8 bits to compose its character configurations. It divides these 8 bits into two 4-bit groupings; the initial 4-bit grouping is established as the equivalent of zone punches, and the second grouping, the equivalent of digit punches. The relationship of these 8 bits is illustrated in Fig. 3-6.

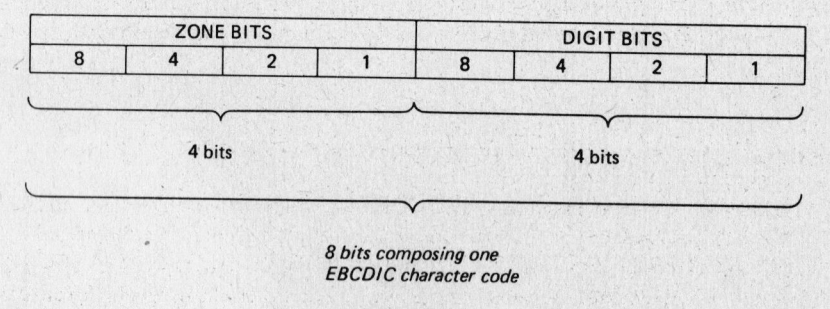

ZONE BITS				DIGIT BITS			
8	4	2	1	8	4	2	1

4 bits | 4 bits

8 bits composing one EBCDIC character code

Fig. 3-6

3.79 What are the EBCDIC equivalents for Hollerith's zone and digit punches?

The EBCDIC equivalents of zone and digit punches are shown in Table 3-5.

Table 3-5 EBCDIC Equivalents to Hollerith's Zone and Digit Punches

		Hollerith Zone Punches			
		12-Zone Punch	11-Zone Punch	0-Zone Punch	No Zone Punch
EBCDIC Zone Bits	8	1	1	1	1
	4	1	1	1	1
	2	0	0	1	1
	1	0	1	0	1

		Hollerith Digit Punches									
		1	2	3	4	5	6	7	8	9	0
EBCDIC Digit Bits	8	0	0	0	0	0	0	0	1	1	0
	4	0	0	0	1	1	1	1	0	0	0
	2	0	1	1	0	0	1	1	0	0	0
	1	1	0	1	0	1	0	1	0	1	0

3.80 How are the EBCDIC equivalents configured?

The first consideration is that the bits associated with EBCDIC all use 0s and 1s to represent their code configurations. The use of 0s and 1s parallels the use of bits in BCD. Effectively, a 1 indicates that a bit is used (and is therefore ON), whereas a 0 means that the bit is not used (and is therefore OFF).

3.81 What are the EBCDIC equivalents for the zone punches?

The EBCDIC equivalent of the Hollerith 12-zone punch is 1100 (reading the 8, 4, 2, and 1 bits downward). The 11-zone punch has a 1101 bit configuration, whereas the 1110 grouping is equivalent to the 0-zone punch. The No Zone equivalent, used with numeric character codes in EBCDIC, has a 1111 bit format.

3.82 What are the digit equivalents in EBCDIC?

The equivalents of the digit punches in EBCDIC are similar to BCD's digit codes. If 0s and 1s were substituted for the blanks and dots of the BCD code, the codes would be identical.

The EBCDIC code for 1 is the grouping 0001 (reading the 8421 bits downward). In that configuration a 1 is positioned against the 1 bit and denotes its usage in formulating the code. The EBCDIC configuration 0010 defines the code for a 2-digit punch, with the 1 associated with the 2 bit of the digit grouping. The 3 punch is defined in EBCDIC as 0011, where 1s are positioned against the 2 and 1 bits (thus totaling 3). Advancing this concept, the 4 punch is a 0100-bit configuration (the 1 matched against the 4 bit alone); the 5 punch carries a 0101 grouping (1s placed against the 4 and 1 bits); the 6 punch noted as the 0110 bits (1s posted against the 4 and 2 bits); and the 7 punch configured as 0111 (1s used in the 4, 2, and 1 bits). The 8- and 9-digit punch equivalents are represented by the 1000 and 1001 groupings (the 1s positioned against the 8 bit and the 8 and 1 bits, respectively).

3.83 Can the EBCDIC codes for alphabetic and numeric characters be related to the Hollerith code?

Yes. A three-step procedure similar to that used with BCD is used to construct the EBCDIC code configuration.
Step 1. Determine the Hollerith code punches for a given character or number.
Step 2. Determine the EBCDIC equivalents for the zone and digit punches defined in step 1.
Step 3. Combine the EBCDIC equivalents of step 2 to form the code for that character or number.

3.84 Applying the three-step procedure of Problem 3.83, what is the EBCDIC code for the character D?

The code for the character D is constructed as follows:
Step 1. The Hollerith code for D consists of a 12-zone and 4-digit punch.
Step 2. The EBCDIC equivalent of a 12-zone punch is 1100, and the EBCDIC equivalent of a 4-digit punch is 0100.
Step 3. Combining the EBCDIC equivalents, the resulting code for the character D is 1100 0100.

3.85 Using the same procedure, what is the EBCDIC code for the character L?

The EBCDIC code for the character L is constructed as follows:
Step 1. The Hollerith code for L consists of an 11-zone and 3-digit punch.
Step 2. The EBCDIC equivalents for the 11-zone and 3-digit punches are 1101 and 0011, respectively.
Step 3. Combining these equivalents, the EBCDIC code for the character L is 1101 0011.

3.86 What is the EBCDIC code for the character V?

The Hollerith code for V consists of a 0-zone and a 5-digit punch, which is converted to an EBCDIC code of 1110 0101. The EBCDIC zone grouping of 1110 identifies the 0-zone punch, whereas 0101 is the EBCDIC digit equivalent of a 5-digit punch.

3.87 Applying the three-step procedure, what is the EBCDIC code for the number 6?

The three-step procedure outlining the EBCDIC code for 6 is as follows:
Step 1. The Hollerith code for the number 6 involves a No Zone punch and a 6-digit punch.
Step 2. The EBCDIC equivalent of the No Zone punch is 1111, and the EBCDIC equivalent of a 6-digit punch is 0110.
Step 3. Combining the EBCDIC equivalents, the EBCDIC code for the number 6 is 1111 0110.

3.88 Why does EBCDIC stress the use of 0s and 1s in its format?

The designers of the EBCDIC code desired to more closely parallel the actual storage of data inside the computer. The use of 0s and 1s simulates the impulses (or electrical states) by which data are stored.

3.89 Are the data really stored in terms of 0s and 1s inside the computer?

Data stored inside the computer are actually stored in the form of electric impulses. The use of 0s and 1s to represent this storage mode simplifies the task of understanding how data are stored. The use of 0s and 1s makes it easier to explain the structure of EBCDIC, for example.

3.90 What term is used to define the use of 0s and 1s in the representation of computer storage codes?

The use of 0s and 1s is referred to as *binary notation*. This reference results from the fact that the use of binary notation is related to base 2. The only digits permitted in a base 2 numbering system are 0 and 1.

3.91 Is the use of binary notation effective in representing computer storage codes?

Yes. Binary notation closely parallels the actual impulses used by computers to store data.

3.92 Is EBCDIC the only code to use binary notation?

No. Many computer codes use binary notation to represent their data. The EBCDIC code uses it directly, denoting its codes in terms of 0s and 1s. The BCD code uses binary notation in a different way. The BCD code uses dots and blanks—the equivalent of 1s and 0s—to note the use of bits and therefore, to construct and represent its codes. In effect, both BCD and EBCDIC use binary notation to represent their character codes. See Table 3-6.

Table 3-6 EBCDIC and Hollerith Codes

EBCDIC 8 4 2 1 8 4 2 1	Character	Hollerith Code Punches	
		Zone	Digit
1 1 0 0 0 0 0 1	A	12	1
1 1 0 0 0 0 1 0	B	12	2
1 1 0 0 0 0 1 1	C	12	3
1 1 0 0 0 1 0 0	D	12	4
1 1 0 0 0 1 0 1	E	12	5
1 1 0 0 0 1 1 0	F	12	6
1 1 0 0 0 1 1 1	G	12	7
1 1 0 0 1 0 0 0	H	12	8
1 1 0 0 1 0 0 1	I	12	9
1 1 0 1 0 0 0 1	J	11	1
1 1 0 1 0 0 1 0	K	11	2
1 1 0 1 0 0 1 1	L	11	3
1 1 0 1 0 1 0 0	M	11	4
1 1 0 1 0 1 0 1	N	11	5
1 1 0 1 0 1 1 0	O	11	6
1 1 0 1 0 1 1 1	P	11	7
1 1 0 1 1 0 0 0	Q	11	8
1 1 0 1 1 0 0 1	R	11	9
1 1 1 0 0 0 1 0	S	0	2
1 1 1 0 0 0 1 1	T	0	3
1 1 1 0 0 1 0 0	U	0	4
1 1 1 0 0 1 0 1	V	0	5
1 1 1 0 0 1 1 0	W	0	6
1 1 1 0 0 1 1 1	X	0	7
1 1 1 0 1 0 0 0	Y	0	8
1 1 1 0 1 0 0 1	Z	0	9
1 1 1 1 0 0 0 0	0	No Zone	0
1 1 1 1 0 0 0 1	1	No Zone	1
1 1 1 1 0 0 1 0	2	No Zone	2
1 1 1 1 0 0 1 1	3	No Zone	3
1 1 1 1 0 1 0 0	4	No Zone	4
1 1 1 1 0 1 0 1	5	No Zone	5
1 1 1 1 0 1 1 0	6	No Zone	6
1 1 1 1 0 1 1 1	7	No Zone	7
1 1 1 1 1 0 0 0	8	No Zone	8
1 1 1 1 1 0 0 1	9	No Zone	9

3.93 How can EBCDIC configurations be verified?

Table 3-6 defines the EBCDIC and Hollerith codes for all alphabetic and numeric characters. Using Table 3-6, readers may check the EBCDIC configurations for any code constructed.

THE ASCII CODE

3.94 What does the term *ASCII* refer to?

The term *ASCII* represents the American Standard Code for Information Interchange, the name applied to another major code used in the computer field.

3.95 Who developed the ASCII code?

The ASCII code was developed by a group of computer manufacturers in an attempt to standardize the codes to be used with terminals and with the telecommunication of data between these devices.

3.96 Is the ASCII code used solely with terminals?

No. In addition to its use with terminal devices, the ASCII code is used in many of the smaller computer systems for the internal storage of data within their primary storage units. For example, many home computers rely on the ASCII code for data storage.

3.97 Is the structure of the ASCII code related to the Hollerith code?

No. One of the most important characteristics of the ASCII code is its independence from the Hollerith code. The structure of its code depends on the order of the alphabet (A to Z) and numerical sequence (0 to 9). As such, it does not possess specific equivalents for Hollerith's zone and digit punches.

3.98 Is the structure of the ASCII code similar to any other code?

Yes. The appearance of the ASCII code is quite similar to the EBCDIC format in that both use a total of 8 bits to compose a character. It subdivides these 8 bits into two 4 groupings: The first 4 bits are referred to as the *zone configuration*; and the second 4 bits, as the *digit bits*. Although referred to as "zone" and "digits" bits, they do not represent the zone and digit punches of the Hollerith code.

3.99 What are the zone-bit configurations employed with ASCII?

The three zone configurations used with the ASCII are 1010, 1011, and 0101. The 1010 and 1011 groupings are used with alphabetic character codes, whereas the 0101 grouping is used solely with numeric codes.

3.100 What characters are associated with the zone codes 1010 and 1011?

The characters A through O use the 1010 bits, and the 1011 bits are reserved for the alphabetic characters P–Z.

3.101 Can the digit bits be assigned the values of 8, 4, 2, and 1 in the construction of the ASCII codes?

Yes. The last 4 bits of the ASCII code are assigned those values and used as the 8, 4, 2, and 1 bits of other codes.

3.102 Assuming the sequenced structure of the ASCII code, what is the ASCII code for the character A, and what is the rationale used?

The ASCII code for the character A is 1010 0001. The zone configuration used with the characters A to O is 1010. The last 4 digits, 0001, finds the 1 in the 1-bit position. These last four bits add up to 1, which reflects the fact that A is the first letter of the alphabet.

3.103 Does the ASCII code for B reflect the fact that it is the second letter of the alphabet?

Yes. The ASCII code for B is 1010 0010. The zone bits are consistent with their use for the characters A to O. In the last 4 bits, the 1 is placed in the 2-bit position. Adding these last 4 bits, they total 2—the number representative of the second letter of the alphabet.

3.104 What is the ASCII code for C?

The ASCII code for C is 1010 0011. The zone bits are 1010, while the digit bits are 0011. In these last four bits 1s are placed in the 2- and 1-bit positions. Adding these last two bits totals 3, the number representative of the third letter of the alphabet, C.

3.105 What character carries the ASCII code of 1010 1111?

Since it carries the zone configuration of 1010, it must be a character A to O. Since 1s are positioned against the 8, 4, 2, and 1 bits, these total 15. The fifteenth letter of the alphabet is O.

3.106 What purpose does the ASCII code for P serve?

The ASCII code for P, 1011 0000, serves as the basis for the characters Q to Z. It is the sixteenth character of the alphabet, and all characters following it must add 16 to the sum of their digit bits.

3.107 How is that basis evident in the ASCII code for Q?

The ASCII code for Q is 1011 0001. The zone bits are 1011, those used with the characters P to Z. The digit configuration totals 1, which added to 16 equals 17. The seventeenth character of the alphabet is Q.

3.108 What is the ASCII code for T?

The ASCII code for T, the twentieth alphabetic character, is 1011 0100. The zone configuration is 1011. The digit grouping is 0100, with 1 positioned at the 4 bit. The total of these bits is 4, which added to 16 equals 20.

3.109 What character is indicated by the ASCII code 1011 1010?

The ASCII code of 1011 1010 represents the character Z. The zone configuration of 1011 is used with the characters P to Z. The digits 1010 find 1s placed against the 8- and 2-bit positions, totaling 10. The sum of 10 and 16 is 26, and Z is the last, and twenty-sixth, letter of the alphabet.

3.110 How are ASCII codes configured for numeric characters?

Numeric codes in ASCII are constructed in a fashion similar to EBCDIC. The zone grouping for all numbers 0 to 9 is 0101. The digit groupings use 8-, 4-, 2-, and 1-bit positional grouping, adding those quantities associated with the placement of 1s in the code. The resulting digit groupings in ASCII are identical to EBCDIC. The major difference between the EBCDIC and ASCII codes for numeric characters is the use of the 0101 zone bits in ASCII.

3.111 Assuming the similarity to EBCDIC, what is the ASCII code for 6?

The ASCII code for 6 is 0101 0110. The zone grouping is 0101. The digit bits find 1s in the 4- and 2-bit positions, which total 6.

3.112 What is the ASCII code for 9?

The ASCII code for 9 is 0101 1001. The zone configuration of 0101 is followed by digit bits of 1001. In the digit grouping, 1s are placed in the 8 and 1 positions, which total 9.

3.113 How can the ASCII codes for alphabetic and numeric characters be reviewed?

Table 3-7 offers the ASCII codes for A to Z and 0 to 9.

Table 3-7 ASCII Codes for Alphabetic and Numeric Characters

Bit Configuration	ASCII	Bit Configuration	ASCII
1010 0001	A	1011 0011	S
1010 0010	B	1011 0100	T
1010 0011	C	1011 0101	U
1010 0100	D	1011 0110	V
1010 0101	E	1011 0111	W
1010 0110	F	1011 1000	X
1010 0111	G	1011 1001	Y
1010 1000	H	1011 1010	Z
1010 1001	I	0101 0000	0
1010 1010	J	0101 0001	1
1010 1011	K	0101 0010	2
1010 1100	L	0101 0011	3
1010 1101	M	0101 0100	4
1010 1110	N	0101 0101	5
1010 1111	O	0101 0110	6
1011 0000	P	0101 0111	7
1011 0001	Q	0101 1000	8
1011 0010	R	0101 1001	9

Review Questions

3.114 The standard punch card consists of 10 rows and 80 columns. (*a*) True, (*b*) false.

3.115 The three types of characters used with 80-column cards are numeric, alphabetic, and alphameric characters. (*a*) True, (*b*) false.

3.116 In the Hollerith code alphabetic characters are represented by a zone punch and a digit punch. (*a*) True, (*b*) false.

3.117 Numeric character codes in Hollerith are defined by punches in the rows equivalent to the number desired. (*a*) True, (*b*) false.

3.118 The Hollerith code for the character N consists of a 12-zone and 5-digit punch. (*a*) True, (*b*) false.

3.119 Special-character codes may require one, two, or three punches per card column (*a*) True, (*b*) false.

3.120 Card fields should be large enough to accommodate the largest item of data to be stored within that field.   (*a*) True, (*b*) false.

3.121 Alphabetic data items are usually right-justified when punched onto card fields.   (*a*) True, (*b*) false.

3.122 In BCD the code for the character L consists of the B, 2, and 1 bits.   (*a*) True, (*b*) false.

3.123 In BCD the code for the character U consists of the A, 2, and 1 bits.   (*a*) True, (*b*) false.

3.124 The BCD and ASCII and EBCDIC codes are directly related to the Hollerith code.   (*a*) True, (*b*) false.

3.125 In EBCDIC each code must consist of a series of eight 0s and 1s.   (*a*) True, (*b*) false.

3.126 The EBCDIC code for the number 4 is 1111 0100.   (*a*) True, (*b*) false.

3.127 By utilizing the digits 0 and 1, EBCDIC is said to use "binary notation."   (*a*) True, (*b*) false.

3.128 Character codes in ASCII are defined on a positional basis.   (*a*) True, (*b*) false.

3.129 The ASCII code for the number 3 is 1111 0011.   (*a*) True, (*b*) false.

3.130 The ASCII code for the character X is 1011 1000.   (*a*) True, (*b*) false.

3.131 The top edge of the 80-column card is referred to as the   (*a*) 9 edge; (*b*) 12 edge; (*c*) zone edge; (*d*) no reference exists.

3.132 A characteristic associated with the Hollerith code is   (*a*) a unique code for each character; (*b*) a standardized code format; (*c*) the punching of only one character code per card column; (*d*) all of the above.

3.133 The Hollerith code for the character V is   (*a*) 11-zone and 5-digit punch; (*b*) 12-zone and 5-digit punch; (*c*) 0-zone and 5-digit punch; (*d*) 0-zone and 6-digit punch.

3.134 The card field defined for a telephone number, including dashes, would be classified as a(n)   (*a*) alphabetic field; (*b*) alphameric field; (*c*) numeric field; (*d*) *b* or *c*.

3.135 The code used with a 96-column card is   (*a*) ASCII; (*b*) EBCDIC; (*c*) BCD; (*d*) Hollerith.

3.136 In BCD the code for the number 7 consists of the   (*a*) B, A, and 7 bits; (*b*) B, A, 4, 2, and 1 bits; (*c*) 4, 2, and 1 bits; (*d*) none of these.

3.137 In EBCDIC the equivalent of a 12-zone punch is   (*a*) 1100; (*b*) 1101; (*c*) 1110; (*d*) 1111.

3.138 The EBCDIC code for the character Y is   (*a*) 1111 1000; (*b*) 1110 1001; (*c*) 1111 1001; (*d*) 1110 1000.

3.139 Which of the following is an appropriate zone code for ASCII?   (*a*) 1100; (*b*) 0101; (*c*) 1110; (*d*) 1111.

3.140 The computer code developed to standardize the codes used with terminal devices was   (*a*) ASCII; (*b*) BCD; (*c*) EBCDIC; (*d*) Hollerith.

3.141 The ASCII code for the character M is   (*a*) 1101 0100; (*b*) 1010 1101; (*c*) 1011 0100; (*d*) 1011 1101.

3.142 The concept of the punch card and code was originated by _____.

3.143 The 80-column card is often referred to as the _____ punch card.

3.144 When the numbers on the card are facing the user, we state that the card is positioned _____.

3.145 Rows 12, 11, and 0 on the 80-column card are defined as the _____ rows.

3.146 On the punch card, _____ define particular card columns that are set aside for specific items of data.

3.147 A field established to handle ZIP code data could be defined as a(n) _____ field.

3.148 Normally, alphameric fields are _____-justified.

3.149 The bits used to compose BCD data are the _____ bits.

3.150 In BCD the equivalent of an 11-zone punch is a(n) _____.

3.151 A total of _____ bits is necessary to compose an EBCDIC character code.

3.152 The EBCDIC code for the character T is _____.

3.153 In ASCII the zone digits used with numbers are _____.

3.154 In ASCII the zone bits used with the characters P to Z are _____.

3.155 The ASCII code for the number 9 is _____.

Answers: 3.114 (b); 3.115 (b); 3.116 (a); 3.117 (a); 3.118 (b); 3.119 (a); 3.120 (a); 3.121 (b); 3.122 (a); 3.123 (b); 3.124 (b); 3.125 (a); 3.126 (a); 3.127 (a); 3.128 (a); 3.129 (b); 3.130 (a); 3.131 (b); 3.132 (d); 3.133 (c); 3.134 (b); 3.135 (c); 3.136 (c); 3.137 (a); 3.138 (d); 3.139 (b); 3.140 (a); 3.141 (b); 3.142 Hollerith; 3.143 standard; 3.144 faceup; 3.145 zone; 3.146 fields; 3.147 numeric; 3.148 left; 3.149 B, A, 8, 4, 2, 1; 3.150 B bit; 3.151 8; 3.152 1110 0011; 3.153 0101; 3.154 1011; 3.155 0101 1001.

Supplementary Problems

3.156 Complete the table below, filling in the proper codes for the character indicated.

Character	Hollerith	BCD	EBCDIC	ASCII
G				
M				
X				
5				
I				
Q				
W				
3				

3.157 Examine the following list of data items and define each item as being a numeric, alphabetic, or alphameric field and indicate the potential size of the field.

    Street address   Time of day
    Social security number   Net pay
    Today's date   Price per gallon of gas
    Sex   Unit cost of carpeting
    Hours worked   Horoscope sign
    Name of a car   Job description
    Test grade   Bowling average
    City   Part description

3.158 From your personal experience give examples of situations in which punch cards are used. Explain why you think the cards are used.

3.159 Why is the 0 row on the 80-column card considered to have a dual purpose?

3.160 Illustrate how the following data items would be right- or left-justified in the field sizes indicated.

Data Item	Justification	Field Size	Field Type
350.6	Right	6 columns	Numeric
OREGON	Left	10 columns	Alphabetic
280ZX	Left	8 columns	Alphameric
52	Right	7 columns	Numeric
CHICAGO	Left	12 columns	Alphabetic
7/28/89	Left	10 columns	Alphameric

Glossary

Alphabetic character. One of the letters A to Z.

Alphabetic field. A field consisting solely of alphabetic characters.

Alphameric field. A field that can contain any combination of numeric, alphabetic, and special characters.

ASCII (American Standard Code for Information Interchange). Computer code developed to standardize codes used on terminal devices; independent of the Hollerith code.

Binary-Coded Decimal (BCD). The computer code used with 96-column cards, which uses the 6 bits of B, A, 8, 4, 2, and 1.

Binary notation. A method of representing numeric data using only 0s and 1s, the digits that make up a binary (base 2) numbering system.

Card column. The basic unit of a punched card capable of containing the code for exactly one character.

Card field. A consecutive number of card columns set aside to contain specific items of data.

Digit punches. Punches in the 0 to 9 rows on an 80-column card.

EBCDIC (Extended Binary-Coded Decimal Interchangeable Code). A computer code, used for the internal storage of data, which consists of eight 0s and 1s.

80-column card. The standard punch card, consisting of 80 columns, that uses the Hollerith code.

Hollerith. The creator of the Hollerith code and card.

Hollerith code. The code used with the 80-column card.

Left-justification. The placement of data in the leftmost positions, or columns, of a field.

96-column card. The physically smaller version of the Hollerith card that uses BCD to code data and that is used solely with the IBM System/3 computer systems.

Numeric characters. The digits 0 to 9.

Numeric fields. Fields consisting solely of numeric data.

Right-justification. The placement of data in the rightmost positions, or columns, of a field.

Row. One of twelve horizontal components on the 80-column card.

Special characters. Any character that is not considered alphabetic or numeric.

Zone punches. Punches in the 12, 11, and 0 rows of the 80-column card.

Zone rows. The 12, 11, and 0 rows of the 80-column card.

Chapter 4

Input and Output Devices

4.1 CARD-RELATED DEVICES

A computer system utilizes many types of input and output devices to process data and disseminate information to its users. In systems that are card-oriented, three devices are generally evident, namely, the card reader, the card punch, and the card reader/punch.

Card readers are input devices classified as either serial card readers or parallel card readers. *Serial card readers* read data on a column-by-column basis and are exemplified by *photoelectric-cell card readers*. *Parallel card readers* read data from the card on a row-by-row basis. *Brush card readers* fall into the category of parallel card readers. Generally, serial card readers attain higher reading speeds than parallel card readers.

Card punch devices are normally found in computer systems that must output large quantities of cards. Using a card punch to prepare cards is more efficient than keypunching because the data to be punched are fed directly from the computer.

The device most often found in card-oriented systems is the *card reader/punch*. This device combines an input and an output capability in one unit and satisfies a diverse group of operational needs.

A concept associated with the use of cards is the *unit-record concept*. This concept is based on the principle that a punched card becomes a record of one unit of data. All data related to one transaction generally are keyed onto one card to expedite processing.

4.2 PRINTING DEVICES

The preparation of printed materials is assigned to a variety of printing devices that may be integrated into a computer system. Generally, the printing device chosen reflects the user's needs and the technology available.

Printers are classified as either impact or nonimpact. *Impact printers* utilize some object to strike the paper, leaving the character image on its surface. *Nonimpact printers* utilize chemical, electrostatic, laser, or other means to produce their outputs. Nonimpact printers normally exhibit the highest printing speeds, but they can print only one copy of output at a time. Each type of printing device has its own operational advantages and limitations.

A specialized form of printing device is the plotter. *Plotters* are used to produce continuous-line drawings, pictorial displays of data, and graphical analyses not possible with conventional printers.

4.3 TERMINALS

Because of the increase in online processing operations, terminals have become an integral part of most computer systems. Terminal devices offer both softcopy and hardcopy outputs, depending on user needs. The most common terminal device is the *cathode ray tube* (*CRT*), which displays its output on a television-like screen. *Hardcopy terminals*, which provide a printed output, are now also commonplace. Some specially designed terminals can produce both hardcopy and softcopy outputs as needed.

Other specialized terminal devices are also available to satisfy a variety of user needs. *Video display terminals* support retail sales and similar operations, and *data collection terminals* are used to speed the input of data from remote job locations. Terminal devices that operate with verbal inputs or outputs are being perfected, but they have not yet reached full operational use. Also available are color terminal devices. Currently, terminal devices that provide color hardcopy and softcopy outputs are being perfected and should replace conventional terminal devices.

4.4 INTELLIGENT DEVICES

The word *intelligence* when applied to I/O devices implies that the unit possesses operational features not normally found in conventional devices. *Intelligent terminals*, for example, possess the ability to monitor the entry of input data. This feature, referred to as *editing*, is not found in regular terminal devices. *Intelligent printers* also exist and exhibit the capacity to operate on an online and offline basis. Intelligent printers can perform a variety of office documentation tasks in addition to printing outputs.

Printing subsystems offer a high-speed printing capability, and they can utilize normal paper stock. They use low-power lasers to produce various type sizes and type faces and duplicate any sort of customized letter format. Printing subsystems may attain printing speeds in excess of 20,000 lines per minute.

4.5 WORD PROCESSING (WP)

Word processing (*WP*) is defined as the computerized preparation of office paperwork ranging from single letters to multipage reports. Many of the previously discussed printing and terminal devices play a major part in word processing activities.

Word processing systems are small computer systems designed to support an office's word processing operations. These systems will usually consist of a CRT, magnetic disk storage, and a printing device. Intelligent printing devices are sometimes substituted for printers in word processing systems to add a specialized printing capability. These devices enable the preparation of multipage reports with the data coming directly from the computer.

Using word processing systems, it is possible to transmit data between distant offices, bypassing conventional postal services. Such transmission of reports is called *electronic mail*. *Automatic typesetters* are word processing devices that receive all data directly from the computer and prepare films directly from manuscripts for subsequent printing.

4.6 DATA PROCESSING TECHNIQUES FOR BUSINESS

Many special techniques have been developed to help business in the rapid processing of large amounts of data. *Magnetic ink character recognition* (*MICR*) was developed to handle the processing of bank checks. *Optical character recognition* (*OCR*) enables the direct entry of input data utilizing specially shaped characters.

The compact storage of computer-generated outputs is accomplished via *computer output microfilm* (*COM*). Printed outputs are photographed onto individual microfilm records called *microfiche*. The computerized identification and retrieval of microfilm records is called *micrographics*. This technique was developed to assist those organizations having extensive libraries of microfilm records and needing rapid access to data within them.

CHAP. 4] INPUT AND OUTPUT DEVICES 55

Solved Problems

CARD-RELATED DEVICES

4.1 What card-oriented devices are normally found within computer systems?

The devices generally used in the computerized processing of cards include the card reader, the card punch, and the card reader/punch.

4.2 What function does the card reader serve?

The card reader serves as an input device and provides a means for sensing data punched onto punch cards. Data read from cards are transmitted to the CPU for processing.

4.3 Do card readers exist that handle both types of punch cards?

No. Card readers are designed to handle either the 80-column or the 96-column card; one device does not handle both types of cards. Generally, a computer system restricts its card processing operations to one type of card. Whereas the 80-column card is the most commonly used, the 96-column card is restricted to the IBM System/3 Series of computers. Because of its greater usage, this text will focus on devices that employ the standard punch card.

4.4 What are the two classes of card readers?

Card readers are either photoelectric-cell or brush readers. Each card reader derives its name from the manner in which it reads card data.

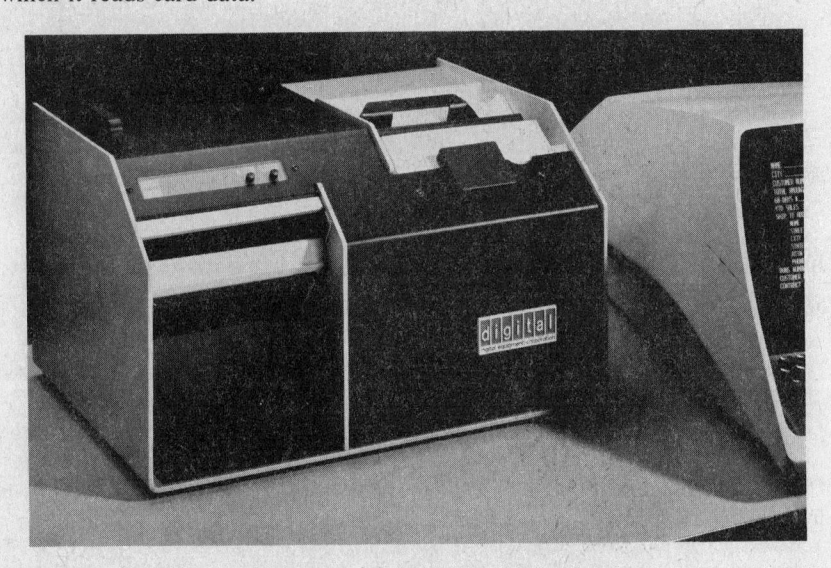

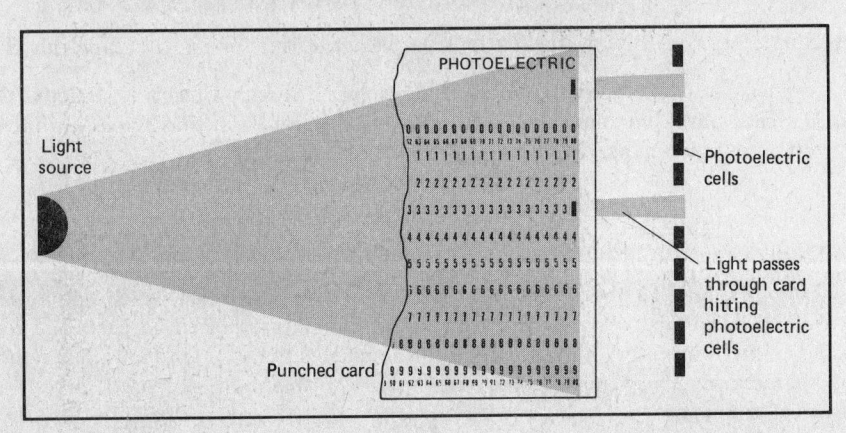

Fig. 4-1 Photoelectric-cell card reader. (*Digital Equipment Corp.*)

4.5 How is the photoelectric-cell card reader used?

Photoelectric-cell card readers, as shown in Fig. 4-1, read their data on a column-by-column basis. A series of 12 photoelectric cells senses the punches appearing within each card column as the card passes beneath the cells. The sensing of data begins with column 1 and continues to column 80.

4.6 What designation is applied to the reading of data on a column-by-column basis?

Card readers that read data on a column-by-column basis are referred to as serial card readers. This designation recognizes the sequential reading of data from cards on an individual-column basis, beginning with card column 1.

4.7 What is the operational opposite of the serial card reader?

The parallel card reader is the direct opposite of the serial card reader. The parallel card reader senses its data on a row-by-row basis and must read the entire card before transmitting its data. In contrast, the serial reader inputs each column's data as that column is read.

4.8 Which type of card reader is faster?

Because of the manner in which they read data, serial card readers are considerably faster, averaging 300–500 cards per minute more than parallel card readers.

4.9 What type of reader is the brush card reader?

Brush card readers are parallel card readers. These devices use a series of 80 brushes to read data from the surface of the card.

4.10 Which is a faster device: the photoelectric-cell or brush card reader?

The photoelectric-cell reader is faster; it is a serial reader, and these devices are generally faster than parallel readers.

4.11 Which of these two types of card readers is currently more popular?

Use of the brush reader is on the decline. The photoelectric-cell card readers are being adopted because of their higher reading speeds.

4.12 If the card reader serves an input function, of what purpose is the card punch?

The card punch is strictly an output device, punching information received directly from the CPU onto cards. The card punch enables the direct punching of card data, thus bypassing the delay inherent in other card preparation methods.

4.13 What type of outputs would a card punch prepare?

The outputs prepared by the card punch might be payroll cards on which employees will record the hours worked in the upcoming week, inventory cards that are placed on parts and removed when that part is issued from inventory, or accounts receivable cards that contain the total amount of dollars owed to an organization. An example of an accounts receivable card, prepared directly by the computer, is illustrated in Fig. 4-2.

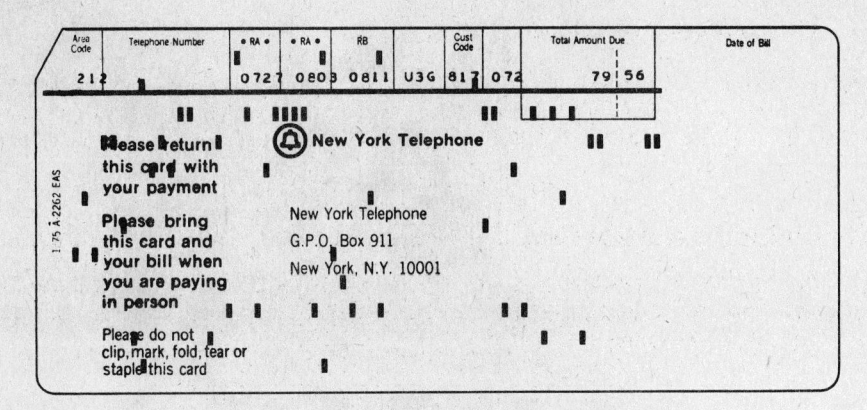

Fig. 4-2 A punched accounts receivable card.

4.14 What term is sometimes applied to the card outputs described in Prob. 4.13?

The previously discussed card outputs may be referred to as *turnaround documents* because after they are used, they are returned to the organization for subsequent processing. In the turnaround document in Fig. 4-2, the card is prepared with the amount due the telephone company; it is then sent to the customer to be returned with the payment. Once received by the telephone company, the card is input to the computer and becomes the basis for updating the customer's bill for the following month.

4.15 What is the operational importance of turnaround documents?

The use of cards that are directly prepared by card punches speeds the processing of data. A card is prepared, sent to the customer who then returns it, and then reused as input for the next phase of processing. The use of turnaround documents eliminates the necessity to prepare intermediate paperwork, which would add additional steps to the processing sequence and slow the overall process.

4.16 Occasionally the term *unit record* is applied to cards that represent a business transaction. What does the term *unit record* represent?

This term refers to the unit-record concept that was developed for the use of computer cards. The concept defined the use of a punched card as the *record* of a *unit* of data describing a transaction. Essentially, one card was to contain one complete unit of data for one transaction. Once that unit of data was punched onto a card, that card became a record of that unit of data.

4.17 Was the unit-record concept specifically applied to card processing operations?

Yes. The unit-record concept was established for cards at a time when cards were the primary means of processing data. The development of other computer media made the concept obsolete since the unit-record concept can be applied only to the use of punched cards.

4.18 Is there a device that combines the operational features of the card reader and the card punch?

Yes. The card reader/punch combines the I/O features of these two devices into one unit. The card reader/punch is physically one device, which normally has separate card reading and card punching units on either side of the device. Figure 4-3 shows a card reader/punch unit.

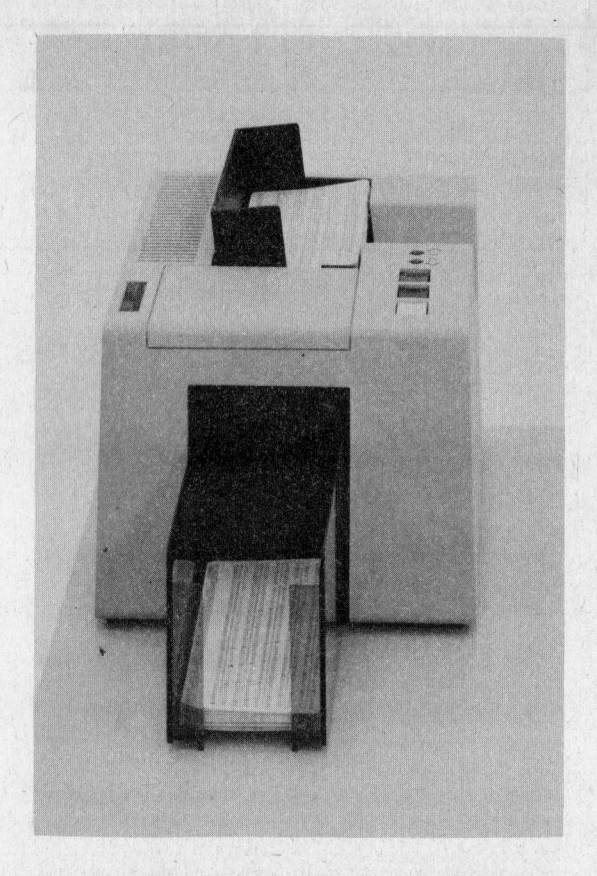

Fig. 4-3 The IBM 3501 card reader/punch. This is one of the many varieties of card reader/punches available currently. (*IBM*)

4.19 In relation to the other units, when is the card reader/punch incorporated into a computer system?

When an organization uses cards as a major data processing medium, then the card reader/punch should be an integral component of its computer system. This provides that organization with a dependable card reading and punching capability.

4.20 When would separate card reading and punching units be desirable?

When there is minimal use of cards or no card punching operations or only the *entry* of card data, the card reader is an ideal secondary input device. The card punch is best suited for those situations in which there is a high volume of card punching and where it has been decided to use only one device for this activity. Generally, when a large volume of card punching is anticipated, multiple card punches are installed in the computer system to improve the efficiency of this effort.

4.21 What are the relative operational speeds of these card-oriented devices?

Table 4-1 denotes the operational speeds normally associated with card readers, punches, and reader/punches. These speeds are measured in CPM (cards per minute).

CHAP. 4]   INPUT AND OUTPUT DEVICES   59

Table 4-1 A Comparison of Card Devices and Speeds

Device	Reading Speed	Punching Speed
Card reader	600–3000 CPM	
Card punch		300–1200 CPM
Card reader/punch	600–2400 CPM	150–1000 CPM

PRINTING DEVICES

4.22 What operational role do printing devices play in computer systems?

Printing devices provide printed output of processed information in the form of reports, listings, or other kinds of documentation.

4.23 What are the two classes of printing devices?

In general, printers are classified as being either impact or nonimpact printers.

4.24 What are the differences between impact and nonimpact printers?

The two classes of printers differ in the manner in which they prepare their outputs. *Impact* printers function in a manner similar to a typewriter, requiring the slug on which the desired character appears to strike the carbon ribbon and paper. In doing this, the character's image is printed on the paper. Nonimpact printers do not touch the paper; rather, printing is accomplished by a laser, electrostatic, chemical, or thermal means.

4.25 Why is there such diversity in printing devices?

Manufacturers developed a variety of printers to meet the diverse needs that exist among users.

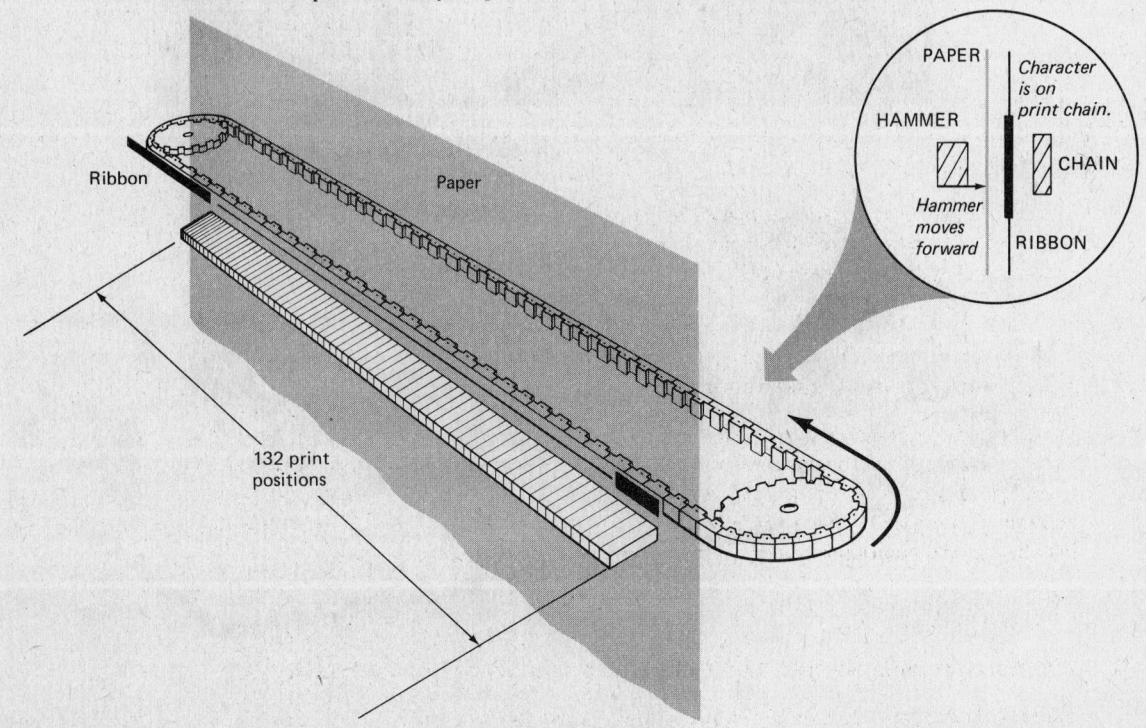

Fig. 4-4 Four types of printers.

60 INPUT AND OUTPUT DEVICES [CHAP. 4

4.26 Which impact printing devices are currently the most popular?

At this time the most widely used printing devices are the *chain printer*, *band printer*, *dot-* or *wire-matrix printer*, and *daisy-wheel printer*. These devices, shown in Fig. 4-4, vary in the manner in which they print, and they work at different speeds.

(b) The newly introduced band printer.

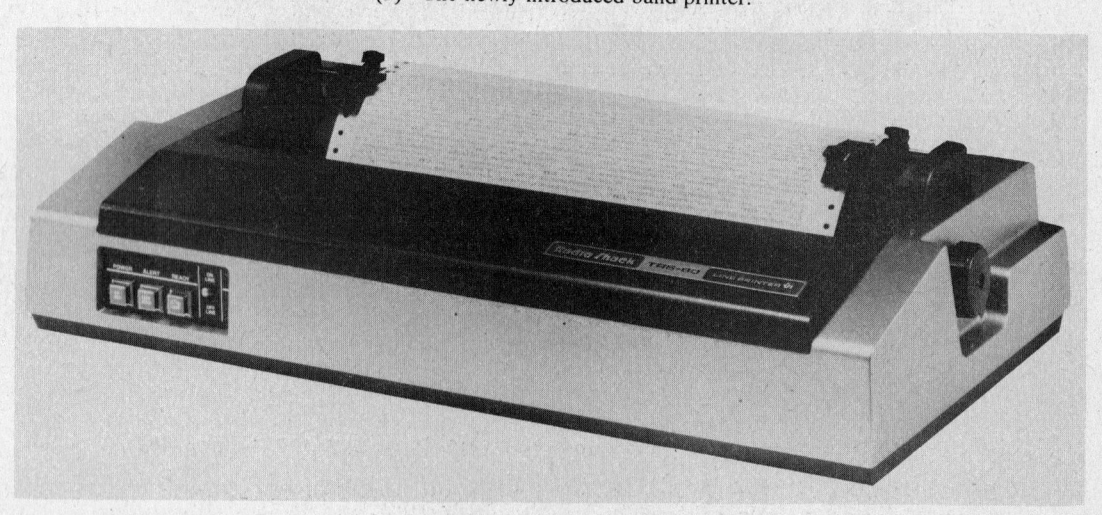

(c) A wire-matrix printer. (*Radio Shack*)

Fig. 4-4 (*cont.*)

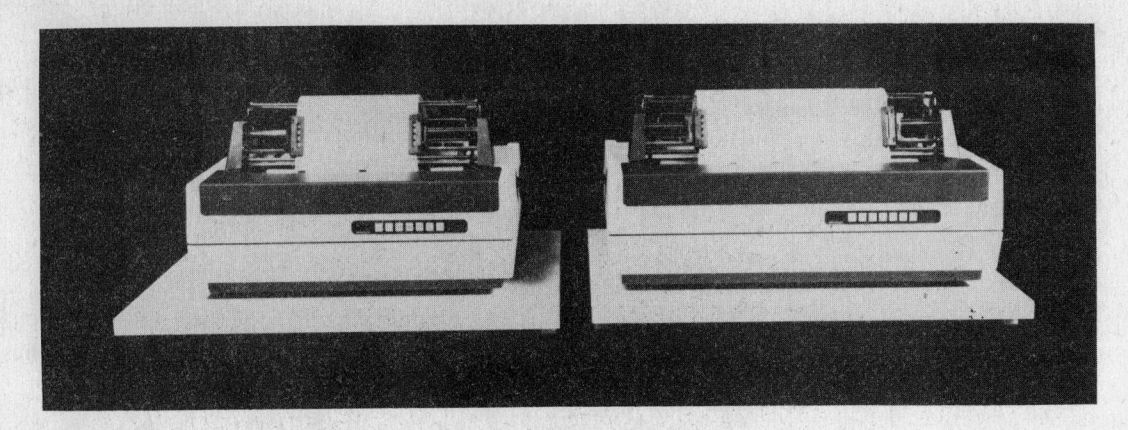

(d) The daisy-wheel printer. (*Wang*)

Fig. 4-4 (*cont.*)

4.27 Which is the fastest printer?

The chain printer (Fig. 4-4a) is the fastest of current impact printers, attaining speeds in excess of 2400 lines per minute (LPM). It derives its name from the fact that the characters used in printing are linked together on a flexible chain that rotates within the chain printer. As this chain rotates in front of the position in which the desired character is to be printed, a magnetized head moves forward to strike the chain. This movement presses the paper, carbon ribbon, and character slug on the chain together, thus creating the printed character on the paper. It is the speed of this printing mechanism that gives chain printers their high-speed capabilities.

4.28 Where is the chain printer most effectively used?

The chain printer is the mainstay of most DP centers because it provides reliable, high-speed printing while producing crisp, legible outputs. Organizations that rely on printed documents and that generate a considerable amount of hardcopy outputs will use the chain printer.

4.29 How does the band printer relate to the chain printer?

The band printer (Fig. 4-4b) is constructed similarly to the chain printer but with two distinctions. First, the band printer does not attain as high a printing speed, and second, it utilizes a metal band for printing instead of a flexible chain. The rotating band functions the same as a chain, but the band printer's top speed is approximately 600 LPM.

4.30 What differences are associated with the band printer?

The band printer has a lower printing speed and is therefore better suited to organizations that are not solely paper-oriented and can operationally withstand the slight delay in receipt of printed materials that may result from its lower printing speed. Another factor is the lower cost of the band printer. Many companies feel that the band printer's lower cost more than compensates for any potential delays that may arise. Also, with the band printer, print heads can easily, and thus frequently, be replaced to vary the typefaces with which reports are printed. Changing print heads is not as easy on the chain printer; in addition, there is a limit to the number of typefaces available for printing.

4.31 How can the differences between the chain and band printers be summarized?

Chain printers offer high printing speeds but have only a few conventional typefaces; they are best used in organizations that handle a high volume of printed reports and documentation. Band printers cost less, work at slower speeds, and have interchangeable bands and thus many typefaces; they are best used in organizations that require a lower level of printing support.

4.32 How does the dot- or wire-matrix printer compare to the chain and band printers?

The wire-matrix, or dot-matrix, printer offers a much slower printing speed, and it is not designed for the heavy volume of a paper-oriented DP center. It is a reliable medium-speed printer, which is competitively priced.

4.33 What is the operating speed of the wire-matrix printer?

The wire-matrix unit can attain a speed of 900 characters per minute (CPM), a much lower speed than either the band or chain printer. (Note that in this case, speed is measured not in lines per minute but characters per minute.) This slower printing speed results from the print mechanism used in the wire-matrix printer. Instead of using a solid character, the wire-matrix device uses a series of wires that extend forward to create a pattern of dots that compose the printed character. The lower speeds result from this wire-matrix print mechanism.

4.34 Considering its lower speed, where is the wire-matrix printer most often used?

The wire-matrix printer lends itself to organizations that have a specific number of printed outputs, limited in scope and size. Wire-matrix units are often incorporated into terminal devices that are used to enter student programs and/or limited amounts of operational data, or they are used to interact with the computer when performing data inquiries against customer files. If printing speeds are not critical, the wire-matrix printer may adequately serve low-level printing needs. Figure 4-4c shows a common wire-matrix device.

4.35 What type of device is the daisy-wheel printer?

The daisy-wheel printer was recently introduced to replace the typewriter as an output device. It is a low-level printing device capable of outputting a few hundred characters per minute. The key to this printer is the daisy-wheel printing mechanism, which rotates to place the desired character in position for printing.

4.36 What special features does the daisy-wheel offer?

The daisy-wheel printer shown in Fig. 4-4d illustrates some special features available with these devices. It is a *twin-head, bidirectional printer*. The "twin-head" designation means that it uses two daisy-wheels, thus offering two typefaces. The bidirectional feature allows the data to be printed from left to right and from right to left. This bidirectional approach is much quicker, as the print-heads do not have to return to the left margins.

4.37 Where is the daisy-wheel printer used?

Organizations requiring a low-level printing device for preparing office paperwork can effectively use the daisy-wheel printer. It is competitively priced, offers a wide range of interchangeable printing styles, and can prepare many forms of hardcopy outputs.

4.38 Currently what other special printing options are available with impact printers?

In addition to the previously described types of printing devices, color printing devices capable of outputting reports and graphs in four colors have been recently introduced. Figure 4-5 shows one type of color printer.

4.39 Do nonimpact printers function in the same way as their impact counterparts?

No. Whereas impact printers must strike the paper with some type of object to create the character image, nonimpact printers produce hardcopy without touching the paper.

4.40 What major means of nonimpact printing exist?

Nonimpact printers may employ *thermal, electrostatic, laser,* or *ink-jet* printing techniques to print data. Figure 4-6 illustrates these four types of nonimpact printing devices.

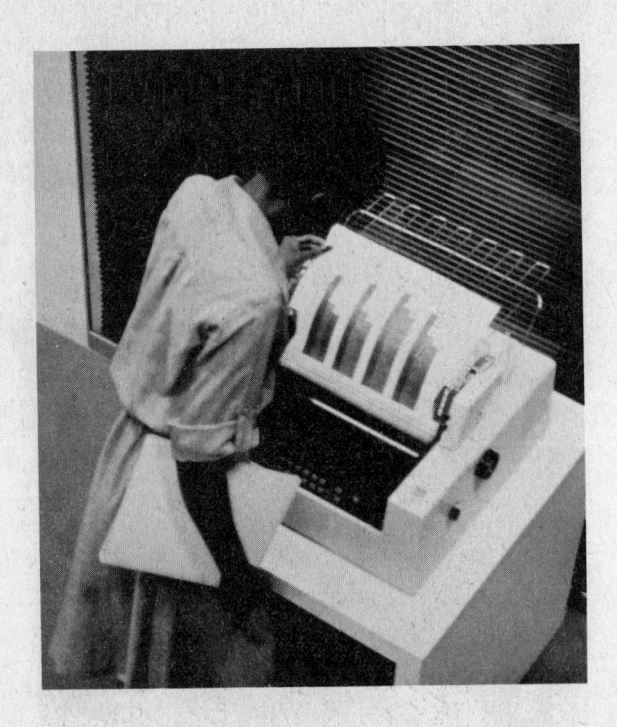

Fig. 4-5 The IBM 3287 Color Printer has a multicolor printing capability. (*IBM*)

(*a*) A thermal printer. (*Texas Instruments*)

Fig. 4-6 Nonimpact printers.

(b) A high-speed electrostatic printer. (*Honeywell Corp.*)

(c) A laser printer. (*Xerox Corp.*)

(d) An ink-jet printer. (*IBM*)

Fig. 4-6 (*cont.*)

4.41 How does a thermal printer operate?

The thermal printer of Fig. 4-6a uses heat to print data on chemically treated paper. The printing mechanism is a heating element that moves across each line to create the desired images. The top speed of thermal printers is 220 characters per second.

4.42 Why is the thermal printer in Fig. 4-6a attached to a telephone?

The printer in Fig. 4-6a is portable and thus may be carried easily from office to office. The thermal printer is not designed for the heavy printing responsibilities that impact printers within an active DP center assume. It is a low-level printing device suited for limited printing services.

4.43 Are any nonimpact printers appropriate for use in a high-output-oriented DP environment?

The nonimpact printers illustrated in Fig. 4-6b and c are suited for high-speed printing activities. The electrostatic printer of Fig. 4-6b and the laser printer of Fig. 4-6c can attain speeds of about 18,000 lines per minute and can handle almost any printing assignment.

4.44 How do the electrostatic and laser printers operate?

Electrostatic printers employ a printing process similar to that of a duplicating machine, using the electronic placement of carbon-like particles to create the desired character shapes. Laser printers use a high-intensity light source to burn images onto paper at remarkably high speeds. Newly developed laser printers have exceeded printing speeds of over 21,000 lines per minute, which is equivalent to printing a 200-page book in one minute (200 lines equal approximately 1 book page). This means that a nonimpact printer would be capable of printing a 600-page book in three minutes.

4.45 How does the printer of Fig. 4-6d differ from the others?

The ink-jet printer literally shoots particles of electronically charged ink onto the paper surface (drawn in a magnetic field) to create the desired characters. The ink-jet printer offers a low-speed printing capability of almost 90 characters per second. It has a replaceable cartridge with an ink supply of 4 million characters.

4.46 Is the ink-jet a conventional printing device?

The ink-jet printer was originally designed as an offline printer for use in an office setting. It can perform a variety of offline printing tasks, including the preparation of letters, addressed envelopes, and mailing labels. With special modifications, it can be attached to a computer to act as an online printer.

4.47 What are the advantages and disadvantages of impact and nonimpact printers?

Nonimpact printers offer higher speeds than impact printers, but they can print only one page at a time. Reports that are composed of multiple sheets of paper and carbons, referred to as *multi-ply forms*, cannot be printed on nonimpact printers. This may be a major consideration for some users.

Impact printers tend to provide a clearer and crisper output, which is easier to reproduce. Because nonimpact printers offer many typefaces, a more attractive format is possible. Also, nonimpact printers tend to be quieter because they do not strike the paper.

4.48 How is the proper printing device chosen?

Potential users should evaluate their printing needs by carefully cataloging their printing requirements as to number of copies, frequency of output, single or multiple sheets, paper size, and budget. The printer chosen should reflect these factors. Any organization handling a high volume of printed outputs should examine high-speed printers of both types. Low-level printing activities are generally better handled by impact printers unless unusual conditions exist. Some offline printing tasks might be better handled by nonimpact printers such as the ink-jet device.

(a) A plotter. (*Cal Comp*)

(b) Line drawings produced by a plotter. (*Cal Comp*)

Fig. 4-7

4.49 Are all printers either impact or nonimpact devices?

No. One printer that is neither an impact nor a nonimpact device is the *plotter*. The plotter enables the printing of continuous-line drawings, which are not possible with impact and nonimpact printers. Figure 4-7 illustrates a plotter and the type of output it can produce.

4.50 Why can't conventional printers prepare continuous-line drawings?

Conventional printing devices print their data on an individual-character basis and are therefore incapable of drawing a continuous line that curves, breaks, or follows divergent paths. Plotters specialize in printing those types of diagrams.

4.51 How are plotters used?

Plotters are used to construct diagrams drawn from the fields of, for example, civil engineering, space exploration, mathematics, science, electrical engineering, architecture, art, interior design, and industrial design. Plotters may be online to prepare computer-directed outputs or produce outputs resulting from data analysis. Without plotters, it would take many hundreds of hours to prepare the same diagrams manually.

4.52 What techniques do plotters use to print their diagrams?

Plotters may use conventional printing techniques of pen-and-ink, but they may also use electrostatic and dot-matrix devices. Electrostatic devices are similar to photocopying machines, whereas dot-matrix diagrams are composed by varying the density of dots per square inch. Some plotters offer the capability of preparing diagrams directly on microfilm.

4.53 What size diagrams are prepared by plotters?

Diagrams prepared by plotters may range in size from 7 by 9 inches to 60 inches per square. Many plotters permit the use of different color inks to highlight special features.

TERMINALS

4.54 Why has the terminal become so important in DP operations?

The terminal has become an integral part of online processing, and with the increase of these activities, it is the major vehicle for performing I/O operations.

4.55 What are the two major types of terminal devices?

The two principal types of terminals are the cathode ray tube (CRT) and hardcopy terminal, as shown in Fig. 4-8a and b, respectively. The CRT provides a visual, or softcopy, output, whereas the hardcopy terminal offers a printed, tangible output.

4.56 Are there devices that combine both softcopy and hardcopy features?

Some terminal devices can provide both a visual display and printed output. These devices permit the rapid display of a series of records and, when necessary, the documentation of a record.

4.57 Where might this dual capacity be effectively used?

The hardcopy/softcopy terminal is often used in hospital administrative activities. Nurses and administrative personnel can rapidly scan the files until a particular patient's record is found. The terminal can then print that patient's record for subsequent reading by the consulting physician.

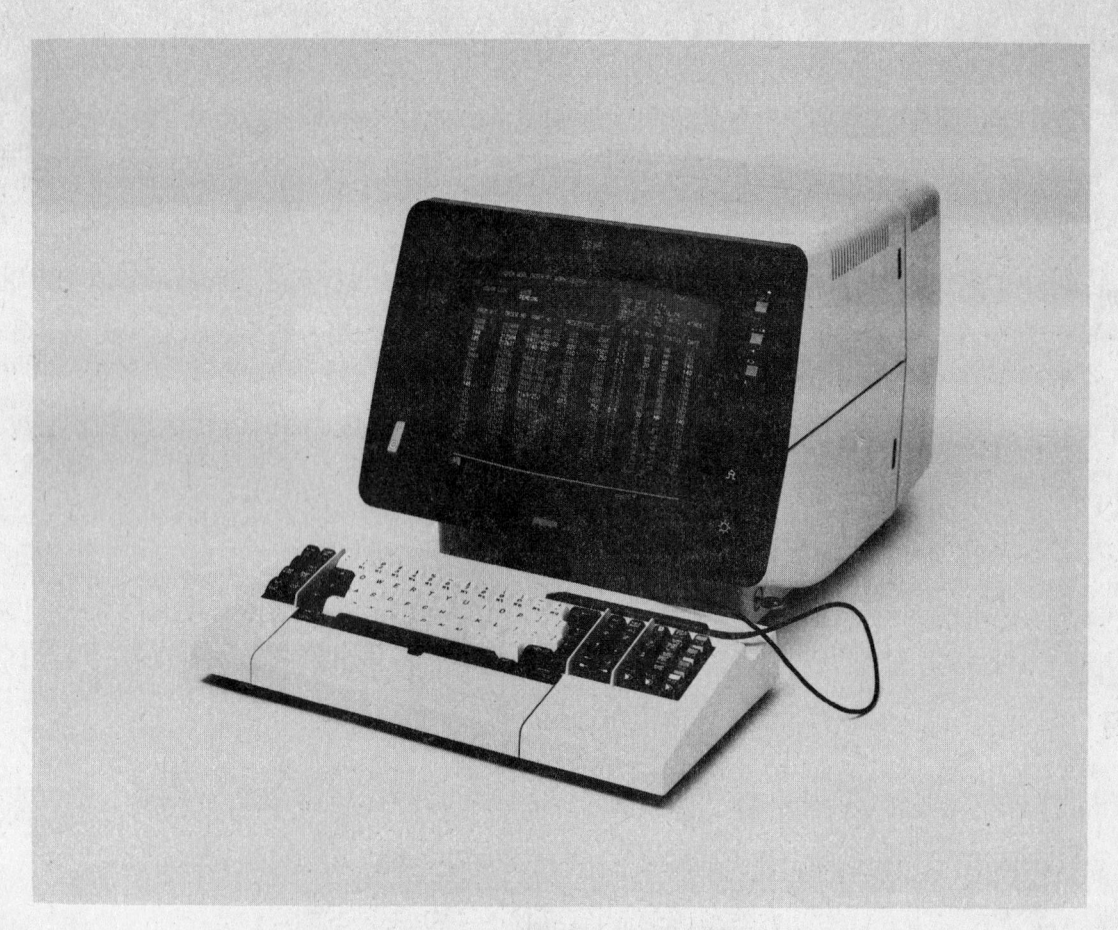

(a) A color display terminal. (*IBM*)

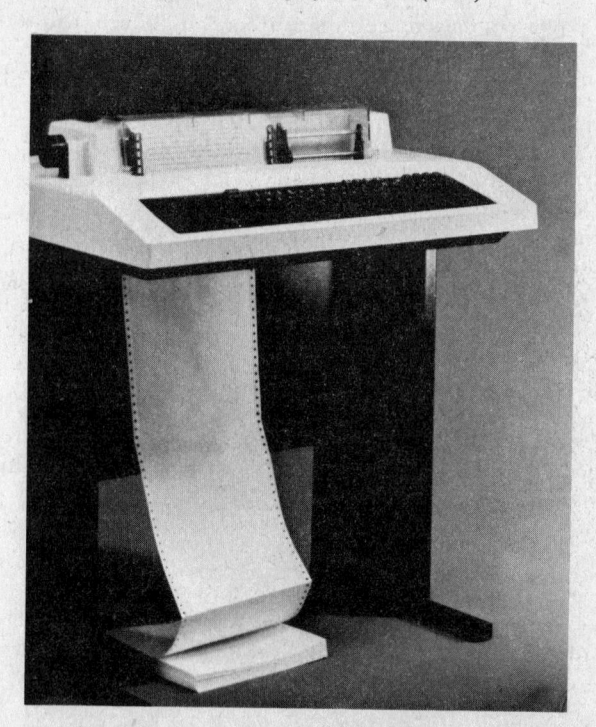

(b) A hardcopy terminal. (*Digital Equipment Corp.*)

Fig. 4-8 Terminal devices can provide both pictorial and printed types of outputs, depending on the device.

4.58 Can some CRTs perform a variety of tasks?

Currently many of the newly introduced CRTs possess more than just the ability to display data on a screen. Newer devices can prepare graphs (in up to nine colors) and can display pictures that assume the form of graphic displays. One such device is the IBM 3279, which serves as a CRT, color-display terminal, and graphics terminal.

4.59 Are there specialized terminal devices to handle unique business applications?

Terminal devices have been modified for specialized applications. For example, a specialized form of terminal device utilized to support the handling of retail sales data is the video display terminal, Fig. 4-9a. The terminal has a limited input keyboard and visual output capability. Customer data are entered via the keyboard, and confirmation of the data is displayed on its screen.

4.60 How is the video display terminal used?

Many retail sales outlets employ video display terminals to verify credit card purchases. Account data are input via the terminal and sent to the computer. After verifying the account, acceptance (or denial) of the sale is flashed on the video display terminal's screen.

4.61 Of what purpose is the data collection terminal shown in Fig. 4-9b?

Many manufacturing companies utilize data collection terminals to collect and input data from plants far distant from the main computer. These devices are distributed throughout a plant at key locations. Employees enter data using a limited keyboard, and the data collection terminal signals whether each data item was successfully received. Rejected items are immediately reentered until accepted.

(*a*) A video display terminal.

Fig. 4-9 Terminal devices have been designed to support the computerized processing of data in a variety of applications.

(b) A data collection terminal. *(IBM)*

Fig. 4-9 *(cont.)*

4.62 Is it possible to input data by simply speaking to the computer?

Currently under development (and refinement) is the *voice input* device. The device, which physically resembles a small stereo speaker, accepts spoken data and inputs it directly to the computer.

4.63 Has the voice input device been developed sufficiently for full operational use?

No. Though great strides have been made, the voice input device has not been fully perfected. One version of the voice input device can accept 500 words, spoken in 12 dialects. A drawback to voice input units is the imprecise speech patterns of its potential users.

4.64 Can the computer output information in a verbal form?

Using an *audio response unit*, the computer can respond with spoken results that follow predetermined speech patterns. The audio response unit, which also looks like a speaker, is often used in computerized telephone and message-switching systems to respond to callers who have dialed incorrectly.

INTELLIGENT DEVICES

4.65 When used with the name of a device, what does the term *intelligent* mean?

The word *intelligent*, when added to a device's name, means that the device has certain features that enable it to perform duties exceeding those of normal devices. Essentially, intelligent devices have certain (limited) offline processing capabilities.

4.66 What features could be incorporated into a terminal device to make it intelligent?

An intelligent terminal is capable of more than just interacting with an online system. It can also check the accuracy of data input via its keyboard, and it sometimes offers a full-scale printing capability.

CHAP. 4]   INPUT AND OUTPUT DEVICES   71

4.67 What term is applied to the monitoring of input data by an intelligent terminal?

The intelligent terminal's verification of input data is referred to as *editing*. This device enables users to substantially lessen the amount of incorrect data entering the system.

4.68 How is the editing performed?

The intelligent terminal has a buffered storage area in which the format applied to input data is stored. Any data item keyed into the intelligent terminal must conform to this format or it is rejected. Rejected data that cannot be properly rekeyed into the system are returned to users for correction.

4.69 Can other physical features be incorporated into intelligent devices?

Yes. Intelligent devices may possess a disk storage capacity and multiple input keyboards. Figure 4-10 shows two types of intelligent terminals. In Fig. 4-10a the device possesses a keyboard, full-line printing capability (of 132 characters), and disk storage capacity. Both input data and its supervisory format may be retained in this disk storage area. In Fig. 4-10b multiple keyboards are used collectively to speed the entry of input data.

(*a*) An intelligent terminal system with hardcopy printing capability. (*Burroughs*)

(*b*) The IBM 3760 allows four operators to enter data at the same time. (*IBM*)

Fig. 4-10 Intelligent terminals provide a variety of features not normally incorporated into regular terminal devices.

4.70 Do intelligent printing devices exist?

Yes. In addition to intelligent terminal devices, intelligent printers are also currently available. These printing devices can be used as either online or offline printers. Figure 4-11 illustrates an intelligent printer.

4.71 What operational services can intelligent printers supply?

Intelligent printers provide both offline and online capabilities. As an online device, the intelligent printer provides a conventional printing capability for hardcopy outputs. As an offline device, it is controlled by a set of instructions that directs its operation. In both modes this printer can not only print report data but also output information on both sides of a page, collate pages, and prepare each report packet for binding. About all the operator/secretary has to do is start its operation and then walk around to the back of the machine to pick up the finished reports.

Fig. 4-11 The IBM 6670 Information Distributor is an intelligent printing device that can prepare printed documents in many formats.

4.72 What printing speeds are attainable by intelligent printers when preparing reports?

Intelligent printing devices offer average speeds of eighteen to thirty-six pages per minute. The current cost of these devices may range as high as $75,000 when all special features are included.

4.73 At that price what is the advantage of the intelligent printer?

Intelligent printers offer the user a conventional and special printing capability in one device. They can undertake normal printing tasks or handle the preparation of special report packets. In this latter capacity, intelligent printers speed the preparation of materials since data are fed directly from the computer to the device. This online hookup avoids the delay in printing caused by intermediary human assistance.

4.74 Are there other devices that can provide multioperational printing capabilities?

Yes. A device that offers a multifaceted printing capability is the IBM 3800 printing subsystem, Fig. 4-12. This device is a laser printer that uses a low-power light beam.

4.75 What special characteristics does the IBM 3800 computer possess?

The IBM 3800 is a high-speed, nonimpact printer that can attain speeds of 18,000 lines per minute. It combines a duplicating and printing capability that permits users to employ conventional paper stock rather than special custom-made forms. Using a three-step process, the 3800 can duplicate stationery; add any special effects, printing, and symbols; and enter customer or invoice data onto the newly produced statement. It offers up to 20 styles of printed characters, ranging from pica to Gothic, permits many levels of shadings to be positioned on the form, and can duplicate many special symbols.

Fig. 4-12 The IBM 3800 Printing Subsystem is a laser printer that has a high-speed printing capability for users with high-volume printing needs. (*IBM*)

4.76 What are the merits of the IBM 3800?

It saves on paper, avoids the expense of buying special and custom-made forms, prepares user-designed outputs, and works at high speeds. Its disadvantages are that it produces only one copy at a time, and its cost can exceed $500,000.

4.77 What other companies produce devices similar to the IBM 3800?

Printing subsystems are also available from Honeywell, Xerox, Siemens, and Wang.

WORD PROCESSING (WP)

4.78 What does the term *word processing* mean?

The term *word processing* refers to the computerized preparation of a variety of office correspondence and paperwork. Word processing tasks may range from the preparation of form letters to annual reports.

4.79 What accounts for the advent of word processing activities?

Business managers realized that many repetitive office tasks could be computerized, thus speeding their preparation while freeing office staff for other responsibilities.

4.80 What are some examples of word processing applications?

Word processing can be applied, for example, to the preparation of letters being sent to all retiring employees or to all applicants denied acceptance to an educational program. In both instances each letter would contain personal information, which would preclude the use of a form letter. To have each letter typed manually would be prohibitively time-consuming and expensive. Word processing (WP) equipment, online to the computer, can accomplish the task in a fraction of the manual time by preparing the required paperwork and entering individual data drawn directly from the computer's files. At most only one person need monitor the task to ensure that each letter is properly handled.

4.81 What were the first levels of word processing equipment?

Initial word processing devices were essentially electronic typewriters, equipped with limited forms of card and disk storage. Referred to as "mag typewriters," these devices offered limited WP support and were primarily oriented toward the preparation of letters or short memos.

4.82 Are current WP activities equally restricted?

No. The advent of new technologies broadened the scope of word processing operations. It is now possible to prepare not only lengthy letters, memos, or legal documents but also lengthy multipage reports, manuscript pages, or microfilm.

4.83 Are word processors individual or multiple devices?

Word processing units are no longer individual typewriting devices as they now consist of many specialized devices that accommodate a variety of printed outputs.

4.84 What devices might make up a word processing system?

As depicted in Fig. 4-13, a word processing system can consist of a CRT, magnetic disk storage unit, and a printer. Data keyed in via the CRT are retained on disk until printing, when they are released for output. The disk capacity of this system is vast, being able to retain over 300,000 pages of output. The speed and type of printer vary, reflecting user needs.

Fig. 4-13 A word processing system with a CRT, disk storage, and a printer. (*Wang*)

4.85 Who might require the retention of that quantity of data?

News-oriented organizations, public relations firms, and law offices are just a few of the organizations that could benefit from the storage of many pages of information. They could prepare press releases well ahead of time and store prepared legal briefs and court papers or copyrighted stories prior to their publication. Using a few simple commands, the word processing system could produce as many copies as needed.

4.86 What additional advantage is served by having materials stored within a WP system?

Using the system's CRT, users can edit all or part of the articles stored on disk and retain those corrections. The online editing of articles is a great time-saver since it eliminates the need to type, read, retype, and reread documents. Corrections can be made any number of times directly via the CRT, with minimal delay, until the manuscript is acceptable.

CHAP. 4] INPUT AND OUTPUT DEVICES 75

4.87 What type of printing device is normally incorporated into a word processing system?

Printing devices often used with WP systems are the wire-matrix, band, and daisy-wheel printers. The daisy-wheel is often favored because of its interchangeable typefaces and low cost.

4.88 What other types of printing devices are effectively used in word processing operations?

Intelligent printers of the type discussed in Probs. 4.70–4.77 are frequently tied into a word processing system to provide high-speed, multifaceted printing.

4.89 What new technology is available with these types of intelligent devices?

An intelligent device frequently incorporated into word processing systems is the Wang Image Printer, Fig. 4-14. This device combines an electrostatic printing technique with fiber optics. *Fiber optics* speeds transmission by sending data over glass wires and electrostatically outputting results in high print resolution. The Image Printer prepares crisp and legible outputs and offers a variety of character sizes, page formats, and printing styles.

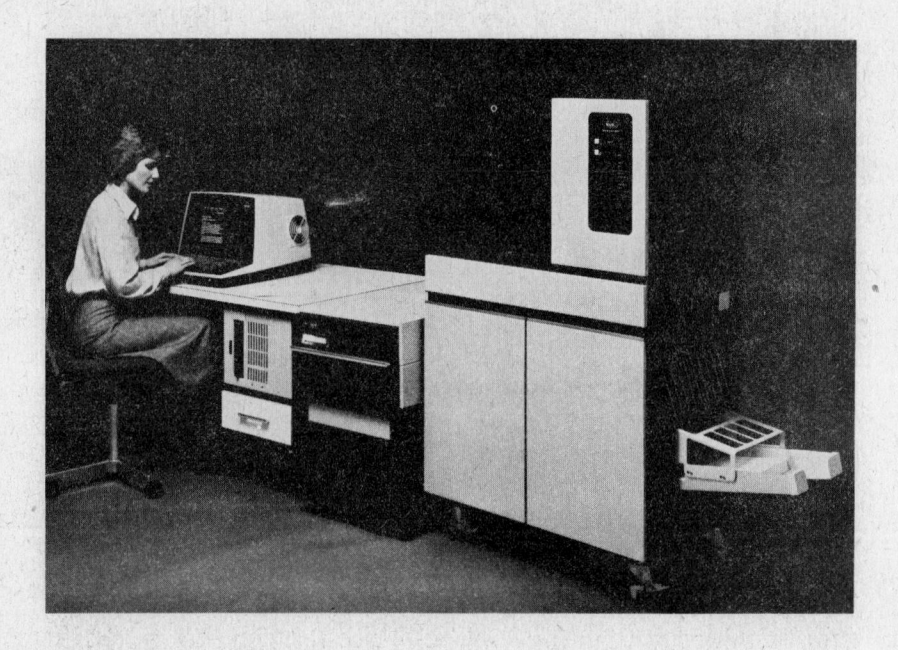

Fig. 4-14 This intelligent printer employs fiber optics to prepare its outputs. (*Wang*)

4.90 Has the Image Printer been used in any highly specialized applications?

Yes. The Image Printer has been involved in telecommunications activities where data are transferred between computers separated by many miles. Reports originated in one system are transferred to and printed at the receiving computer by an Image Printer. Thus materials are made immediately available at distant offices and postal delays are avoided.

4.91 Is there any special term applied to the transfer of letters to and their subsequent printing at a distant office?

Yes. The term originated for this type of informational, electronic transfer of printed materials is *electronic mail*. This technique of transferring printed materials via computerized systems is in its infancy and represents one of the fastest growing aspects of the computer field.

4.92 In addition to electronic mail, what other new techniques have been introduced to prepare printed materials?

To assist in the preparation of manuscripts, automatic typesetting devices have been developed. These devices accept data directly from the computer and print this material onto film. The film produced is then used to prepare galley proofs, from which books are actually printed and bound. This direct printing of material on film offers publishers considerable savings. Figure 4-15 shows an automatic typesetting device.

Fig. 4-15 A word processing system with an automatic typesetting device. (*Wang*)

DP TECHNIQUES FOR BUSINESS

4.93 Why have special DP techniques been developed for selected applications or jobs?

The answer to this question lies in the volume of data being handled. There are certain tasks that by their very nature must be handled by computers or else they would never economically (or speedily) be processed. As manual procedures prove inefficient, computerized procedures must be created and instituted.

4.94 Give an example of an application that could not be economically handled without computerized procedures.

Consider the processing of checks written by most people when paying bills or making purchases. It is estimated that over 3 billion checks are written each year in the United States. Without some form of computerized support vehicle, that volume of checks could not be speedily processed. Manual procedures, acceptable in prior years at lower levels of check use, would now be inadequate.

4.95 What technique was introduced to handle the computerized processing of checks?

The data processing technique applied to the handling of checks is magnetic ink character recognition, or simply MICR. The key to this technique is the use of specially created characters that are printed at the bottom of each check (Fig. 4-16).

CHAP. 4] INPUT AND OUTPUT DEVICES 77

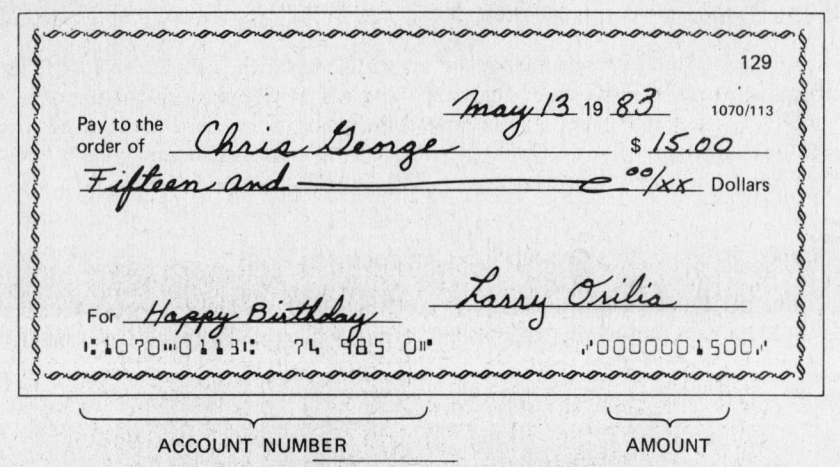

(a) MICR characters appear at the bottom of this check.

(b) MICR reading device. (*IBM*)

Fig. 4-16 MICR characters are printed onto bank checks to speed their eventual processing.

4.96 How are the MICR characters used?

Each check is printed with a unique account number, appearing on the lower left-hand corner of the check. After the check is cashed, a second set of digits, giving the amount of the check, is added to the lower right-hand corner of the check.

4.97 How is the MICR-coded check processed?

The completely coded check is then read by an MICR reading device as the check passes through the device from left to right. The account number is read first, followed by the amount of the check. These data are then placed in secondary storage (either tape or disk) from which they are read and processed. Using this operational sequence, data are rapidly input to the computer for processing; thus the time-consuming manual task otherwise necessary is avoided.

4.98 Are OCR techniques similar to MICR?

The initials OCR stand for optical character recognition, which is similar to MICR in its use of specially shaped characters. There the similarity ends. Whereas MICR requires the use of special magnetic ink, OCR does not. OCR characters may be written in pencil or regular ink. What is important is the shape of the OCR characters.

4.99 How are OCR characters conventionally processed?

Handwritten OCR character data may be read by OCR scanning devices, which sense the character shapes directly from the manually prepared form. OCR readers are usually online, thereby permitting the ready entry of input data.

4.100 What newer means are available for sensing OCR data?

OCR *reading wands*, which are similar in shape to fountain pens and have light sensors in their tips, are used to sense data directly from documents containing these characters. Use of the wand reader eliminates the need to pass OCR-coded forms through OCR readers.

4.101 Where has wand reading been used successfully?

Wand readers are successfully used in retail sales operations. Attached to devices that act as both cash registers and data collection terminals, the wand reader is used to read sales data directly from OCR-coded sales tags. These devices are referred to as *point-of-sale* (*POS*) *terminals*. The use of POS terminals greatly improves the handling of sales data and speeds customer transactions. Figure 4-17 illustrates the specially shaped OCR characters and a sales tag on which they are coded.

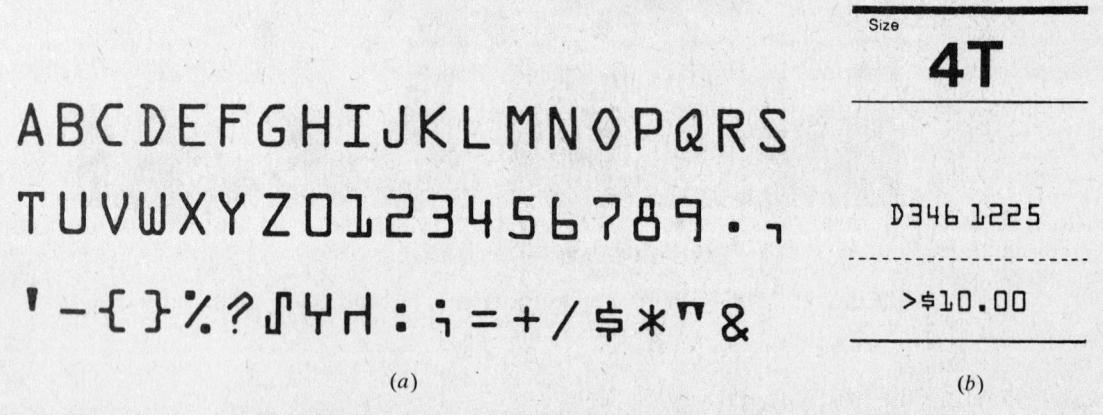

Fig. 4-17 The specially shaped characters associated with Optical Character Recognition (OCR).

4.102 In what other types of applications have OCR techniques been used?

OCR characters are now used by many states in their handling of driver registrations, motor vehicle registration renewals, and license plate certifications. Many magazines also use OCR characters when renewing customer subscriptions. Currently on the rise is the use of OCR characters on monthly customer statements. Stubs returned with payments contain OCR-coded data that are read directly into the system to update a customer's account.

4.103 Is storage of computer-generated outputs a problem?

Organizations that use a vast quantity of printed outputs repeatedly face the problem of what to do with those outputs. Printed outputs can occupy a considerable space, especially if those outputs must be retained for any length of time. An organization may suffer from paperwork logjams if storage does not receive proper planning and consideration.

4.104 Does a solution exist to the retention of voluminous computer outputs?

Yes. Computer output microfilm, or, simply, COM, is used to read computer output permanently on microfilm that can be accessed later.

4.105 How are outputs recorded onto microfilm?

Outputs are recorded onto individual microfilm records called microfiche. Microfiche are prepared in two fashions. The original method used was to photograph hardcopy outputs, thus producing the microfiche records. A newly introduced technique enables certain intelligent printers to directly prepare microfiche of output from the computer, thus bypassing the hardcopy output of that data. A device capable of this latter technique is the Wang Image Printer.

4.106 What is the storage capability of microfiche?

Approximately 25,000 pages of printed outputs can be stored within 1 inch of microfiche.

4.107 What problems in COM led to the development of micrographics?

Again the problem of access to records became critical. When many microfilm records are involved, access to an individual microfiche should be fast. Rapid access to microfilm records is provided by micrographic techniques.

4.108 How do micrographic devices retrieve individual records on microfilm?

The retrieval of microfilm via micrographics is accomplished in two steps. The initial step involves determining the location of the desired record on microfilm. This is performed by searching a computerized index of all retained microfiche on a small computer system. Once the desired microfiche is identified, special terminal devices called *microimage terminals* actually retrieve the microfiche and display its contents.

4.109 How successful are microimage terminals?

A microimage terminal can provide access to almost 6000 microfiche records within a 5-second time span. Once the location of a desired microfilm is identified, retrieval of that microfiche is assigned to the microimage terminal.

4.110 Where have micrographic techniques been used?

Police departments have successfully used micrographics in surveillance operations, identification of dangerous addresses, and investigations of past criminal activities. Virtually any organization that requires ready access to a microfilm library of records could profit from the application of micrographics.

Review Questions

4.111 The card reader/punch is restricted to input operations only. (*a*) True, (*b*) false.

4.112 Generally, brush card readers are faster than photoelectric-cell card readers. (*a*) True, (*b*) false.

4.113 The unit-record concept is specific to punch cards. (*a*) True, (*b*) false.

4.114 The two classes of printing devices are impact and electronic printers. (*a*) True, (*b*) false.

4.115 Daisy-wheel printers offer a low-speed printing capability and the ability to interchange wheels for the mixing of typefaces. (*a*) True, (*b*) false.

4.116 Thermal printers offer printing speeds that can exceed those of some impact printers. (*a*) True, (*b*) false.

4.117 Nonimpact printers can easily produce multi-ply forms as well as prepare single-page outputs at high speeds. (*a*) True, (*b*) false.

4.118 The term *hardcopy/softcopy terminal* is incorrect since terminals cannot offer both forms of output. (*a*) True, (*b*) false.

4.119 Voice input devices and audio response units offer verbal I/O capabilities to a computer system. (*a*) True, (*b*) false.

4.120 Intelligent terminal devices offer additional operational features not normally found on conventional terminals. (*a*) True, (*b*) false.

4.121 Word processing systems may use CRTs, printers, and disk devices. (*a*) True, (*b*) false.

4.122 Intelligent printers are not used within word processing systems. (*a*) True, (*b*) false.

4.123 Both OCR and MICR require the use of specially treated inks and character shapes. (*a*) True, (*b*) false.

4.124 The computerized input of sales data is possible using POS terminals. (*a*) True, (*b*) false.

4.125 Microimage terminals are instrumental to micrographic operations. (*a*) True, (*b*) false.

4.126 Card readers that read data on a column-by-column basis are referred to as (*a*) serial card readers; (*b*) column card readers; (*c*) parallel card readers; (*d*) brush readers.

4.127 The printing device whose outputs appear as a series of dots is the (*a*) chain printer; (*b*) band printer; (*c*) wire-matrix printer; (*d*) daisy-wheel printer.

4.128 Which of the following devices attains the highest printing speeds? (*a*) band printer; (*b*) chain printer; (*c*) daisy-wheel printer; (*d*) wire-matrix printer.

4.129 The nonimpact printer that uses a printing process similar to that of a duplicating machine is the (*a*) thermal printer; (*b*) electrostatic printer; (*c*) laser printer; (*d*) ink-jet printer.

4.130 The printing device capable of attaining a printing speed of 18,000 lines per minute is the (*a*) chain printer; (*b*) thermal printer; (*c*) band printer; (*d*) laser printer.

4.131 Visual outputs are defined by the term (*a*) hardcopy; (*b*) softcopy; (*c*) photocopy; (*d*) all of the above.

4.132 The terminal device used in retail sales that possesses a limited I/O capability is the (*a*) CRT; (*b*) visual display terminal; (*c*) video display terminal; (*d*) hardcopy terminal.

CHAP. 4] INPUT AND OUTPUT DEVICES 81

4.133 The monitoring of input data using intelligent terminals is called (a) validation; (b) verification; (c) error checking; (d) editing.

4.134 An operational characteristic associated with printing subsystems is (a) laser printing; (b) high-speed printing; (c) multiple character styles; (d) all of the above.

4.135 The direct preparation of photographic films used in printing is accomplished via (a) hardcopy printers; (b) automatic typesetters; (c) intelligent printers; (d) printing subsystems.

4.136 The computerized technique applied to the processing of checks is (a) COM; (b) MICR; (c) OCR; (d) micrographics.

4.137 The computerized retrieval of microfilm records is the result of (a) COM; (b) MICR; (c) OCR; (d) micrographics.

4.138 The card punch is solely a(n) _____ device.

4.139 Cards used for accounts receivable purposes and returned with payments are referred to as _____ documents.

4.140 Nonimpact printers are not required to _____ the paper and perform their printing using other methods.

4.141 The device that provides its characters for printing on a flexible metal strip is the _____ printer.

4.142 A printer capable of printing in both directions is referred to as a _____ printer.

4.143 The _____ printer may be used as an offline printing device to perform a variety of office tasks.

4.144 The specialized printing device that can prepare continuous-line drawings is called a _____.

4.145 The rapid input of manufacturing data from remote locations is accomplished via the _____ terminal.

4.146 Printing devices that offer special printing features are referred to as _____ printers.

4.147 The computerized preparation of office paperwork is defined as _____.

4.148 The transmission of documentation between remote offices via word processing systems is called _____.

4.149 The technique that requires the manual entry of specially shaped characters is _____.

4.150 The recording of computerized outputs onto microfilm is referred to as _____.

4.151 Individual microfilm records are referred to as _____.

Answers: 4.111 (b); 4.112 (b); 4.113 (a); 4.114 (b); 4.115 (a); 4.116 (a); 4.117 (b); 4.118 (b); 4.119 (a); 4.120 (a); 4.121 (a); 4.122 (b); 4.123 (b); 4.124 (a); 4.125 (a); 4.126 (a); 4.127 (c); 4.128 (b); 4.129 (b); 4.130 (d); 4.131 (b); 4.132 (c); 4.133 (d); 4.134 (d); 4.135 (b); 4.136 (b); 4.137 (d); 4.138 output; 4.139 turnaround; 4.140 strike; 4.141 band; 4.142 bidirectional; 4.143 ink-jet; 4.144 plotter; 4.145 data collection; 4.146 intelligent; 4.147 word processing; 4.148 electronic mail; 4.149 optical character recognition (OCR); 4.150 computer output microfilm (COM); 4.151 microfiche.

Supplementary Problems

4.152 What are the differences between impact and nonimpact printers? Describe how selected devices in each category function.

4.153 How might micrographics be used effectively to support the retrieval of newspaper microfilm records in a library?

4.154 Explain the difference between serial and parallel card readers. Why do serial card readers have higher reading speeds?

4.155 Cite examples from your surroundings of the use of OCR characters in retail sales, education, and government.

4.156 Why would word processing speed the preparation of paperwork in the office? Do you think offices of the future will depend totally on word processing operations?

4.157 Take a position in favor of or against electronic mail. Do you think that it could revolutionize current interoffice correspondence procedures? Explain.

Glossary

Audio response unit. An I/O device that outputs its information in the form of spoken words.

Automatic typesetter. An output device that directly records information on photographic film from which printed documents are produced.

Band printer. An impact printer that uses a metal band of characters to print output.

Bidirectional printer. A printer that can print data from left to right and vice versa.

Brush card reader. A card reader that reads data off the card's surface on a row-by-row (parallel) basis.

Card punch. An output device that punches information directly onto cards.

Card reader. The input device responsible for the reading of data coded onto punched cards.

Card reader/punch. An I/O device capable of reading and punching card data.

Cathode ray tube (CRT). A terminal device utilizing a keyboard for the input of data and a television-like screen for the display of information.

Chain printer. An impact printer that uses a flexible chain of characters in its printing of outputs.

Computer output microfilm (COM). A technique to record printed outputs on microfilm.

Daisy-wheel printer. An impact printer whose printing element is a rotating wheel on whose spokes characters are positioned.

Data collection terminal. A terminal device, with limited I/O capabilities, used to speed the input of data from remote locations or sites.

Editing. The term applied to the correction of input data by intelligent terminals.

Electronic mail. The electronic transmission of printed reports to far distant word processing systems and their immediate output upon receipt.

Electrostatic printer. A nonimpact printer that uses electrostatic technology to prepare its printed outputs.

Hardcopy terminals. Terminal devices that provide only printed outputs.

Impact printer. A printer whose print mechanism strikes the paper.

Ink-jet printer. A nonimpact printer, frequently used on an offline basis, that prints data using an ink-jet to spray characters onto the paper surface.

Intelligent printer. A printing device whose additional operational features make it more than just a conventional printer.

Intelligent terminal. A terminal device equipped with editing features.

Laser printer. A nonimpact printer that utilizes a low-power light beam to output its printed materials.

Magnetic ink character recognition (MICR). A technique applied to banking that employs specially shaped characters and a magnetic ink on checks to facilitate processing.

Microfiche. The individual pieces of microfilm on which material is recorded.

Micrographics. The computerized identification and retrieval of microfilm records.

Multi-ply form. A printed form composed of multiple sheets of paper, usually interspersed with carbon paper.

Nonimpact printer. A printer that does not have to strike the paper in order to produce a printed output.

Optical character recognition (OCR). A technique that utilizes special character shapes to speed the input of data.

Parallel card readers. Card reading devices that read data on a row-by-row basis.

Photoelectric-cell card reader. A card reader that utilizes photoelectric cells to sense punched data.

Plotter. A printing device capable of outputting continuous-line drawings and other pictorial outputs.

Point-of-sale (POS) terminal. A terminal device, which also serves as a cash register, that is designed to speed the input of sales data.

Serial card reader. A card reader that reads punched data on a column-by-column basis.

Thermal printer. A nonimpact printer that uses a heating element to burn data onto chemically treated sheets.

Turnaround documents. Documents which are initially sent to customers and returned with payment to directly enter processing and update accounts.

Twin-head printer. A daisy-wheel printer that concurrently uses two daisy-wheels to prepare hardcopy outputs.

Unit-record concept. The principle associated with use of punched cards whereby the card is used as a record of one unit of data.

Video display terminal. A terminal device with a limited I/O capability, used to display sales/credit information.

Voice input device. An input device that permits verbal input data to computers.

Wire-matrix printer. An impact printer that utilizes a matrix of wire ends to compose the characters appearing as output. (May be referred to as dot-matrix printer.)

Word processing (WP). The computerized preparation of office paperwork.

Word processing system. A small computer system, used to support word processing activities, normally consisting of a CRT, magnetic disk storage, and a printing device.

Chapter 5

Information Processing Systems

5.1 ONLINE PROCESSING SYSTEMS

One of the more currently popular approaches to data processing is the use of *online processing systems*, that is, systems that permit the user to interact directly with the computer. Organizations that use online systems generally have their processing results available almost immediately. Prior to the development of online processing, *batch processing* was the primary vehicle for handling business data. With batch processing, data are accumulated over a period of time and processed at regular intervals. Computer cards were the main source of input in batch processing operations.

Terminals are an integral part of online processing operations. The term *telecommunications* was developed to describe the computerized processing of data via terminals and telephone lines. *Teleprocessing* refers to telecommunication operations that involve CRTs.

Online processing activities may be in the form of online processing, real-time processing, time-sharing, and remote-job-entry (RJE) stations. *Online batch processing* systems accumulate data in online files, with that data processed at predetermined intervals. *Real-time* systems process data immediately. *Time-sharing* systems enable many users to concurrently share the resources of the same computer system. *Remote-job-entry* stations enable the online interaction of users with remote computers, with output being retrieved in a printed format. The direct interaction of users with their supporting computer on an online basis is sometimes referred to as *interactive processing*. *Service bureaus* offer users online data processing services on a rental basis.

5.2 DATA COMMUNICATIONS FACILITIES

Modern data communications operations may utilize telegraph lines or satellites to transmit computerized data. Telephone lines are either leased lines or dialed services. *Leased lines* are specially strung by a common carrier, whereas *dialed services* are available via the conventional telephone.

Three classes of data communications are the narrowband channel, voice-grade channel, and wideband channel. *Narrowband channels* offer the lowest transfer rates, with *voice-grade channels* assuming the midrange and *wideband channels* offering the highest data transfer rates.

5.3 MULTIPROGRAMMING AND MULTIPROCESSING

Though the terms *multiprogramming* and *multiprocessing* appear similar, each has its own distinct operational characteristics. *Multiprogramming* identifies the concurrent handling of many programs retained within one CPU. *Multiprocessing* defines the simultaneous execution of two or more instructions in two or more CPUs. Time-sharing is an example of multiprogramming, whereas a network of computers is an example of multiprocessing.

5.4 DISTRIBUTED DATA PROCESSING SYSTEMS (DDPS)

The concept of multiprocessing provides the basis of a *distributed data processing system* (*DDPS*). Distributed data processing systems offer the rapid distribution of information throughout an organization, computer support to all levels of management, and access to a group of files. The term *database* identifies the integrated collection of files to which a distributed system has access.

DDP systems assume many configurations. In one configuration a centrally located computer interacts with computers that supply operational data to the database. In a second configuration a smaller system performs all the preparatory work necessary in the processing of data.

5.5 DISTRIBUTED WORD PROCESSING SYSTEMS (DWPS)

Distributed word processing systems (*DWPS*) are distributed systems that handle word processing operations between computer systems. DWPS permit electronic mail activities to be easily accomplished. Special software systems have been developed to support word processing activities within DWPS.

Solved Problems

ONLINE PROCESSING SYSTEMS

5.1 What is the function of an online processing system?

Online processing systems permit the direct communication of data to a computer system without extensive delays and interruptions.

5.2 Are these types of systems popular today?

Yes. With improvements in communications technology, online processing systems are becoming increasingly popular. These systems focus their processing potential on the direct transmission of data to distant computers, thus speeding the processing of that material. Organizations employing online systems obtain their results almost immediately.

5.3 Prior to the advent of online processing systems, what type of data processing approach was conventionally employed?

In the past the most commonly employed system was batch processing. With batch processing, data were accumulated over a specific period of time and then processed. This delay always caused the results to be less current than desired.

5.4 What I/O medium was normally associated with batch processing operations?

The punch card was the medium most commonly used in batch processing. The association of punch cards and batch processing resulted from the fact that keypunching the cards was a time-consuming operation. The delays created by keypunching caused delays in processing, which resulted in the accumulation of "batches" of data destined for processing.

5.5 Would the processing of a weekly payroll be a good example of batch processing?

Yes. Batch processing operations all rely on a regular processing cycle of some type, be it weekly, monthly, quarterly, or annually. Payroll data are accumulated over the period of a week and then processed. The *batch* of payroll data is keyed onto cards from which paychecks are prepared.

5.6 What other type of application could qualify as batch processing?

The monthly processing of inventory data would also be batch processing. Inventory data are batched over a month's time and processed at that month's end. Inventory data keyed onto cards are accumulated and then processed.

5.7 If cards were successfully used in batch processing, why did some organizations switch to online processing?

Though batch processing was usually satisfactory, online processing offered the advantage of no delays in processing or in obtaining up-to-date information.

5.8 If cards and related devices are the primary support for batch processing operations, what supports online processing activities?

Online processing is supported by a variety of terminal apparatus, some of which was reviewed in Chap. 4. Using these and other devices, data are transmitted over telephone lines and communications systems to computers for immediate processing. Access to the information produced is on an online basis also.

5.9 Do terminal devices complement online processing activities?

Yes. Using terminal devices, it is possible to minimize processing delays and to interact rapidly with the computer. With the direct entry of input data, the information produced from processing is readily available to all users.

5.10 What term describes the combined use of terminals and telephone systems to process data?

The term *telecommunications* was developed to describe the computerized processing of data transmitted via telephone systems and terminal devices. When CRTs and other visual I/O devices are used in telecommunications activities, the term *teleprocessing* may be used to describe the complete processing of data entered from them. The use of online devices greatly speeds the handling of data and eliminates lengthy delays that hinder processing.

5.11 Are telecommunications operations restricted to terminal devices?

No. All types of peripheral devices, including many newly introduced I/O devices, are now integral parts of telecommunications operations. For example, intelligent terminal devices are frequently used in online processing because of their keyboard (input) and printing (output) capabilities. They provide a ready access to data held in computerized files and the ability to document those facts.

5.12 Are telecommunications activities restricted to the use of telephone lines?

No. At the inception of telecommunications operations, telephone lines were the primary vehicle for data communication. Today, though telephone lines handle the bulk of the communications between users and their computers, other more highly sophisticated means of data transmission exist. Currently, telecommunications may involve satellites, microwave transmissions, selected radio wavelengths, national digital wire services, and lasers. These technologies represent just a few of the means available to transmit computer-related data in the support of online processing activities.

5.13 What forms of online processing currently exist?

Online processing activities may assume many configurations depending on hardware and user requirements. Online processing activities that have been defined by specific terms are real-time processing, time-sharing, and remote job entry (RJE).

5.14 How might banking activities be supported by an online system?

Many banks use online processing systems because these systems permit immediate access to savings and checking account records. Consider a banking organization that uses intelligent terminals at its local branches to interact with the bank's main computer. Banking data are entered by tellers, as needed, and posted against the appropriate customer records. The use of terminal devices provides immediate online access to banking data. Without online processing systems, direct access to these data would not be possible.

CHAP. 5] INFORMATION PROCESSING SYSTEMS 87

5.15 Might a retail sales organization benefit from an online processing system?

A retail organization, highly reliant on the use of credit cards, could successfully utilize online processing. Using video display terminals, sales clerks could immediately verify the status of a customer's charge account. Data drawn from the credit card, via that specialized terminal device, could be checked directly against the customer's account. All devices in this retail system would be online to the computer to ensure the rapid response to credit checks.

5.16 What happens when the computer is inoperative and cannot support online processing?

This question often arises in the discussion of online systems. Organizations reliant on online processing systems must have a set of backup procedures to be used until the computer can be brought online. Some organizations merely incorporate manual procedures and continue to function. Other organizations have backup computers that assume the processing workload.

5.17 In addition to backup systems, how can an online system be replaced?

Occasionally the type of hardware chosen to support an online system can be used during difficult operational periods or when the computer is inoperable. Consider the intelligent terminals used in Prob. 5.14, each equipped with a limited disk storage capacity. Should the computer be inoperative for a short time, the terminal's disk capacity could be used as a reserve storage area to retain data from transactions completed during that period. When the computer is again operative, it can contact each terminal and request the input of the data that were temporarily retained. The computer's contact of each terminal and request for its data are operationally referred to as *polling*. Note that it is not always possible to use intelligent terminals in this fashion, but it does offer an alternative to an online system that is temporarily out of service.

5.18 Is the accumulation of data on intelligent terminal devices referred to as "online batch processing"?

No. "Online batch processing" is a newly developed term that refers to an online processing operation in which data are accumulated within the main computer for subsequent processing. The data are accumulated by a secondary storage disk file since they are received from online devices located at distant centers. At the end of a specific period of time (e.g., daily), the data are immediately processed. The advantage of online batch processing is that it minimizes the batch cycle, the delay in converting data to a computerized format, and the actual processing of data.

5.19 How might a manufacturing plant use online batch processing?

Consider a manufacturing plant that utilizes data collection terminals to enter production data directly from locations within its production shops. Data on all project costs, completion times, material usage, and personnel involved are entered via the online data collection terminals of a main computer. Within that system are disk files that are capable of accepting and temporarily holding this production data. By using this system, production data are made available for processing throughout the day. At the end of each 8-hour shift, production data within the file are processed, thereby maintaining all related files in their most current state. Essentially, each batch of production data is entered via an online device and kept in an online file. When directed, the computer accesses this file to process its batch of data.

5.20 When might an online batch system be preferred to a strictly online system?

If the application does not economically warrant a full online system or the data being handled are not sufficiently critical to justify immediate processing, batching of data is a viable economic alternative. The online aspects of an online batch system speed the input and subsequent processing of that data.

5.21 Is time-sharing similar to online batch processing?

No. Though another form of online processing, time-sharing is not the equivalent of online batch processing. Time-sharing may involve the transmission of data to a distant main computer; however, what is more important is how that computer is used. In a time-sharing operation, many users share the resources of a single computer system at the same time. Essentially, the computer shares its resources with many users, responding to the needs of each user. This type of online support capitalizes on the fantastic processing speeds of current computers.

5.22 What advantages does time-sharing offer to potential users?

For individuals that do not require the full-time support of a computer system or cannot afford the expense of a full computer system, time-sharing offers many positive points. The expenses incurred by a time-shared user may only include the cost of a terminal, telephone service, and the rental of computer time; thus the greater expense associated with a privately owned or leased system is avoided. Disadvantages of time-sharing are the potential lack of data security, the unavailability of the system should it be fully employed by other users, and faulty telephone lines or an inoperative system.

5.23 What are the two most widely used versions of time-sharing operations?

Time-sharing operations may be divided into two categories: time-sharing from a commercially available system or time-sharing with an organization. In the first instance, a user rents time-sharing support from a computer center that makes its services available to any organization. In the latter case, the organization owns the computer and permits users through all levels of management to tie into that system. With either method, the level of time-sharing support is the same.

5.24 Why is time-sharing often referred to as *interactive processing*?

The reference to *interactive processing* results from the fact that during time-sharing operations, users can interact directly with the computer in the processing of their programs. Users can respond to queries initiated by the computer, issue commands to direct processing, or input data on an as-needed basis.

5.25 Who might benefit from the support of time-shared services?

Accountants, architects, engineers, bankers, financial analysts, programmers, and college students have all successfully used time-sharing operations. Professionals from all fields can temporarily tie into time-sharing systems to answer questions and solve problems directly related to their work. At many schools students have completed their initial programming exercises with the aid of time-shared services.

5.26 What term is applied to DP organizations that rent time-sharing services to the general public?

DP organizations renting time-sharing support are often referred to as *service bureaus*. These agencies generally offer, in addition to time-sharing, a variety of data processing services, including the processing of payroll, accounts receivable, accounts payable, and inventory. Service bureaus can fully process a portion of the workload at a variety of rates.

5.27 How does a remote-job-entry (RJE) station relate to time-sharing?

A remote-job-entry station, or RJE, provides a vehicle for interacting with a distant computer on an online basis. It is essentially an I/O device that is quite similar to an intelligent terminal device. An RJE possesses an input capability (generally a keyboard) and a printed output capacity that is sometimes coupled with a CRT for rapid softcopy displays. Using this device, it is possible to access data retained on files within a centrally located computer.

Access to the computerized files is accomplished via the RJE on an online basis. The RJE can directly access data or, when necessary, interact with the computer on a time-sharing basis.

5.28 Do service bureaus sometimes employ RJE stations to service their customers?

Yes. Service bureaus will frequently install RJEs at the customers' offices to facilitate the transmission of data between their DP center and the bureau's computer system. The use of an RJE speeds the entry of data to the computer where it is processed and returned to the user as output. The RJE also supports user inquiries. In many cases the RJE provides an attractive economic alternative to the separate devices often used in online processing.

5.29 Is there an example of an organization that might effectively employ an RJE station?

Police and criminal justice organizations frequently use RJEs in their DP activities. The RJE supports the online processing activities now commonplace in most police organizations. File inquiries, time-shared activities, and the hardcopy output of investigative information are all possible with RJE devices.

5.30 How does real-time processing differ from online processing?

Whereas online activities may incur and tolerate delays in data processing, real-time systems will process all data immediately, without interruption. Instantaneous processing is an integral characteristic of real-time systems.

5.31 Are real-time systems large computer systems?

Yes. Generally, real-time systems are quite large since they support organizations that require instantaneous data processing. Real-time configurations usually possess large CPUs, extensive disk storage capacities, and many I/O devices. These systems commonly exceed $1 million in cost and exhibit the highest operating speeds. The complex nature of real-time systems requires that they be large enough to support a variety of tasks. Their size makes them expensive and suited to organizations that can afford (and require) their services.

5.32 What types of organizations require real-time support?

Real-time, online processing systems support national defense, weather forecasting systems, regional and municipal police organizations, large corporations with international offices, airline and car rental companies, and stock exchanges. Generally, any organization that handles a large volume of critical data that are sensitive to the passage of time will use a real-time system.

5.33 Why would an airline utilize a real-time reservation system?

A real-time reservation system enables an airline to continually update and change its customer reservations files. Because passenger reservations are voluminous and critical to planning and to servicing aircraft, these data must be processed immediately. Any delays in handling reservations data could result in customer dissatisfaction or in the misallocation of aircraft support resources, which could lead to financial loss.

A similar need for real-time computing exists in the system that supports the stock exchanges. Considering the volume of stock traded and the speed with which these data must be reported, real-time is the only system that can provide the necessary support. Imagine the chaos that would result from the inability to promptly report stock trades to the entire financial community.

DATA COMMUNICATIONS FACILITIES

5.34 What is the basis of all online processing systems?

All online data processing depends on the user's direct interaction with the computer. To facilitate the telecommunication of data, some form of communications line must exist.

5.35 What types of communications services are available?

Many types of communications services exist, ranging from the conventional telegraph line to more exotic forms of transmission such as satellites. The most commonly employed mode of data communication is the telephone line.

5.36 How are telephone lines used in telecommunications?

Data communications services in the form of telephone lines are generally divided into the categories of leased lines and dialed service. These services are provided by a common carrier, such as AT&T, to support online processing.

5.37 What are leased lines, and how are they used?

Leased lines are telephone lines that are specially strung between users and their supporting online systems. These lines are available to users on a twenty-four-hour basis. Generally, the common carrier charges a flat fee on a monthly basis.

5.38 What other terms are applied to leased lines?

The terms *private* or *dedicated lines* are sometimes used to describe leased lines. These terms refer to lines that are strung specifically to support online processing, and they are rented on a scheduled basis.

5.39 How does dialed service differ from leased lines?

Dialed service is used as a conventional telephone might be used. Users must dial a specific telephone number to access a computer. Since a limited number of lines are made available for these purposes, users must compete for access to the system. When all lines are in use, the user is denied access to that computer.

5.40 Does the denial of access with dialed service occur with leased lines?

No. Since each line is tied directly to the computer, the user of leased lines cannot be denied access unless the computer is inoperative.

5.41 What is a general guideline to costs for dialed service?

With dialed services, users pay only for the time they use. The rate applied depends on the area, distance, and cost structure permitted by licensing agencies.

5.42 Is there a dialed service that is currently popular with many users?

One of the most widely used dialed services, which is actively promoted, is the wide area telephone service, or WATS line. With WATS support, a flat fee is charged for calls within certain regions. Costs for this service vary between geographical areas and companies.

5.43 What are the merits of dialed or leased services?

Naturally, the service chosen should reflect the needs of the individual user. Leased lines may prove more economical for users anticipating high levels of activity. Leased lines generally provide a superior level of transmission since the lines are dedicated to one use. In contrast, dialed services are better suited to lower levels of use since the user pays only for the time involved. Also dialed services offer users some operational flexibility. Wherever the user has access to a telephone, access to the computer is possible. (Consider how portable terminals might be used effectively by salespeople who have access to dialed services while visiting their clients.)

5.44 What are the three classifications of data communications services that deal with data transfer?

The three classes of data communications services are narrowband, voice-grade, and wideband channels. Narrowband channels offer the lowest data transfer rates, and wideband channels offer the highest rates. Voice-grade channels occupy the midrange of data transfer rates.

5.45 What are the characteristics of narrowband channels?

Narrowband channels offer the lowest data transfer rates and use telegraph lines to transmit data. The largest common carrier, Western Union, offers this type of service. Narrowband channels can support a maximum transfer rate of 600 bits per second.

5.46 What are the characteristics of voice-grade channels?

Voice-grade channels represent the midrange of transmission rates, handling from 600 to 2400 bits per second. Voice-grade channels handle the vast majority of online processing activities. Conventional telephone lines used in dialed service activities are examples of voice-grade channels.

5.47 What are the characteristics of wideband channels?

Wideband channels offer the highest data transfer rates, exceeding 2400 bits per second. Data communications that involve coaxial cables, microwave transmission, or transmission of data via satellites are examples of wideband channel activities.

5.48 What other vehicles are being used to facilitate data communication activities?

A national digital service is currently available that can handle over 50,000 bits per second. Researchers are designing a satellite facility that will utilize lasers to transmit data at speeds of 1 million bits per second. Future projects, sponsored with government and corporate funds, are envisioned to launch additional satellites to support telecommunications activities. Recent studies have projected that by 1985 existing satellite transmission resources will reach 100 percent usage.

MULTIPROGRAMMING AND MULTIPROCESSING

5.49 Do the terms *multiprogramming* and *multiprocessing* represent the same operational features?

No. Though the terms appear similar, they represent totally different operational capacities.

5.50 What does multiprogramming represent?

Multiprogramming identifies a computer's ability to concurrently process a group of programs temporarily sharing the same CPU. Though only one program can have instructions executed at any one time, the computer can rapidly shift from one program to another stored in the CPU.

5.51 Why is the computer restricted to the execution of only one program at a time during multiprogramming?

A computer is always restricted to the processing of only one program at any given moment because it can execute only one instruction at a time. However, because it can process at a fantastic speed and jump from one program to another, the computer is able to provide a continuous stream of data.

5.52 What is the importance of having programs concurrently share primary storage during multiprogramming?

Having more than one program in the primary storage unit at a time enables the computer to execute instructions from one program and then shift to another program.

5.53 During multiprogramming, why does it appear that the computer is executing many programs simultaneously?

The computer cannot execute two or more programs simultaneously. However, its high processing speed gives the appearance that it is executing many programs at once when it is actually only moving rapidly among them.

5.54 What operational feature assists in the orderly execution of programs during multiprogramming?

Multiprogramming is governed by a computer system's operational software, which controls the orderly execution of programs and their concurrent storage within the CPU. Without this operational software, multiprogramming is not possible.

5.55 Where, for example, might multiprogramming be used?

A time-sharing environment offers a fine illustration of the use of multiprogramming. Multiple users share the same computer, which concurrently contains the programs undergoing execution. The computer executes programs as needed, shifting from program to program, under direction of its operational software.

5.56 Who might benefit from the application of multiprogramming?

All users who desire to improve the efficiency of their computer system can benefit from multiprogramming. For example, with multiprogramming, one user in a retail organization could examine a customer's credit status while another user handles inventory changes. In a commercial time-sharing system, an accountant, research engineer, and architect, for example, could have their programs stored concurrently in the computer where they would be executed as needed. A service bureau would utilize a multiprogramming environment to satisfy the needs of its many users, concurrently handling their jobs as they enter the system.

5.57 How does multiprogramming differ from multiprocessing?

Whereas multiprogramming is accomplished within one CPU, multiprocessing requires two or more CPUs. *Multiprogramming* is defined as the processing of programs concurrently held in a CPU. *Multiprocessing* is defined as the simultaneous execution of instructions from two or more programs, in two or more CPUs. As previously discussed, a CPU can execute only one instruction from one program at any given moment. Thus, in order to execute two instructions simultaneously, two CPUs must be involved.

5.58 What are the critical terms related to multiprogramming and multiprocessing?

The terms *concurrently* and *simultaneously* are associated with multiprogramming and multiprocessing, respectively. Programs are held concurrently in multiprogramming operations whereas two or more instructions are simultaneously executed in multiprocessing.

5.59 What is required to operate multiprocessing systems?

Multiprocessing requires the use of two or more CPUs within a computer system network. Usually multiple computers, within a network of computer systems, are simultaneously executing instructions at separate sites, with each program servicing an individual system's needs.

5.60 What type of organization might benefit from multiprocessing?

Any organization that utilizes multiple computer systems to satisfy its DP needs would benefit from multiprocessing. For example, stock-brokerage houses use multiprocessing to monitor stock transactions and service their customers. National weather organizations require a multiprocessing environment to field, process, and project weather conditions throughout the United States. Insurance companies use multiple computers at various levels of their organizations to service clients, independent agents, and salespeople. Criminal justice and court systems use multiple systems to access police data and to prepare trial documentation, as well as to track down criminal records.

5.61 Is it possible for a computer within a multiprocessing network to utilize multiprogramming?

Yes. It is perfectly feasible for a computer to use multiprogramming in its data handling activities while it is an integral part of a multiprocessing system. The use of multiprogramming identifies that system's ability to respond to the needs of many programs.

DISTRIBUTED DATA PROCESSING SYSTEMS (DDPS)

5.62 From what concept is the basis for distributed data processing systems (DDPS) derived?

The operational configurations associated with DDPSs are derived from the principles of multiprocessing. The DDPS structure involves multiple computer systems that form a network or overall system to support an organization. In the majority of cases the computers comprising the DDP system interact with each other.

5.63 Since multiple systems are involved, what are the major objectives of the DDPS structure?

The primary objectives of distributed data processing systems are (1) computer support at the various levels of the organization, (2) distribution of data throughout the entire system, and (3) access to the collective files of the overall network.

5.64 Do DDP systems provide adequate support at all organizational levels?

Yes. A DDPS configuration is made up of computers from many levels of the organization. The individual computers within a DDPS are generally tailored to provide maximum support at all organizational levels. Multiprocessing systems are more expensive than conventional, non-integrated systems, but offer a higher level of support to users.

5.65 How do distributed systems make data more readily accessible to the organization?

Instead of moving data manually through the organization, DDP systems utilize computers to distribute that same data at higher rates of transfer. Computers with the DDPS configuration automatically move data to the proper files or users, without delay. Thus all data are immediately available for use in decision making.

5.66 Why is the update of the DDPS collective files important?

Distributed data processing systems generally handle large quantities of data because of their structure and capabilities. It is beneficial to the system's efficiency that data be handled a minimal number of times and that duplicate files do not exist. Thus DDP systems will frequently use files that are common to computers within the structure. Common files are used more efficiently than scattered duplicate files; thus they eliminate waste, unnecessary programming effort, and minimize the handling of critical data slated for use in more than one file.

5.67 How might a DDPS configuration function?

An example of a distributed data processing system is shown in Fig. 5-1. In this configuration, a centralized computer is the focal point of processing. It coordinates the interaction of the three smaller computer systems and controls access to the system's database. The database is made up of files that contain data common to the entire system. The main system handles all requests for data from the database, enables the distribution of these data throughout the system, and efficiently posts new data within the files of the database.

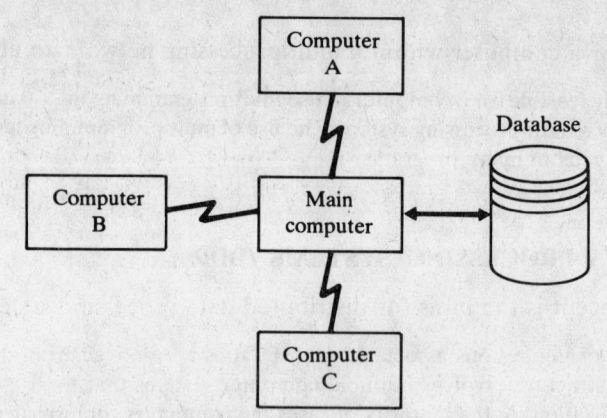

Fig. 5-1 A distributed data processing system in which three computer systems are supervised by the larger main computer system. Access to the database is controlled by the larger system.

5.68 Where might a DDPS structure of this type be employed?

This type of distributed data processing system might support
(a) Retail sales organizations where small computers are located at local stores to monitor sales activity and feed data to a larger corporate computer. The larger system has access to the database, which contains charge sales, inventory, and marketing files.
(b) Manufacturing organizations where smaller systems support production activities at each plant and then feed data to a larger computer that coordinates all production data within a manufacturing database.
(c) Service organizations that use computers at their local sales offices to handle small-business activities and communicate with the main computer at the highest supervisory level. This setup enables salespeople to draw data from a corporate database in their sales activities. Some examples of businesses that use this operational configuration are local insurance sales offices, regional sales offices for farm and industrial equipment, and satellite clinics of large hospitals or medical centers.

5.69 Are there distributed data processing configurations in which a smaller computer acts as controller to a larger system?

The multiprocessing configuration of Fig. 5-2 illustrates a DDPS setup in which a smaller system acts as a preprocessor for a larger system that interacts with a database. The smaller computer is sometimes referred to as a *slave computer* since it performs all the preparatory tasks necessary for data processing by the larger system or *master computer*. In this network users can employ a variety of terminal devices to access the slave computer, which monitors all requests for data accessed via the master computer.

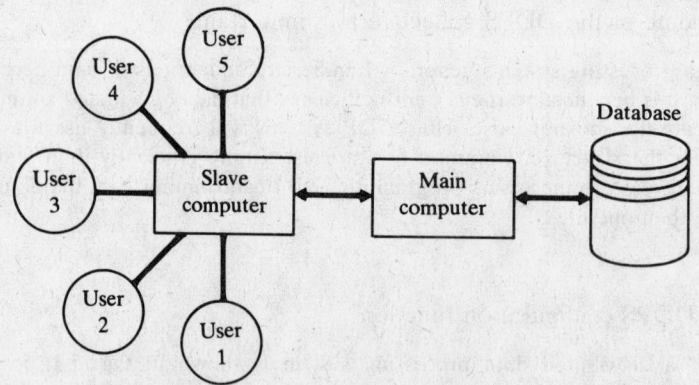

Fig. 5-2 A distributed data processing system in which data input from users is initially handled by the slave computer. All preparatory tasks are assigned to and performed by the smaller system. Access to the database and major processing activities is the responsibility of the larger computer system.

CHAP. 5]   INFORMATION PROCESSING SYSTEMS

5.70 Is the interaction of the slave and master computer efficient?

The use of these two computer distributed systems is quite efficient because operational responsibilities are assigned according to the capabilities of each system. The slave computer is assigned to handling requests for information and to the slower preparatory tasks needed for processing. Thus the larger computer is not bogged down by those tasks and can concentrate on rapidly retrieving data from the database and related processing. Each system focuses its attention on those activities it is best suited for and performs them efficiently.

5.71 What type of organization uses the slave/master computer configuration?

The configuration shown in Fig. 5-2, where access to the slave computer is through terminal devices, is used by computerized ticket sales agencies. The slave computer prepares the request for reservations while the larger system scans the database of ticket availabilities for suitable matches.

In other similar configurations, terminals are replaced by small computers at local offices that are online to the slave computer. A three-level computer configuration is often used in police investigative work. The local smaller systems handle informational requests relative to local ordinances and reports. When checks are required at higher levels, requests are transferred from local computers to the slave computer so that a search of a police database in the master computer can be made. This relationship exists between many statewide police organizations and municipal localities that cannot afford to retain vast amounts of data on their computers.

5.72 What term is applied to computer systems in which a large computer acts as the focal point of processing data from other smaller systems?

A DDP system that utilizes a main computer system (or a slave/master configuration) at the heart of its DP activities is usually referred to as a *centralized data processing system*. That term identifies the fact that a main computer is at the center of that network's processing. Many large organizations use centralized systems to monitor and control their DP activities.

DISTRIBUTED WORD PROCESSING SYSTEMS (DWPS)

5.73 Are DWP and DDP systems related?

Distributed word processing systems are extensions of the principles associated with distributed data processing systems. DWP systems are distributed networks that focus on word processing operations.

5.74 Which distributed configuration do most DWP systems assume?

Most distributed word processing systems are centralized so that individual word processing systems are tied to a centrally located main system. Memos, letters, and other office paperwork are prepared by the smaller WP systems and then fed to the main system for distribution throughout the network.

5.75 Would electronic mail exemplify DWPS operations?

Yes. The preparation of documents via electronic mail offers a fine example of distributed word processing operations. Paperwork prepared at one WP station is sent, via the central computer, to other WP centers in the network.

5.76 Can databases be incorporated into a DWPS?

Yes. Many DWPS configurations rely on databases to retain letters, correspondence, and other forms of paperwork for reference. Access to materials retained in the database is permitted via the main computer, which can accept documentation from any of the satellite WP systems.

5.77 What types of organizations can utilize DWPS?

Publishing companies, law offices, municipal governments, advertising agencies, and newspaper organizations are just a few of the groups that benefit from distributed word processing systems. Any organization that handles large quantities of printed material is a potential adopter of DWPS. Each of the preceding organizations handles a high volume of printed material, storing that information for varying periods of time. Repeated access to that material is facilitated via the DWPS, which also permits users to make online corrections to the printed material. Use of the DWPS permits users to enter data from a variety of WP systems and output that material at other centers. The distribution of multiple copies at various office centers is easily accomplished.

5.78 Has special software been developed to support operations in DWPS?

Yes. A special software system called *Applied Text Management System* (*ATMS*) is now available from IBM for distributed word processing systems. This software permits users to enter documentation, store it within a database, recall it any number of times, make online corrections, and direct the output of the data, in any number of copies, to specified locations. Other software similar to ATMS is available from other manufacturers that duplicate its features.

Review Questions

5.79 Online processing systems handle data directly and thereby minimize the delay normally asssociated with batch processing. (*a*) True, (*b*) false.

5.80 The processing of monthly credit card statements is an example of a batch processing operation. (*a*) True, (*b*) false.

5.81 CRTs and other terminal devices are an integral part of both batch processing and online processing activities. (*a*) True, (*b*) false.

5.82 Telecommunications activities are restricted to the use of terminal devices only. (*a*) True, (*b*) false.

5.83 Real-time processing provides instantaneous access to data and the update of those records. (*a*) True, (*b*) false.

5.84 Leased lines are specially strung lines that offer 24-hour access to the user's computer. (*a*) True, (*b*) false.

5.85 Telegraph lines are an example of voice-grade communications services. (*a*) True, (*b*) false.

5.86 It is possible to execute two instructions in one CPU at exactly the same time. (*a*) True, (*b*) false.

5.87 Multiprocessing systems must utilize multiple CPUs. (*a*) True, (*b*) false.

5.88 The larger of two computers in a DDPS is referred to as the *master computer* and is assigned the preparatory processing tasks and control of access to the corporate database. (*a*) True, (*b*) false.

5.89 DWPS are distributed processing systems that focus their attention on word processing activities. (*a*) True, (*b*) false.

5.90 A DWPS is perfectly suited to the performance of electronic mail operations. (*a*) True, (*b*) false.

5.91 The computer medium normally associated with batch processing is (*a*) punch cards; (*b*) magnetic disks; (*c*) paper tapes; (*d*) hardcopy terminals.

5.92 Telecommunications activities that specifically utilize CRTs are referred to as (a) online batch processing; (b) RJE processing; (c) teleprocessing; (d) none of the above.

5.93 The concurrent processing of multiple programs that share the resources of the same system is called (a) batch processing; (b) time-sharing; (c) online batching; (d) multiprocessing.

5.94 DP organizations that rent their services are called (a) DP centers; (b) online agencies; (c) service bureaus; (d) all of the above.

5.95 The data communications service that possesses a data transfer rate of 600 to 2400 bits per second is (a) narrowband channels; (b) voice-grade channels; (c) wideband channels; (d) satellite channels.

5.96 The concurrent processing of multiple programs in time-sharing is representative of (a) multiprogramming; (b) online batch processing; (c) multiprocessing; (d) a and b.

5.97 The operational mode most closely associated with a distributed DP system is (a) multiprogramming; (b) multiprocessing; (c) remote-job-entry storage; (d) online batch processing.

5.98 A primary objective of a distributed data processing system is (a) to support all levels of an organization; (b) to distribute data throughout the total system; (c) to access the system's database; (d) all of the above.

5.99 A special word processing software system developed to support DWPS activities is (a) DDPS; (b) RJE; (c) ATMS; (d) BPIS.

5.100 Processing activities that accumulate data over a period of time and process that data at regular intervals are referred to as _____ activities.

5.101 The combined use of terminals and telephone communications for online processing is defined by the term _____.

5.102 The computer's systematic contact of intelligent terminal devices containing stored data is called _____.

5.103 The interaction of time-shared users and their computer is sometimes called _____ processing.

5.104 With _____ service, users are required to dial the computer to gain access to its CPU.

5.105 Microwave transmissions fall into the category of _____ channels.

5.106 The simultaneous execution of two instructions in two CPUs is called _____.

5.107 A collective group of organized files in a DDPS may be referred to as a _____.

5.108 In a multiprocessing DDPS environment, the preprocessing handling of data is assigned to the smaller _____ computer.

5.109 The distributed network that focuses its activities on a main computer is often referred to as a _____ system.

Answers: 5.79 (a); 5.80 (a); 5.81 (b); 5.82 (b); 5.83 (a); 5.84 (a); 5.85 (b); 5.86 (b); 5.87 (a); 5.88 (b); 5.89 (a); 5.90 (a); 5.91 (a); 5.92 (c); 5.93 (b); 5.94 (c); 5.95 (b); 5.96 (a); 5.97 (b); 5.98 (d); 5.99 (c); 5.100 batch processing; 5.101 telecommunications; 5.102 polling; 5.103 interactive; 5.104 dialed; 5.105 wideband; 5.106 multiprocessing; 5.107 database; 5.108 slave; 5.109 centralized.

Supplementary Problems

5.110 From your daily environment, look for examples of online processing activities. Use the following list of applications to assist your research.
  (a) Online banking activities at your local savings bank branch office
  (b) Credit card checks performed at retail sales outputs
  (c) Purchasing the tickets for a play, concert, or sports event from a department store
  (d) Buying or trading shares of stock

5.111 Examine the following list of online processing applications, and in your own words describe how these data might be processed.
  (a) Offtrack betting on horse races
  (b) Making reservations for airline tickets
  (c) Obtaining a computerized printout of an insurance policy at a local sales office
  (d) Using a time-shared system in the design of skyscrapers by an architect or structural engineer.

5.112 Explain the differences between multiprogramming and multiprocessing.

5.113 Explain why electronic mail technology could be readily supported by a DWP system.

5.114 (a) Consider why a national retail sales organization might want to use a distributed data processing system to monitor its sales activity, cash flow, and inventory levels.
  (b) Why are police organizations utilizing distributed processing networks in their law enforcement activities and in the apprehension of criminals?

Glossary

Applied Text Management System (ATMS). A specialized software, available from IBM, that supports distributed word processing operations in DWP systems.

Batch processing. The data processing method whereby batches of data are accumulated over a period of time and processed at regular intervals (e.g., weekly payroll data, daily sales data, and monthly customer credit reports).

Database. A collection of files grouped as one entity in a distributed system that facilitates rapid and efficient access to large quantities of operational data.

Dedicated line. Another term for a leased line.

Dialed service. Data communications lines that are also utilized as telephone lines, whereby the computer is accessed by dialing it on a phone.

Distributed data processing system (DDPS). A multiprocessing configuration that focuses its energies on efficiently handling data processing activities throughout an organization.

Interactive processing. A term that describes the interaction of a user and an online computer system (e.g., programming in a time-sharing system).

Leased line. A specially strung line, leased from a common carrier, that solely connects users to their supporting computer systems.

Master computer. In a multiprocessing system the larger of two or more interacting computers for which all preparatory work is performed and which usually controls access to a database if it exists.

Multiprocessing. The concurrent storage and handling of multiple programs within the same CPU.

Multiprogramming. The simultaneous execution of two or more instructions in two or more CPUs.

Narrowband channels. The lowest level of data-communications service, providing transfer rates of less than 600 bits per second.

Online batch processing. A processing approach whereby data are batched within an online environment and processed at timely intervals, thereby minimizing the delay normally associated with batch processing.

Online processing system. A computer system that relies on telecommunications to handle all phases of processing and support devices that are online.

Polling. The technique whereby an online computer sequentially contacts intelligent devices in the system to access data that have accumulated over a period of time.

Private line. Another term for a leased line.

Real-time processing. An online processing configuration whereby data are instantaneously processed within the system, and access to all online files is immediate.

Remote-job-entry (RJE) station. A peripheral device that provides an I/O capability that is usually part of an online processing system and located at a remote site; used to access data from online files and record the information retrieved in a printed format.

Service bureau. A DP organization that rents computer time, time-shared support, or a variety of data processing services to users that do not possess their own computer support.

Slave computer. The smaller of two computers that performs all preparatory work for a larger central computer within a multiprocessing system.

Telecommunications. The computerized processing of data via data communications lines involving many types of I/O devices.

Teleprocessing. Telecommunications activities that specifically involve CRTs and other visual I/O devices.

Time-sharing. The processing approach whereby many users concurrently share the resources of the same computer.

Voice-grade channels. The midrange of data communications services that handles transfer rates of 600 to 2400 bits per second.

Wideband channels. The highest range of data communications service transferring more than 2400 bits per second.

Chapter 6

Introduction to Program Languages

6.1 EARLY PROGRAMMING LANGUAGES

The first programming languages, called *machine languages*, were extremely technical and of the lowest operational level. They were difficult to use, even for the smallest tasks. These languages required the programmer to work with data items, their individual storage areas, and the indexing from one instruction to the next. The correction of program errors was a tedious and lengthy task. Machine language instructions were composed of an *operation* (*op*) *code* and an *operand*. The operation code defined the task to be performed, and the operand identified the data to be worked on.

The next major language to evolve from machine language was *assembly language*. Though also a low-level language, it possessed new, advantageous features. It permitted the use of symbols and codes in its instructions and thus represented a symbolic programming language. Each symbol or code, referred to as a *mnemonic*, designated the operation to be performed by the instruction.

A special instruction introduced with assembly language was the *macroinstruction*, commonly called *macro*. The macro, a single instruction, provided access to a group of related instructions to handle a specific task. The macro became the operational equivalent of the *predefined subroutine*. The conversion of assembly language instructions into machine language is accomplished by a translating program called an *assembler*.

6.2 HIGH-LEVEL LANGUAGES

High-level languages are easier than low-level languages for the users to learn and understand, and they offer many operational advantages to programmers. For example, high-level languages are easier to debug. In the *debugging* process, a *compiler* seeks out *syntax* errors; when such errors are detected, the compiler invokes its self-documentation feature to record their existence. Each language develops its own set of rules, or syntax.

High-level languages are machine-independent, so they can be used on a variety of computer models. In addition, these languages are in a standardized format to simplify their use.

Compilers are used to convert *source programs*, written by the programmer, into machine language for execution by the computer. When punched onto cards, a *source deck* results, which is how the source program is input. Source programs may be entered via online terminals. In *compilation* the source program is converted into the *object program*—which is in machine language—for execution. If errors are detected by the compiler, the compilation is stopped and the program is *abended* and removed from the flow of processing.

High-level languages may be categorized as either problem-oriented or procedure-oriented languages. *Problem-oriented languages* are restricted to only one type of application, whereas *procedure-oriented languages* can be applied to a wide variety of program solutions.

6.3 MODERN PROGRAMMING LANGUAGES

Currently available high-level programming languages assume many different formats to satisfy the wide range of user needs. Among the oldest languages is *FORTRAN*, developed by IBM in the late 1950s. FORTRAN possesses a rigid syntax and an algebraic format to simplify its use with formulas. It was designed for *scientific applications* involving lengthy computations.

Whereas FORTRAN was applied to scientific problems, *COBOL* became the major language of business. It easily handled work involving computer files, their creation and update, and the preparation of the multiple I/O formats used in the reporting of business and management reports. COBOL utilizes an English-like format to simplify its comprehension. It is a wordy language, requiring many statements to handle the simplest of tasks. However, its file manipulative and I/O abilities far outweigh that drawback.

PL/1 was designed to incorporate the best features of both COBOL and FORTRAN, but it never succeeded in exciting the imagination of most users. It is used primarily with IBM systems and microcomputers. PL/1 provides a powerful analytic language.

RPG was created for those organizations that required a report-oriented language to produce the diverse group reports needed by management. RPG is programmed using a selective group of specially coded sheets on which all program particulars are specified. It does not possess the file manipulation capabilities of COBOL, but it does have the ability to prepare a multitude of reports.

BASIC is an interactive language that permits users to interact with an online computer during time-sharing. BASIC employs a simple syntax to code its statements and has relatively few operational rules. Its algebraic format is easily applied. Because of its simplicity, BASIC is a major language in the home computer market.

PASCAL is a relatively new language, which also has an algebraic format. Its syntax was developed to take full advantage of *structured programming* principles, which emphasize modular solutions. PASCAL's syntax can assist in preparing sound program logic, reducing errors, and minimizing debugging time.

6.4 PROGRAM EXECUTION

The execution of programs within a computer system, by design, must follow a predetermined series of events. Initially, the source program is written by the programmer and *desk-checked* (i.e., manually checked) prior to its entry for processing. The source program can be input in the form of cards or keyed directly into the computer via an online terminal.

Accompanying all programs upon input are a series of control instructions. These statements, drawn from an operational control language, detail what processing options will be invoked during the program's processing. *Job control language* (*JCL*) represents a common operational control language.

Control statements will result in the application of the proper compiler, which will convert the source program into machine language. Control statements help maintain an effective *jobstream* of programs to maximize efficient use of the computer. Because of the specific and complex nature of their syntax, most control languages are not easily mastered.

6.5 PROGRAM SPECIFICATIONS

Program specifications, detailing what considerations compose a particular program, vary extensively among organizations. Despite this diversity, some level of documentation must describe the I/O formats and processing that a program will perform. Three forms often used in program documentation are the *multiple card layout form*, *printer spacing chart*, and *record layout form*.

The *multiple card layout form* is used when punched cards are involved in processing. The form can describe cards used for both input and output purposes. The *printer spacing chart* is used to document the appearance of printed outputs. All features of a printed report may be detailed on the printer spacing chart. These features may include column headings for data, totals of many related items, margins, and any comments regarding how the forms are to be handled.

The formats of any files used in the processing effort can be detailed using the *record layout form*. On this form it is possible to describe all fields composing the record format upon which a file is constructed. The order and appearance of every field can be detailed. The record layout form can be used for both tape and disk files.

Solved Problems

EARLY PROGRAMMING LANGUAGES

6.1 In comparison to the levels of current programming languages, what were the early computer languages like?

The first computer languages were extremely low level and designed for the rudimentary computers of that day. They were not designed to simplify the programmer's task but to parallel the actual processing of data within the computer.

6.2 What were the disadvantages of these early languages?

These languages were extremely difficult to use because they were constructed in a technical format, using only numbers. Programmers were required to break down operational tasks to their smallest elements, often needing hundreds of statements to perform the simplest of tasks. Program instructions had to define the individual data items, as well as the primary storage positions being used. An error in any instruction resulted in a major rewriting effort, as all storage positions and instructions subsequent to the error required alteration. These reprogramming efforts could consume twice the labor hours needed to code the original instructions.

6.3 With these obstacles, why were these languages used?

They were used because they were the only languages available. The level of sophistication that exists today was not available then, as the supporting technology did not exist. With the advancement of software, new languages became available to simplify the writing of codes and handling of diverse problems.

6.4 How were the early programming languages related to the languages developed later on?

The early languages became the foundation for later programming languages. The structure of the first languages was oriented to defining the simplest instructional format that the computer could handle, and the most efficient in processing data.

6.5 What were the first languages called?

The first computer languages were called *machine languages* because they were the languages used by the computer. Machine language is the language that the computer uses to process data and execute all instructions. Even today, though software are written in sophisticated languages, the actual execution of programs occurs in machine language.

6.6 What format does machine language assume?

Machine language instructions generally assume a numeric format, as shown in Fig. 6-1. These instructions utilize strings of numbers to define processing operations, that is, the tasks to be undertaken and the data to be used. To visualize the tedious nature of machine language programming, consider what an entire program consisting of thousands of instructions in that format would be like.

```
50  00A3D8
```

Fig. 6-1 In this machine language instruction, 50 is the op code and the 6 digits following are the operand.

6.7 What parts of the machine language format were made part of languages developed later?

Two critical components of machine language instructions are the operation (op) code and the operand. The op code defines the processing task to be performed by the specific instruction. The *operand* defines both the data to be worked on and the data's actual location in storage. Within a single instruction, the op code and the operand define the processing and data to be used.

6.8 Why were the op code and operand incorporated into newer languages?

Because they are essential to the execution of all machine language instructions and thus the processing of data, they were made part of newer languages. Though they do not assume the same format in newer languages, the op code and operand are built into those instructional formats and executed to effect processing.

6.9 What major development followed machine languages?

The next milestone in the evolution of programming languages was assembly language. It was also a low-level language, but unlike machine language assembly language permitted the use of symbols and codes. Thus, instead of having to use numbers, programmers could use a coded entry to indicate a processing operation.

6.10 What designation was applied to assembly languages?

Assembly languages were referred to as the first *symbolic programming languages* because they permitted the use of coded entries. Table 6-1 denotes some of the codes that are used with assembly language. These codes, called *mnemonics*, became the equivalent of the op code and denoted the operation to be performed.

Table 6-1 Assembly Language Codes

Operation	Mnemonic Code
Addition	A
Subtraction	S
Multiplication	M
Division	D
Compare	C

6.11 What advantages did the use of mnemonics offer?

It simplified the programmer's task, as references to operations and data items were simplified. Instead of using a string of numbers, the programmer specified the operation to be performed using only a few characters. Figure 6-2 shows a series of assembly language statements.

LABEL	OP CODE	OPERAND
	BALR	15, 0
	LM	2,3,34(15)
	BCR	15,2
ABC	DC	00000000
X	DC	F1F5F7F9
	DC	0000F6F6
OPEN2	MVI	12(13),1255
	BCR	15,14
	A	5,X

Fig. 6-2 A program excerpt illustrating assembly language's coded syntax.

6.12 In addition to an op code, what other features compose an assembly language instruction?

The instructional format used with assembly language consists of a label, op code, and operand, thus paralleling the original format of machine language instructions. The label provides a means of identification for the specific instruction in much the same way that a name identifies an individual in a line of people. The op code and operand identify the operation to be performed and the data items to be worked on, respectively.

6.13 What other special feature was introduced with assembly language?

The concept of macroinstruction, or macro, was introduced with assembly language. A *macro* is a special assembly language statement that when executed generates a series of assembly language instructions that accomplish a complete operational task.

6.14 Why was macro introduced?

Macroinstructions were developed for I/O operations, as well as other assembly language tasks. A macroinstruction is used to identify a group of related instructions and refers to them by one instruction, the macro. Programmers found that when writing code in assembly language, the same instructions were written repeatedly to execute I/O operations. To simplify this task for everyone, the I/O instructions were specially stored within the computer and identified by a specific macroinstruction. The programmer need only specify that macro's name to gain access to those instructions and thus complete the I/O instructions, rather than writing the I/O instructions each time they are needed.

6.15 What is the equivalent of a macro in many current languages?

The current equivalent of a macro is the predefined subroutine, which defines a specific set of instructions associated with a particular operational task or feature. The predefined subroutine is identified by a specific coded name, which when invoked within a program provides access to that set of instructions.

6.16 How are predefined subroutines formulated?

Predefined subroutines in various languages are available from the manufacturer, or they may be written by programmers and incorporated into the computer's operational software. In either case, specification of the required coded phrase will make the predefined subroutine available for use.

6.17 What is an example of a predefined subroutine?

A predefined subroutine commonly found in many languages is the instructional set used to compute the square root of a number. When the need arises, the programmer can request use of the square root instructions by specifying its code name. Other predefined subroutines may include instructions for trigonometric functions, statistical tables, or converting data into special computerized formats.

6.18 How are assembly language and machine language related?

Assembly language is a symbolic programming language that uses symbols and coded entries to perform specific operations. This format is markedly different from the numeric codes of machine language. However, despite this difference, the assembly language must be converted to machine language in order to be executed.

6.19 What operational software is employed to accomplish this necessary conversion?

The conversion of assembly language to machine language is accomplished using an assembler, which is part of a computer system's operational software. The assembler is a translating program that converts the assembly language program into machine language prior to its execution.

6.20 What was the significance of the development of the assembler?

One of the first translating programs to be written, the assembler became a prototype for similar software written for subsequent languages.

HIGH-LEVEL LANGUAGES

6.21 Practically speaking, what drawbacks were associated with the machine and assembly languages?

Both of these low-level languages were very difficult to use, so that writing programs consumed vast amounts of time. Also the search for and correction of errors, called *debugging*, often took even greater amounts of time. Users needed highly technical backgrounds to become proficient in these languages.

6.22 Again, from a practical standpoint, why was this a disadvantage?

For the computer to be universally accepted, the languages available to support its usage had to be easy to learn and apply. As long as existing languages were overly technical, they hindered computer adoptions. Use of a computer was too difficult for general application to be feasible.

6.23 How did computer manufacturers deal with this problem?

The computer industry recognized that the marketability of their product was seriously affected by the complexity of the existing programming languages and moved to simplify the structure of software.

6.24 What was the outcome of these efforts?

The major move toward an easier software product culminated in the development of high-level languages. This advancement was not simply the creation of one language but was an industry-wide effort to introduce new languages that adhered to certain conventions and met certain standards.

6.25 What characteristics are associated with high-level languages?

Generally, the following four characteristics are associated with high-level languages:
(1) Machine independence
(2) Use of a compiler
(3) Self-documentation features
(4) Standard language format

6.26 What does machine independence mean?

Machine independence refers to the fact that a language may be run on any series of computer systems without alteration. A disadvantage of low-level languages was that they were executable on one computer only and could not be processed elsewhere. Major changes were necessary to software written in that language before it could be processed on another system. Often the necessary changes required labor time that was equivalent to starting from scratch.

6.27 What is the impact of using a compiler?

A compiler is a translating program similar to the assembler utilized with assembly language. The term *compiler* is the general name applied to many translating programs that are used in the conversion of high-level languages to machine language.

6.28 Why was the compiler necessary?

Great emphasis was placed on simplifying the appearance and use of high-level languages. However, the simplified format developed for humans still had to be converted to machine language for execution. The compiler was the translating program that accomplished the conversion of the source program (in that language) to the object program (in machine language).

6.29 What do the terms *source program* and *object program* mean?

The source program is the original program written by the programmer in the required high-level language. It is the source program that is entered into the computer for execution. When the source program is input in the form of punched cards, the cards containing the program are referred to as the *source deck*. The source program enters processing and is converted by a compiler into machine language. The resulting machine language program is called the *object program* and is in actuality the program executed by the computer. The term *compilation* is often used to describe the conversion of the source program into the object program.

6.30 What other special operational feature is assigned to compilers?

Each high-level language is formulated within certain rules to which programmers must adhere. These rules are referred to as the *syntax* of a language. During the compilation process, the compiler will seek out syntax errors in the source program. If no syntax errors are found, the program is permitted to run to completion. If, however, syntax errors are detected during compilation, the program is prevented from running. The operational software overseeing the computer system, of which the compiler is an integral part, will invoke a set of instructions and purge the program from the system. Removal of the incorrect program frees the computer to do other work. When a program is flushed from the system because of syntax errors, the program has *abended*.

6.31 How does the computer record syntax errors?

It is the self-documentation feature of high-level languages that records syntax errors in the source program. *Self-documentation* means that the computer, via its operational software, is automatically instructed to record syntax errors for the programmer. The resultant list of syntax errors becomes a debugging guide for the programmer. In Fig. 6-3 the list of errors resulting from a COBOL program illustrates the product of the self-documentation feature of a high-level language.

CARD	ERROR MESSAGE	
	IKF1100I-W	16 SEQUENCE ERRORS IN SOURCE PROGRAM.
17	IKF2049I-C	NO OPEN CLAUSE FOUND FOR FILE.
120	IKF3001I-E	COMPUTE-RTN NOT DEFINED. STATEMENT DISCRDED.
144	IKF1007I-W	EQUAL NOT PRECEDED BY SPACE. ASSUME SPACE
204	IKF3026I-E	IDENTIFIER-2 OMITTED IN MOVE STATEMENT.

Fig. 6-3 In this example, errors are listed by their card number, whereas other languages may use dollar signs ($) to identify errors beneath the line in which the error appears.

6.32 Why are high-level languages in a standardized format?

The standardized format provides a level of uniformity for a given high-level language. Each computer manufacturer generally adds special touches to standard versions of a language to make them more attractive to potential adopters. The standard format of the language ensures that users will obtain a minimum set of instructions with which most programmers are familiar and which support most applications of the language.

6.33 What are the two categories into which high-level languages may be divided?

High-level languages may be classified as problem-oriented languages and procedure-oriented languages. *Procedure-oriented languages* are high-level languages that may be applied to any problem because they can support a variety of processing modes. *Problem-oriented languages* are more specialized languages that limit their usage to selected applications.

6.34 Which language classification offers the programmer the most flexibility?

Procedure-oriented languages, because of their diverse format, offer the programmer a wider range of options. These languages handle problems from both the scientific and business fields with a minimum of difficulty.

CURRENT PROGRAMMING LANGUAGES

6.35 When did high-level languages become prominent?

The use of high-level languages became popular in the early 1960s, subsequent to the surge in software development from NASA's space exploration work. The successful use of computers in these research efforts spurred manufacturers to develop languages to support other areas.

6.36 What language is considered the precursor of current programming languages?

The language considered to be the precursor of current high-level languages is FORTRAN. FORTRAN, a contraction of *FOR*mula *TRAN*sition, was developed in the late 1950s by IBM.

6.37 What format does FORTRAN assume?

FORTRAN has an algebraic format since the language was designed for scientific purposes. It readily handles data manipulations involving complex formulas.

6.38 How are applications in the areas of science characterized?

In general, *scientific applications* are characterized as having a high level of computations but a limited amount of I/O activity. Conversely, *business applications* possess a high volume of I/O operations and few complex manipulations. Using the designations of scientific and business applications, it is possible to distinguish between those two types of problems and the work that each requires.

6.39 Does FORTRAN use a highly structured format?

FORTRAN possesses an exacting syntax, the rules of which cannot be violated. It dictates what types of statements are usable, where and when. Most statements utilize an algebraic format that may intimidate individuals who are not comfortable with mathematical notations. Figure 6-4 shows an excerpt from a FORTRAN program and illustrates the algebraic nature of its statements.

```
LINE    STATEMENT
        WRITE(3,20)
   20   FORMAT(1H ,'SOLVING A PARABOLIC EQUATION')
    4   READ(1,50)A,B,C,X
   50   FORMAT(4F7.2)
        Y = A*X*X + B*X + C
        WRITE(3,70) X,Y
   70   FORMAT(1H ,'FOR A VALUE OF X = ',F7.2,  Y = ',F14.7)
        END
```

Fig. 6-4

6.40 What language followed the development of FORTRAN?

The next major language to follow the introduction of FORTRAN was COBOL. *COBOL* (*CO*mmon *B*usiness *O*riented *L*anguage) was specially developed by a consortium of manufacturers and users for business applications.

6.41 What made COBOL so different?

Instead of using an algebraic format, COBOL's syntax adopted an English-like appearance. Statements in COBOL look like sentences drawn from paragraphs. Figure 6-5 illustrates the English-like format that characterizes COBOL.

```
MULTIPLY HOURS-IN BY RATE2 GIVING GROSS-PAY.
MULTIPLY GROSS-PAY BY .0645 GIVING FICA-DED.
ADD OT-PAY-N, GROSS-PAY GIVING TOT-PAY.
SUBTRACT FICA-DED FROM TOT-PAY GIVING SUBTOT1.
SUBTRACT FICA-DED-2 FROM SUBTOT1 GIVING SUBTOT2.
WRITE PRINT-REC FROM PAY-LINE1 AFTER ADVANCING 2 LINES.
MOVE SPACES TO PRINT-REC.
```

Fig. 6-5 These statements from a payroll program are representative of COBOL's appearance and syntax.

6.42 Why did the industry switch to a nonscientific format?

The move to an English-like syntax was deliberate. It was an effort to relieve the anxiety associated with use of formulas and to enable people to read through a program and understand it. The logic and computations of a COBOL program are not shrouded in a haze of algebra.

6.43 Are there other advantages to COBOL?

COBOL also has enhanced file manipulation abilities. A drawback associated with FORTRAN is its inability to facilitate file handling operations. COBOL was designed to overcome this problem and readily handles a variety of file operations with a few standard statements.

6.44 What are the disadvantages to using COBOL?

COBOL is a rather wordy language, often requiring many statements to accomplish one task. Programs written in FORTRAN consisting of ten statements might require forty to fifty statements in COBOL because of COBOL's syntax. Also the COBOL compiler is quite large and requires a CPU size sufficient to retain it and the programs undergoing execution. Considering these drawbacks, however, COBOL is nevertheless well worth the effort and can properly support a variety of business applications.

6.45 What language was developed to incorporate the best features of COBOL and FORTRAN?

The language developed to combine these features was *P*rogramming *L*anguage/*1*, or simply PL/1. Created by IBM and used solely with their computers, PL/1 was intended to combine the best operational features of COBOL and FORTRAN.

6.46 What drawbacks were encountered in the adoption of PL/1?

The widespread adoption of PL/1 was hindered by the fact that the language could be run only on IBM systems. Users possessing different hardware could not use it. Many users were reluctant to convert their existing software, which was satisfactorily conforming to current and projected needs, to PL/1. They were not convinced the conversion was economically justifiable. In many instances the powerful processing potential of PL/1 was not necessary for the average user.

6.47 Is PL/1 a powerful programming language?

PL/1 offers a tremendous processing potential to users requiring data manipulative capacities. It easily manipulates data for complex numeric analyses and can examine strings of alphabetic data to identify patterns of repeated characters used in coding schemes. These analytic techniques, which would require many statements in other languages, can be initiated in a few PL/1 statements. Since these activities are highly specialized and unique to selected organizations, PL/1 has not achieved the level of success expected by its developers. Figure 6-6 offers an overview of PL/1 statements.

```
              CTOT = 0.0 :
    MAINLP:
              OPEN FILE(SPOT) SEQUENTIAL INPUT:
              ANSK = TYPE2:
              GRD = 9:
              CTOT = CTOT + CUM5:
              PUT DATA(SPPR,L):
              IF CTCT = TEST THEN LPEND ELSE MAINLP:
```

Fig. 6-6 These statements are representative of the PL/1 syntax, which employs algebraic and English-like terms.

6.48 Considering the capacities of COBOL, FORTRAN, and PL/1, why was RPG introduced?

The acronym *RPG* represents the *R*eport *P*rogram *G*enerator computer language. Introduced subsequent to COBOL, this language has an entirely different operational capacity. RPG is designed to simplify the preparation of reports for management to be used in their decision-making activities.

6.49 How does RPG differ from other languages?

Though it possesses the file manipulation, computational, and I/O capabilities, the primary operational purpose of RPG is the preparation of printed reports. It enables users to access computerized files and develop a variety of printed report formats. Using a highly structured set of input forms (Fig. 6-7, page 110), users input coded entries to create the desired fields and formats to compose the reports they need.

6.50 How might RPG be used within a DP center and in relation to other languages?

The extended use of RPG depends on the level of file activity within the data processing operation. If only a low level of activity is needed as within a batch processing environment, RPG might prove sufficient. Files could be updated using it, with all reports generated using the RPG syntax. In a larger, more active system, other languages would handle the updating of files, and RPG would be reserved just for the preparation of reports. This specialized use of languages takes advantage of each language's best features and improves the overall efficiency of DP operations.

6.51 Are the special coding sheets vital to RPG programming?

Yes. The special coding sheets shown in Fig. 6-7 are critical to successful programming activities in RPG. All program instructions are coded on these sheets and are the basis for laying out report formats and the mode of accessing data from the required computerized files. Without these special coding sheets, it is virtually impossible to program in RPG.

6.52 In what types of computer systems is RPG used?

RPG is employed primarily within IBM systems, in particular, their System 32, 34, and 38 computers. These are generally small computer systems, possessing low-level data processing capacities. These systems are generally used within conventional batch processing operations, providing more than adequate support for their users.

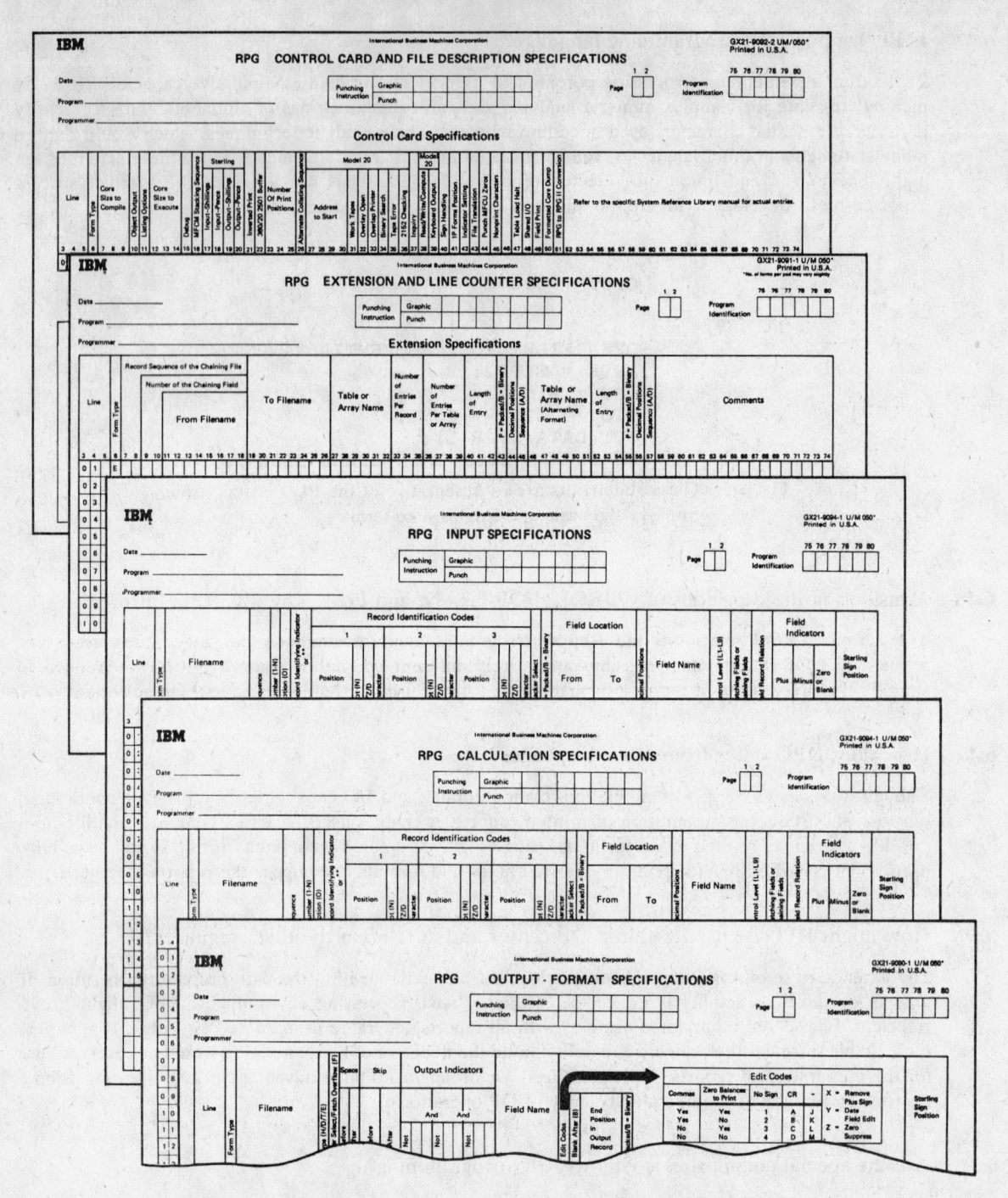

Fig. 6-7 RPG requires the use of specially designed coding sheets.

6.53 Which of the currently popular languages was developed to support time-sharing?

BASIC was created by Dr. John Kemeny to simplify the learning of computer languages and to enable students to interact with computers to apply their skills.

6.54 Where is the BASIC language used?

BASIC is used in conjunction with large and small computer systems, as well as many small home computers. It is used at schools to teach programming skills and computer use, and it is offered by service bureaus to users to perform selective data processing tasks.

```
100 FOR I = 1 TO 100
110 READ N$, H, R
120 IF H = -999.99 THEN 2000
130 G = H*R
140 F = G*.0645
150 N = G-F
160 PRINT N$,G,F,N
170 NEXT I
    .
    .
    .
2000 END
```

Fig. 6-8 A segment from a BASIC program that computes net pay for employees.

6.55 What format does BASIC assume?

BASIC has an algebraic format similar to FORTRAN, but its rules are not as rigorous. BASIC has far fewer rules than other languages, which partly explains its popularity. Within hours, students using BASIC can commence work on the computer. BASIC was introduced to overcome student reluctance to learning languages that were overly technical and overregulated. An excerpt of a BASIC program is shown in Fig. 6-8.

6.56 Why is BASIC referred to as an *interactive language*?

When using BASIC in time-sharing, users interact with the computer on a statement-by-statement basis. Users enter individual statements to which the computer reacts, and conversely, users will respond to computer-generated commands. It is this one-to-one interaction that provides the basis for *interactive processing*.

6.57 Is BASIC the only interactive language?

No. BASIC is one of a group of interactive languages currently available to users. Interactive versions of FORTRAN and COBOL exist today, as well as many other interactive languages.

6.58 Why is BASIC incorporated into many of the home computers?

Because of the ease with which it is learned, its simple and relatively few rules, and its interactive capabilities, BASIC has become a principal language associated with home computers. First-time computer users can quickly develop an understanding of BASIC and utilize their home computer to perform desired tasks.

6.59 Is BASIC the only language found on home computers?

No. Another major home computer language is PASCAL. PASCAL was developed to offer a powerful, yet easily learned, programming language that could be applied to scientific problems. It is somewhat more difficult than BASIC but not as demanding as FORTRAN.

6.60 What format does PASCAL use?

PASCAL has an algebraic format, but it possesses characteristics that reinforce the use of structured programming principles. Structured programming represents a group of programming principles that are applied to improve program logic, simplify solutions, eliminate foolish errors, and minimize the time spent on debugging poorly written software. PASCAL's syntax emphasizes the use of structured concepts (presented in Chap. 8) and permits their application.

6.61 Is PASCAL's syntax difficult to master?

Once concepts associated with structured solutions are understood, PASCAL programming is readily accomplished. It takes somewhat more time, when compared to BASIC, to master PASCAL. A sample of PASCAL statements is shown in Fig. 6-9.

```
BEGIN
    REDS:=0;
    BLKS:=0;
        BEGIN
            READ(KEY);
            IF KEY=1 THEN REDS:=REDS + 1
                ELSE BLKS:=BLKS + 1;
        END;
    WRITELN(REDS,BLKS)
END.
```

Fig. 6-9

PROGRAM EXECUTION

6.62 Considering the differing formats of the high-level languages, what procedures are used to facilitate their execution within computer systems?

Though their formats may vary, currently available programming languages undergo a strict series of operational tasks. Essentially, the same series of tasks is undertaken by the computer whether it uses COBOL or FORTRAN or any other high-level language. A different compiler may be used, but it must be used at exactly the same point within the operational sequence.

6.63 Starting from scratch, what is the first task in a representative operational sequence?

The initial step in the sequence is the writing of the source program by the originating programmer. This program must include all I/O operations and computations. Once written, before converting the program to a computer-acceptable input medium, the programmer desk checks the source program. The term *desk check* describes a checking procedure instituted by the programmer to ensure the correctness of the source program. In doing a desk check, the programmer reads through the source program looking for errors, verifying the variables and the computations used, and catching any glaring omissions.

6.64 Once the desk check is completed, what is the next task?

The desk check precedes the conversion of the source program into a format that can be directly input to the computer. Programmers have two options: (1) keypunch the source program onto cards, which are subsequently input via a card reader, or (2) key the source program directly to the computer by using an online terminal. The option chosen will depend on the resources available within the supporting computer system and the operational procedures in effect within that DP organization.

6.65 With the source program input, what operational software is brought into play?

With entry of the source program into the system, the internal execution of its processing commences. The system must ready the appropriate compiler to convert the source program into machine language.

6.66 What instructions define which compiler to use?

Though the names vary among manufacturers, every computer system has an operational control language that is used in processing programs. One of the more popular terms is *job control language*, or *JCL*. JCL instructions are added to the source program during its input. The JCL instructions alert the computer to what processing features and options should be incorporated within the processing of a particular program.

6.67 What purpose do the JCL instructions serve?

JCL instructions provide a means of communicating with the operational software of a particular system. Using JCL, it is possible to select and control how, when, and where the source program is executed.

6.68 What control features can a system's JCL invoke?

JCL instructions will define the compiler needed to support processing, the hardware involved in processing, the execution of I/O operations, the tasks undertaken when errors are encountered, and the steps required to end one program and start the next. JCL statements are critical to the effective processing of a series of jobs, called a *jobstream*, within computer systems.

6.69 Are JCL statements easily mastered?

No. The JCL language is an extremely difficult language to learn because of its complex structure. It uses many coded entries whose positioning can define many different operational tasks. The juxtaposition of just two control codes can define two diverse tasks. It normally takes many years to master a computer system's operational control language.

6.70 Do operational languages vary from system to system?

Yes. Another difficulty associated with control languages is that they are machine dependent. Though there are carryovers, each control language is different and must be mastered separately. A shift from one manufacturer's system to another requires the computer personnel to learn the new system's control language.

6.71 What will result from the system's use of the compiler?

Invoking the compiler, defined via the JCL accompanying the source program, results in the conversion of the source program to machine language. During this conversion the compiler is constantly scanning for syntax errors. If errors are detected by the compiler, the program will not be executed. A program containing no syntax errors is compiled and permitted to run to completion.

6.72 Can a program be compiled but still encounter errors during its execution?

Yes. A program may contain no syntax errors, but it may possess faulty logic. Thus, even with a clean compilation, the subsequent execution of the program could reveal errors in logic. This type of problem occurs frequently and causes programmers to expend great quantities of debugging time. Similarly, a program may be compiled without error, only to encounter bad input data, which will cause the program to abort.

PROGRAM SPECIFICATIONS

6.73 How do programmers get their software projects?

Programming jobs are normally assigned by the manager of the programming area. Though much verbal discussion may ensue throughout the initial phases of the project, the programmer must receive documentation describing the project under consideration.

6.74 What purposes will that documentation serve?

The documentation received by the programmer may describe an input format, a printed report format, an explanation of the file used in processing, or the limitations applied to the program to be run.

6.75 What form may be used to describe inputs?

A form often used to describe card input is the multiple card layout form (Fig. 6-10). This form may be used to describe from one to six different card formats. In Fig. 6-10 two card formats are illustrated. Data relating to one salesperson are coded onto cards 1 and 2. Note that both cards contain the salesperson's number to ensure that the cards are associated with the same salesperson.

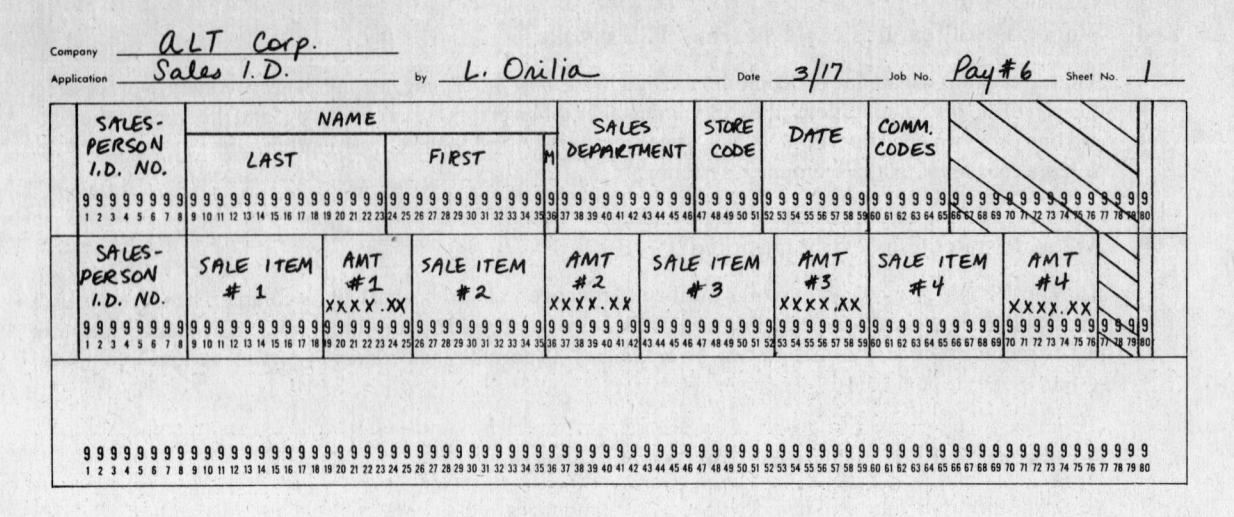

Fig. 6-10 The multiple card layout form.

6.76 What is the rationale for using two cards?

One card cannot contain all the data related to the individual salesperson. Examining the cards, it is possible to note the specific nature of each card. Card 1 holds data related to the salesperson's identity that will not undergo radical changes. Card 2 contains sales data that will change as sales are achieved.

6.77 What is an advantage of this multiple card setup?

One card contains relatively static data and thus will remain unchanged for a long time. Sales transactions will follow on card 2 since they will vary daily. As sales exceed the capacity of card 2, more cards may be added using exactly the same format. As many cards as necessary may be added, without undue difficulty.

6.78 What document is used for recording printed outputs?

The printer spacing chart is the form used to record the format of printed reports resulting from processing. Printed outputs are vital to the success of any organization since they provide the information used in decision making. Figure 6-11 illustrates the printer spacing chart used to record the sales data taken from the two sales cards in Fig. 6-10.

6.79 What facts are garnered from examining the printer spacing chart?

The printer spacing chart details features of the report to be printed. These features include all headings and column headings used, what fields compose the output and their order of appearance, the positioning of these fields, and the use of any totals within the report's format. An examination of Fig. 6-11 reveals the following:
(1) Each salesperson's data will consist of at least two lines.
(2) Line 1 will contain the salesperson's data, beginning with salesperson number.
(3) Line 2 will identify each sales transaction and amount, by its transaction date. As many lines as necessary will use this second line format.
(4) After the last sales transaction is printed, a total will appear reflecting the sum of all sales activities for that individual salesperson.
(5) The report will print only one salesperson per page.
(6) Each field in the report is defined by the number of positions used and its relation to adjacent fields.

The printer spacing chart is designed to lay out all printed report formats on a position-by-position basis.

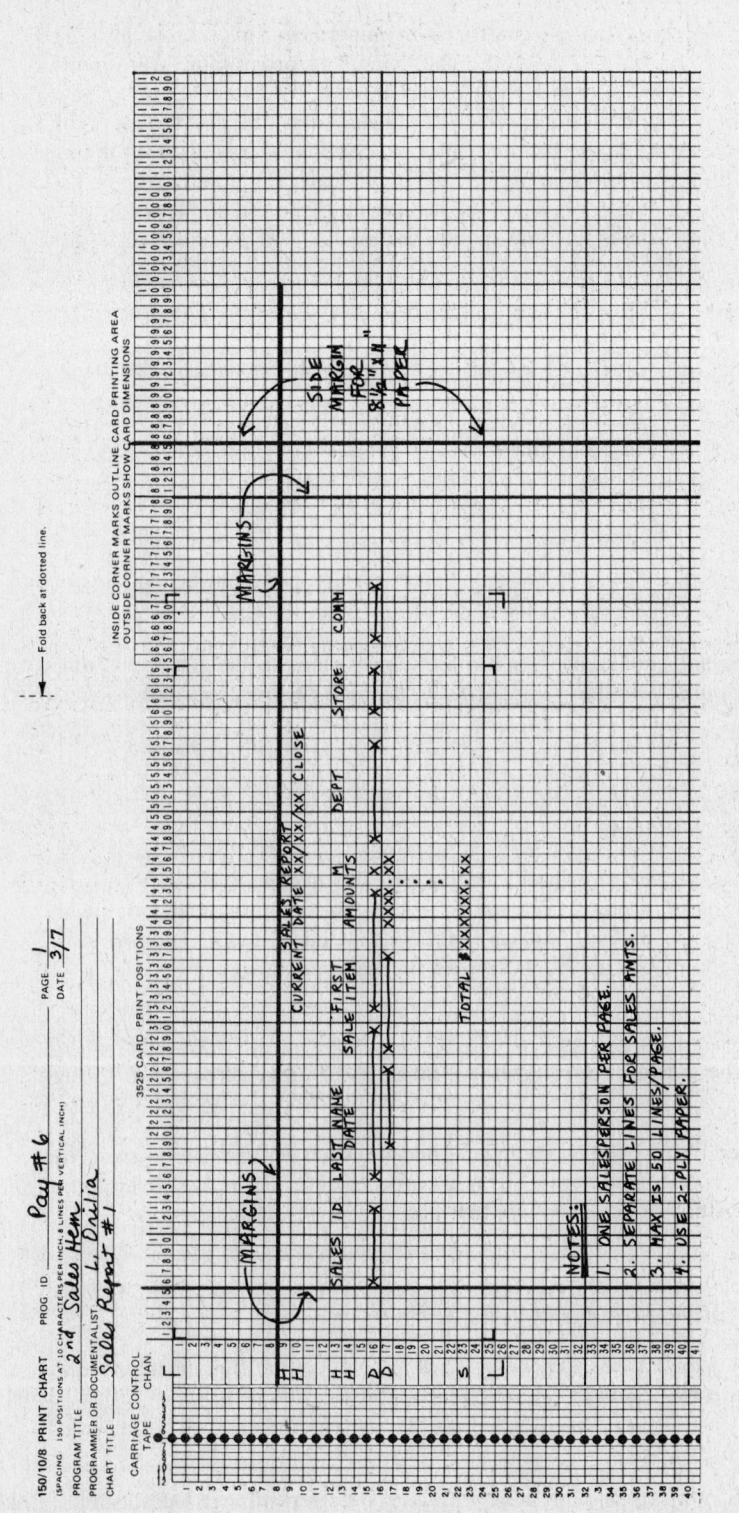

Fig. 6-11 A printer spacing chart.

Fig. 6-12 A record layout form.

6.80 Why is this level of detail necessary?

Using the detailed layouts depicted on printer spacing charts, programmers can prepare the programs necessary to produce reports. As each character is carefully positioned, the programmer can literally count the number of characters to be used and note how they should appear. For example, the first field on the printer spacing chart of Fig. 6-11 is salesperson number. By observation, the programmer could assess that it is eight positions long, uses the column heading Sales No., and is the first field on the first line of that page. Similarly, the positioning of the summary field Total is carefully noted. It consists of eight positions (to include a decimal point), appears beneath the last amount printed, and is preceded by the label Total. The printer spacing chart carries this information pictorially, without the need of long explanations.

6.81 In addition to the multiple card layout form and the printer spacing chart, what other forms can programmers use?

A third type of document encountered by the programmer is the record layout form. This particular form is used to detail the contents of a tape or disk file, on a field-by-field basis.

6.82 How does the programmer detail the fields composing the record from which the file is constructed?

Each field is laid out in exactly the order and appearance that it will assume within the file. Figure 6-12 (page 115) illustrates the record format that could be used to compose a salesperson's file from the cards shown in Fig. 6-10.

6.83 What facts are gained from the record layout form?

The form details each field composing the record of each salesperson. The first field of every record is the salesperson number field, consisting of 8 digits. The file is ordered in ascending order, using the numeric data in that field. Fields drawn from the input cards follow that initial field to complete the record's format. All fields composing the record match those used on the input cards.

6.84 In examining the record layout, the salesperson number field appears only once, even though it appeared on both cards. Why?

The salesperson number field was used twice, once on each card, because each card had to be associated with a specific salesperson. On the record layout form, this field appears once as the first field and all other fields follow it. Its first appearance is sufficient to identify that record with a salesperson.

6.85 How long is the salesperson record illustrated in Fig. 6-12?

The record format used for the salesperson's file is 133 characters long. Notice that it is shorter than the number of card columns identified with two cards.

6.86 Are there other nonstandard documentation features available to programming personnel?

Many organizations develop forms that are unique to their organizations and satisfy their specific needs. Also, programmers may use a variety of memos or notes to assist their preparation of software. Everyone develops some personalized form to assist the work. The three forms shown in Figs. 6-10–6-12 are standard and are used throughout the DP field.

6.87 Is there any singular documentation format that is used to completely describe a program solution?

Program documentation is generally unique to each organization and, as such, assumes different formats. The purpose of program documentation is to describe all aspects of the problem defining all inputs, outputs, and records. This description is normally accomplished using a variety of charts, diagrams, and written narratives. The extent and level of the documentation are unique to the organization. One of the first tasks undertaken by programmers is to research the documentation used by that organization. It provides a consistent link between projects.

6.88 Why have flowcharts not been mentioned in the discussion of program documentation?

Flowcharts are analytic tools that outline the logic used in writing a program. This topic is so important and complex that it has been reserved for an entire chapter. Chapter 7 reviews the topic of flowcharting and describes their preparation.

Review Questions

6.89 High-level languages were among the first languages used with computer systems. (*a*) True, (*b*) false.

6.90 The op code of a machine language instruction defines the operation performed by that instruction. (*a*) True, (*b*) false.

6.91 Three components of assembly language instructions are the label, op code, and operand. (*a*) True, (*b*) false.

6.92 An assembler is the translating program used specifically with assembly language and RPG. (*a*) True, (*b*) false.

6.93 Compilers are used to convert the object program into the source program. (*a*) True, (*b*) false.

6.94 Source programs are initially written by the programmer. (*a*) True, (*b*) false.

6.95 Object programs consist of machine language statements. (*a*) True, (*b*) false.

6.96 Procedure-oriented languages are used in a wide range of program applications. (*a*) True, (*b*) false.

6.97 FORTRAN's algebraic format is perfectly suited to scientific applications. (*a*) True, (*b*) false.

6.98 COBOL programs are rather lengthy, despite COBOL's concise algebraic format. (*a*) True, (*b*) false.

6.99 PL/1 was successfully adopted by many non-IBM computer users because of its unique processing features. (*a*) True, (*b*) false.

6.100 Structured programming is designed for the writing of better and more logical software but is of little value during the debugging process. (*a*) True, (*b*) false.

6.101 Control over a program's execution is exercised via some form of operational control language. (*a*) True, (*b*) false.

6.102 Mastering of a control language is accomplished over a period of time because of its complexity and detail. (*a*) True, (*b*) false.

6.103 Sound program documentation is critical to programmers' understanding of the task assigned to them. (*a*) True, (*b*) false.

6.104 Machine language instructions have a(n) (*a*) algebraic format; (*b*) numerical format; (*c*) English-sentence format; (*d*) alphabetic format.

6.105 The first symbolic language was (*a*) machine language; (*b*) FORTRAN; (*c*) assembly language; (*d*) RPG.

6.106 The equivalent of a macro is a(n) (*a*) program; (*b*) operand; (*c*) predefined subroutine; (*d*) assembler.

6.107 A characteristic of a high-level language is (*a*) machine dependence; (*b*) use of an assembler; (*c*) self-documentation feature; (*d*) all of the above.

6.108 A high-level language that is applied to only one type of programming application is referred to as a (*a*) problem-oriented language; (*b*) procedure-oriented language; (*c*) low-level compiler; (*d*) macro language.

6.109 The computer language possessing an English-like format is (*a*) PASCAL; (*b*) RPG; (*c*) PL/1; (*d*) COBOL.

6.110 The language requiring the use of special coding sheets is (*a*) FORTRAN; (*b*) RPG; (*c*) PASCAL; (*d*) COBOL.

6.111 BASIC may be referred to as a(n) (*a*) interactive language; (*b*) time-sharing language; (*c*) high-level language; (*d*) all of the above.

6.112 The manual verification of a program code prior to its conversion to an input medium is called (*a*) desk checking; (*b*) validation; (*c*) preprocess checking; (*d*) all of the above.

6.113 Hardcopy outputs are defined using a(n) (*a*) card layout form; (*b*) printer spacing chart; (*c*) record layout form; (*d*) I/O operational chart.

6.114 The description of records composing a computerized file are defined via the (*a*) card layout form; (*b*) record spacing chart; (*c*) record layout; (*d*) file format sheet.

6.115 In machine language the programmer must specify the actual _____ locations of the data items used in processing.

6.116 In machine language instructions the data to be worked on are defined by the _____.

6.117 The coded entries of assembly language instructions are referred to as _____.

6.118 In assembly language a group of related instructions is accessible using a _____.

6.119 The correction of programs is referred to as _____.

6.120 A _____ is the general name assigned to translating programs, used with high-level languages.

6.121 The rules governing the writing of statements in a language are defined as its _____.

6.122 A program application involving basic arithmetic operations and a high level of I/O activity is defined as a _____ application.

6.123 _____ was designed to incorporate the best features of COBOL and FORTRAN.

CHAP. 6] INTRODUCTION TO PROGRAM LANGUAGES 119

6.124 A language primarily designed for preparation of management-oriented reports is _____.

6.125 The application of structured programming principles is an integral part of the _____ language.

6.126 When the source program is punched onto cards, the resulting cards are referred to as the _____.

6.127 A popular form of control language is _____.

6.128 A _____ refers to the continuous processing of a series of jobs within a computer system.

6.129 A series of card formats involved in processing is detailed using a _____ form.

Answers: 6.89 (b); 6.90 (a); 6.91 (a); 6.92 (b); 6.93 (b); 6.94 (a); 6.95 (a); 6.96 (a); 6.97 (a); 6.98 (b); 6.99 (b); 6.100 (b); 6.101 (a); 6.102 (a); 6.103 (a); 6.104 (b); 6.105 (c); 6.106 (c); 6.107 (c); 6.108 (a); 6.109 (d); 6.110 (b); 6.111 (d); 6.112 (a); 6.113 (b); 6.114 (c); 6.115 primary storage; 6.116 operand; 6.117 mnemonics; 6.118 macro; 6.119 debugging; 6.120 compiler; 6.121 syntax; 6.122 business; 6.123 PL/1; 6.124 RPG; 6.125 PASCAL; 6.126 source deck; 6.127 JCL; 6.128 jobstream; 6.129 multiple card layout.

Supplementary Problems

6.130 Why do you think the developers of COBOL chose an English-like syntax instead of an algebraic instructional format?

6.131 In your own words describe the syntax associated with BASIC, FORTRAN, PL/1, and PASCAL. What similarities do you observe?

6.132 What advantages do programmers derive from the use of multiple card layout forms, printer spacing charts, and record layout forms?

6.133 In your own words describe the execution process from the preparation of the source program to the processing of the object program.

6.134 Describe the differences between a business application and a scientific application. Why would a business application involve a high volume of I/O activity?

6.135 Examine the classified ads within your local trade journals and newspapers. Prepare a list of the various programming languages referred to in these ads. Why do you believe so many different languages exist?

Glossary

Abended. The cancellation of a program's execution prior to its planned end, due to error conditions of some type.

Assembler. The translating program specifically used with assembly language to convert its programs to machine language.

Assembly language. A low-level language that was developed after machine language; the first symbolic programming language; used symbols or codes to define operations.

BASIC. The interactive language developed by Kemeny to support time-sharing activities.

Business application. A programming application characterized by relatively simple computations and a high level of I/O activity.

COBOL. A programming language that has an English-like format, which was designed to handle business-related software.

Compilation. The compiler's conversion of the source program into machine language.

Compiler. The translating programs that convert source programs to object programs (in machine language).

Debugging. The assessment and correction of errors in program software.

Desk check. The manual checking of source programs prior to their conversion to a computer-acceptable input medium.

FORTRAN. One of the older high-level languages that utilizes an algebraic format; used for scientific problems; handles complex formulas easily.

Interactive processing. The online interaction between users and their supporting computer system; frequently associated with time-sharing.

Job control language (JCL). A control language used by computer personnel to invoke special operational features to assist or control the processing of programs.

Jobstream. The continuous flow of programs or jobs through a computer system.

Machine language. The only instructional language that computers understand; the original language developed for computers.

Macroinstruction (macro). A specially coded assembly language instruction that provides access to a group of instructions that handle a specific problem or operational task.

Mnemonics. The symbolic codes used within assembly language that identify operational tasks.

Multiple card layout form. A program documentation form that can detail the format of from one to six cards used in processing.

Object program. The machine language program that results from the compiler's conversion of the source program.

Operand. The component of an instruction that defines the data or variables to be worked on.

Operation (op) code. The instructional component that defines the operation to be performed by the program instruction.

PASCAL. A programming language that relies on an algebraic format and the use of structured programming principles.

PL/1. A programming language designed by IBM to incorporate the best features of COBOL and FORTRAN.

Predefined subroutine. A specific set of instructions, identified by a special coded name, that handles one special task.

Printer spacing chart. A program documentation form used to detail the exact format of printed outputs.

Problem-oriented languages. Programming languages that can be applied to only one type of application.

Procedure-oriented languages. Programming languages that can be applied to a wide variety of problems in many fields.

Record layout form. A program documentation form used to detail the fields composing the record format of a computerized file.

RPG. A programming language that utilizes specially coded sheets to prepare printed reports.

Scientific application. A programming application characterized by low levels of I/O activity and the processing of complex formulas and arithmetic manipulations.

Source deck. The group of cards onto which the source program is punched.

Source program. The original problem written by the programmer.

Structured programming. A highly specialized approach of preparing programs to improve logic and reduce errors.

Symbolic programming language. A programming language in which symbols or codes are used to represent operational tasks.

Syntax. The rules that govern the writing of instructions in a specific language.

Chapter 7

Flowcharting

7.1 FLOWCHARTING DOCUMENTATION

A *flowchart* is a pictorial representation of the flow of logic in a processing application. Each symbol in the flowchart represents a specific step within that approach and dictates the order to be used. Flowcharts provide a means of documenting the work of data processors and offer management a vehicle for supervising the work in progress.

The two most frequently encountered flowcharts are *systems flowcharts* and *program flowcharts*. Of the two, systems flowcharts are the broader, more encompassing diagrams, detailing the flow of information through any part of an organization. Systems flowcharts document both manual and computerized data processing activities. Program flowcharts are restricted to defining the logic used in writing a computer program. Program flowcharts assist in the development of sound and logical software. They enable programmers to test potential solutions and to gauge the progress of their work.

Each flowchart is composed of specific symbols, with each symbol reflecting a specific operational use. One set of symbols is reserved for use with program flowcharts, with a much larger set of symbols set aside for systems flowcharts.

7.2 PROGRAM FLOWCHART LOOPS

Flowchart symbols are placed within a flowchart to represent the logical flow of data through the EDP cycle of input, processing, and output. Symbols used within program flowcharts include the terminal symbol, input/output (I/O) symbol, annotation symbol, and processing symbol. *Terminal symbols* open and close program flowcharts and are often referred to as *START* and *STOP* symbols. *I/O symbols* denote input and output operations. Narratives (e.g., READ and PRINT) written into I/O symbols denote the I/O operation to be performed. *Annotation symbols* permit the entry of descriptive comments within the text of the flowchart. Arithmetic manipulations and processing activities of any type are defined within *processing symbols*.

Data handled within each symbol are identified by unique datanames. Processing activities may be written out or defined by formulas in which only one dataname exists to the left of the equal sign. Symbols may be used to represent fundamental arithmetic operations (that is, +, −, /, ∗).

The specifications related to a problem are usually defined within its narrative. The flowcharter should extract from that problem narrative key points from which to prepare the flowchart. The datanames used for the flowchart are selected by the flowcharter and should reflect the data to be processed.

Most flowcharts open and close with terminal symbols. Input operations normally precede processing activities, which set the stage for outputting the results of processing. The repetitive handling of data is accomplished via the *flowchart loop*. Integral components within the looping sequence are the decision and unconditional branch.

The *decision* enables use of the *last record check* (*LRC*), which is a test to determine whether the last record has been fully read and processed. LRC decisions are normally placed immediately after the opening *READ symbol* at the beginning of the flowchart loop. Decisions also permit the flowchart to choose between two alternative paths. The *unconditional branch*, or *GO TO*, permits the branching back to a prior READ operation to commence processing of the next loop. Branches leaving decisions are referred to as *conditional branches* and may be identified by the terms YES and

NO. Input/output symbols are sometimes identified as *READ* and *PRINT symbols* to simplify reference to them. *Connector symbols* may be used to represent unconditional branches to complete a looping sequence.

7.3 LOOPING SEQUENCES

An LRC decision enables the handling of an unspecified amount of data. Flowcharts that involve a predetermined amount of data are constructed using a *counter*, which permits an exact number of loops to be executed. Three components are necessary to construct a counter. First, the counter must be initialized prior to the start of looping (that is, $K = 1$). This step is defined as an *initial condition* and represents just one of the tasks performed prior to processing.

A second counter component is the *counter decision* where a test is performed to determine whether the desired number of loops has been executed (that is, 'IS $K = 25$?'). The counter decision is normally positioned at the end of the processing loop, prior to the branch back to restart the loop. On the NO branch of the counter decision is its *increment*, the third key factor of a counter. The counter increment increases the counter by 1 as each loop is completed (that is, $K = K + 1$). The YES branch of the counter decision may lead to a STOP symbol or another phase of processing.

The creation of *literals* within PRINT symbols permits the output of column headings and special labels to highlight printed data. Column headings are defined as initial conditions and create characters that define the data items that are printed beneath them. Each individual heading is encased within a pair of single quotation marks, defining the desired string of characters. Special labels are similarly created but are usually seen at the end of reports to highlight summaries of data and identify critical data items.

Automated looping sequences may be defined using flowcharting techniques. One technique is to use two processing symbols to define the start and end of a loop, in much the same manner as a counter. The automated looping mechanism defines the same operational steps as does the counter but is simpler to represent. In the example shown in Fig. 7.8 (Probs. 7.83–7.88), processing symbols containing the terms FOR and NEXT were used to define the start and end of a looping sequence, respectively.

7.4 ACCUMULATORS

An *accumulator* provides a means of developing grand totals or subtotals, which are an integral part of handling data from many people or transactions. Functioning like a running total, the accumulator permits updating at each repetition by adding new data to the existing total. The updated total is then retained for the next loop and becomes the basis for the next total. This updating process continues until looping ceases and the accumulated total is output.

Two critical components for an accumulator are its initialization and its update. The initial condition that establishes an accumulator may appear as $T = 0$ within a processing symbol. Similarly, the update may be written as $T = T + AMT$, where an AMT is added to the accumulator (T) on each flowchart loop. When the last loop is complete, the accumulated total for T is output usually preceded by a special label.

The number of accumulators used within a flowchart reflects the number of totals needed to support processing. If three grand totals are required, then three accumulators would be used. Each would carry a unique name (that is, T1, T2, and T3), and each would have its own update (that is, $T1 = T1 + A$, $T2 = T2 + B$, $T3 = T3 + C$).

It is also possible to combine accumulators and counters within a flowchart solution. Each must be separately initialized, and each must invoke its components within separate flowchart symbols. Both initial conditions will appear prior to the loop's start, with the accumulator update contained in the loop. The counter decision will appear at the loop's close, with the counter increment on its NO branch. The YES branch will contain the output of the accumulated total and any other processing deemed necessary.

7.5 ADDITIONAL FLOWCHARTING CONCEPTS

A flowchart will reflect the particular problem being solved. As such, a flowchart may contain multiple decisions, two or more accumulators, and as many literals as required to properly output the desired information. As long as each technique is properly defined with its initial conditions and represented by the appropriate symbols, they may be incorporated into a flowchart. Thus, for example, two accumulators will respectively require two initial conditions and two accumulation statements for proper processing.

Multiple decisions may be used to choose between alternative paths or critical data items during processing. In addition to distinguishing between equality, decision symbols may represent inequality, that is, less than or greater than conditions. The decision should always be formulated as a question with specific choices to be made.

Computations involving percentages should also be scrutinized. When using percents, it is important to use the decimal equivalent of the desired percentage rate to ensure the accuracy of the computation.

Multiple outputs may result from any processing activities. When separate outputs are necessary, they should be denoted by individual I/O symbols containing the desired printed data.

Solved Problems

FLOWCHARTING DOCUMENTATION

7.1 What is a flowchart?

A flowchart is a diagram that pictorially represents the flow of logic related to a specific processing solution. Using the flowchart diagram, the steps involved in that solution are positioned in the exact order of execution.

7.2 What purpose does the flowchart serve?

The flowchart serves as a valuable piece of documentation, as well as a visual reference to the problem being considered and the solution suggested for it.

7.3 Why is that documentation important?

Documentation enables the data processors to assess the work being performed and the solution. Currently, many DP professionals are constrained within their work schedules by their flowchart documentation. They must show their flowcharts to their managers, who evaluate these solutions in relation to the entire project. Only if the solution is approved may the processors proceed to the next level of program development.

7.4 What are the two most frequently used types of flowcharts?

Systems flowcharts and program flowcharts are the types of flowchart documentation most commonly encountered.

7.5 What are the differences between them?

The systems flowchart is a broader flowchart encompassing the flow of data within an organization. It is designed to describe a diverse group of processing activities. In contrast, the program flowchart has a more limited scope, restricted to the steps within a program solution. Essentially, the program flowchart details the logic that should be used to write the instructions that compose a program.

7.6 In what way does the systems flowchart serve a broader function?

Systems flowcharts describe an overall level of processing within an organization, where processing activities occur with and without the aid of computers. Program flowcharts describe steps, which when converted to some computer language, are executed inside the computer.

7.7 Which type of flowchart will be discussed in this chapter?

Because of the complexity associated with developing systems flowcharts, this chapter will discuss only program flowcharts. Chapter 9, however, will discuss the preparation of systems flowcharts.

7.8 When is the program flowchart written?

The program flowchart is prepared and checked well before the software is written. This is an essential step in developing a program because it affords the opportunity to lay out the logic of the proposed solution.

7.9 Why does flowcharting precede the writing of the program?

It is important to detail the logic of a program before writing instructions. If the logic is incorrect, then a great number of program statements will have to be rewritten. If, however, the program flowchart contains faultless logic, the writing of instructions can be efficiently performed.

7.10 How does the preliminary preparation of flowcharts assist in program preparation?

The initial writing of flowcharts helps the programmer in many ways. First, it permits programmers to document their progress, and it also illustrates that they are developing an organized approach to the solution. Second, the flowchart enables the testing of many solutions without having to write the program. By examining a flowchart, it is possible to discern whether a particular approach will be effective. Using flowcharts, programmers can communicate their ideas to their associates and gain insights into the suggested programming approach.

7.11 What symbols are used with program flowcharts?

The symbols used with program flowcharts are illustrated in Fig. 7-1. These symbols have specified predefined meanings, as indicated. Each is used to represent a specific task or type of program instruction. Subsequent problems will illustrate the use of these symbols.

PROGRAM FLOWCHART SYMBOLS

Terminal symbol indicates the beginning and end of a flowchart.

Processing symbol notes program instructions that assist in or perform manipulations of data.

Predefined process symbol defines a set of instructions within a program with a specific purpose; the set is always accessed as a unit.

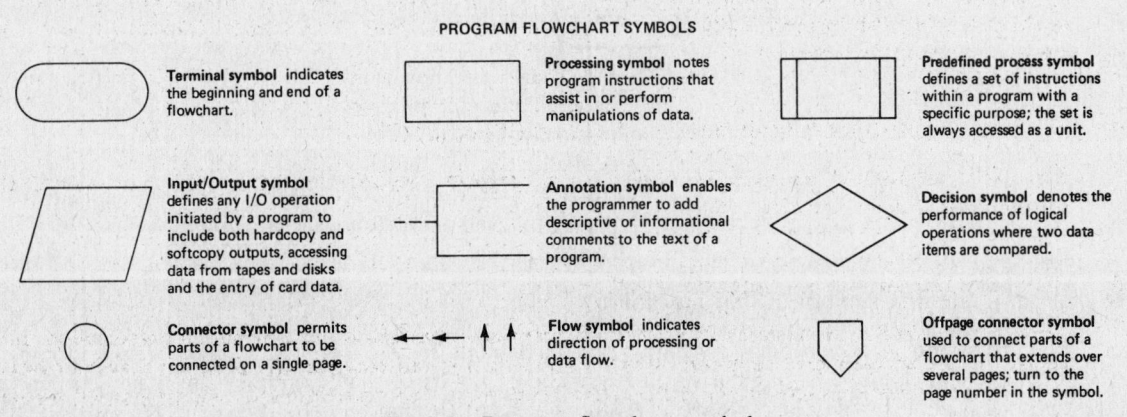

Input/Output symbol defines any I/O operation initiated by a program to include both hardcopy and softcopy outputs, accessing data from tapes and disks and the entry of card data.

Annotation symbol enables the programmer to add descriptive or informational comments to the text of a program.

Decision symbol denotes the performance of logical operations where two data items are compared.

Connector symbol permits parts of a flowchart to be connected on a single page.

Flow symbol indicates direction of processing or data flow.

Offpage connector symbol used to connect parts of a flowchart that extends over several pages; turn to the page number in the symbol.

Fig. 7-1 Program flowchart symbols.

7.12 Are other symbols available for flowcharting?

Yes. Many other flowcharting symbols are available, but they are restricted to systems flowcharts (see Chap. 9). This chapter will present only those symbols related to program flowcharts.

PROGRAM FLOWCHART LOOPS

7.13 How are flowcharting symbols positioned?

The symbols composing a flowchart are logically positioned to describe how data should be processed. Their placement should detail every step in the handling of that data. Any user reading the flowchart should be able to follow the logic used.

7.14 Is there any general flow that can be followed in detailing the steps composing a flowchart?

The steps representing the EDP cycle are often a useful general guide to laying out a flowchart solution. Data are generally input, prior to processing, which precedes the output of these results. The order of these three EDP operations provides a general rule of thumb for preparing a flowchart.

7.15 How might a preliminary flowchart be constructed?

A simple introductory flowchart is shown in Fig. 7-2. This flowchart represents the computation of a gross pay amount and related I/O operations. To simplify these initial discussions, the flowchart has been deliberately kept at a low level.

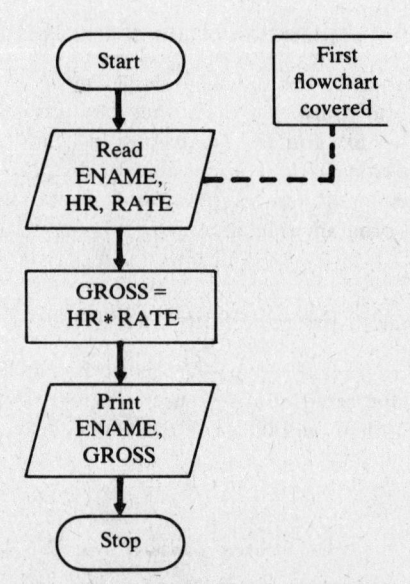

```
        Start              First
                         flowchart
                          covered
         │
         ▼
    Read ENAME,  ─ ─ ─ ─ ┘
    HR, RATE
         │
         ▼
    GROSS =
    HR * RATE
         │
         ▼
    Print
    ENAME,
    GROSS
         │
         ▼
        Stop
```

Fig. 7-2 Flowcharts use their symbols to define the processing activities to be performed. This flowchart introduces the terminal, I/O, processing, and annotation symbols.

7.16 What is the first symbol of that flowchart?

The first symbol of our opening flowchart is called a *terminal symbol*. Terminal symbols are used to open and close flowcharts, denoting the starting and ending points of that diagram. Note that the opening terminal symbol contains the narrative START, whereas its closing counterpart contains the word STOP.

7.17 What other terms are applied to the two terminal symbols?

Computer jargon permits users to refer to the opening and closing terminal symbols as *START* and *STOP symbols*. These references provide an alternative to the tediousness of repeatedly stating a terminal symbol noting a START and STOP narrative. Over the years, the use of START and STOP symbols became an accepted equivalent for terminal symbols containing those narratives.

7.18 What name is applied to the parallelogram used with the second flowchart symbol?

The second flowchart symbol is referred to as an *input/output symbol*, or simply an *I/O symbol*. The I/O reference denotes the dual use of this symbol for both input and output operations.

7.19 How does the flowcharter distinguish between input and output operations?

The narrative used within the I/O symbol denotes whether an input or output operation should be performed. If the term READ or INPUT is used, an input operation is indicated. The use of PRINT or WRITE would denote an output operation.

7.20 What operation is noted within the initial I/O symbol of the flowchart in Fig. 7-2?

The first I/O symbol of this flowchart notes an input operation involving three items of data. The symbol instructs the READing of data for an employee's name (ENAME), hours worked (HR), and hourly rate of pay (RATE). The word READ denotes the input of those data items.

7.21 Of what significance are the terms ENAME, HR, and RATE?

Those three terms are called *datanames* since they refer to the data that will be input for processing. They provide a unique form of reference for each data item slated for input. That item of data will be referred to by that specific dataname, throughout the flowchart, whenever it is involved in any form of processing.

7.22 Who picks the datanames used?

The programmer is usually free to select the datanames most appropriate for the data handled. The only ground rules followed are that the datanames chosen be used with only one specific data item and that the datanames be used consistently throughout the flowchart. Thus, though HR and HRS are similar, they are two distinct datanames. Only one of those datanames would be used consistently throughout a flowchart to represent any hours data used in processing.

7.23 What purposes do the commas serve in that initial I/O symbol?

Commas serve to separate the three datanames for input, as directed by the I/O symbol. Generally, the comma is reserved for delineating variables in either input or output operations.

7.24 What symbol is attached to the I/O symbol by a dashed line?

The three-sided rectangle attached to the READ I/O symbol is called an *annotation symbol*. The annotation symbol is used to add descriptive comments that assist in the user's comprehension of the flowchart's purpose. These comments do not affect processing, nor do they initiate any processing activities. To emphasize the advisory status of annotation symbols, a dashed line is used to attach them to other symbols within the flowchart.

7.25 What comment has been added to the flowchart in Fig. 7-2?

The annotation symbol indicates that the flowchart illustrated is the FIRST FLOWCHART COVERED. The comment is placed within the three-sided annotation symbol and attached to the first I/O symbol by a dashed line.

7.26 Why are advisory comments necessary?

Annotation symbols enable flowcharters to add comments to flowcharts that help advise or clarify points in the diagram. They are very helpful when creating reminders that highlight critical data items or point out potential trouble spots within processing or I/O operations.

7.27 Where are processing operations defined?

Processing operations are defined within the processing symbol, which is a rectangle. The third symbol of our flowchart, a processing symbol, contains the narrative GROSS = HR * RATE. The use of a formula is well-suited to processing operations since it offers a shorthand method of expressing computations.

7.28 Must formulas always be used in processing symbols?

Though formulas offer a shorthand convention, it is possible to express computations using a sentence-like structure. Thus the prior calculation could have been properly expressed as MULTIPLY HR BY RATE GIVING GROSS. The flowcharter will use the method with which he or she feels most comfortable and which is best suited to the problem being studied. Formulas will be used in this book whenever possible because of their concise notation.

7.29 Are there any conventions that are normally followed when specifying formulas in processing symbols?

Yes. One common convention is to place only one dataname to the left of the equal sign in the formula. Because this format parallels the structure of many modern computer languages, the conversion of flowcharts to those languages is simplified.

7.30 What symbols are generally used to represent arithmetic operations?

In the computation of GROSS in Fig. 7-2, an asterisk * was used to denote multiplication. The fundamental arithmetic operations are represented by the plus sign + for addition, minus sign − for subtraction, and the slash / for division. Parentheses may be used in any computation to ensure the accuracy of the formula expressed.

7.31 What variables are output in the flowchart's second I/O symbol?

The second I/O symbol denotes the undertaking of an output operation because of the word PRINT. The two datanames noted are ENAME and GROSS, representing the two items slated for output. The order of output is indicated by the order in which the datanames are expressed. Thus ENAME is printed first on a line followed by the GROSS amount.

7.32 How is the flowchart closed?

The flowchart in Fig. 7-2 closes with a terminal symbol, the word STOP. The STOP symbol denotes the flowchart's end and the cessation of any processing activities. No operational symbols should follow the STOP symbol.

The following narrative refers to Probs. 7.32–7.41.

The task to be performed is to compute a sales commission. Input to the problem are a salesperson's name and three sales amounts. Add up the three sales amounts to compute a total sales amount. The salesperson's commission is 10 percent of the total sales amount. Print out the salesperson's name, total sales amount, and the commission derived from those sales.

7.33 What flowchart can be prepared for the problem stated in the narrative?

Figure 7-3 illustrates the flowchart for the problem. Note that the entire flowchart consists of six symbols, including both START and STOP symbols at its beginning and end. It is longer than the flowchart in Fig. 7-2 since more computations are undertaken.

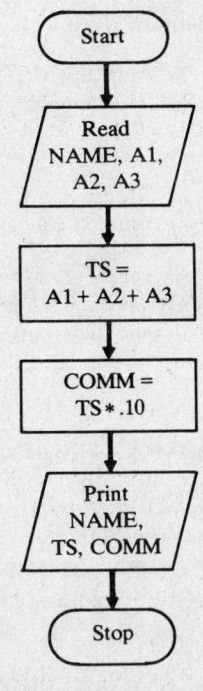

```
                    ┌─────────┐
                    │  Start  │
                    └────┬────┘
                         ▼
                    ╱─────────╱
                   ╱  Read   ╱
                  ╱ NAME, A1,╱
                 ╱  A2, A3  ╱
                ╱──────────╱
                     │
                     ▼
                 ┌────────┐
                 │  TS =  │
                 │A1+A2+A3│
                 └────┬───┘
                      ▼
                 ┌────────┐
                 │ COMM = │
                 │ TS*.10 │
                 └────┬───┘
                      ▼
                ╱──────────╱
               ╱   Print  ╱
              ╱   NAME,  ╱
             ╱  TS, COMM╱
            ╱──────────╱
                  │
                  ▼
             ┌─────────┐
             │  Stop   │
             └─────────┘
```

Fig. 7-3

7.34 What facts pertinent to the construction of the flowchart may be extracted from the flowchart narrative?

From reading the narrative, the following facts can be determined:
 (a) Four items are input—a salesperson's name and three sales amounts.
 (b) The three sales amounts are added to create the total sales amount.
 (c) Commissions are calculated at 10 percent of the total sales amount.
 (d) The printout will contain the salesperson's name, total sales amount, and commission.
 (e) The flowchart serves only one person.
By detailing these facts, the major factors presented within the problem narrative that will compose our flowchart solution have been analyzed. Each of these five items is reflected in the flowchart in Fig. 7-3.

7.35 What is the purpose of the first symbol following the START symbol of the flowchart?

The first I/O symbol of this flowchart defines a READ operation and brings in four data items. Input are the salesperson's name (NAME) and three sales amounts (A1, A2, and A3). The datanames A1, A2, and A3 are used to identify uniquely each of the three sales amounts.

7.36 Why is it necessary to define each sales amount by its own dataname?

Unique datanames enable the flowcharter to independently access items of data and separately use them in processing operations. It is not sufficient to state that three sales amounts exist. Each sales amount must be defined by its own dataname. Using three separate datanames simplifies the computation of commissions.

7.37 After inputting the salesperson's name and three sales amounts, what computation follows?

With the data provided, it is possible to compute the total sales amount, which is needed for computing commissions. Note that in this flowchart two consecutive processing symbols exist. Their relationship is deliberate. The first processing symbol contains the computation of the total sales amount TS, and the second processing symbol reflects the computation of a commission COMM.

7.38 What conventions are characteristic of these processing operations?

Each processing task is configured as a formula, with only one variable positioned to the left of the equal sign. Each formula uses the predefined symbols for addition, which is a plus sign +, and for multiplication, which is an asterisk *.

7.39 Why can an output operation commence after total sales amount and commission are computed?

Those two results are required entries for output. Thus when they exist, it is possible to print them. The second I/O symbol of this flowchart directs their output, along with the salesperson's name. Note that within this PRINT operation, datanames are separated by commas for legibility.

7.40 Though only NAME, TS, and COMM are readied for output, would it have been possible to also print the three sales amounts?

Yes. It would have been possible to print A1, A2, and A3, but that option was not specified by the problem narrative. When establishing a problem's criteria, the flowcharter is free to select an output format. In this case a choice was made not to output the three sales amounts.

7.41 After output of the required data, what does the flowchart direct?

The flowchart closes with a STOP symbol, noting its completion. Only one person's data are handled by this type of flowchart.

7.42 What limitation on data processing is imposed by a flowchart for one person?

Flowcharts designed to support the processing of only one person's data exclude in their design the repetitive processing of data that is a cornerstone in the computerized handling of data. Most business activities require the repeated handling of data, with the computer at the heart of this repetitive processing cycle. As such, flowcharts must offer the capability to graphically depict all steps composing this repetitive activity.

7.43 What terms are applied to these repetitive processing activities?

The series of steps repeated within the context of a flowchart is referred to as a *flowchart loop*. The flowchart loop enables the repeated processing of data, via the same processing steps, with new data input on each loop. New data are input and then processed within the loop, with the same process being repeated on the next loop. Figure 7-4 (page 131) illustrates a looping sequence incorporated into the flowchart solution of Fig. 7-3.

7.44 What is the purpose of the diamond-shaped symbol positioned in the flowchart in Fig. 7-4?

The diamond-shaped symbol represents a *decision symbol*, which is used for logical operations. As stated in the earlier discussion of the CPU's arithmetic-logic unit, logical operations involve comparisons of data. These comparisons may entail the test of two items of data to determine which is larger or smaller, or if equality exists, or if additional data exist that are to be processed.

7.45 What purpose does the decision serve in this flowchart?

The decision symbol serves two purposes in the flowchart in Fig. 7-4. First, it serves to verify the existence of (or lack of) data to be processed. The decision's second purpose is to enable the creation of a looping sequence, which permits data to be processed for more than one person.

CHAP. 7] FLOWCHARTING 131

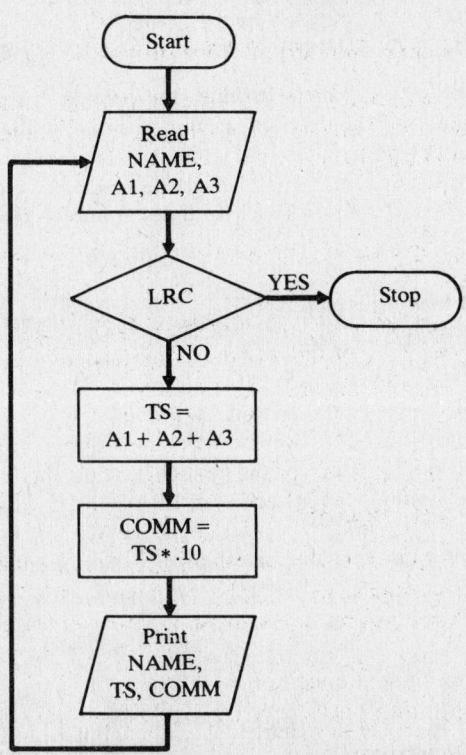

Fig. 7-4 The flowchart in Fig. 7-3 is redrawn to incorporate a loop to permit the processing of more than one person's data. The diagram also details the use of a last record check (LRC) and an unconditional branch.

7.46 How does the decision verify the existence of data slated for processing?

The decision symbol is positioned after the I/O symbol that inputs the salesperson's name and three sales amounts. It contains the initials *LRC*, which represent the words *last record check*. The LRC decision may be viewed as asking, "Has the last record been read and processed?" If the answer to that question is no, then processing is to continue. If the response is yes, then processing will cease in this problem. The rationale for positioning the LRC after the READ operation is simple; if the last record has been read and processed, then no additional data are input and processing may cease. If additional data are to be input, then the data should enter processing. Because of the widespread use of the last record check condition, the initials LRC are used to identify it.

7.47 How does the decision symbol represent the two alternative paths that processing may follow?

The exits from a decision symbol are called *conditional branches*, as the branch chosen to exit the symbol depends on the answer to the condition (question) proposed by the decision. The LRC poses the question, "Has the last record been read and processed?" There are two possible answers—yes or no. As such, the two conditional exits branches of the LRC decision are identified as the YES and NO branches. If the last record has been fully read and processed, the YES branch is taken. If not, the NO branch directs the flow of processing to where data items are to be processed.

7.48 What general conditions are usually associated with the YES and NO branches of the LRC?

Normally the NO branch leads to normal processing of data within the flowchart loop, whereas the YES branch will lead the flow of processing out of the loop. The logic used is that if a data item is read, it will enter processing. If no data are read, then the last record or data item has been processed, and it is time to exit from the loop in which processing occurs. Obviously, data items that do not exist cannot be processed.

7.49 Are there any guidelines for composing the conditional statements used within decisions?

Yes. Generally, a conditional statement assumes the form of a question, so as to create YES or NO alternatives for branching from the decision. In this example, the initials LRC are used because of their common usage to represent the conditional statement. However, in another decision the question 'IS HOURS = 40?' might be used to determine which employees have worked a 40-hour week. By phrasing the condition in this manner, the YES or NO conditional branch from the decision is readily established.

7.50 How is the flowchart loop illustrated in Fig. 7-4?

To analyze the looping sequence of this flowchart, the reader must examine the NO branch of the LRC and proceed down the steps that compose that leg of the flowchart. The computation of the total sales amount and commission precede the output of the salesperson's name, total sales, and commission amounts. Note that these same steps were evident in the flowchart in Fig. 7-3. The difference in the second flowchart is the loop created by the branch leaving the PRINT I/O symbol of Fig. 7-4. This branch leaves the PRINT symbol (a contraction of PRINT I/O symbol) and directs the flow of processing back to the READ symbol (a similar contraction of READ I/O symbol), where the next salesperson's data are read. Thus, after printing one salesperson's data, the flowchart loops back to get the next person's data.

7.51 How long will the looping sequence continue?

The processing resulting from the flowchart loop will continue until the last record is processed. When the last salesperson's data items are read and processed, the LRC will react to that condition and cause the flow of processing to exit the YES branch.

7.52 Is there any specific name given to the branch that leaves the PRINT symbol and flows back to the READ symbol?

Yes. The flowline leaving the PRINT symbol is referred to as an *unconditional branch*. This name is derived from the fact that no deviation from its intended course is permitted. The flow of processing is unconditionally directed toward the READ symbol. Because of its directed use, the unconditional branch is referred to as a *GO TO*, a designation noted within many computer languages.

7.53 What is the net effect of the GO TO, or unconditional branch?

The unconditional branch to the READ symbol at the top of the loop completes the loop and enables the repetitive processing of salespersons' data. In this flowchart the looping sequence will continue until the last record is fully processed. When no more data exist, processing will cease, which will lead directly to the YES branch of the LRC.

7.54 Can a looping sequence, defined with the aid of an LRC, be incorporated into almost any flowchart?

Yes. The application of the LRC is easily accomplished and lends itself to almost any type of problem. Consider the flowchart resulting from the problem narrative that follows.

The following narrative refers to Probs. 7.55–7.59.

This flowchart relates to the computation of the average unit cost paid for inventory items. Input to the problem are the item's number and the four prices paid for that inventory item. To compute the average unit cost, add the four prices and divide that sum by 4. Print out only the item number and the average unit cost. As an unlimited number of items are to be worked on, use a last record check to control the looping sequence.

7.55 What important facts can be drawn from the flowchart narrative?

Five data items are input to include an item number and four prices. These four prices are averaged, with the resultant average and its item number output. A last record check is to be used since an unspecified number of data items will be processed. Whenever the number of data items to be processed is not stated, an LRC should be used to control the looping sequence of the flowchart solution.

7.56 What symbols compose the flowchart solution shown in Fig. 7-5?

The flowchart denotes its opening with a START symbol, which precedes the READ symbol denoting the input of data. This READ symbol is positioned before the LRC, which will verify the processing of the last data item. The NO branch of the LRC leads to a processing symbol, that contains the formula needed to compute the average unit price. A PRINT symbol follows, denoting the output of an item number and its average price. An unconditional branch to the READ symbol at the top of the loop completes the flowchart's looping sequence. The YES branch of the LRC directs the close of the flowchart via a STOP symbol.

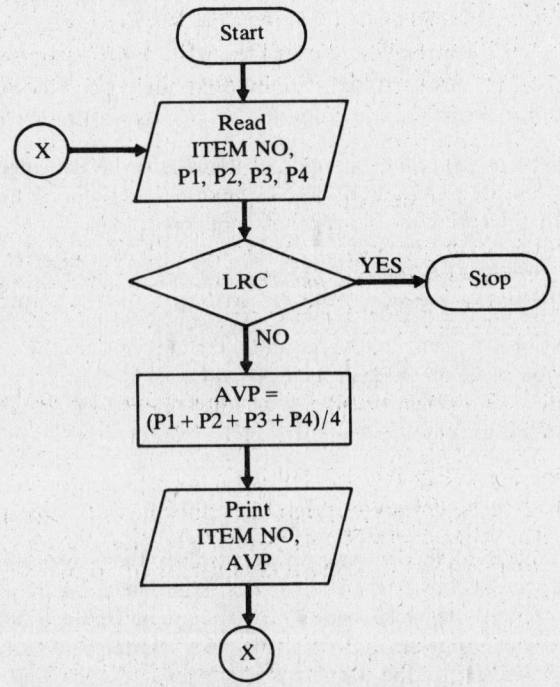

Fig. 7-5 In this flowchart, a looping sequence provides for the repeated processing of inventory data.

7.57 In Fig. 7-5, the unconditional branch is noted with two circular symbols, not a solid line. Why?

Flowcharters are permitted to use two graphical techniques to represent unconditional branches. In Fig. 7-4 a solid line was chosen to represent an unconditional branch. In Fig. 7-5 the unconditional branch is represented with two connector symbols. The use of these matching symbols replaces solid lines while offering identical operational features.

7.58 Why are connectors used instead of the solid flow lines for unconditional branching?

In large flowcharts, many unconditional branches may exist. Rather than have solid flow lines intersecting, flowcharters adopted the convention of using connectors for unconditional branches. This convention requires that two connectors be used for each unconditional branch, that a flow-line arrow point toward one connector, and that the second flow line leave the second connector and enter the symbol being branched to. In addition, the same identifying mark must be placed within both connectors to indicate the relationship of both connectors to each other. Note that in Fig. 7-5 there is an X in both connectors to indicate that these two symbols match.

7.59 Why are parentheses used in the computation of the average unit price?

The use of parentheses more closely duplicates the computer's handling of that computation. Without the parentheses, that formula would have been written as follows:

$$AVP = P1 + P2 + P3 + P4/4 \quad \text{(Wrong)}$$

This computation would have been interpreted by the computer as noting the addition of P1, P2, P3, and one-quarter of P4. Only P4 would have been divided by 4, not the sum of the four prices. To ensure that the sum of the four prices is divided by 4, parentheses are placed around the addition of P1, P2, P3, and P4. The formula

$$AVP = (P1 + P2 + P3 + P4)/4 \quad \text{(Correct)}$$

will result in the sum of four prices and the division by 4 of that sum to produce the average unit price.

LOOPING SEQUENCES

7.60 When the number of data items to be processed is unknown prior to processing, a last record check is used to control the looping sequence. What type of controlling technique can be used when an exact number of loops are needed to process an exact number of data items?

A *counter* is used when a specified number of loops is to be executed. The counter is a flowcharting technique that enables the execution of an exact number of loops. It literally counts through each loop, one loop at a time, monitoring the exact number of repetitions.

7.61 What components are necessary in the construction of a counter?

Three components are necessary to incorporate a counter into a flowchart:
(1) The initialization of the counter at its initial value of 1
(2) The counter decision, which determines whether the proper amount of loops have been performed
(3) The increment of the counter by a factor of 1

7.62 How are these three components expressed within flowcharts?

A dataname is assigned to the counter to accomplish these processing activities. In this book the dataname K will represent a counter. The counter is initialized at 1 by using the computation $K = 1$. A counter decision is represented by a conditional statement within a decision. For exactly sixteen loops the counter decision would appear as 'IS $K = 16$?' The counter increment that increases the counter by 1 prior to each loop would utilize the formula $K = K + 1$.

7.63 Whereas $K = 1$ and 'IS $K = 16$?' are in accepted forms of a formula and a conditional statement, how can the counter increment $K = K + 1$ be interpreted?

Although the formula $K = K + 1$ is algebraically incorrect, it is perfectly valid for flowcharting and its subsequent use within programs. The accuracy of this formula results from how the formula is handled. Paralleling the computer's processing, the right side of the formula is handled first. The result of adding 1 to K increases the current value of K by 1 for the next loop. To retain this increased value, it is stored back in K—the value on the left-hand side of the equal sign. On each loop the old value of K is increased by 1 and then stored back in K for the subsequent loop in which the same increment is repeated.

The following narrative refers to Probs. 7.64–7.70.

A flowchart must be constructed to show the steps in computing net pay. Input to the problem are an employee's name, hours worked, and hourly rate of pay. Gross pay is computed by multiplying hours worked by rate of pay. FICA deductions are computed at 6.85 percent of gross pay. Net pay is computed by subtracting the FICA deductions from gross pay. Output each employee's name, gross pay, FICA deduction, and net pay. As exactly 54 employee payrolls are to be processed, use a counter to control the looping sequence. (*Note*: For discussion purposes the computation of the FICA deduction has been deliberately simplified in this problem.)

7.64 What important facts can be drawn from the preceding flowchart narrative?

Three items of data are input to include an employee's name, hours worked, and rate of pay. The three formulas used in the computation of net pay are:

(1) GROSS = hr * RATE
(2) FICA = GROSS * 0.0685
(3) NETPAY = GROSS − FICA

The output will consist of the employee name, gross pay, FICA deduction, and net pay. A counter will control the execution of 54 loops, processing the paycheck for one employee on each loop.

7.65 What symbols compose the flowchart shown in Fig. 7-6?

In Fig. 7-6, note that the initialization of the counter K = 1 is placed within a processing symbol immediately following the START symbol. The input of the three required data items is defined by an I/O symbol, which signals the start of the flowchart loop. These processing symbols define the successive computations of GROSS, FICA, and NETPAY, prior to their output along with the employee's name.

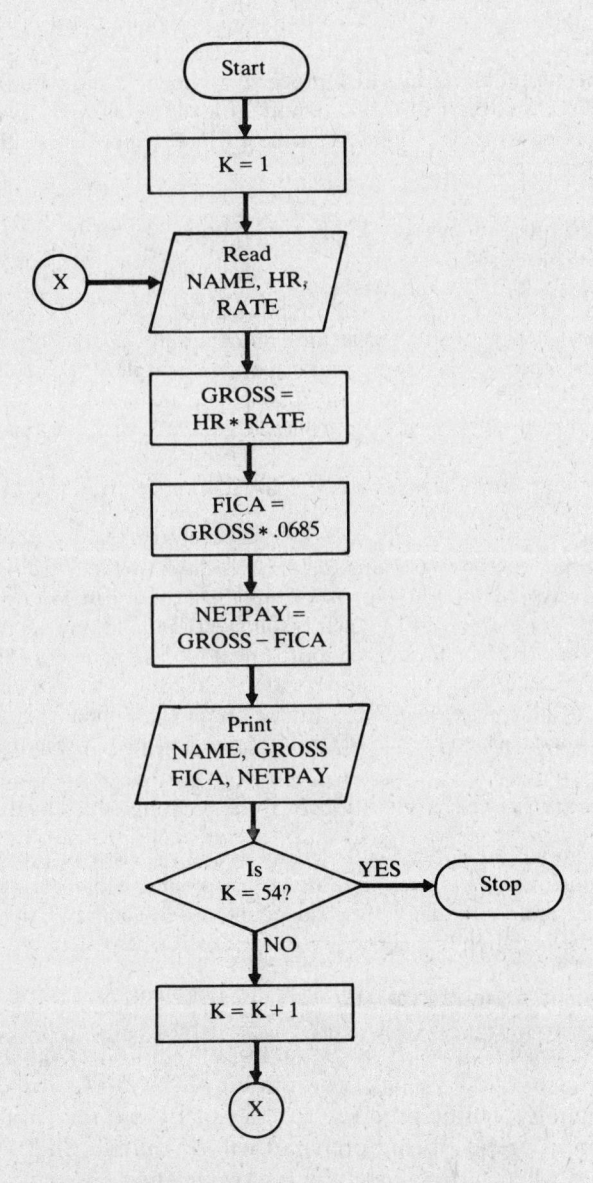

Fig. 7-6 This flowchart shows the use of a counter.

136   FLOWCHARTING   [CHAP. 7

The output of these data items denotes the completion of processing an employee's payroll data and also defines the end of the loop. The counter decision 'IS K = 54?' is positioned at the loop's end. If the fifty-fourth loop has not been completed, the counter is incremented by a factor of 1 using the formula K = K + 1. The flowchart then unconditionally branches back to the READ symbol to begin the flowchart loop for the next employee's data. If the fifty-fourth employee's payroll data have been processed, the YES branch of the counter decision is taken and the flowchart is closed.

7.66 Why is the counter initialization of K = 1 positioned before the start of the flowchart loop?

The initialization (K) of the counter at 1 must be performed before the looping sequence can commence. Thus it must be placed prior to the READ symbol, which denotes the start of the flowchart loop. This initialization is representative of many operations that are performed prior to the start of a looping sequence and that are called *initial conditions*. Initial conditions define values or perform processing operations that must be completed prior to the looping sequence. Other initial conditions are discussed in subsequent problems.

7.67 Why was it necessary to sequence the processing operations, as shown?

The positioning of the processing related to the computation of GROSS, FICA, and NETPAY was dictated by the logic of each task. GROSS has to be computed first because it is needed to compute FICA. Both FICA and GROSS are needed to calculate NETPAY. Essentially, the data required for each formula dictate the order in which processing operations are to be performed. Note that with the processing of NETPAY, the data items required for output become available and the printing of those four data items is possible. For this reason the PRINT symbol is positioned after the three processing symbols at the loop's end.

7.68 Why is the counter decision 'IS K = 54?' placed after the I/O symbol outputting the employee's payroll data?

Whereas the LRC is always positioned after the READ symbol commencing the flowchart loop, the counter decision is always positioned at the end of the flowchart loop. This positioning ensures that all processing activities composing the flowchart loop are completed since the counter decision is capable of determining whether the desired number of loops has been performed. The counter decision is always placed at the end of the flowchart loop, which is generally noted by an output operation of some type.

7.69 Why is the counter increment K = K + 1 always positioned on the NO branch of the counter decision?

If the last loop has not been performed, the response to the conditional statements of the counter decision must always be NO. In Fig. 7-6, until the fifty-fourth loop is completed, the answer to 'IS K = 54?' must be NO and the NO branch is followed. Thus at any value of K less than 54, the counter will have to be increased by 1 to prepare for the next loop's processing. Since the NO branch leads to the unconditional branching that starts the next loop, the counter increment of K = K + 1 is positioned on the NO branch of the counter decision. In this example two connector symbols are used to identify the unconditional branch back to the READ symbol, the first task within the looping sequence.

7.70 Must all flowcharts, at the completion of their looping sequences, end with a STOP symbol?

No. Not all flowcharts end with a STOP symbol noting the close of processing activities. For the sake of brevity and simplicity, this has been the case in this chapter. However, in problems that follow, the YES branches exiting from both the LRC and counter decisions will denote the end of one phase of processing and the initiation of a second set of processing activities.

The following narrative refers to Probs. 7.71–7.81.

The problem to be solved relates to the computation of an average unit price for inventory items. The discussion will refer to the flowchart shown in Fig. 7-5, with the exception that instead of using a last record check, a counter will be used to process exactly 100 inventory items. In addition, column headings for the inventory report being prepared will be output, and the line 'ALL PROCESSING DONE' will be printed when processing activities are finished.

7.71 The placement of the LRC in Fig. 7-5 differs from that of the counter decision in Fig. 7-7. Why?

In Fig. 7-5 the last record check is positioned after the READ symbol to immediately determine whether the last record has been read and processed. The LRC is used in this flowchart because an unspecified amount of data are to be handled. In Fig. 7-7 the counter decision is properly positioned at the end of the flowchart loop to verify the processing of the one-hundredth loop. The use of the counter is possible since a known number of data items is to undergo processing.

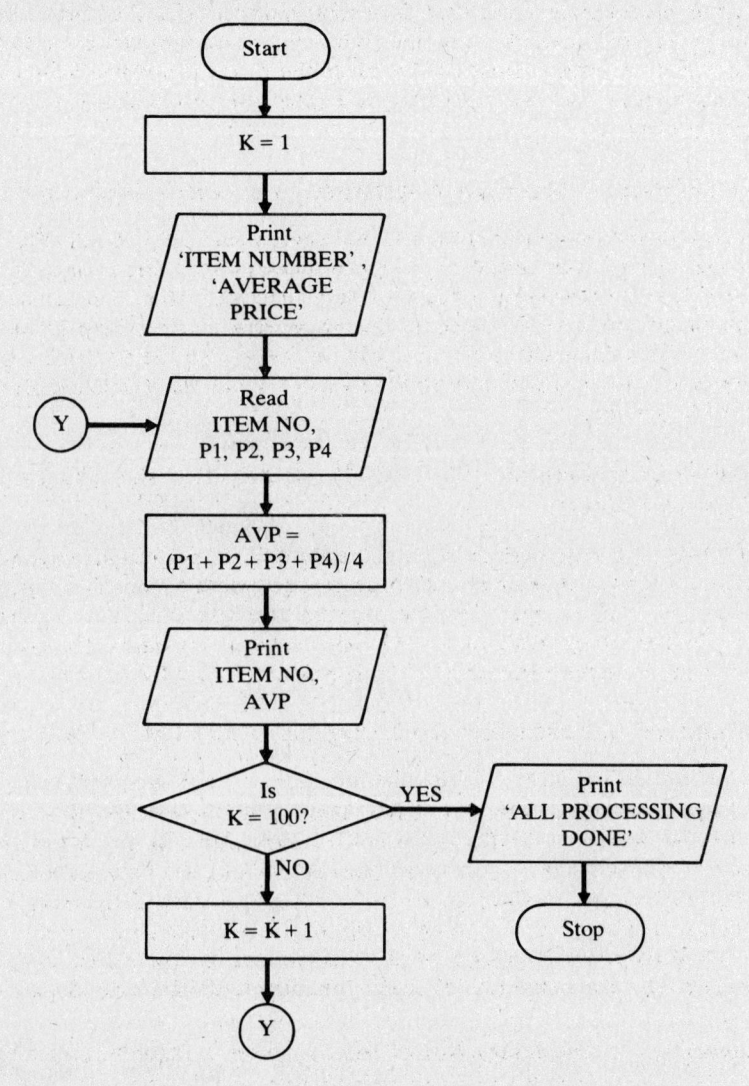

Fig. 7-7 This flowchart contains literals and a counter to execute one hundred loops.

7.72 What relationship exists between use of an LRC and a counter to control the looping sequence?

The last record check and the counter assume separate operational responsibilities. If the amount of data to be processed is known, a counter may be used to control the repetitive processing of data. If an unspecified amount of data is to be used, the LRC should be used to control the looping sequence. Each technique is used differently; thus, if an LRC is used, a counter is not, and vice versa.

7.73 In Fig. 7-7 what flowchart symbols relate directly to the use of a counter?

Three symbols relate directly to the incorporation of a counter into the flowchart solution of Fig. 7-7. The processing symbol containing the initial condition K = 1 initializes the counter K at a starting value of 1. The counter decision, 'IS K = 100?' checks for the completion of the 100th loop. The counter increment of K = K + 1, positioned on the NO branch of the counter decision, increases the value of K by 1 on each loop before branching to start the next loop.

7.74 What is the purpose of the PRINT symbol following the processing symbol containing K = 1?

This symbol will direct the output of the column headings appearing on the inventory report, as requested in the flowchart narrative. This I/O symbol directs the printing of 'ITEM NUMBER' and 'AVERAGE PRICE', the two headings that will appear on this report above each column of data.

7.75 What is the purpose of the single quotation marks around ITEM NUMBER and AVERAGE PRICE?

The single quotation marks are placed at the start and end of these terms to define literals. A *literal* is a specially created string of characters, defined within a PRINT symbol using single quotation marks, that output the characters contained within the quotes. In this problem two literals are defined—ITEM NUMBER and AVERAGE PRICE.

7.76 In defining the literal 'ITEM NUMBER', will an actual number or the 11 characters of the term be printed?

This question highlights a common misconception associated with the use of literals. Many people incorrectly believe that the literal will output an actual data item. This is not the case. Only the characters contained within the single quotes are printed, nothing more. In this case 11 characters are output: 4 characters for ITEM, 6 characters for NUMBER, and 1 blank for the space between both words. Blanks occupy one position on output and must be accounted for.

7.77 How many positions are accounted for in the literal 'AVERAGE PRICE'?

A total of 13 characters are defined within that literal. Seven characters for AVERAGE, five characters for PRICE, and one blank compose that 13-character literal. The literal 'AVERAGE PRICE' will appear as the second column heading following 'ITEM NUMBER'. Again the literal will result in the printing of the 13 characters previously specified. The 100 numbers representing each average price will be printed beneath that column heading.

7.78 Why are the literals composing the column headings printed prior to commencement of the processing loop?

The PRINT symbol containing the literals for column headings appears prior to the flowchart loop to ensure that these headings are output on the top of the report. With this printing atop the first page, all other outputs must appear beneath them. Thus the output of actual item numbers and their average prices will appear beneath the headings.

7.79 Can the output of these literals be considered an initial condition?

Yes. As the printing of column headings must be accomplished prior to the start of the looping sequence, the output of literals may be classified as an initial condition. Both the initialization of the counter and the output of column headings are considered initial conditions to processing in this problem. As these two operations are independent of each other, either the I/O or the processing symbol may appear first without affecting the flowchart's logic.

7.80 What is the purpose of the literal on the YES branch of the counter decision?

The literal 'ALL PROCESSING DONE' serves two functions. One, it indicates the close of processing activities as it is output only after the 100th item is processed. Two, it also demonstrates that it is possible to initiate processing activities on the YES branch of a counter decision, after the looping sequence is completed.

7.81 What term may be associated with this closing literal?

This type of literal is often referred to as a *special label* because it attempts to highlight a particular aspect of the processing effort. It cannot be referred to as a column heading since it does not appear at the top of a report but at its end. Special labels are literals that may appear alone or be positioned adjacent to other output data to highlight their existence or to explain their use. Subsequent problems will illustrate this point and other uses of special labels.

7.82 Are counters the only means of creating a looping sequence for a specific number of repetitions?

No. Many computer languages possess the capability to establish an automated looping sequence that parallels the counter mechanism, yet is easier for the programming personnel to write. Though these techniques are unique to their languages, flowcharters have developed a variety of ways to graphically portray these automated looping sequences.

7.83 Do automated looping sequences possess the same operational impact as counters?

Yes. Automated looping sequences generally achieve the same results as counters. To observe this, examine Fig. 7-8 (page 140), in which an automated looping sequence is applied to the flowchart shown in Fig. 7-7. Compare the solution of Fig. 7-8 to that of Fig. 7-7 to see the differences and similarities of both solutions. Essentially, the differences between the solutions lie with the means of controlling the looping sequence, with all other processing activities being the same.

7.84 What symbols do the flowcharts of Figs. 7-7 and 7-8 have in common?

The symbols found in both flowcharts include the START and STOP symbols, which open and close the flowcharts, respectively; the initial PRINT symbol, which creates the column headings of 'ITEM NUMBER' and 'AVERAGE PRICE'; the READ I/O symbol, which inputs the item number and four prices; the processing symbol, which details the computation of the average price for each item; the PRINT symbol inside the loop, which outputs the item number and average price for each item on each repetition; and the PRINT symbol noting the final literal of 'ALL PROCESSING DONE'.

7.85 What is the purpose of the two processing symbols associated with the automated looping sequence?

The first processing symbol associated with the automated looping sequence contains the statement FOR K = 1 TO 100 DO. This instruction defines the start of the flowchart looping sequence. It establishes a loop counter K, at a starting value of 1, that is to run to a value of 100. This statement directs the performance of 100 loops, where the counter K will run from 1 to 100. The NEXT K statement identifies the loop's end and represents the position of the counter decision, increment, and unconditional branch back to the processing symbol containing the FOR statement to commence the loop's handling of the next data item.

7.86 Besides their operational impact, what visual aspects do the processing symbols containing the FOR and NEXT statements add to the flowchart of Fig. 7-8?

These processing symbols help to visually frame the flowchart loop. The processing symbol containing the FOR defines the loop's start, whereas the NEXT notes its end.

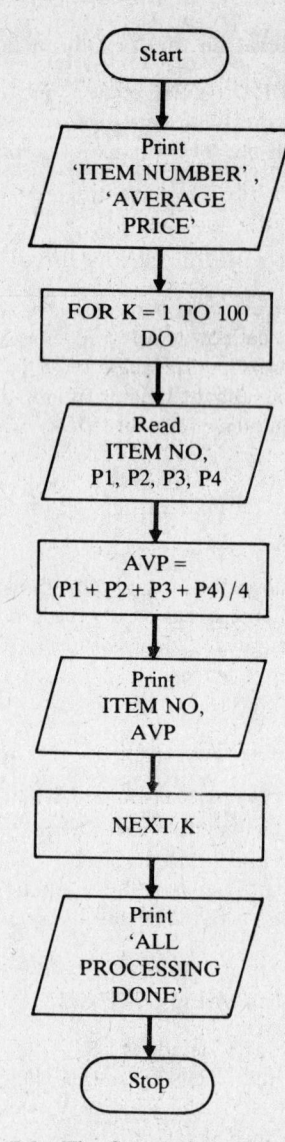

```
              ┌─────────┐
              │  Start  │
              └────┬────┘
                   ▼
           ╱─────────────╲
          ╱    Print      ╲
         ╱ 'ITEM NUMBER',  ╲
         ╲   'AVERAGE      ╱
          ╲    PRICE'     ╱
           ╲─────────────╱
                   ▼
          ┌─────────────────┐
          │ FOR K = 1 TO 100│
          │      DO         │
          └────────┬────────┘
                   ▼
           ╱─────────────╲
          ╱    Read       ╲
          ╲   ITEM NO,    ╱
           ╲ P1,P2,P3,P4 ╱
            ╲───────────╱
                   ▼
          ┌─────────────────┐
          │     AVP =       │
          │ (P1+P2+P3+P4)/4 │
          └────────┬────────┘
                   ▼
           ╱─────────────╲
          ╱    Print      ╲
          ╲   ITEM NO,    ╱
           ╲    AVP      ╱
            ╲───────────╱
                   ▼
          ┌─────────────────┐
          │     NEXT K      │
          └────────┬────────┘
                   ▼
           ╱─────────────╲
          ╱    Print      ╲
         ╱     'ALL        ╲
         ╲   PROCESSING    ╱
          ╲    DONE'      ╱
           ╲─────────────╱
                   ▼
              ┌─────────┐
              │  Stop   │
              └─────────┘
```

Fig. 7-8 The flowchart in Fig. 7-7 is redrawn to accommodate an automated looping sequence.

7.87 What happens in relation to the NEXT instruction when the 100th loop is completed?

Prior to the 100th loop, the flow of data will branch from the NEXT back to the FOR to commence processing on the next loop. When the 100th loop is completed, the flowchart will direct the flow of data through the NEXT and onto the symbol that immediately follows it. This is always the case. When the desired loop limit is attained, processing will pass through the NEXT and to the symbol immediately following it.

7.88 Is this the only graphical way to depict an automated looping sequence?

No. The technique employed in Fig. 7-8 represents only one way of recording an automated looping sequence. Other looping mechanisms exist, and they will be reviewed at length in Chap. 8. This graphical approach was presented to provide a simple means of detailing an automated looping procedure and to serve as an introduction to future discussions on this topic.

ACCUMULATORS

7.89 Whereas a counter affords control over a looping process, what role does an accumulator play in flowcharting?

Accumulators provide the means for obtaining subtotals or grand totals involving data from several transactions. An *accumulator* is a running total that enables the addition of data on successive loops, updating the total held within it after each addition.

7.90 How does an accumulator function as a running total?

A data item is added into the accumulator, creating a new subtotal. On the next loop the accumulator has another data item added to it and updates the subtotal again prior to the next loop. Each successive loop adds another amount into the accumulator, creating a new subtotal. Each new subtotal is retained in the accumulator, where it is updated on the next loop. The update of the accumulator occurs on each loop until the last data item is encountered and the looping ceases. At that point the total stored in the accumulator is considered a final total since no new data will be added to it.

7.91 What three processing activities are associated with use of an accumulator?

The three processing activities required to construct and use an accumulator within a flowchart are:
(1) The initialization of the accumulator at 0
(2) The update of the accumulator by the desired amount
(3) The output of the total accumulated amount at the end of the looping sequence

7.92 How are these three activities incorporated into a flowchart solution?

The initialization and update of the accumulator are represented as processing activities within processing symbols. The output of the accumulated total is provided within a PRINT symbol, generally at the close of processing.

The following narrative refers to Probs. 7.93–7.100.

This problem involves the computation of individual sales commissions and the grand total of all commissions paid. The headings used in this problem are 'SALESPERSON', 'TOTAL SALES', and 'COMMISSION'. Input to the problem are the salesperson's name and three sales amounts. The total sales amount is calculated by adding the three sales amounts. The individual sales commission is computed at 20 percent of the total sales amount. Individual sales commissions are accumulated on each loop to generate the grand total of all commissions paid. Output the name, total sales amount, and commission for each salesperson. After processing the last salesperson's record, print out the accumulated total of commissions paid preceded by the label 'COMM. PAID = '. Because an unspecified number of salespeople exist, use an LRC to control looping.

7.93 In the flowchart of Fig. 7-9 (page 142), what symbols relate to the use of an accumulator?

Three symbols relate directly to the use of an accumulator. The processing symbol containing the computation $T = 0$ initializes the accumulator at 0 and ensures that adding starts from 0. The processing symbol within the flowchart loop containing $T = T + C$ is the second symbol containing an accumulator-related operation. This formula enables the addition of each salesperson's commission into the accumulator. The third symbol associated with the accumulator is the I/O symbol on the YES branch of the LRC. This symbol directs the printing of the accumulated total of all commissions paid.

7.94 Why does the initialization of the accumulator $T = 0$ appear prior to the start of the flowchart loop?

The computation $T = 0$ is an initial condition specifically related to using an accumulator. It is logically positioned after the START symbol and prior to the start of the flowchart loop, which is the READ operation. Note that the initialization $T = 0$ is grouped with the output of the column headings, which are initial conditions within this solution.

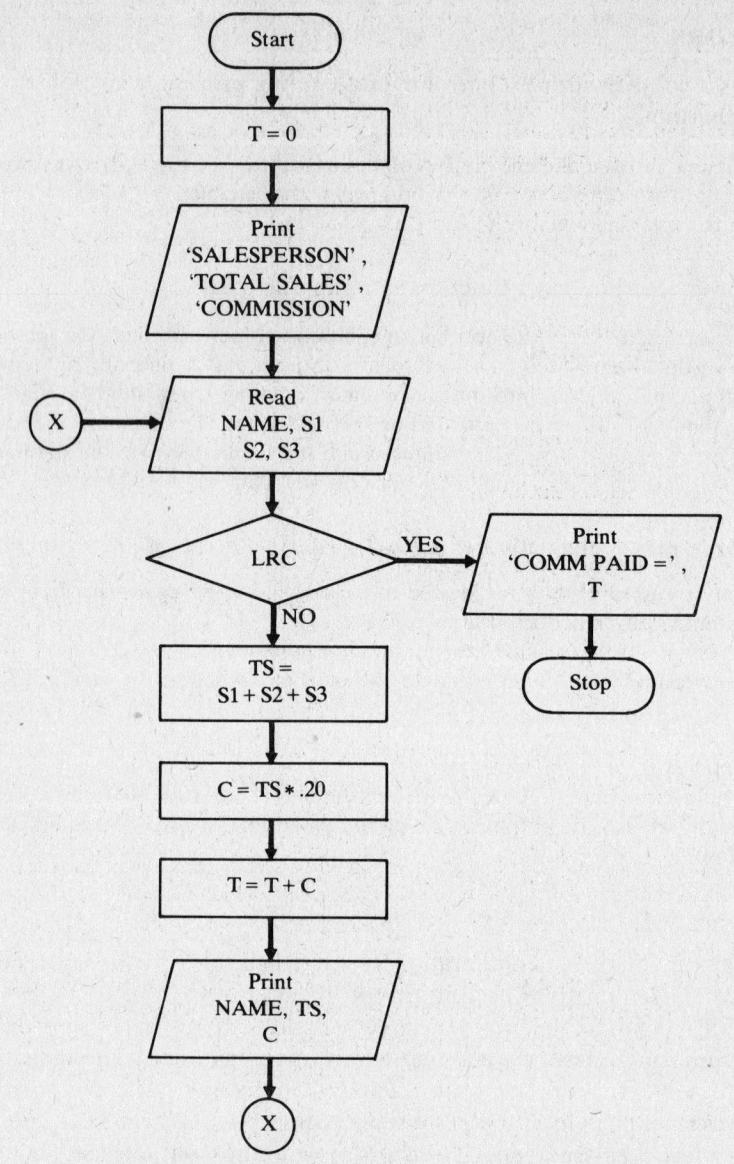

```
            Start
              │
              ▼
           T = 0
              │
              ▼
           Print
       'SALESPERSON',
        'TOTAL SALES',
         'COMMISSION'
              │
              ▼
   ┌──X──▶   Read
   │      NAME, S1
   │       S2, S3
   │          │
   │          ▼
   │        ╱ ╲          YES         Print
   │       ╱LRC╲───────────────▶  'COMM PAID =',
   │       ╲   ╱                        T
   │        ╲ ╱                         │
   │         │ NO                       ▼
   │         ▼                         Stop
   │       TS =
   │    S1 + S2 + S3
   │         │
   │         ▼
   │     C = TS * .20
   │         │
   │         ▼
   │      T = T + C
   │         │
   │         ▼
   │       Print
   │      NAME, TS,
   │         C
   │         │
   └─────────X
```

Fig. 7-9 An accumulator is included in this flowchart. The accumulator requires an initialization, an update, and the output of the total computed.

7.95 Why are there two initial conditions?

One initial condition relates to the initialization of the accumulator, whereas the second defines the output of column headings. These initial conditions were dictated by the problem narrative, which directed the output of three column headings and the use of an accumulator to total the commissions paid to all salespeople.

7.96 Does the T = 0 computation relate to the accumulator's processing of T = T + C?

These two computations are uniquely related in the first processing loop. This results from the fact that 0 is the first value supplied for T and added to the first computed commission amount. As in earlier examples, the right side of the equal sign is handled first and the result stored in the dataname on the left of the equal sign. In T = T + C the commission C is provided by the computation preceding that symbol (C = TS * 0.20, where TS is 'TOTAL SALES'). The value for T results solely from the initialization of the accumulator since there is no formula or input by which T is defined on the first loop. As each commission is added to it, T is then updated on each successive loop.

7.97 How does the T = T + C computation function?

On the first loop a value of 0 is used for T and added to C, with that commission amount stored back in T. On the second loop a new commission amount is added to the old T amount, producing a new accumulated subtotal that is stored back in T. On the third loop, another new C is added to the old T, producing a new accumulated total that is stored in T. This processing continues until data are exhausted. In effect, the new commission amount is added to the previously accumulated total, updating it, and producing a new value of T for the next loop. When the last data item is processed, the total retained in the accumulator becomes the final accumulated total and is ready for output.

7.98 Why is the I/O symbol containing the printing of the accumulated total T positioned on the YES branch of the LRC?

The YES branch of the LRC denotes that the last record has been read and processed and no other input data exist. If no new data exist, then no additional commissions will be calculated and the accumulator will remain unchanged. Thus it is time to output that total, before the close of processing.

7.99 Why does the output of T carry a special label?

The special label preceding the output of T highlights its appearance and identifies it for the user. Without the label formed by use of a literal, the accumulated total of T would be printed without identification. It would look like simply a number at the bottom of a page. Using a special label clarifies the purpose of that total.

7.100 What other steps compose the flowchart solution in Fig. 7-9?

After the initial START symbol, two initial conditions are established. The first is the initialization of the accumulator T = 0, and the second is the printing of headings. The READ symbol begins the flowchart loop and precedes the LRC decision, which controls looping. The NO branch of the LRC leads to normal processing activities, which sequentially compute the total sales amount TS by adding the three sales amounts, compute the commission amount C, and increment the accumulator using T = T + C. The output of the salesperson's name NAME, total sales amount TS, and commission C complete the flowchart loop and precede the unconditional branch back to the READ symbol to restart the looping sequence. Two connectors are used to define the unconditional branch. The YES branch of the LRC leads to the output of T and the close of processing.

7.101 Can accumulators be used with counters?

Yes. It is possible to incorporate both accumulators and counters in the same flowchart solution, where the number of data items is known and the need for an accumulated total is identified.

The following narrative refers to Probs. 7.102–7.105.

The problem relates to the computation of net pay and the accumulation of the net pay paid to exactly 63 employees. Input to the problem are the employee's name, hours worked, and hourly rate of pay. Gross pay is equal to hours times rate. FICA is 6.83 percent of gross pay. Net pay is computed by subtracting FICA from gross pay. Accumulate the total net pay for each employee after its computation. Output each employee's name, gross pay, FICA, and net pay under the headings of 'NAME', 'GROSS', 'FICA', and 'NET'. After processing the last employee, output the accumulated total with the label, 'NET PAY TOTAL = '. Use a counter to control looping for the 63 employees.

7.102 What facts unique to this problem can be drawn from the narrative?

The problem involves the use of a counter to control looping and an accumulator to compute grand total of net pay paid. Three initial conditions are involved to include the initialization of the accumulator T = 0, the initialization of the counter K = 1, and the output of column headings. The counter decision is positioned at the loop's end, with the increment K = K + 1 on the NO branch and the output of the accumulated total of net pay on the YES branch. See Fig. 7-10.

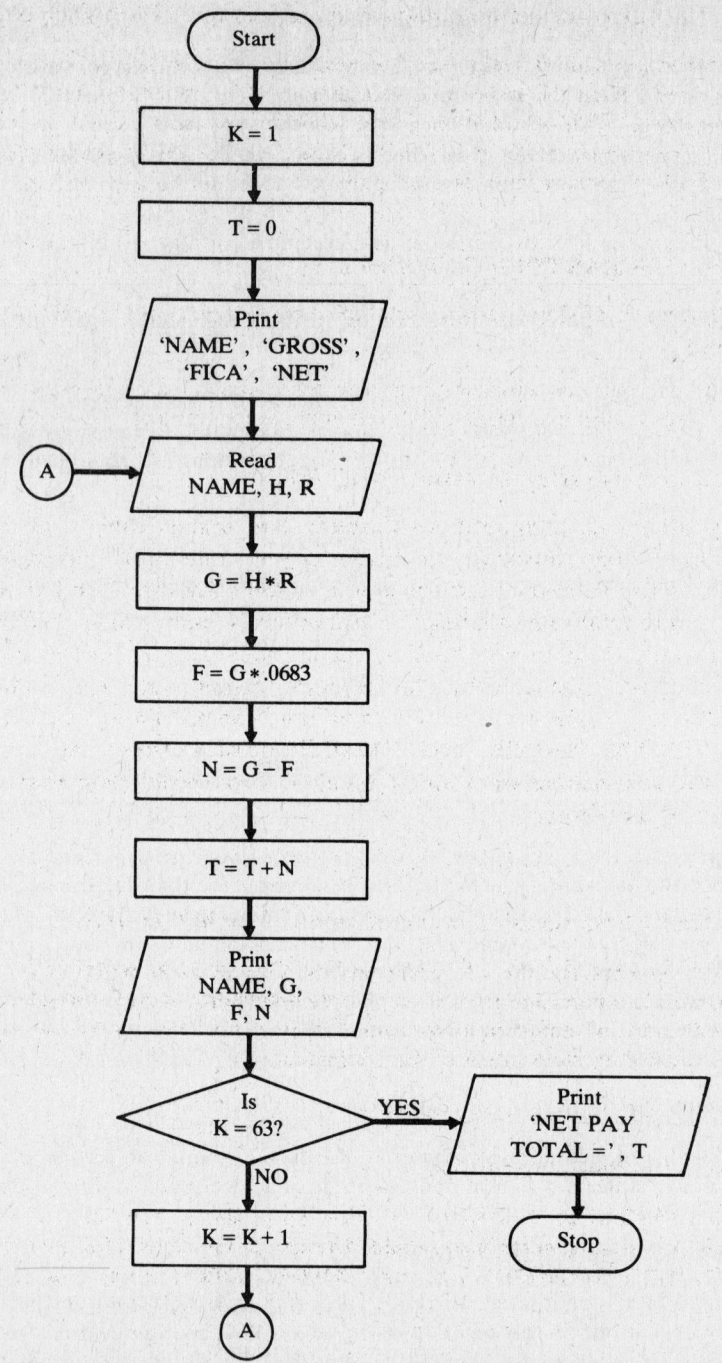

Fig. 7-10 This flowchart contains both an accumulator and counter.

7.103 Can the three initial conditions be reordered?

The three initial conditions may appear in any order, but all three must appear prior to the READ operation, the first task of the loop. The three initial conditions are necessary for processing to properly continue.

7.104 Why does the accumulation of net pay appear after its computation?

The accumulation of T, via T = T + N, appears after the computation of net pay since that is when N becomes available for processing. Following the T = T + N processing step, the output of the employee's data, which includes N, is initiated.

7.105 Why does the output of the accumulator appear on the YES branch of the counter decision?

Until data for the sixty-third person are processed, the flow of data passes through the NO branch of the counter decision. When the last employee's data are fully processed, the YES branch is taken as no further data exists. With no additional data to be processed, the total net pay accumulated may be printed. This total is preceded by its own label, NET PAY TOTAL = , to highlight its existence. The STOP symbol closes the flowchart following this output.

ADDITIONAL FLOWCHARTING CONCEPTS

7.106 Is the preparation of flowcharts restricted to problems that incorporate one decision and one accumulator?

Flowcharting solutions may utilize as many decisions, accumulators, counters, and literals as required to satisfy the problem narrative. The number of flowcharting techniques used reflects the proposed solution.

The following narrative refers to Probs. 7.107–7.115.

The problem relates to computation of sales commissions using two different rates and accumulating the commissions paid to all employees. Input to the problems are the salesperson's name and three sales amounts. Total sales is computed by adding the three sales amounts. The commission rates used relate to the total sales amounts. If total sales is greater than $175, the commission rate is 15 percent. If the total sales is less than or equal to $175, the commission rate is 12 percent. Commission amounts are calculated by multiplying the commission rate by the total sales amount. Output the salesperson's name, total sales amount, and commission beneath the column headings of 'SALESNAME', 'TOTAL SALES', and 'COMMISSION'. Output the accumulated total of all commissions paid to salespeople when looping ends with a special label. An unspecified number of salespeople are to be processed.

7.107 What flowchart characteristics are noted in this flowchart narrative?

The problem requires the use of two decisions. One decision performs an LRC, with the second determining which commission rate to use. An accumulator is required to total the commissions paid to all salespeople. The required outputs include column headings, individual salesperson's data, and a special label preceding the printing of the accumulator.

7.108 What initial conditions are needed?

Two initial conditions are utilized in this flowchart. The first initial condition of T = 0 defines the accumulator used to total commissions paid. The second initial condition generates the column headings of 'SALESNAME', 'TOTAL SALES', and 'COMMISSION'. See Fig. 7-11.

7.109 Why is a last record check used?

The LRC decision was chosen because an unspecified number of salespeople are slated for processing. The LRC assists in controlling the looping sequence.

7.110 Why does the second decision use the conditional statement 'IS TS > 175?'

This second decision will enable the flowchart to branch to the correct commission rate. It is determining whether the total sales amount TS is greater than > 175 dollars. The decision uses the symbol > for greater than instead of spelling it out. Also note that the $ is omitted from the conditional statement— the $ is a special character and, as such, should not be part of the numeric field 175. The use of the $ would compromise the integrity of the numeric field and invalidate the decision.

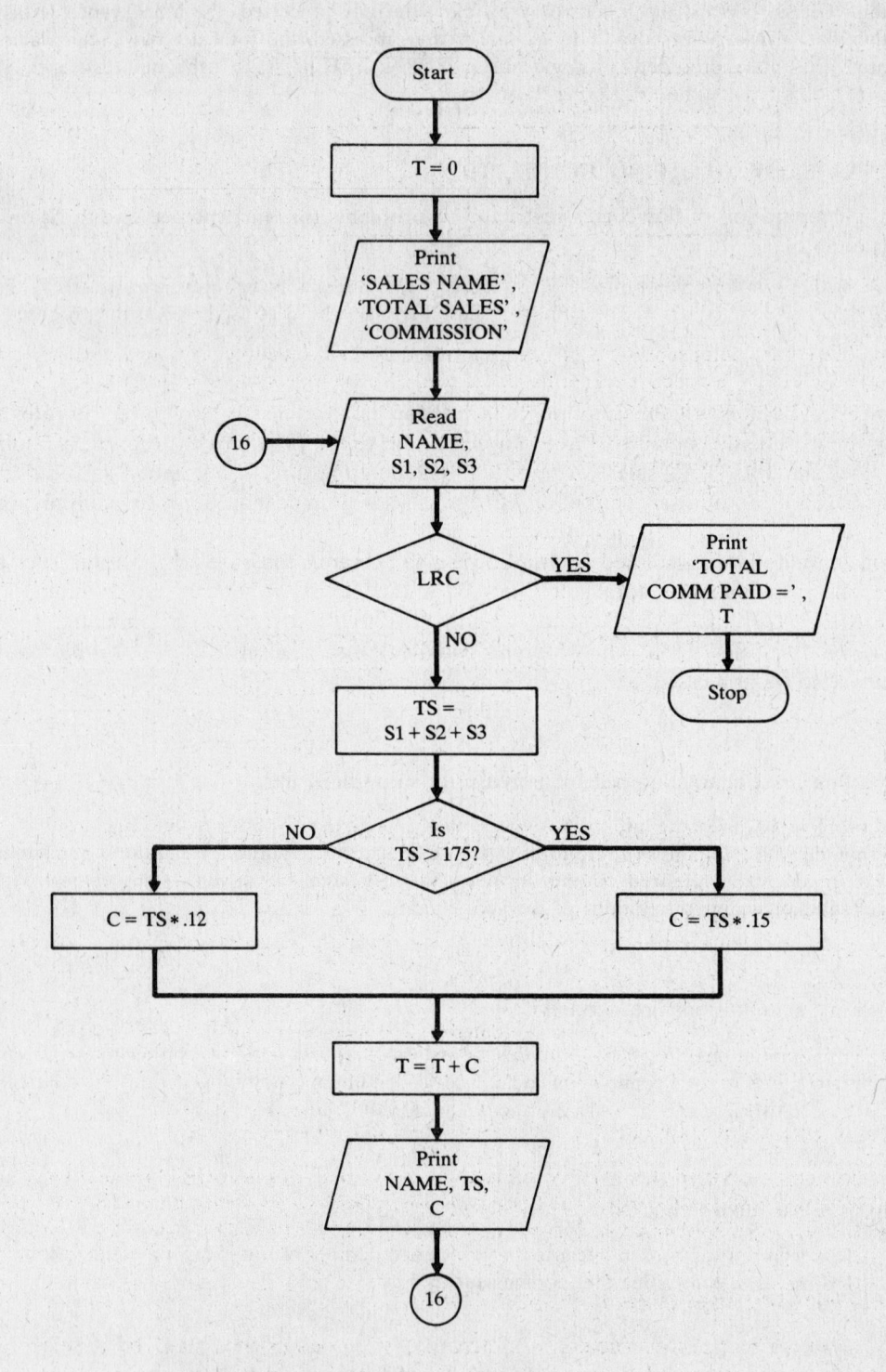

Fig. 7-11 This flowchart demonstrates the use of an accumulator, multiple decisions, and literals.

7.111 What other symbols may be used to denote inequalities in a decision?

A total of six fundamental symbols may be used to create relationships with conditional statements, as listed in Table 7-1.

Table 7-1 Conditional Symbols

Symbol	Meaning	Symbol	Meaning
=	Is equal to	≠	Is not equal to
<	Is less than	≤	Is less than or equal to
>	Is greater than	≥	Is greater than or equal to

7.112 Why do the two conditional branches of the total sales decision carry different commission computations?

The different formulas represent the two rates to be used in computing each salesperson's commission. The formula chosen depends on the response to the conditional statement. If $TS > 175$, then the YES branch is chosen and a rate of 15 percent is used. If $TS \leq 175$, the NO branch is followed and the commission is computed using a 12 percent rate. The flow of logic through this decision dictates that one or the other path be chosen. Despite the branch followed, the flowchart directs the accumulation of the commission via $T = T + C$ since all commission amounts are added into that grand total.

7.113 Why is 0.15 or 0.12 included in the computation of commissions rather than 15 percent or 12 percent, respectively?

The percent figures were not included in the computation of commissions because the equivalent decimal amounts were required. The formula called for the use of 0.12, not 12 percent, when performing the calculation. The use of the decimal equivalent of percentages ensures that the computation will be properly represented.

7.114 What steps follow the accumulation of C?

The output of the salespeople's data follows the accumulation of their commissions. The output of the salesperson's name, total sales, and commission will appear beneath the headings printed at the start of processing. The unconditional branch following the PRINT symbol restarts the looping sequence, which will continue until the LRC condition is met.

7.115 How does this flowchart close?

With satisfaction of the LRC, the accumulated total of commissions T is printed with the special label 'TOT COMM PAID = .' This label highlights that amount. The flowchart closes following that output.

7.116 Can an accumulator be used to count individual data items by a factor of 1?

It is possible to accumulate a total by a single unit value of 1. This is a special form of accumulator that looks like a counter but is not. It is frequently used when the need to count people or single objects exists. The sample flowchart that follows incorporates such an accumulator and multiple decisions.

The following narrative refers to Probs. 7.117–7.122.

A flowchart must be constructed to determine the commissions paid to a select group of salespeople. Input to the problem are the salesperson's name and commission paid. The task is to determine how many salespeople have achieved the status of $1000 or more in commissions. If the commission amount is greater than or equal to $1000, accumulate the commission amount and add 1 to the total of salespeople in that category. If not, read the next salesperson. For the chosen salespeople, output their names and commissions beneath appropriate column headings. At the end of looping, output the number of people in the $1000 plus category and the accumulated total of the commissions paid to that total. Print these totals on separate lines using the labels, 'NUMBER:' and 'COMM TOTAL = '. An unspecified number of salespeople are processed.

7.117 How many accumulators are required for this problem?

Two accumulators are needed to facilitate the processing related to the salespeople in the $1000 plus group. One accumulator T1 is used to add up the commissions paid to those salespeople. The second accumulator T2 is used to add up the number of people in that category. The formula for accumulating commissions is $T1 = T1 + C$, whereas the salesperson's accumulator is $T2 = T2 + 1$. The increment of 1 in the accumulator is deliberate since we will add salespeople one person at a time. See Fig. 7-12.

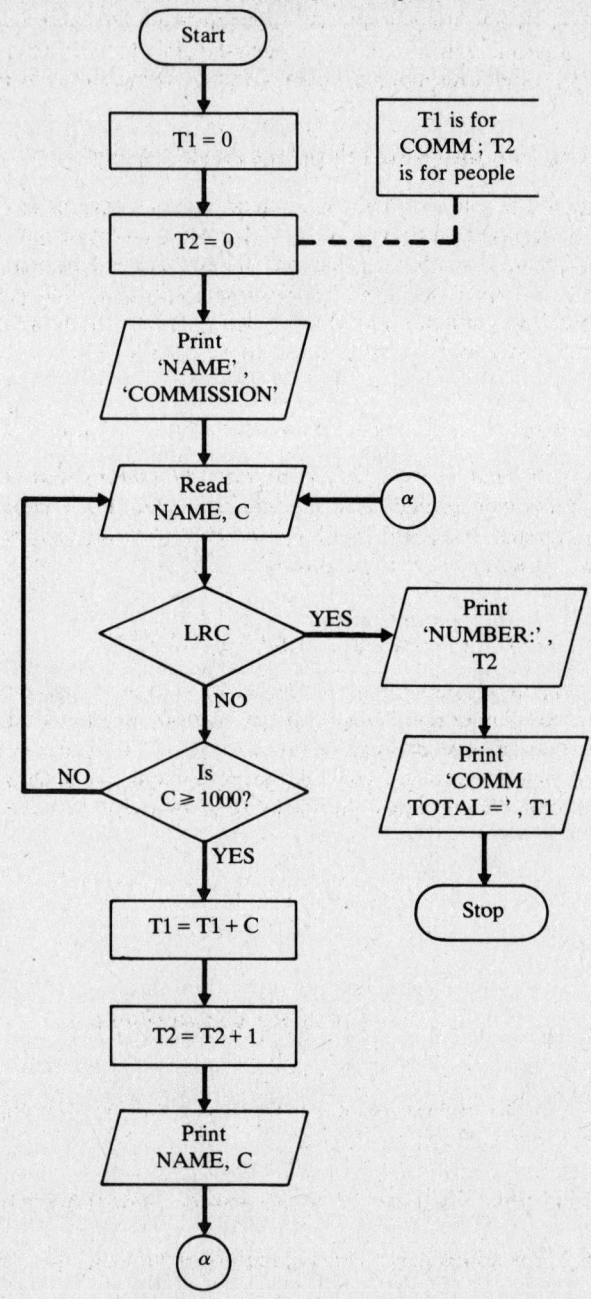

Fig. 7-12 In this flowchart, two accumulators are required to compute the total commission dollars paid and the number of people being paid commission.

7.118 Is the T1 = T1 + 1 computation a counter?

The similarity in formulas often leads people to mistakenly conclude that T1 is a counter. It is not. The T1 = T1 + 1 represents a special form of an accumulator, by which T1 is increased by a factor of 1. Another difference lies in their initialization values. T1 was initialized at 0, whereas a counter is initialized at 1.

7.119 Why are the two accumulators on the YES branch of the 'IS $C \geq 1000$?' decision?

The positioning of the accumulators relates to the purpose of that decision. The decision helps distinguish between salespeople with commission amounts that are less than $1000 and greater than or equal to $1000. A YES to the conditional statement denotes that the salesperson falls into that category, and thus the accumulators should be updated. The T1 accumulator is increased by C, with T2 incremented by 1. A NO response directs the flowchart back to read the next salesperson's data.

7.120 Is it appropriate to position two decisions consecutively?

Yes. If the logic of the solution dictates the need for two consecutive decisions, then they are used. This was the case for the solution drawn in Fig. 7-12. After inputting data via the READ symbol, the LRC was positioned. The next symbol was logically the decision testing whether the commission amount input was greater than or equal to $1000. This test was critical to determining what steps would ensue. If $C \geq 1000$, then the accumulator would be updated. If not, the flowchart would unconditionally branch back to the READ symbol to input the next salesperson's data.

7.121 What device serves as a reminder of the purpose of T1 and T2?

The accumulators T1 and T2 were initialized at the flowchart's start. Attached to their initial processing symbols were annotation symbols that identified T1 and T2 as accumulators for totaling commission dollars and the number of people in the select $1000 plus category, respectively. The use of annotation symbols serves as a reminder of their purpose.

7.122 Why are two I/O symbols used to output T1 and T2?

The problem narrative called for each accumulated total to be output on its own separate line. To accomplish this and denote that separate output operations should be undertaken, two PRINT symbols were used. The first I/O operation will print the number of people in the special commission group T2, and the second, outputting the total number of commission dollars attained by that group T1. The printing of T2 before T1 presents no difficulty since they may be handled separately.

Review Questions

7.123 A flowchart offers a pictorial review of the steps composing a processing approach but does not detail the logic of that solution. (*a*) True, (*b*) false.

7.124 Flowcharts are not generally prepared before writing required software. (*a*) True, (*b*) false.

7.125 Terminal symbols are used solely to close program flowcharts. (*a*) True, (*b*) false.

7.126 Computations involving the use of formulas are detailed using processing symbols. (*a*) True, (*b*) false.

7.127 Unconditional branches enable the flowchart to distinguish between two alternative paths and branch accordingly. (*a*) True, (*b*) false.

7.128 Counters are initialized at a value of 1. (*a*) True, (*b*) false.

7.129 Literals are groups of characters defined within single quotation marks, in PRINT symbols. (*a*) True, (*b*) false.

7.130 Automated looping sequences are defined within many program languages and duplicate the impact of a counter. (*a*) True, (*b*) false.

7.131 The output of an accumulator generally occurs after the looping sequence has been completed. (*a*) True, (*b*) false.

7.132 Program flowchart solutions generally restrict the number of accumulators used to a limit of two. (*a*) True, (*b*) false.

7.133 It is not possible to concurrently utilize a counter and an accumulator in a program flowchart solution. (*a*) True, (*b*) false.

7.134 Performing computations involving percentages, the decimal equivalent to the percentages is used. (*a*) True, (*b*) false.

7.135 Accumulators may not increment by a factor of 1 since only counters may utilize that particular form of computation. (*a*) True, (*b*) false.

7.136 Two PRINT symbols will denote the output of data on separate lines. (*a*) True, (*b*) false.

7.137 The printing of payroll data is depicted in a program flowchart using the (*a*) START symbol; (*b*) processing symbol; (*c*) I/O symbol; (*d*) annotation symbol.

7.138 Descriptive comments are added to a program flowchart using the (*a*) I/O symbol; (*b*) annotation symbol; (*c*) processing symbol; (*d*) all of the above.

7.139 Conditional and logical operations are defined via the (*a*) decision symbol; (*b*) I/O symbol; (*c*) processing symbol; (*d*) connector.

7.140 The repetitive processing of data in a flowchart may be defined via a(n) (*a*) counter; (*b*) LRC; (*c*) automated looping sequence; (*d*) all of the above.

7.141 Symbols used to represent unconditional branching are the (*a*) GO TO symbols; (*b*) connectors; (*c*) branch symbols; (*d*) all of the above.

7.142 The counter increment of $K = K + 1$ is normally positioned (*a*) on the YES branch of the counter decision; (*b*) as an initial condition prior to the start of looping; (*c*) on the NO branch of the counter decision; (*d*) anywhere within the flowchart loop.

7.143 Processing activities performed prior to the start of the loop sequence are defined as (*a*) initial conditions; (*b*) preprocessing actions; (*c*) literals; (*d*) opening statements.

7.144 Grand totals may be created and computed with a program flowchart using a(n) (*a*) counter; (*b*) LRC; (*c*) accumulator; (*d*) literal.

7.145 The update of an accumulator (that is, $T = T + A$) is normally positioned (*a*) as an initial condition; (*b*) on the NO branch of the LRC; (*c*) on the YES branch of a counter decision; (*d*) after any decision symbol within the flowchart.

7.146 An initial condition that could be encountered in a program flowchart would be (*a*) $K = 1$; (*b*) $T = 0$; (*c*) the output of column headings; (*d*) all of the above.

7.147 A _____ flowchart depicts the flow of information through an organization.

7.148 The _____ offers a general guideline to the flow of data in a program flowchart.

7.149 A _____ symbol is computer slang for a terminal symbol containing the word START.

7.150 Individual items of data are referred to in program flowcharts by the use of _____.

7.151 When specifying the use of a formula in a processing symbol, only one dataname is positioned to the _____ of the equal sign.

7.152 The question contained within the decision symbol is referred to as a _____ statement.

7.153 An unconditional branch may be referred to as a _____.

7.154 Literals used to highlight totals at the end of a report are referred to as _____.

7.155 Accumulators are initialized at a value of _____.

7.156 In a decision the symbol < refers to _____ a specific amount.

Answers: 7.123 (*b*); 7.124 (*b*); 7.125 (*b*); 7.126 (*a*); 7.127 (*b*); 7.128 (*a*); 7.129 (*a*); 7.130 (*a*); 7.131 (*a*); 7.132 (*b*); 7.133 (*b*); 7.134 (*a*); 7.135 (*b*); 7.136 (*a*); 7.137 (*c*); 7.138 (*b*); 7.139 (*a*); 7.140 (*d*); 7.141 (*b*); 7.142 (*c*); 7.143 (*a*); 7.144 (*c*); 7.145 (*b*); 7.146 (*d*); 7.147 systems; 7.148 EDP cycle; 7.149 START; 7.150 datanames; 7.151 left; 7.152 conditional; 7.153 GO TO; 7.154 special labels; 7.155 zero (0); 7.156 less than.

Supplementary Problems

For each of the flowchart narratives that follow, prepare a complete flowchart to best represent the processing described.

7.157 Compute gross pay and net pay. Headings to the problem are: 'EMPLOYEE NAME', 'GROSS PAY', 'FICA', and 'NET PAY'. Input to the problem are the employee's name, hours worked, and pay rate per hour. Gross pay is computed by multiplying hours by rate. FICA is withdrawn at 6.25 percent of gross pay. Net pay equals gross pay minus FICA. Output each employee's name, gross pay, FICA deduction, and net pay. An unspecified number of people are to be processed, so use an LRC to control looping.

7.158 Determine an average sales price. Input to the problem are a sales item's name and 4 retail prices at which it could be purchased. The average price for that item is computed by adding the 4 sales prices and dividing that sum by 4. Print out the name of the sales item and the average price for that item. Headings on this report should appear as 'SALES ITEM' and 'AVG SALES PRICE'. As exactly 30 sales items are slated for this pricing problem, use a counter to control the execution of flowchart loops.

7.159 Compute average pay amounts. A company desires to ascertain the average salary it pays to its employees, so it will read through its pay records to compute this number. Input to the problem are each employee's name, his or her regular pay total, overtime pay amount, and special payment totals. All the payment amounts are added to compute a total gross pay. This total is acccumulated on each loop for every one of the 705 employees on file. For each employee, output his or her name, regular total pay, overtime pay, special pay amount, and the total of those three amounts. When looping ceases, the accumulated total of all gross pay is divided by 705 to produce the average salary paid to employees. Output this computed average using the label 'AVG SALARY PAID = '. Use a looping technique of your choice to control the looping sequence.

7.160 Determine the cost of a special inventory and the number of items within it. Input to the problem are the item's number, its description, unit cost of the item, and the quantity held in inventory. Compute the inventory cost of that item by multiplying its unit cost by the quantity held in inventory. If the unit cost of that item exceeds $50 per unit, accumulate the total inventory cost of that item and add 1 to the total number of items falling into that category. For every item read, print out its item number, description, unit cost, quantity, and total inventory cost. When looping stops, print out on a separate line this total cost of that $50 plus inventory and the number of items in that special category. An unspecified amount of data exists. (*Hint*: This problem may require the use of an LRC and two accumulators.)

7.161 Accumulate total sales and sales taxes in a retail establishment. Input to the problem are the item sold and its price. Sales tax is added to the price, being computed as 4.25 percent of the sales price. The sales tax is added to the original price for the total sales price. Accumulate both the sales tax and total sales price computed for each sales item. On each loop print the item sold, sales price, sales tax, and total sales price. When looping ends, print out the two accumulated totals using the labels 'TOTAL SALES TAX PAID = ' and 'TOTAL SALES = '. Use an LRC since the amount of data processed will vary between applications. Choose your own column headings.

7.162 Identify the levels of salespeople in an organization. Input to the problem are a salesperson's name, total sales made, and commissions earned. If the commission amount ≤ 500, that salesperson belongs in category 1. If commission > 500, the salesperson is a category 2 salesperson. The problem requires that you accumulate the number of people in each category and add up the commissions earned by those salespeople. On each loop print each salesperson's name, total sales made, commissions earned, and a literal of either 'CAT1' or 'CAT2'. The column headings 'SALESPERSON', 'TOTAL SALES', 'COMM EARNED', and 'CATEGORY' should appear atop the report. When looping ends, print out the four accumulated totals using four separate special labels on separate lines. Choose your own labels. An unspecified number of sales records is processed.

Glossary

Accumulator. A flowchart technique that enables the computation of subtotals and/or grand totals.

Annotation symbol. A three-sided rectangular symbol that is used to add descriptive comments to flowcharts.

Conditional branches. The multiple exits from a decision symbol that are taken in relation to the flowchart's response to the conditional statement within that decision.

Connector symbol. A small circular symbol that represents unconditional branching activities in a flowchart.

Counter. A flowchart technique to control the looping sequence in a flowchart, for an exact number of loops.

Decision symbol. The diamond-shaped flowchart symbol used for logical operations to determine the relationship between two values.

Flowchart. A graphic representation of the flow of logic for a processing application.

Flowchart loop. The repetitive processing of a series of steps to facilitate the handling of more than one data item.

GO TO. Flowchart slang for an unconditional branch.

Initial conditions. Processing activities that must be accomplished prior to the commencement of looping or the main processing effort.

Input/output (I/O) symbol. A parallelogram-shaped symbol used to denote input and output operations within a flowchart.

Last record check (LRC). The decision operation that checks whether the last record has been fully read and processed, in order to determine whether looping should continue.

Literals. The headings or special labels used when outputting data, created within the pairs of single quotation marks that define each.

PRINT symbol. Flowchart slang for an I/O symbol containing the word PRINT.

Processing symbol. The rectangular symbol in which all processing activities are represented.

Program flowchart. A flowchart that details the logic and steps composing a program solution.

READ symbol. Flowchart slang for an I/O symbol containing the word READ.

START symbol. Flowchart slang for a terminal symbol containing the word START.

STOP symbol. Flowchart slang for a terminal symbol using the word STOP.

Systems flowchart. A flowchart that details the flow of information through an organization; more encompassing than a program flowchart.

Terminal symbol. Denotes the beginning and end of a flowchart solution.

Unconditional branch. A branching operation from which no deviation is possible; often used to branch to the READ symbol at the start of a loop to continue the looping sequence and processing.

Chapter 8

Structured Designs

8.1 TOP-DOWN DESIGN CONCEPTS

Top-down, or *structured*, *designs* were introduced to improve the problem-solving capabilities of users and to overcome the difficulties with bottom-up techniques. *Bottom-up techniques* offered partial nonintegrated solutions, often duplicating processing efforts. The top-down approach requires examining the interaction of all components and developing modular solutions for each major component within a solution.

The major objectives of structured designs are the elimination of GO TOs, the preparation of logical designs, construction of modular components, greater operational definition, and improved documentation. These objectives are designed to produce well thought-out, logically correct solutions. The modular structure of top-down designs offers users flexibility in updating or modifying resultant solutions, as well as dividing the initial problem into workable units. The documentation provides a ready means of project control and of assessing the progress made, while acting as a reference for deriving information about data handling procedures.

8.2 HIPO DOCUMENTATION

A critical feature of structured designs is the documentation. Rules normally applied to these designs require that each module be unique, possess a clear operational purpose, and offer only one entry and exit point. These rules enable users to attack each module separately, focusing on their operational role and their interface with other modules.

A form used to initially record top-down designs is the *structure chart*. This form looks like a corporate organization chart, with modular components positioned in their relative logical order. The top-most module of the structure chart is the *main control module*, with modules at the lowest level referred to as *processing modules*. Modules at intermediary levels are called *processing and control modules*. The hierarchy of modules relates directly to their operational purposes. The structure chart serves as a planning tool by subdividing the solution into its modular components.

A form prepared from the structure chart is the *visual table of contents*. The visual table of contents also uses a hierarchical format, but it incorporates a numbering scheme to identify each module within its structure. These numbers act as an identification code and assist in defining the subdivision of each level within the design.

Both of the preceding documents can be incorporated into a *HIPO package*, that is, documentation fully detailing the operational aspects of a structured design. The term *HIPO* represents *hierarchy plus input-process-output*. The HIPO package includes a visual table of contents overview HIPO and detail HIPO diagrams, and miscellaneous documents. The visual table of contents provides an overview of the total design. The *overview HIPO diagram* describes the general purpose of modules at the higher levels of a visual table of contents. The *detail HIPO diagrams* relate to the lower levels of a top-down design, detailing specific aspects of processing performed by that module. The miscellaneous category may include any paperwork deemed necessary by the user, such as flowcharts, written narratives of processing, and forms detailing any aspect of an I/O design.

8.3 CONTROL BLOCK STRUCTURES

Control block sequences are used to describe the processing undertaken within structured solutions. Three control sequences commonly used include the processing sequence, the IF/THEN/ELSE sequence, and the looping sequence. Each of these control block structures is graphically represented by its own set of symbols.

The *processing sequence* describes the consecutive processing of multiple statements. Conditional operations involving decisions and their branches are detailed via the *IF/THEN/ELSE sequence*. Repetitive processing actions are expressed using the *looping sequence*, which incorporates a decision and branching operations. Flowcharts may be prepared describing any processing using these three control sequences.

8.4 STRUCTURED DESIGN TECHNIQUES

Structured programming refers to the application of top-down principles to software development. The use of structured concepts results in better software, cost savings, and simplified debugging.

Three looping techniques used with structured concepts are the *FOR/NEXT*, *DO/WHILE*, and *DO/UNTIL*. The FOR/NEXT offers an automated looping sequence to execute an exact number of loops. The DO/WHILE and DO/UNTIL are conditional looping sequences, relating to the execution of a loop to satisfaction of a conditional value. The DO/WHILE stipulates that looping continue while a specific condition exists. The DO/UNTIL directs that looping continue until a specific condition occurs.

An input technique used with structured programming is the *priming read*. This technique positions one input prior to the looping sequence and a read operation at the loop's close. This second read is considered more efficient when exiting the looping sequence. Problems 8.72–8.86 deal with the priming read and DO/UNTIL looping sequence.

Groups of related statements are grouped together in modules, which are graphically defined via the *predefined process symbol*. Each module is identified by a narrative within that symbol. Each module is referenced within the main flowchart and detailed within a smaller flow diagram. The RETURN processing symbol at the end of each module's flowchart denotes the return to processing within the main flowchart. The use of modules expresses principles related to the use of *subroutines* in programs.

8.5 PSEUDOCODE

Pseudocode offers a hypothetical language with which to detail the logic of structured solutions. It complements the use of flowcharts, drawing its logic from these pictorial solutions. The pseudocode solution assumes the appearance of a program, using many language-like statements. These instructions are meant to simplify documentation and enhance the actual coding of software. Top-down concepts are easily coded in pseudocode solutions.

8.6 THE PERSONNEL INVOLVED

Top-down designs may be individually analyzed or prepared on a group basis, depending on the scope of the project. A *chief programmer team* (*CPT*) is a group of programming personnel often assigned to large top-down projects. The CPT group usually consists of a chief programmer, an assistant, team members, and librarian. All documentation prepared by the CPT is carefully cataloged.

Review of structured designs is accomplished via informal and formal design reviews. The *informal design review* is a preliminary analysis that attempts to monitor the initial direction of the team's work. The *formal design review* is more structured, requiring a detailed analysis of every module's function and processing effort. *Structured walkthroughs* are rigorous examinations of a module's activities. These detailed analyses are essential in uncovering discrepancies and critical omissions in the structure of designs being implemented.

Solved Problems

TOP-DOWN DESIGN CONCEPTS

8.1 What does the term *top-down design* mean?

The phrase *top-down design* represents a computerized data processing approach to problem solving, as applied to the preparation of computer-related solutions. As they focus on application of the same principles, the terms *top-down design* and *structured design* are interchangeable. Top-down designs are applied to software solutions, as well as to other problems, such as improving the flow of information through organizations.

8.2 Why were top-down design principles introduced?

With the improvement of computer hardware, organizations needed to improve their software and methods of handling data. In their efforts to satisfy user demands, many DP personnel took shortcuts which, for convenience sake, bypassed conventional approaches and accepted practices. The result was a confusing jumble of programs and approaches that were undecipherable. Instead of designing software and procedures that were properly integrated, DP personnel devised approaches that attacked problems on a piecemeal basis and did not interact. This approach toward problem solving, referred to as the *bottom-up technique*, proved inefficient and costly.

8.3 What is wrong with the bottom-up technique?

The bottom-up approach offers partial solutions to computer-related problems. These design techniques look only at a specific part of the problem not at the whole. Thus each bottom-up solution is independent and is not integrated into a totally operative approach. This type of individualized solution often duplicates other aspects of previously developed solutions, wastes money in unnecessary rework, consumes computer resources and personnel, and occupies periods of time that might be more advantageously used.

8.4 How do structured design approaches overcome the difficulties associated with bottom-up designs?

By offering an integrated approach to designing computer-oriented solutions, structured designs offer a real plus. The top-down design approach forces an examination of the whole problem, not just portions of it. Not only are individual problems scrutinized but their direct impact on the entire computer function is assessed. Essentially, solutions are not designed in a vacuum, which would result in expensive rework. In this fashion, overlapping solutions are avoided, labor power is more efficiently used, and more work is produced for the same dollar figures.

8.5 How recently were structured principles introduced?

Technical papers addressing the principles of structured design solutions were presented in the mid-1960s. Though well received, many data processors could not initially assess their importance on a practical basis. Much of the then-available software and design philosophies would not permit the application of those principles. However, as the nature of computer-related solutions expanded and supporting technology improved, many users sought to apply top-down design principles and benefit from their usage.

8.6 What are the major characteristics of top-down design solutions?

The primary considerations implemented via structured design solutions are:
(1) The elimination of GO TOs
(2) The development of more logical solutions
(3) The construction of modular units
(4) More well-defined and organized solutions
(5) Improved documentation

CHAP. 8] STRUCTURED DESIGNS 157

8.7   How does the elimination of unconditional branching, via GO TOs, improve design strategies?

In bottom-up designs, GO TOs were frequently used to connect the diverse components of those solutions and compensate for faulty logic. Proponents of structured principles believed that the elimination of GO TOs would force programmers to design better software. In nonsoftware applications in which informational handling is critical, the same logic applies. If data handling procedures are clearly defined and well conceived, then the amount of lost time resulting from the confusion of not knowing what to do or whom to contact is minimized, and the overall efficiency of the entire computer support system is improved.

8.8   How does this result in more logical solutions?

Minimizing unconditional branching forces the development of more tightly designed solutions since design elements must now flow logically from one unit to another. The structured design approach directs the user to look at the entire structure of the solution, identifying individual components within it and their relationships to each other. Detailing all aspects of a solution ensures that no major omissions exist and that the relationships between component units are properly defined. The establishment of the hierarchy of every unit within a solution ensures that each unit is logically positioned, that data flow properly between units, and that the interface of each unit is clearly defined.

8.9   Why are modular units critical to top-down designs?

It is the modular construction of top-down designs that enables the identification of the individual units composing a structured solution. By defining each unit within its own module, it is possible to totally design all aspects of that module. Remember that by delineating all aspects of a top-down solution, we have defined the interface of component units and each unit's operational responsibility. Thus the programmer can work on an individual module, knowing that it is unique and will properly integrate with all other components.

8.10   On a practical basis, what advantages does the modular structure afford?

Treating each component module independently affords greater flexibility. For example, the programmer may separately configure and work on each module, knowing that they will interface. With respect to design modifications, modular components are readily handled. The addition or deletion of modules is easily accomplished since each module is a separate entity. Its removal will not radically alter the design, nor will the addition of another module following it. Changes are effected within a module without affecting other modules. As a hypothetical example, a programmer has five coded procedures in handling customer complaints, with each procedure within its own module. It is possible to change the third coded procedure without affecting any of the others. The elimination of procedure 2 will not alter coded modules 1, 3, 4, and 5. Similarly, modules representing coded procedures 6 to 8 may be easily handled, their addition affecting none of the other modules. The structure of top-down solutions was carefully designed with this concept in mind, because it offered a real plus to its adopters.

8.11   How do the preceding factors help create more well-defined and logically organized solutions?

All three factors result in the user's carefully detailing all aspects of a solution and defining the modules that compose it, their operational requirements and interface, and the logical placement of each module. These results cannot be achieved without detailed prior planning and extensive analysis of the problem under study.

8.12   Does the structured design approach afford its users any assistance in the area of documentation?

Yes. A major characteristic of the top-down design approach is the excellent documentation it affords its users. It mandates that all aspects of a solution be properly recorded throughout its development. This necessity forestalls the spotty documentation often associated with other less-demanding techniques. Documenting the top-down solution ensures that all component units are fixed in their proper position and provides an opportunity to assess the correctness of this logic. No additional work may be performed without certifying the overall logic of the solution offered. This rationale prevents the numerous false starts and incomplete approaches often associated with poorly integrated and ill-conceived solutions.

8.13 How does proper documentation help in project management?

The proper documentation of the top-down solution ensures project continuity. If a designer leaves the project, his or her replacement may gain knowledge of the project by carefully examining the documentation. The project manager can assess the progress made on the project by scanning existing documentation. Evaluation of the project's correctness is also assessed by examining the documentation prepared. The documentation of any project is of considerable importance to management. Structured designs stress this aspect of the technique.

HIPO DOCUMENTATION

8.14 What form does the documentation supporting structured designs assume?

Structured designs are visually documented in a variety of ways. Some top-down diagrams are similar to flowcharts, others are more like corporate organization charts. Additional documentation was developed to highlight special aspects of top-down designs.

8.15 Are there any general rules for developing structured designs?

Yes. Three rules usually apply when developing structured designs, namely,
(1) A modular component within a solution should be unique and independent of all other modules.
(2) The operational purpose of each module should be clear.
(3) Each module should offer only one entrance and one exit.

8.16 Why should each module be unique?

One of the major characteristics of a top-down design is its modular structure, whereby each module defines one specific operation. If the module is ill-conceived, it will not project its purpose but may partially service one or more tasks and duplicate steps existing in other modules. Designing unique modules ensures that each module will efficiently process one task that is not duplicated elsewhere and that the module can be accessed independently without affecting another module.

8.17 Why should each module's purpose be clearly defined?

This second point reinforces the concept that each module serve one operational purpose. Each module groups together those operations that support the processing of one specific task. The advantages of this approach are that errors are readily identified within their respective modules, modules do not become unwieldy in size and complexity, and analysis of each module's purpose is simplified.

8.18 How is each module affected by having only one exit and entrance?

This requirement is a technical feature that ensures the proper passage of control between modules. Each module is logically accessed and control passes between modules in an orderly sequence. The single entrance and exit make it impossible to haphazardly jump between modules or create gaps in the flow of data.

8.19 Where are these rules applied?

These rules are used in preparing documents related to top-down designs. One of the initial documents encountered is the *structure chart*, as shown in Fig. 8-1.

8.20 Of what purpose is the structure chart?

The structure chart is in a format similar to a corporate organization chart, in which managerial positions at all levels of an organization are detailed. Within the structure chart each module or block identifies a specific operational task and its relationship to the whole solution.

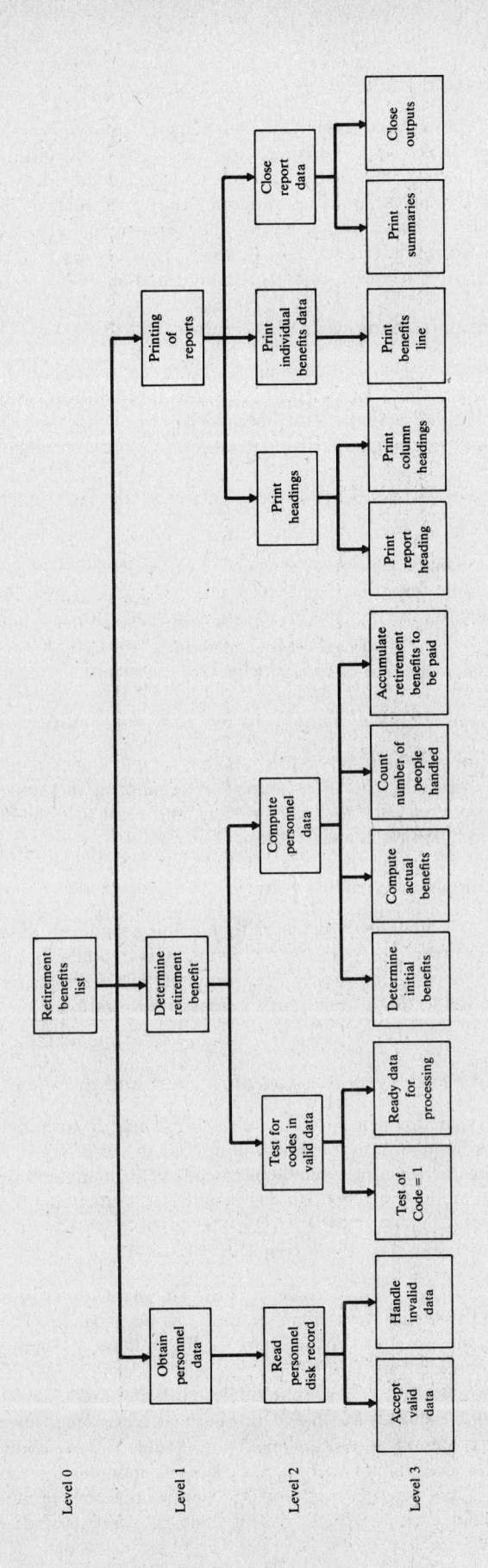

Fig. 8-1 Structure chart prepared for writing a program on retirement benefits.

8.21 What titles are assigned to modules on each level of the structure chart?

The topmost level of a structure chart, level 0, is called the *main control module*, which states the overall purpose of the chart. The succeeding levels composing the middle of the structure chart are referred to as *processing and control modules*. These intermediary modules, identified as levels 1 and 2 in Fig. 8-1, classify the majority of processing components composing the structure chart. These modules dictate the logic applied to the solution and describe the responsibilities assigned to each module. The modules at the lowest level on the structure chart are called the *processing modules* and represent the lowest level of processing support. In Fig. 8-1 processing modules are indicated at level 3.

8.22 How are the levels used in working with the structure chart?

The use of levels reinforces the top-to-bottom analysis technique associated with top-down designs. The flow of logic proceeds down each leg of the structure chart until all processing activities within that leg are completed. Then processing activities are undertaken in the next leg. Each module is logically positioned within the overall solution, with its relative level and position noted in the structure chart.

8.23 From Fig. 8-1, what respective titles are assigned to modules from each level of the structure chart?

Level 0 contains only one main control module, which is called Retirement Benefits List. Two levels of processing and control modules exist in this structure chart. On level 1, one module is identified as the Determine Retirement Benefit module. The Read Personnel Disk Record module is a processing and control module on level 2. Level 3 contains the most processing modules, with the Print Column Headings module appearing in the rightmost leg of the structure chart.

8.24 What advantages are immediately evident from use of the structure chart?

By dividing the problem into workable units, it is possible to assign each module a specific task within the overall solution. The structure chart has helped in organizing the steps to the solution and in detailing the relationship between each module. In effect, the chart is a blueprint of the solution, with each module identified in relation to its assigned task.

8.25 What documentation follows the structure chart?

The structure chart serves as a preliminary planning tool defining the levels of tasks to be performed and the logical relationship between components. It details this modular structure and precedes the preparation of the visual table of contents form. This form parallels the appearance of the structure chart but adds a numerical notation to that format. A representative visual table of contents is shown in Fig. 8-2.

8.26 What is the major difference between the structure chart and the visual table of contents?

As both diagrams assume a hierarchical format, the distinguishing characteristic of the visual table of contents is an identification number scheme. Each module of the visual table of contents is assigned a unique identification number by which it is readily accessible. This number denotes the relative position of the module by level and by the organizational leg in which it is situated.

8.27 How is this identification number scheme structured?

Identification numbers are assigned on level-by-level basis. The main control module, level 0, is assigned the number 1.0, which is the highest-level number that can be assigned. The next level of modules represents subdivisions of the main control module, each subdivision defining a separate leg of the solution. As such, each module at the top of that leg receives a distinct identification number that will identify every module within that leg. In Fig. 8-2 modules atop the three distinct legs are assigned, from left to right, the numbers 2.0, 3.0, and 4.0. Modules within each leg are assigned lower-level decimal numbers commencing with that leg's identification number. Thus module 3.0 is subdivided into two modules identified as 3.1 and 3.2. Subdivisions of that level, processing modules, are noted with corresponding numbers. As such, it is clear that modules 3.1.1 and 3.1.2 are subdivisions of module 3.1. This numerical scheme is carried throughout each leg of the visual table of contents and makes reference to any individual module relatively easy.

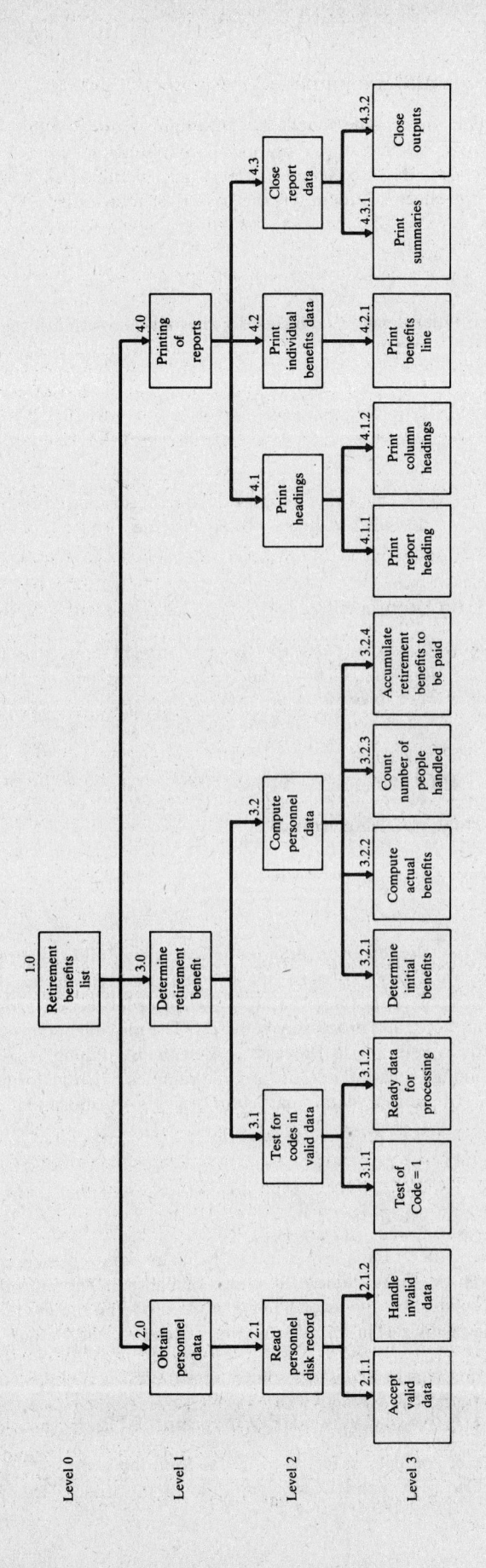

Level 0	**1.0** Retirement benefits list
Level 1	**2.0** Obtain personnel data — **3.0** Determine retirement benefit — **4.0** Printing of reports
Level 2	**2.1** Read personnel disk record; **3.1** Test for codes in valid data; **3.2** Compute personnel data; **4.1** Print headings; **4.2** Print individual benefits data; **4.3** Close report data
Level 3	**2.1.1** Accept valid data; **2.1.2** Handle invalid data; **3.1.1** Test of Code = 1; **3.1.2** Ready data for processing; **3.2.1** Determine initial benefits; **3.2.2** Compute actual benefits; **3.2.3** Count number of people handled; **3.2.4** Accumulate retirement benefits to be paid; **4.1.1** Print report heading; **4.1.2** Print column headings; **4.2.1** Print benefits line; **4.3.1** Print summaries; **4.3.2** Close outputs

Fig. 8-2 The visual table of contents prepared from a structure chart for program related to retirement benefits. Note the identifying numbers on each module.

8.28 What module carries the identification number of 4.3.1?

The number 4.3.1 denotes that the module sought is in the rightmost leg of the diagram, headed by the 4.0 module, Printing of Reports. Advancing to its subdivision, module 4.3 which is labeled Close Report, it can be seen that the next lower level contains the modules 4.3.1 and 4.3.2. The 4.3.1 module, Print Summaries, which is a subdivision of 4.3, identifies the output of totals accumulated during processing.

8.29 How effective is this numbering scheme?

The identification scheme provides a ready reference to any module within a top-down solution. Using the digits provided, access to any module in the visual table of contents is possible.

8.30 Are the visual table of contents and structure chart the sole means of documenting top-down designs?

These forms represent just a few of the forms used to document structured solutions. The paperwork used to fully document top-down designs is called a HIPO package.

8.31 What does the acronym *HIPO* represent?

The acronym *HIPO* represents *hierarchy plus input-process-output*, terms that relate to the modular structure of top-down designs. Note that in both the structure chart and visual table of contents, all aspects of a solution—including input, processing and output operations—were detailed.

8.32 What forms compose the HIPO package?

The HIPO package comprises the following forms:
(1) Visual table of contents
(2) Overview HIPO diagrams
(3) Detail HIPO diagrams
(4) Miscellaneous documents

The visual table of contents has already been described. Overview HIPO diagrams, reserved for the higher-level modules of the visual table of contents, provide an overview to the function of those modules. Detail HIPO diagrams define specifics related to the lower levels of the visual table of contents, including data names, I/O operations, and processing activities. The miscellaneous documents category is a catch-all that includes any forms relevant to processing. Documents falling into this category include flowcharts; detailed charts defining input and output formats; samples of cards, forms, or documents to be used in processing; and narratives that detail particular aspects of processing or provide advisory material.

8.33 How is the overview HIPO diagram used?

A representative overview HIPO diagram is shown in Fig. 8-3. The data represented within the overview HIPO diagram are drawn from the visual table of contents of Fig. 8.3. The information presented atop the overview HIPO diagram defines the application being worked on and the module involved. Note that this form defines all processing activities in terms of input, processing, and output operations.

8.34 Which module is reviewed in the overview HIPO diagram of Fig. 8-3?

Module 3.1 of the visual table of contents in Fig. 8-2 is detailed in the overview HIPO diagram. Module 3.1 represents the Test for Codes in Valid Data, a module in the middle leg of the visual table of contents.

CHAP. 8] STRUCTURED DESIGNS 163

Author Adrian O.	Application Personnel Reporting	Data 9/30/
Module ID 3.1	Description Test for Codes in Valid Data	Page 12 of 23

Inputs	Processing	Outputs
Valid Employee Record	1. Test for a code = 1 in record of employee; valid data used. 2. If match exists, record is readied for processing. Move data to proper data fields. 3. If no match exists, proceed to next employee record.	Employee Record Initialize Data Items

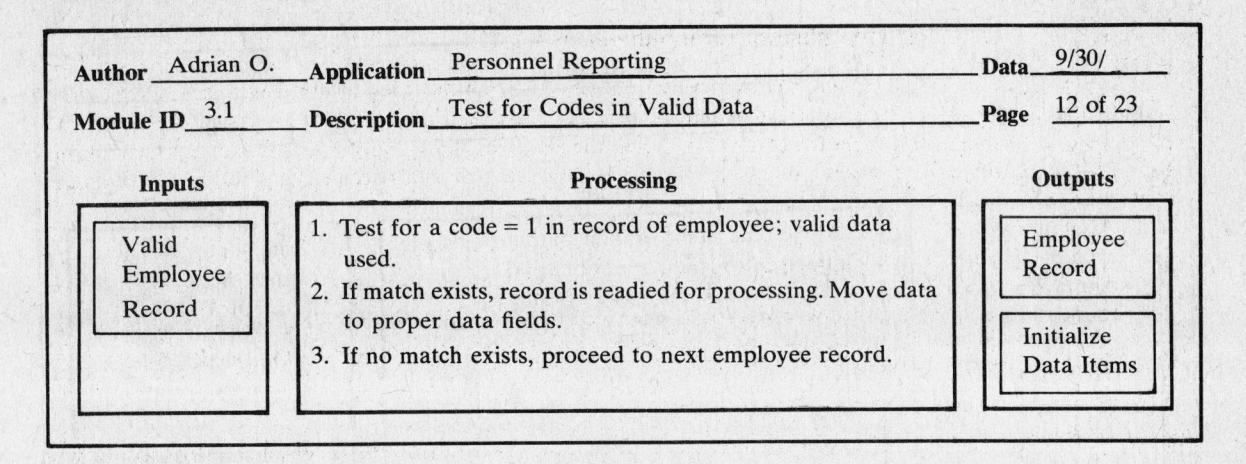

Fig. 8-3

8.35 What information is written in the input, processing, and output sections of the overview HIPO form?

Factors relating to each of those three activities are presented in each section. The input section notes that only valid employee records will enter processing related to that module. The processing section defines three tasks. Task 1 identifies the test for a code equal to 1. Task 2 instructs that if a code of 1 exists, that employee's data be accepted for processing. Task 3 indicates that a no match situation should lead to the input of the next employee's record. The outputs resulting from module 3.1 are the individual employee's record, which is entering processing, and those data items that have been initialized in order that processing continue.

8.36 Why are no specific data items specified in the overview HIPO diagram?

The overview HIPO diagram is exactly that, an overview of that module's function. Processing activities are outlined as to their purpose, with specifics relegated to another piece of documentation. Essentially, all activities related to the module 3.1 are briefly discussed in the overview HIPO diagram.

8.37 Which form is used to represent the specifics of processing for a module?

The detail HIPO diagram assumes the responsibility of detailing all processing activities related to a specific module. Where the overview HIPO form was general, the detail HIPO diagram provides greater depth of coverage. Specific data names, literals, and record formats can be detailed using this form. A detail HIPO diagram is shown in Fig. 8-4.

8.38 How specific is the detail HIPO in Fig. 8-4.

The level of detail regarding each point within the form is quite specific. Data names, literals, and data handling steps are clearly specified. Two accumulated totals are input to this module. Their data names, BEN-TOT and TOT-BEN-DUE, are noted next to an explanation of their purpose. The lone processing step advises to move these accumulated totals to their appropriate output lines. In the output section, two summary lines are to be output. Summary line 1 will use the literal 'NO OF EMPLOYEES DUE BENEFITS =', with summary line 2 requiring the label 'TOTAL DOLLAR ESTIMATE DUE ='.

8.39 Why is it necessary to provide such detail?

Whereas the overview HIPO form is a broad outline, the detail HIPO diagram is designed to provide specifics as to what data are processed when and how. Specific data names, literals, and other related factors are detailed for the programmer's use when writing software.

Author	Vanessa O.	Application	Personnel Reporting	Data	9/30/
Module ID	4.3.1	Description	Print Summaries	Page	22 of 23

Inputs	Processing	Outputs
1. Accumulated total of employees to receive benefits (BEN-TOT) 2. Accumulated total of the benefits due employees (TOT-BEN-DUE)	1. Move data items to their output fields preceded by their special labels.	1. Print summary line 1; use the label 'NO OF EMPLOYEES DUE BENEFITS = ' with BEN-TOT. 2. Print summary line 2; use the label 'TOTAL DOLLAR ESTIMATE DUE = ' with TOT-BEN-DUE.

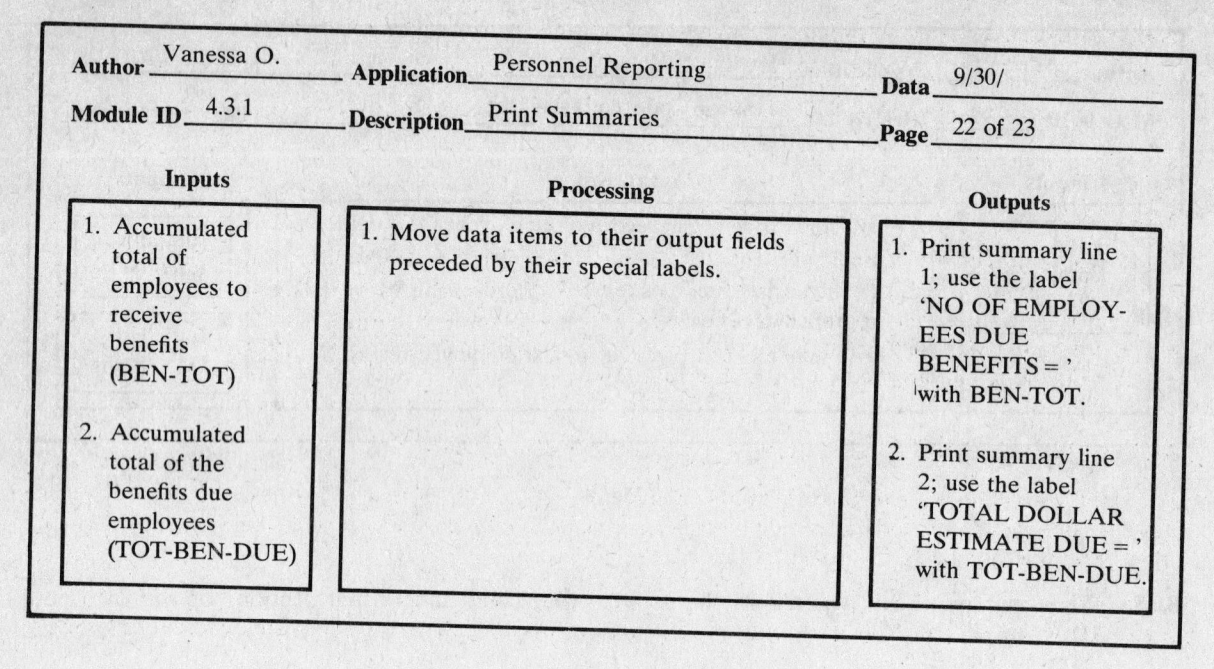

Fig. 8-4

8.40 What other forms usually complete the HIPO package?

Generally, flowcharts accompany the HIPO documentation, although any documentation deemed necessary can be incorporated. This may include written step-by-step narratives, advisory memos, and special notes that could prove helpful in the preparation of software or clarify any points regarding any level of processing activity.

CONTROL BLOCK STRUCTURES

8.41 What special techniques have been developed to support the implementation of top-down design techniques?

Three special processing structures have been developed to accommodate the use of top-down techniques. The three groupings, referred to as *control block sequences*, are extremely useful in representing structured solutions. Figure 8-5 depicts the three control block sequences fundamental to structured designs.

(a) Processing sequence   (b) IF/THEN/ELSE sequence   (c) Looping sequence

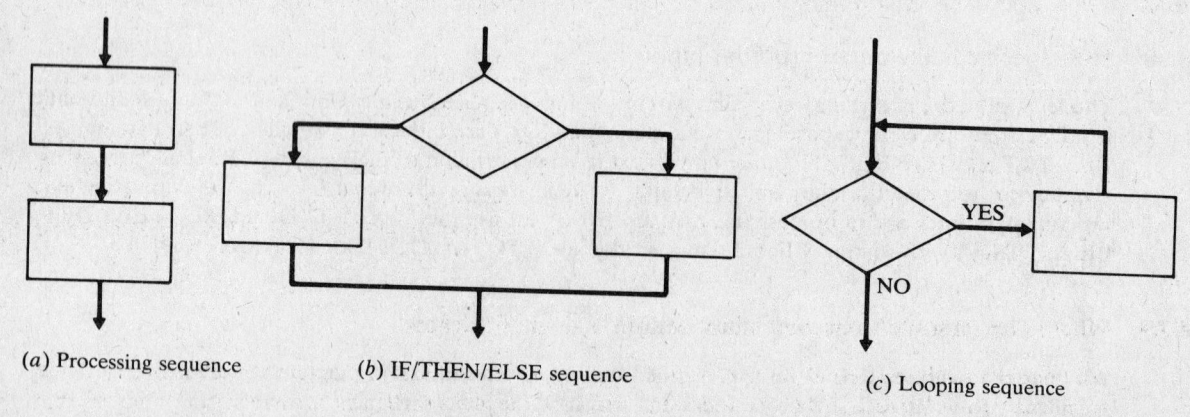

Fig. 8-5 The three control block sequences associated with structured solutions.

8.42 How are a series of processing tasks represented in structured solutions?

Consecutive processing tasks are represented using the control block sequence shown in Fig. 8-5a. Called the *processing sequence*, this control block grouping defines a string of processing tasks in much the same manner as they are depicted on a flowchart.

8.43 What activities are represented via the IF/THEN/ELSE sequence?

The IF/THEN/ELSE sequence, Fig. 8-5b, is used to define decisions and the conditional branches that result from them. The concept of clearly detailing a decision and the tasks related to it are an integral part of the structured philosophy. It is important to define a decision's purpose and position, as well as the operations that result from its execution. The IF/THEN/ELSE sequence addresses those considerations and pictorially represents those tasks.

8.44 Which control sequence defines repetitive processing tasks?

Flowchart loops are defined via the looping sequence, Fig. 8-5c. This sequence has at its heart a decision as to whether the looping should continue. One conditional branch leads to the looping sequence, with the other providing the exit from the loop.

8.45 How are the control block sequences incorporated into flow diagrams to pictorially represent the flow of data?

Figure 8-6 (page 166) illustrates the incorporation of these sequences into a hypothetical flowchart. The flowchart shown illustrates how the three control sequences can interact within one solution.

8.46 Where are the control block sequences evident in the flow diagram of Fig. 8-6?

Though a hypothetical solution, the flowchart of Fig. 8-6 illustrates the blending of these three control sequences. A processing sequence of two blocks is noted at the diagram's beginning. Midway in the flowchart is an IF/THEN/ELSE sequence, where processing sequences are performed in both conditional branches. The flowchart's close notes the use of a looping sequence where an unconditional branch commences the looping sequence. One or all of the control block sequences may be used, with any of the other program flowchart symbols, to diagram a solution to any problem.

8.47 Since the modular concept is an accepted structured design component, how are modules pictorially represented?

Modules composed of related sets of instructions are represented within flow diagrams using the predefined process symbol, Fig. 8-7a (page 166). This symbol represents a module of processing activities designed to handle some aspect of processing.

8.48 How does use of the predefined process symbol differ from the conventional processing system?

The differences between these two symbols are evident in Fig. 8-7b. Using the structure of the IF/THEN/ELSE sequence, it can be seen that the conditional branches possess the two symbols being discussed. On the NO branch there is a lone processing symbol indicating the execution of a single processing operation. This is not the case on the YES branch, where a predefined process symbol is placed. This symbol represents a series of instructions, accessed as a module, that will be executed. The predefined process symbol enables users to directly access a specific group of instructions, thus applying the modular concept.

8.49 How many modules may be defined within a single flowchart?

Any number of modules may be used within a flowchart in response to the needs of the problem. Once referenced in a flowchart, each module must be subsequently detailed in a smaller flow diagram that complements the original flowchart.

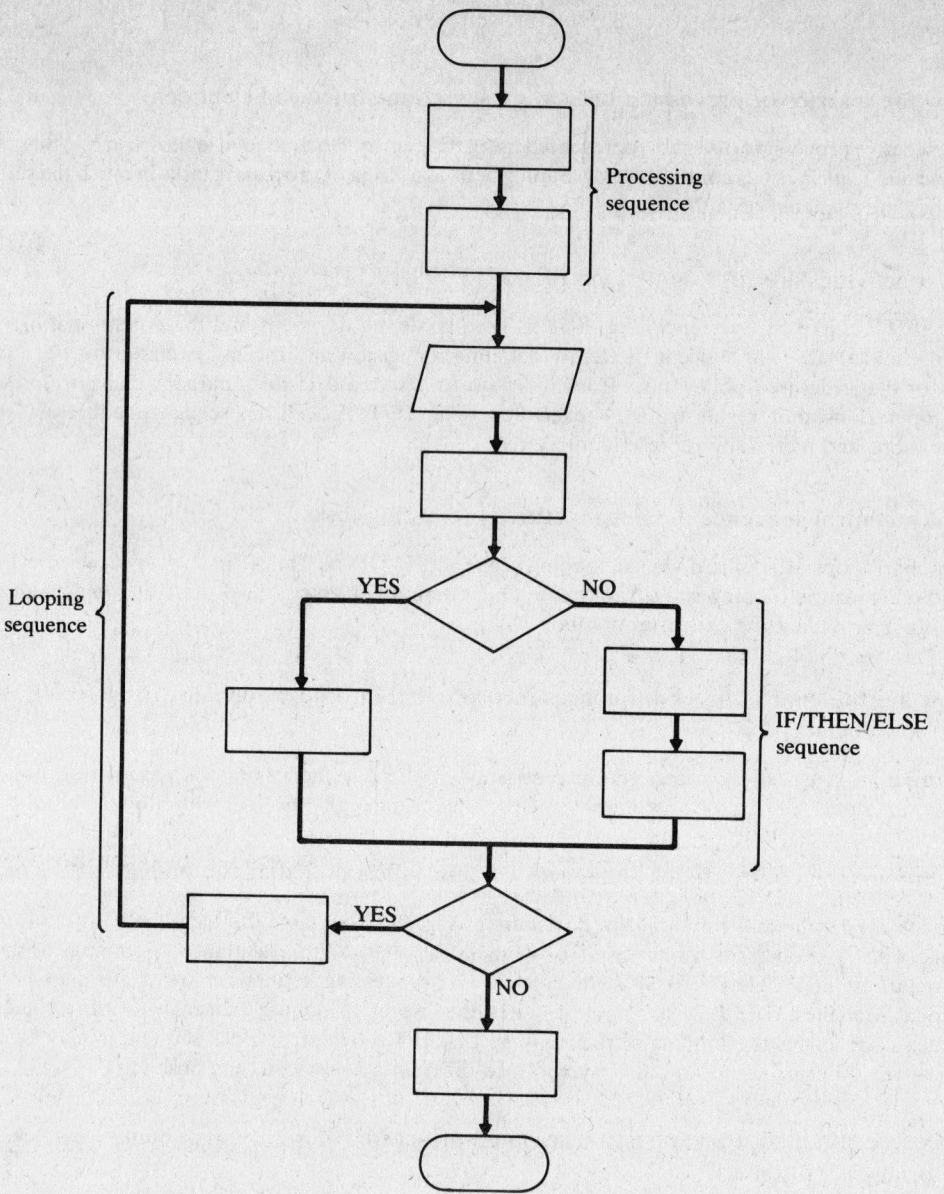

Fig. 8-6 A hypothetical structured diagram sequence in which all of the three control block sequences are employed.

(a) Predefined process symbol

(b) Predefined process symbol within IF/THEN/ELSE sequence

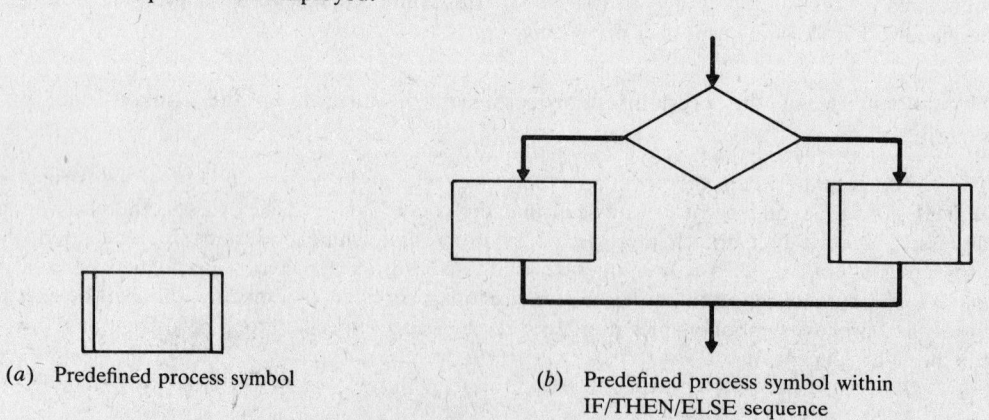

Fig. 8-7 Reference to modules of processing activities is accomplished through a variety of symbolic techniques. A predefined process symbol identifies a module of activities in a flowchart. This symbol is used within an IF/THEN/ELSE sequence to indicate access to that module of processing via a conditional operation.

STRUCTURED DESIGN TECHNIQUES

8.50 Do the modular-related flowcharts follow conventional flowchart principles?

Yes. Flowcharts related to modules defined via predefined process symbols are prepared as any other flow diagram might be. Essentially, they are small flowcharts whose sole purpose is to detail the processing defined within a module.

STRUCTURED DESIGN TECHNIQUES

8.51 What does the term *structured programming* mean?

The term *structured programming* defines the application of top-down design concepts to the writing of software. It implies that structured design principles have been incorporated into programs producing well-conceived, modular constructed, and logically correct software.

8.52 Does structured programming result in better software?

Yes. Practical experience over many years has demonstrated that when properly applied, structured programming produces sound, logically correct, and well-thought-out programs—software that is readily corrected and modified, with the appropriate changes properly documented for subsequent revisions. Programming personnel may find themselves more productive because of the potential efficiencies offered by structured programming efforts.

8.53 How can these efficiencies result in greater productivity?

Savings in personnel costs are gained from expending less time in debugging, searching for unrecorded program modifications, and unraveling convoluted program logic. As top-down concepts result in more logically correct software, their designs are better, easier to follow, and properly documented. Debugging efforts are greatly simplified. Necessary modifications in existing software are as easily handled because they were properly recorded. These savings in laborhours are readily converted into time that can be spent on other projects.

8.54 Have special concepts been developed to support the application of structured programming?

Yes. In addition to the development of the control block sequences, other concepts were developed to support the application of structured programming principles. These concepts relate to the development of looping sequences, the coordination of input data and looping sequences, and the use of hypothetical language to detail program logic.

8.55 Are these additional concepts exclusive of prior flowcharting and control block material?

No. These newer concepts were developed to further refine and enhance the structured programming technique, incorporating ideas related to flowcharting and the control block sequences. It should be obvious that material related to looping is common to flowcharting principles and the application of control block sequences, as well as structured programming. In many instances a technique was specially modified to improve its applicability to a structured design and facilitate data handling activities.

8.56 What structured programming concepts are associated with looping operations?

Three concepts developed in support of structured programming applications and related to repeated processing tasks are:
(1) FOR/NEXT
(2) DO/WHILE
(3) DO/UNTIL
Each possesses its own looping characteristics.

168   STRUCTURED DESIGNS   [CHAP. 8

8.57 How is the FOR/NEXT looping sequence used?

The *FOR/NEXT* is used to define looping sequences in which an exact number of loops must be performed. When a FOR/NEXT is specified, the user has already determined the number of loops that must undergo execution in order to complete processing. The FOR/NEXT simplifies the means of representing the looping sequence.

8.58 Why is the FOR/NEXT the means of representing this repetitive task?

The wording is deliberate, as the FOR/NEXT identifies the looping sequence and the exact number of loops to be performed. However, the actual execution of these loops is accomplished via a specific language. As computer languages vary extensively, the actual instructional format may not utilize the phrase FOR/NEXT but another similar term. The FOR/NEXT provides a vehicle for planning and logically positioning the looping sequence.

8.59 To what flowcharting concept is the FOR/NEXT related?

The FOR/NEXT is closely related to the concept of a counter. The counter (see Chap. 7) is a means of establishing a looping sequence in which an exact number of repetitions is performed. The FOR/NEXT provides an updated means of identifying automated looping sequences in which a predefined number of loops is performed.

8.60 How is the FOR/NEXT graphically represented?

Since no convention has been established for documenting an automated looping sequence like the FOR/NEXT, several graphic means have been employed. Figure 8-8 illustrates the means of denoting the FOR/NEXT looping sequence.

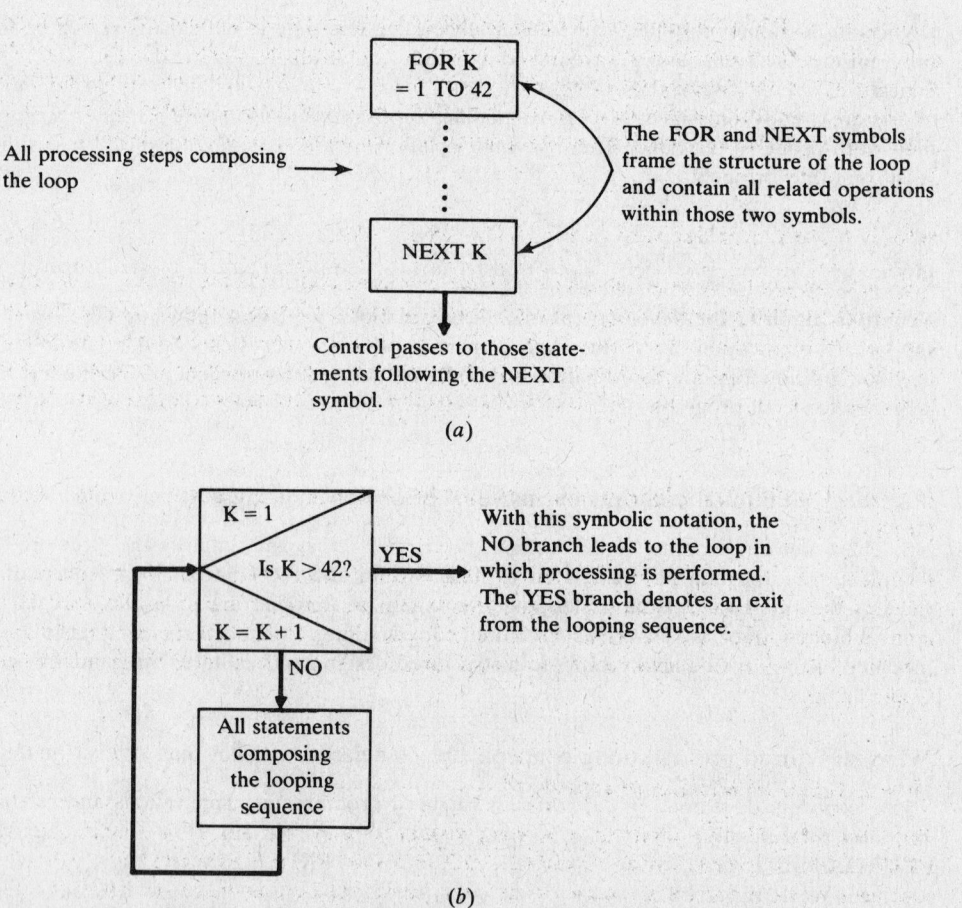

Fig. 8-8 Looping sequences are vital to structured designs.

CHAP. 8] STRUCTURED DESIGNS 169

8.61 How is the looping sequence defined in Fig. 8-8a?

In the flowchart excerpt to Fig. 8-8a, the FOR/NEXT is establishing an automated looping sequence of forty-two loops. The FOR/NEXT is defined via two processing symbols, one at the loop's start and one at the end, respectively. The FOR and NEXT processing symbols frame the looping sequence, positioning all statements composing the loop within the two symbols.

8.62 What is the function of the separate FOR/NEXT symbols?

Each of the FOR and NEXT processing symbols has a distinct purpose. The first FOR symbol establishes the loop's starting point and data relating to the loop's execution. It defines the loop counter as the variable K, initializes K at a value of 1, and stipulates an ending value of 42. The range of K from 1 to 42 effectively establishes the series of 42 loops.

The NEXT processing symbol is equally multifaceted. It determines whether loop 42 has been executed, as a counter decision might. If the forty-second loop has not been completed, the variable K is automatically incremented by 1, the looping sequence is returned to the FOR processing symbol, and looping is continued. If the forty-second loop has just ended, the NEXT processing symbol directs that processing continue onto the symbol following it. The NEXT processing symbol effectively represents the equivalent of a counter decision, a counter increment of 1, and the unconditional branch to the top of the loop. The FOR processing symbol initializes the loop and defines the counter variable to be used and the number of loops to be executed.

8.63 How does the symbol in Fig. 8-8b differ from FOR/NEXT?

The symbol in Fig. 8-8b more closely approximates the activities of a counter-oriented loop. It carries no name since it has a nonstandard shape and function. The three components of this symbol represent the initialization of the looping sequence and its counter ($K = 1$), the increment of the loop counter by one ($K = K + 1$), and the counter decision affecting the number of loops executed (IS K = 42?). This symbol can effect an automated looping sequence when a given number of loops is desired.

8.64 Why is the counter decision of Fig. 8-8b, 'IS K > 42?'

Note that the symbol appears at the loop's start, not at its end. Thus the counter K will reach 42 before it completes the forty-second loop and immediately exit the looping sequence. To avoid the exclusion of that last loop, the counter decision IS K > 42? is used. The forty-second loop is completed, and when K exceeds 42 at the next loop's start, the flow of processing exits the looping sequence via the YES branch. When using this symbol, the NO branch leads to the processing steps composing the loop.

8.65 If the FOR/NEXT defines an automated looping sequence, of what function is the DO/UNTIL?

It too creates a looping sequence, but one that is terminated when a specific condition is encountered. The DO/WHILE also controls a looping sequence with the aid of a conditional operation. the looping will continue until a particular value is found. The DO/UNTIL functions as a loop in which an LRC-type decision is incorporated to control looping. When the control value is input or created, the looping stops.

8.66 How is the DO/WHILE interpreted?

The DO/WHILE also controls a looping sequence with the aid of a conditional operation. The DO/WHILE is interpreted as dictating, "DO the loop WHILE this condition exists." Thus looping continues while a particular condition or value exists. Once that value or condition changes, looping immediately stops. Using the last record check analogy, looping can continue as long as the last record has not been read. When it has been, looping ceases.

8.67 Which of the looping sequences is favored?

Either the DO/WHILE or the DO/UNTIL may be used to create and control a loop in which repetitive processing is possible. The DO/UNTIL is more frequently used, and parallels to it are found in many computer languages.

8.68 What other structured technique is constructed using the looping sequence?

An input technique referred to as the *priming read* combines a looping sequence and the execution of input operations. The priming read utilizes an input operation both in and out ot the loop. The initial input operation is positioned prior to the loop and initializes the first loop's processing. The second input is positioned at the loop's end, prior to its conditional operation. This second input is repeatedly executed as each loop is performed. When the LRC condition is met, the positioning of this second input permits the ready exit from the loop. Figure 8-9 shows the framework of a priming read.

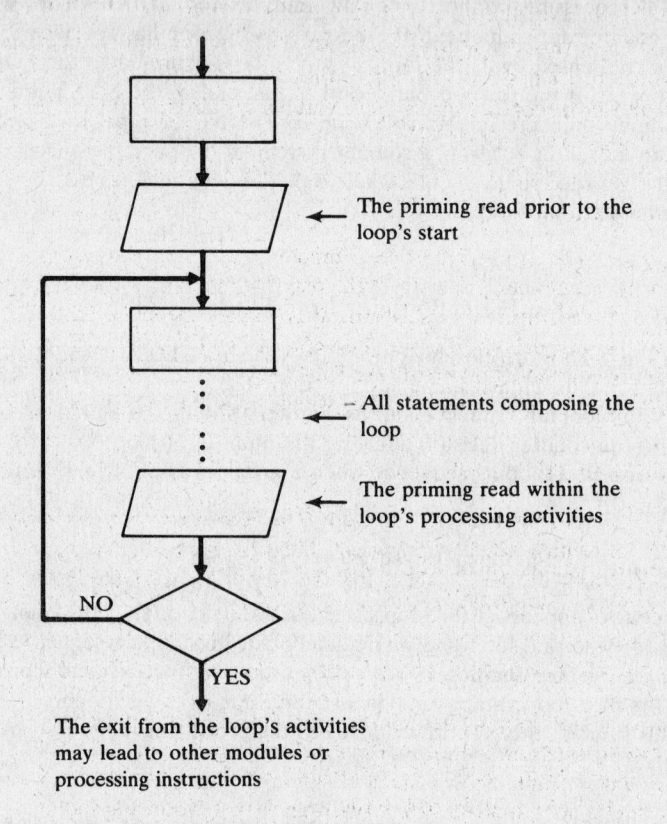

Fig. 8-9 The priming read is an input technique popular in structured designs.

8.69 What is the main objective of the priming read?

The priming read is designed to provide for the ready exit from the looping sequence, when the last data item has been processed. As shown in Fig. 8-9, the input and LRC are positioned at the loop's end. When the LRC condition is met, the exit from the loop permits access to the next module of processing without using an unconditional branch.

8.70 Is the priming read often used?

The priming read is used in many computer languages and readily supports the application of top-down principles. The priming read is a favorite of many programmers.

8.71 What looping technique is generally used with the priming read?

The DO/UNTIL is the looping sequence commonly used with the priming read because they complement each other. Both are designed for unlimited amounts of data, where an LRC decision usually controls the looping sequence. Problems 8.72–8.86 deal with situations in which the DO/UNTIL and priming read are combined to process data.

The following narrative refers to Probs. 8.72–8.77.

Commission rates are computed. A priming read and DO/UNTIL looping sequence are needed as is an accumulator. The report heading consists of three literals: 'NAME', 'UNITS SOLD', and 'COMM PAID'. Inputs to the problem are the salesperson's name (SNAME), units sold 1 (UN1), and units sold 2 (UN2). The total units sales amount (US) is computed by adding the two units-sold figures that are input. If that total is greater than 100, the commission rate is computed by multiplying the total by an average cost of 2.65 and 18.75 percent. If $US \leq 100$, the commission rate is 12.5 percent of the total times the average cost of 2.65. The commission amount computed for each salesperson is accumulated on each loop. Print out each salesperson's name, total units sold, and commission. After the last record is processed, output the accumulated total of all commissions paid (T) preceded by the label 'TOT COMM = $'.

8.72 How is the priming read depicted?

Figure 8-10 (page 172) demonstrates the implementation of the priming read technique. After the initialization of the accumulator $T = 0$ and the printing of headings, the initial input of the priming read is encountered. This READ symbol is outside the loop sequence and is used to prime processing within the first loop. The read that supports the normal loop appears prior to the LRC at the loop's close. This READ symbol inputs data for each loop. With the READ symbol so positioned, the loop may be continued by branching to its top or exited from the LRC when no data exist.

8.73 How is the DO/UNTIL depicted?

The DO/UNTIL frames the looping sequence. The DO portion of the flowchart is represented within a processing symbol, which effectively defines the first symbol of the loop. The close of the looping sequence is defined by the LRC. The narrative within the DO processing symbol advises to continue looping until an LRC condition is met.

8.74 Does the DO/UNTIL satisfactorily represent the control block looping sequence?

Yes. The control block looping sequence is properly documented via the DO/UNTIL. The looping sequence is created to permit the repetitive processing of data. The priming read does not adversely affect the loop, and it complements the application of top-down principles. In Fig. 8-10 connectors were chosen rather than a solid line, to define the branch that closes the loop.

8.75 What other control block sequence is shown in Fig. 8-10?

This flowchart also incorporates the IF/THEN/ELSE control block sequence to determine which commission rate to use. Using the decision IS US = 100?, the proper formula can be selected, and commissions can be computed at either 12.5 percent or 18.75 percent. Note that regardless of which formula is used, the flow of processing returns to the accumulation of C (commissions). The accumulation of commissions precedes the output of sales data and the priming read at the loop's end.

8.76 When the last record is processed, where does processing flow?

Whereas the NO branch of the LRC directs the flow of processing to the top of the loop, the YES branch details an output operation. The output of the accumulated total of commissions T is preceded by the special label, 'TOT COMM = $'. This PRINT symbol appears prior to the STOP symbol that closes the flowchart.

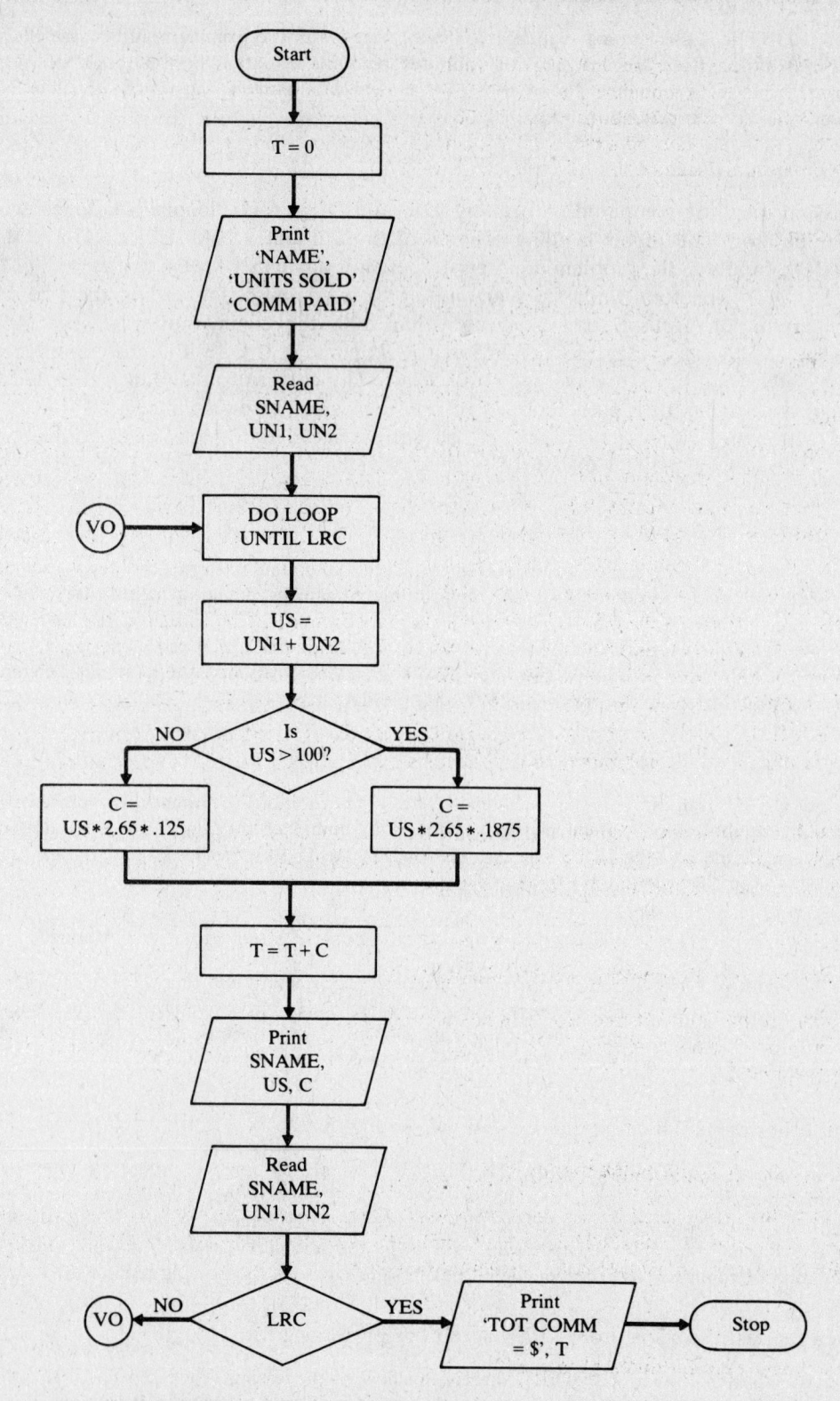

Fig. 8-10 This flowchart illustrates use of a priming read and DO/UNTIL looping sequence.

CHAP. 8] STRUCTURED DESIGNS 173

8.77 Can multiple groups of statements be incorporated into flow diagrams using structured concepts?

Sets of related statements are handled as modules within flowcharts and are defined using the predefined process symbol. Each module is logically positioned within the flowchart and identified by its predefined process symbol. The processing steps composing that module are then detailed in a separate flow diagram, which appears adjacent to the main flowchart. Problems 8.77–8.86 deal with the use and documentation of modules.

The following narrative refers to Probs. 8.78–8.86.

This problem describes the processing and accumulation of union dues. Three separate dues amounts are to be computed for each employee depending on his or her union affiliation. The total dues paid to each union must be accumulated; thus three accumulators are needed. Report headings are 'EMPLOYEE', 'UNION', and 'DUES PAID'. Inputs to the problem are the employee's name NAME, union code UC, and gross pay amount GROSS. Processing related to each union should be handled within its module. A union code of 1 notes a dues rate (R1) of 0.006. The dues paid to this local D1 is computed by multiplying the rate R by the gross pay amount GROSS and adding it to a base fee of $2.50. This dues amount D1 is accumulated separately T1. Print the employee's name, union code, dues amount, and the label 'LOCAL 126'. A union code of 2 notes a rate R2 of 0.008. The dues amount D2 is computed by multiplying this rate by the gross pay amount and adding it to a flat fee of $4.50. This second dues category is totaled within an accumulator T2. Output this employee's name, union code, dues amount, and label 'LOCAL 3351'. The third dues category is similarly handled. It uses a rate R3 of 0.010. This third dues amount D3 is computed by multiplying the rate by the gross pay and adding that to a fee of $6.50. A third accumulator T3 totals dues paid to this third local. Output the employee's name, union code, dues amount, and label 'LOCAL 3'. When processing is complete, output these three accumulated totals with appropriate labels. Use a priming read, LRC, and DO/UNTIL to control the looping sequence. Use modules to define the processing related to each union's dues computation and accumulation. Describe that processing within its own flow diagram.

(*Note*: As the problems become more complex, so do the narratives used to describe the problem. Each narrative must properly detail the processing steps involved for the entire problem, which means adequate documentation and explanation.)

8.78 How are the three accumulators documented?

The three accumulators are detailed using the datanames T1, T2, and T3. They are initialized by the first three processing symbols of the flowchart (Fig. 8-11), with their individual updates situated within their respective modules.

8.79 How are the three modules identified?

Each module is designated by a predefined process symbol, with a narrative indicating each module's number. Each module is logically positioned within the main flowchart, with the symbols composing the module represented in another flow diagram on that page.

8.80 Why are separate modules necessary?

Modules are used to group statements related to a processing activity. The rationale of using modules reinforces concepts related to top-down designs. Modular structures also simplify the appearance of flow diagrams. Modules composed of many instructions, if conventionally drawn, would make that leg of the flowchart unusually difficult to draw, although it would be correct.

Mod 1

- R1 = .006
- D1 = (R1 × GROSS) + 2.50
- T1 = T1 + D1
- Print NAME, UC, D1, 'LOCAL 126'
- Return

Mod 2

- R2 = .008
- D2 = (R2 * GROSS) + 4.50
- T2 = T2 + D2
- Print NAME, UC, D2, 'LOCAL 3551'
- Return

Mod 3

- R3 = .010
- D3 = (R3 * GROSS) + 6.50
- T3 = T3 + D3
- Print NAME, UC, D3, 'LOCAL 3'
- Return

Main flowchart

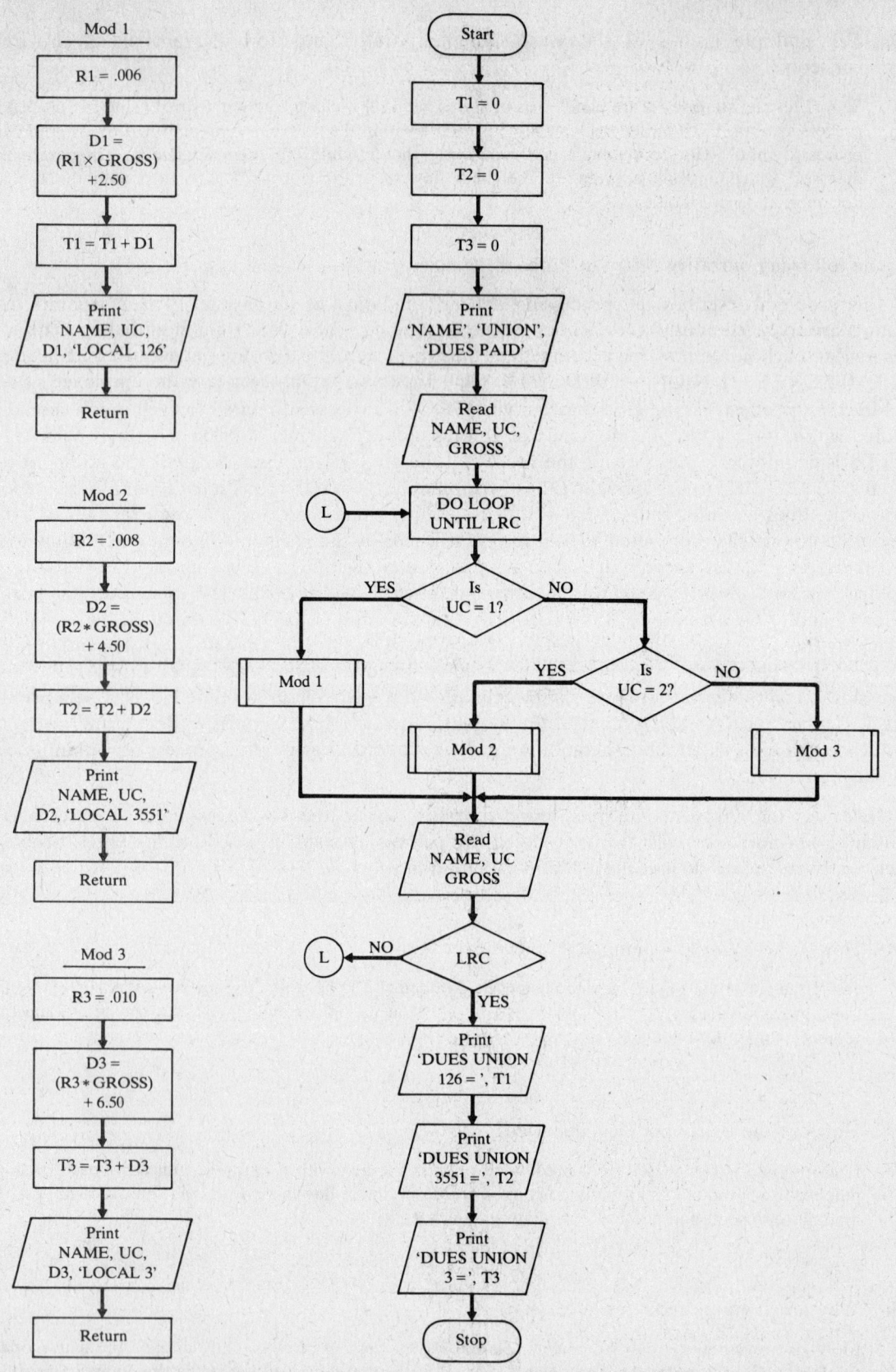

- Start
- T1 = 0
- T2 = 0
- T3 = 0
- Print 'NAME', 'UNION', 'DUES PAID'
- Read NAME, UC, GROSS
- L: DO LOOP UNTIL LRC
- Is UC = 1? YES → Mod 1; NO → Is UC = 2? YES → Mod 2; NO → Mod 3
- Read NAME, UC, GROSS
- LRC? NO → L; YES → continue
- Print 'DUES UNION 126 = ', T1
- Print 'DUES UNION 3551 = ', T2
- Print 'DUES UNION 3 = ', T3
- Stop

Fig. 8-11 These flow diagrams show the use of modules to handle the processing of three coded entries. Each module also appears in the main flowchart.

8.81 What are the differences in the three modules of Fig. 8-11?

Though the processing activities are similar, each module uses different values in processing and has slightly varied outputs. A programmer could not handle these outputs or statements simultaneously, so different instructions in separate modules are the best way to handle them. To prove this point, note that different rates were used, as well as three separate base-rate fees. Processing developed three dues amounts and three accumulators to enable their addition. Outputs for each union code also reflect the three union locals involved in processing.

8.82 What is the purpose of the RETURN processing symbol at each module's end?

The RETURN processing symbol reflects the true nature of the module when subsequently converted to software. In effect, the flow of processing will shift from the main flowchart to the respective module when that module's symbol is accessed. When the processing within that module is complete, the flow of processing returns to the main flowchart where its execution is resumed. The RETURN narrative details the transfer to and from the module, as well as its close.

8.83 How does the switch between a main flowchart and its modules parallel the actual execution of programs?

Consider reading the main flowchart and encountering a predefined process symbol within a loop. To determine the processing performed within that module, the programmer goes to the module's symbols and analyzes those processing steps. After that reading, the programmer switches to the main program where, once again, he or she continues its examination. The computer's execution of the program prepared from that modular flowchart will react the same way. The computer will shift to the module's processing in much the same fashion and return to the main program, once the module's processing is complete.

8.84 What programming concept is derived from the execution of modules, as reviewed in Prob. 8.83?

The concept of a subroutine parallels the processing of a module. A subroutine represents a group of statements that are executed as a single entity. Modules defined in flowcharts are represented as subroutines in programs. The execution of each subroutine will result from the computer's shift to the instructions composing that module.

8.85 Is the priming read evident in Fig. 8-11?

The priming read is used in this flowchart, as is the DO/UNTIL, to control looping. One READ symbol is positioned prior to the loop's start and end. The DO/UNTIL is bracketed by the DO processing symbol at the loop's start and the LRC decision at its end.

8.86 Why are three outputs needed on the YES branch of the LRC?

The three PRINT symbols denote the output of the three accumulated totals, T1, T2, and T3. Each is preceded by a label specially designed for the respective locale. As three separate I/O symbols are used, three lines of output are printed.

PSEUDOCODE

8.87 What is pseudocode?

Pseudocode is a hypothetical language that is used to detail the logic of programs. The statements of pseudocode parallel the structure of computer languages, thus permitting the conversion of its solutions to actual software.

8.88 Is pseudocode a flowcharting technique?

Pseudocode is not a flowcharting technique but a means of detailing the logic of a solution. The terms used by pseudocode look like program instructions and enable users to detail the logical position and type of statements that should be used in processing.

8.89 Can pseudocode solutions be developed from flowcharts?

Yes. The flowchart pictorially depicts the logic of a solution, whereas pseudocode represents that logic in instruction-like statements. Figure 8-12 (page 177) shows the flow diagram paralleling the logic used in the following pseudocode solution.

```
Start
Write headings
Read individual sales data
DO WHILE data exists
   Compute sales totals
   IF sales level is reached
      THEN compute commission using rate 1
      ELSE compute commission using rate 2
   Write individual sales data
   Read sales data
ENDIF last record check
Write closing label
Stop
```

8.90 Is the pseudocode solution an actual program?

The pseudocode solution detailed in Prob. 8.89 is not a program but uses statements that have a language-like appearance. Their structure is designed to help programmers prepare for the subsequent software that is to be written. Note that for almost every symbol on the flowchart, a pseudocode statement is provided. The conversion of the pseudocode solution to an actual program parallels the conversion of the flowchart to pseudocode.

8.91 How is the looping sequence defined in pseudocode?

In the pseudocode solution, the looping sequence is defined using a DO/WHILE. This technique indicates the looping should continue while data exist. The DO/WHILE statement notes the loop's start, with an ENDIF line detailing its close. The ENDIF instruction directs that the loop be closed; if the last record has not been processed, looping will continue.

8.92 Why are the statements between the DO/WHILE and ENDIF indented?

The indentations highlight the position of the loop and the statements composing it.

8.93 Why are statements following the IF line indented?

The indentation of lines commencing with THEN and ELSE highlights the use of an IF/THEN/ELSE control sequence. This conditional uses both of its branches to define two sets of computations. The indenting points toward each of these branches and the processing associated with them.

8.94 Does pseudocode utilize structured design concepts?

Yes. Many top-down techniques are integrated into pseudocode solutions. Figure 8-12 demonstrates the use of a DO/WHILE, priming read, and IF/THEN/ELSE sequence, as well as many conventional flowchart techniques.

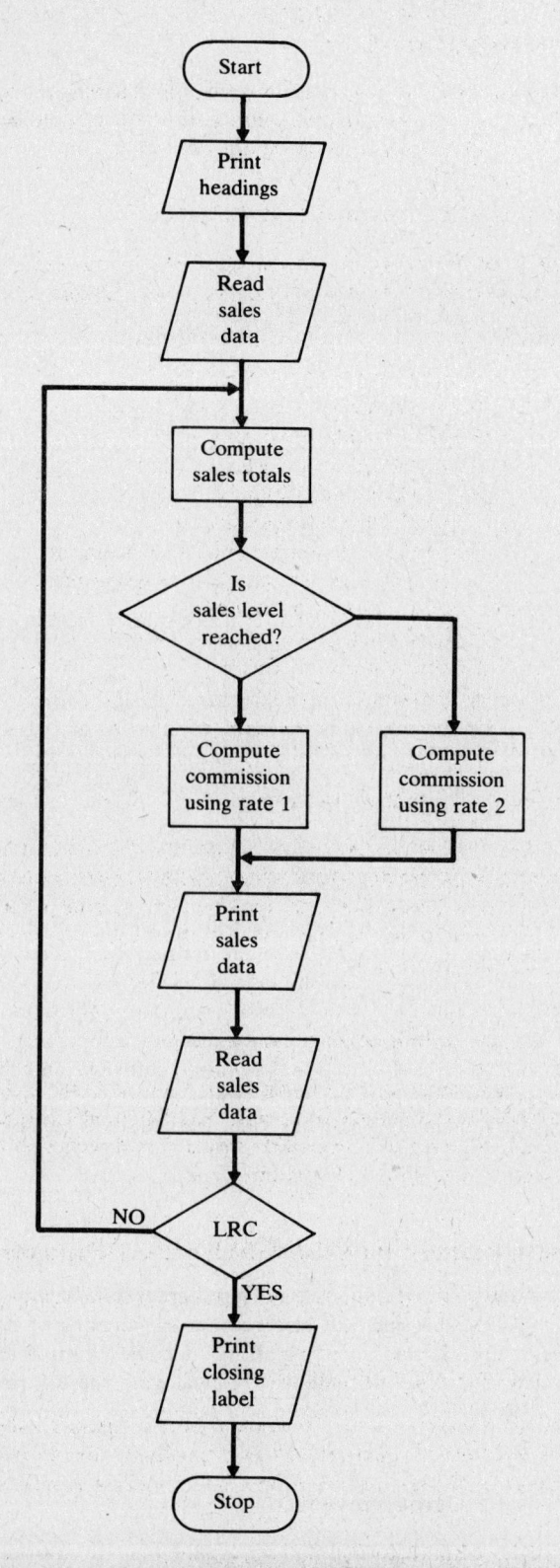

Fig. 8-12 Pseudocode solutions enable users to draft potential software approaches in a hypothetical language format. These solutions are often prepared with the assistance of a flowchart.

8.95 Is pseudocode widely utilized?

No. Although pseudocode is used by many programmers as a planning tool, it has not achieved the level of success anticipated by its proponents. Its detractors feel that it is a duplication of flowcharting efforts and tends to confuse users because of its program-like appearance. Generally, the application of pseudocode is left open as an option to its users.

THE PERSONNEL INVOLVED

8.96 Can top-down techniques be used by individual programming personnel?

Yes. The top-down approach may be used on an individual as well as a group basis, depending on the project being worked on. If a programmer is working on a program that will not interact with any other software, the structured approach is readily applied as the programmer needs it. As is the case most often, large projects require a coordinated effort in which the structured design approach is the keynote tying all aspects of the project together. The modular structure of top-down designs enables project teams to work separately but on a coordinated basis.

8.97 When a large structured project is attacked, is a complete project team put together for this purpose?

Yes. A team of programmers that works on a structured design project may be referred to as *chief programmer team* (*CPT*). This designation is normally used in larger organizations, where formal titles are mandated. In smaller DP centers, this title may be omitted, with the team informally assuming its work responsibilities.

8.98 What individuals compose the CPT group?

The chief programmer team is usually a small select group of programmers, under supervision of one person. The title assigned the leader varies, with the terms *project leader*, *chief programmer*, or *team leader* most often used. The CPT is assigned the task of developing sound, well-conceived software. The chief programmer coordinates all project work, assigns supporting programmers, and assumes responsibility for the more difficult software assignments. Usually supporting the chief programmer is a software specialist who acts as an assistant, writes required software, and checks all software written by the team. Other programmers complete the CPT group, with their number varying in relation to the project's size. A critical CPT member is the librarian, who catalogs and updates all the documentation produced by the team.

8.99 What documentation does the CPT produce?

The CPT will generate many types of paperwork. This chapter has already reviewed the HIPO package and its component parts. The librarian will also receive all versions of flow diagrams, listings of the software under development, diagrams depicting all I/O documents, structure charts, narratives describing the flow of processing, and other documents. By cataloging these forms, a complete record of the CPT's work is created. The documents also serve as a reference for research or subsequent projects.

8.100 How is the work of the CPT group reviewed?

Structured efforts are reviewed on a formal and informal basis. An informal design review is instituted during the early phases of a project to provide an initial review of the work underway. All available paperwork is reviewed, and recommendations are made with regard to potential changes or methods of improving the project's design. This type of intermediary review provides a means of controlling a project, ensuring that its initial direction is proper.

8.101 What type of formal review process is used?

The formal design review, which is a more rigorous review, takes into consideration every piece of documentation. A select group of supervisory people evaluate the documentation related to each module of the proposed design. This review team ensures that all parts of the design properly interface. All I/O documents are rated, procedures for transferring data are examined, the impact of supporting software is evaluated, and, generally, all aspects of the proposed design are assessed. Each module is reviewed in relation to its accuracy, thoroughness, logic, level of detail, clarity, and intended use.

8.102 With the formal review process, what is the purpose of a structured walkthrough?

The structured walkthrough is a review session in which the logic applied to a module's processing is rigorously tested. Structured walkthroughs are used to evaluate the thoroughness of a design, the interface of modules within that design, and the eventual software developed for those modules.

8.103 Is the structured walkthrough a mere formality?

Structured walkthroughs are extremely important and demanding sessions because every aspect of a module's structure is evaluated. Because of the intensity of the walkthrough sessions, these meetings are usually limited to one hour in length, and only one is scheduled per morning or afternoon period. Errors, poor logic, or discrepancies uncovered by the structured review panel are recorded, corrected by CPT personnel, and reviewed at a subsequent structured walkthrough.

8.104 What personnel compose the structured walkthrough panel?

The panel conducting the structured walkthrough is generally composed of no more than five people, with one person acting as moderator. The moderator chairs the review session, recording all pertinent comments regarding actions to be taken, changes, errors, improvements, suggested modifications, and general comments of any type. Other panel members, usually from the programming staff or CPT group, serve on a rotating basis to offer the broadest review base possible. This diversity of opinion permits the widest range of analysis and commentary.

8.105 How much time is provided to the structured walkthrough panel to review materials?

As structured walkthroughs are very detailed analyses, sufficient time must be afforded the panelists to adequately review materials related to any modules. Normally, a 2- to 4-week period is set aside to permit review of pertinent documentation. Moderators are given a week to prepare their summary of the structured walkthrough sessions.

Review Questions

8.106 The construction of integrated, modular units is a characteristic of top-down designs. (*a*) True, (*b*) false.

8.107 Structured designs require the analysis of only one part of a problem and the design of a solution to that module's specifications. (*a*) True, (*b*) false.

8.108 Within a structure chart the module representing the chart's purpose is the main control module. (*a*) True, (*b*) false.

8.109 The visual table of contents uses a number scheme that clearly identifies each module within it. (*a*) True, (*b*) false.

8.110 Overview HIPO diagrams offer a broad review of the lower-level modules within a top-down design. (*a*) True, (*b*) false.

8.111 Consecutive processing operations are represented by the processing sequence, which is a basic control block structure. (*a*) True, (*b*) false.

8.112 When composing structured solutions, a restriction of five or fewer modules is invoked. (*a*) True, (*b*) false.

8.113 The module structure of structured programming solutions does not assist in the debugging process when errors are found. (*a*) True, (*b*) false.

8.114 The priming read is an input technique that uses only one input at the start of the looping sequence. (*a*) True, (*b*) false.

8.115 The priming read is never used with an LRC. (*a*) True, (*b*) false.

8.116 Pseudocode is an actual programming language in which top-down designs are written. (*a*) True, (*b*) false.

8.117 Pseudocode solutions may be developed with the assistance of a flowchart. (*a*) True, (*b*) false.

8.118 Pseudocode solutions use a variety of visual and hypothetical language techniques to document top-down designs. (*a*) True, (*b*) false.

8.119 The CPT moderator plays a critical role in the review of structured design solutions, as well as recording all comments made. (*a*) True, (*b*) false.

8.120 The term that is used interchangeably with top-down design is (*a*) bottom-up design; (*b*) structured design; (*c*) modular design; (*d*) *a* and *b*.

8.121 A characteristic of the structured design approach is (*a*) the development of modular design elements; (*b*) improved documentation; (*c*) more well-defined, organized, and logical solutions; (*d*) all of the above.

8.122 The form directly derived from a structure chart is the (*a*) organization chart; (*b*) flowchart; (*c*) visual table of contents; (*d*) top-down diagram.

8.123 A rule applied to modules of structured design is (*a*) A module may possess more than one purpose. (*b*) Each module should be unique. (*c*) A module must have a minimum of one entry and exit. (*d*) All of the above.

8.124 Specifics related to the lower modules of a structured design are described within a(n) (*a*) structure chart; (*b*) overview HIPO diagram; (*c*) detail HIPO diagram; (*d*) flow diagram narrative.

8.125 The control block structure used to define conditional operations is the (*a*) processing sequence; (*b*) IF/THEN/ELSE sequence; (*c*) looping sequence; (*d*) priming sequence.

8.126 The looping sequence that controls the execution of an exact number of repetitions is the (*a*) FOR/NEXT; (*b*) DO/UNTIL; (*c*) DO/WHILE; (*d*) HIPO loop.

8.127 The equivalent of a module of instructions is represented in a program as a (*a*) DO/UNTIL; (*b*) processing symbol; (*c*) subroutine; (*d*) main control module.

8.128 Within the CPT the person assigned to catalog all documentation is the (*a*) chief programmer; (*b*) program specialist; (*c*) CPT documentalist; (*d*) librarian.

8.129 A specialized form of formal review is the (a) detailed HIPO review; (b) structured design review; (c) structured walkthrough; (d) all of the above.

8.130 Use of the _____ results in partial, nonintegrated solutions that duplicate effort and are costly.

8.131 The elimination of GO TOs is a prime objective of _____ solutions.

8.132 The preliminary hierarchical organization of a top-down solution into its various levels and modules is represented within a(n) _____ chart.

8.133 Modules at the lowest level of a structure chart are referred to as _____ modules.

8.134 A group of documents that detail all aspects of a top-down design compose a _____ package.

8.135 Modules composing top-down solutions are represented within flow diagrams using the _____ symbol.

8.136 The application of top-down design concepts to the preparation of software is referred to as _____.

8.137 The looping sequence that continues while a specific value exists is defined via the _____.

8.138 The flow diagrams representing modules of a structured solution close with a processing symbol containing the narrative _____.

8.139 A hypothetical language used to detail structured solutions is _____.

8.140 The group of programmers assigned to implement structured designs is called the _____.

8.141 The preliminary analysis of a top-down design is performed via a(n) _____ review.

Answers: 8.106 (a); 8.107 (b); 8.108 (a); 8.109 (a); 8.110 (b); 8.111 (a); 8.112 (b); 8.113 (b); 8.114 (b); 8.115 (b); 8.116 (b); 8.117 (a); 8.118 (a); 8.119 (a); 8.120 (b); 8.121 (d); 8.122 (c); 8.123 (b); 8.124 (c); 8.125 (b); 8.126 (a); 8.127 (c); 8.128 (d); 8.129 (c); 8.130 bottom-up technique; 8.131 top-down; 8.132 structure; 8.133 processing; 8.134 HIPO; 8.135 predefined process; 8.136 structured programming; 8.137 DO/WHILE; 8.138 RETURN; 8.139 pseudocode; 8.140 chief programmer team (CPT); 8.141 informal design.

Supplementary Problems

8.142 What are the five major characteristics associated with structured design solutions?

8.143 List and describe the three rules applied to modules within structured designs.

8.144 What are the structure and purpose of the following pieces of HIPO documentation:
(a) Structure chart
(b) Visual table of contents
(c) Overview HIPO diagram
(d) Detail HIPO diagram
(e) Flowchart

8.145 Why is the identifying numbering scheme used with the visual table of contents helpful in detailing each module's position?

8.146 Draw and explain the three control block sequences used within flow diagrams. Are these readily applied to structured solutions?

8.147 What are the function and purpose of the following looping techniques?
  (a) FOR/NEXT
  (b) DO/WHILE
  (c) DO/UNTIL

Use diagrams to support your discussions.

8.148 Using Fig. 8-2, prepare the following diagrams:
  (a) Draw the overview HIPO diagram for module 4.1 of the visual table of contents shown.
  (b) Draw the detail HIPO diagram for module 4.1.1 of the visual table of contents shown.

8.149 Draw the flowchart to satisfy the following problem narrative:

The problem relates to the computation and accumulation of inventory costs. The report headings appearing atop each column are 'PART', 'QUANTITY', 'UNIT COST', and 'INV COST'. Inputs to the problem are the part's name PART, quantity on hand Q, and unit cost of that item UC. The inventory cost of that item INVC is computed by multiplying the quantity on hand and its unit cost. On each loop accumulate the inventory cost of each item. Print out the part's name, quantity on hand, unit cost, and inventory cost of that item. When looping stops, output the accumulated total of all inventory costs, preceded by the label 'TOT INV COST'.

Use a DO/UNTIL and an LRC to control looping, and a priming read to facilitate the input of data. Ensure that the required accumulator is initialized.

8.150 Draw the flowchart to satisfy the following problem narrative.

The computation of overtime pay is accomplished. Two overtime rates are used depending on the employee's overtime code. Two accumulators are needed to separately total each type of overtime amount. The column headings used are 'EMPLOYEE', 'OTC', 'HRS', 'RATE', and 'OT PAY'. Inputs are the employee's name NAME, overtime code OTC, and total hours worked HRS. If the overtime code equals 1, processing related to that code is handled in its own module. The same is true for an overtime code equal to 2.

In module 1, computations related to an overtime code of 1 are presented. The overtime rate R is $7.50 per hour. The number of overtime hours H1 is computed by subtracting 40 from the total hours worked. The overtime pay OT1 is calculated by multiplying the overtime rate by the overtime hours worked. Accumulate this amount into its own accumulator T1 each time this amount is computed. Print out each employee's name, overtime code, total hours worked, overtime rate, and overtime pay.

Module 2 is similarly constructed. The overtime rate R2 for a code of 2 is $10.50. The overtime hours worked H2 is computed by subtracting 40 from the total hours worked. The overtime pay OT2 is calculated by multiplying the overtime rate by the overtime hours worked. Accumulate this overtime pay amount, whenever this figure is computed, in its own accumulator T2. Print out each employee's name, overtime code, total hours worked, overtime rate, and overtime pay. Use a DO/UNTIL with an LRC to control looping and a priming read to input data. When the last record has been processed, output the two accumulated totals using the labels 'TOT OT1 = ' and 'TOT OT2 = ', respectively.

8.151 What are the pros and cons of using pseudocodes to prepare structured solutions? Could pseudocode's language-like appearance work against the user?

Glossary

Bottom-up technique. A nonstructured design approach in which solutions are developed on a nonintegrated basis.

Chief programmer team (CPT). A team of programmers, assigned to the development of structured programming solutions, consisting of a chief programmer, an assistant, supporting programmers, and librarian.

Control block sequences. Three fundamental processing techniques associated with top-down designs to include the processing, IF/THEN/ELSE, and looping sequences.

Detail HIPO diagrams. A HIPO form used with lower-level processing modules, which details all input, processing, and output activities for that module; part of the HIPO package.

DO/UNTIL. A looping technique, used with structured designs, that directs that looping continue until a conditional code is encountered.

DO/WHILE. A looping technique, used with top-down designs, that directs that looping continue while a specific condition is maintained.

Formal design review. A formal rigorous review of a top-down design solution, with careful emphasis placed on each module's function and documentation; exemplified by structured walkthroughs.

FOR/NEXT. A looping technique, associated with structured solutions, by which an exact number of loops are to be performed.

HIPO. An acronym for hierarchy plus input-processing-output.

HIPO package. A group of documents describing all aspects of a top-down solution, consisting of a visual table of contents, overview HIPO diagrams, detail HIPO diagrams, and any other desired documentation.

IF/THEN/ELSE sequence. A fundamental control block sequence representing conditional operations and the resulting branches.

Informal design review. The preliminary, informal review of a structured design to determine whether the project is meeting its intended goals.

Looping sequence. A fundamental control block sequence identifying repetitive processing operations within a loop.

Main control module. The topmost module on a structure chart noting the overall purpose of the chart.

Overview HIPO diagram. A HIPO form used with the higher levels of a visual table of contents identifying the module's overall purpose.

Predefined process symbol. A rectangular-shaped symbol that represents modules of related operations in flowcharts.

Priming read. An input technique, associated with structured solutions, that facilitates exits from looping sequences.

Processing and control modules. The intermediary modules on a structure chart.

Processing sequence. A fundamental control block sequence that represents consecutive processing operations.

Pseudocode. A hypothetical language used to construct the logic of structured design solutions.

Structure chart. A hierarchical chart detailing those modules composing a top-down design solution; it consists of multiple levels and modules.

Structured design. A systematic, modular approach to designing software solutions and improving the flow of information through an organization; emphasis placed on well-conceived modular and logically accurate solutions that eliminate the use of GO TOs.

Structured programming. The application of top-down principles to the design of software.

Structured walkthrough. A rigorous review session, used within the formal design review of a top-down solution, during which all aspects of a design are tested.

Subroutine. A program module composed of related statements that is handled as a single entity.

Top-down design. See *structured design*.

Visual table of contents. A hierarchical chart, similar to a structure chart, in which each module carries with it a unique identifying number.

Chapter 9

Systems Analysis and Design

9.1 THE SYSTEMS GROUP AND ITS ANALYSTS

The term *systems analysis* refers to the evaluation of how well an organization handles the information it generates and distributes through its structure. This analysis is performed by *systems analysts* who work within an organization's *data processing (DP) department*. Analysts work within the systems group, one of the three groups that usually make up the DP department. The remaining two groups are the programming group and the operations group.

The *operations group* contains personnel who work directly with computer hardware and facilitate the handling of data. The *programming group* assumes responsibility for developing all needed software. The *systems group* handles projects involving the evaluation of an organization's information handling abilities.

In performing their function, analysts may work directly with computerized systems as well as manual systems. In either case the analyst is concerned with how efficiently that system handles its data. Though analysts operate on an individual basis, the majority of their systems tasks are performed on a team-like basis. For the purposes of this discussion, a *system* is a way of achieving a stated goal. Systems analysis relates to evaluation of the steps taken to achieve that goal.

The use of analyst teams to perform systems studies has many positive effects. Analysts can share personal experiences common to a system, offer practical advice based on those experiences, suggests areas of research, and collectively brainstorm for new ideas. These group sessions permit analysts to draw on their many years of DP experience, formal schooling, and widespread practical exposure. Depending on the scope of a project, a systems study may take from two to twenty-four months to complete.

9.2 BUSINESS SYSTEMS

The five fundamental business systems are the payroll, personnel, accounts payable, accounts receivable, and inventory systems. Most other versions of business systems are derived from these five fundamental systems.

A *payroll system* consists of all the documentation, computer support, people, and equipment necessary to process data and pay the employees of an organization. This includes preparing paychecks, updating all payroll records, preparing required internal and federal (and state) payroll reports, accounting for the dispersal of deductions to governmental and private agencies, and providing access for any employee inquiries.

Personnel systems describe varied aspects of an organization's work force. The outputs generated by personnel systems are frequently used in compiling federal laborpower reports.

Retail organizations are major users of *accounts receivable systems*, since these systems detail monies that are owed to an organization. Conversely, *accounts payable systems* focus on the monies that are owed by the organization. These two systems parallel each other, requiring the continued maintenance of files, their update, reporting on monies due and owed, providing customer statements and invoices, and recording payments made.

Inventory systems monitor the status of items held in an inventory. These systems report on the quantities of goods on hand, as well as when items should be purchased to replenish stock and what critical items are needed. Inventory systems are crucial to organizations that maintain large and costly inventories.

9.3 SYSTEMS ANALYSIS

When business systems do not function efficiently, systems analysis techniques are used to determine the source of the inefficiencies. When problem areas are uncovered, a *systems design* effort is instituted to correct the deficiencies and create a new system. The entire sequence of analysis and design is traditionally divided into the three major components:

1. Analysis of the existing system
2. Problem definition
3. Design of the new system

In the analysis phase the existing system is scrutinized for problem areas, and the state of the existing system is recorded. In the *problem definition* the problem areas are individually identified after having been uncovered in the analysis effort. In the design of the new system, all aspects of the new system are detailed, including those incorporated to rectify inefficiencies recorded in the problem definition.

The need for a systems analysis effort may stem from management's desire to make organizational changes and seek new markets or from newly passed laws, stiffer competition, changing operational needs, or the obsolescence of existing existing equipment. The request for a systems study may result from a managerial directive, the *scheduled review* of a system, or an analyst's recognition of an inefficient system.

9.4 COLLECTING DATA

The *collection of data* refers to the collection of materials upon which to base the systems analysis. It is a critical phase of the analysis effort since the quality of the analysis depends on the accuracy of the data collected. Analysts will gain the raw data needed for analysis from existing I/O documents, personal observations, personnel interviews, prior systems studies, and examination of procedure manuals.

Existing I/O forms identify the data used by a system and enable analysts to assess the accuracy of those data and the information provided by the system. Personal observations enable the analyst to gain a firsthand knowledge of the system's operation and provide a basis of comparison when evaluating the performance of both the system and personnel. By interviewing the people who work within the system, the analyst views the system's operation from the user's standpoint and can often gain probable solutions to problem areas. Prior systems studies provide a historical perspective from which to judge the existing system's function and structure. Procedure or organization manuals provide a formal view of the system's purpose and a description of jobs related to a system and define the steps constituting procedures used by that system.

Two graphic tools used by the analyst include the printer spacing chart and storage layout form. The printer spacing chart is used to document the appearance of I/O formats in both hardcopy and softcopy. The storage layout form is used to document the contents of a file, sequentially listing each of the fields composing the record format on which that file is based. Both forms appear within the documentation detailing the existing system, the problem definition, and the design of the new system.

9.5 SYSTEMS FLOWCHARTS

Systems flowcharts are diagrams that depict the flow of information through an organization. Special symbols are used to depict the computerized and manual operations used in handling data. Accompanying systems flowcharts are *systems narratives* that detail in a step-by-step basis the operations depicted by the flowchart and logic involved. These forms assist the analyst in both the analysis and design of business systems as they permit the visual documentation of procedures used in the handling of data and the distribution of information.

9.6 DESIGN OF THE NEW SYSTEM

With the analysis of the existing system completed and the preparation of the problem definition, the design of the new system (to replace the existing one) may commence. In this effort a variety of potential alternatives will be developed to afford management a choice of solutions. Each alternative will be developed with sufficient detail to provide management with a sense of that solution's complexity and cost.

Included in this detail are I/O formats, file structures, systems flowcharts of critical procedures, and savings accruable to each approach. The savings and expenses associated with each solution can play a vital part in management's decision. Expenses are prepared from estimates of the personnel, hardware, procedures, and equipment used in the new systems. Savings are computed from reductions in personnel and equipment, the improved handling of information, and efficiencies resulting from the new system's operation.

The new alternative systems are presented to management for their consideration. After selection of one design alternative, management will direct a further investigation of that solution.

9.7 THE FEASIBILITY COMMITTEE

The further investigation of the systems alternative chosen by management is accomplished by a *feasibility study*. The study is performed by a select group of people referred to as the *feasibility committee*. The main purpose of this study is to determine whether the alternative chosen represents a feasible and sound approach to solving the problems uncovered by the systems study.

Composing the feasibility committee are a top executive, senior systems analyst, department representatives, and an outside consultant. Each contributes a level of expertise and knowledge to the committee's work. The top-level executive offers guidance on budget matters, and the senior analyst provides guidelines on systems and procedural information. Department representatives act as informational sources, with the outside consultant serving as an independent voice in the committee's discussions.

The feasibility committee evaluates the alternative solution, preparing critical I/O documents, operational procedures, and cost estimates. An evaluation of the system's feasibility is prepared for management, which must act on those recommendations. The feasibility report is retained within the systems group's library for future investigative efforts.

Solved Problems

THE SYSTEMS GROUP AND ITS ANALYSTS

9.1 What does the term *systems analysis* mean?

The term *systems analysis* refers to the process of evaluating how organizations handle the information they generate and how those facts are distributed throughout their organizational structure. Systems analysis attempts to determine how well an organization uses its information and the accuracy of the information provided.

9.2 Why is this form of analysis important?

How well an organization functions often depends on the information it uses. Businesses that are provided with the best available data stand a far better chance at succeeding in their endeavors. A management equipped with the most current information can respond to changing business conditions and perhaps avoid the pitfalls created by unplanned events.

9.3 Who performs the analysis function?

Systems analysis studies are performed by systems analysts who are assigned the specific responsibility of assessing the efficiency of an organization's information handling activities.

9.4 Where within the organization does the systems analyst work?

The systems analyst works within the systems group of the data processing (DP) department. The systems group represents one of three operational areas in the DP department, as shown in Fig. 9-1. Individuals involved in systems-related studies are teamed together in the systems group.

```
            Data
         processing
         department
        /     |     \
   Operations Programming Systems
     group     group      group
```

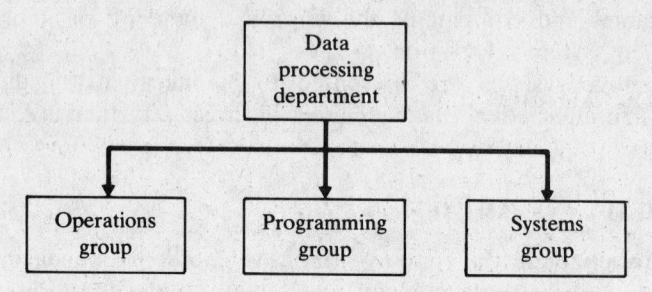

Fig. 9-1 The data processing department of an organization is normally divided into three groups.

9.5 In addition to the systems group, what other groups compose the DP department?

The other units composing the DP department are the programming group and the operations group. The programming group assumes the task of developing the software required by the organization. The operations group is responsible for operating the hardware in the computer system. Both groups interact with the computer directly, whereas the systems group serves the functions of advising and planning.

9.6 Why are these groups differentiated?

The programming and operations groups are directly involved in the handling and processing of data. The systems group evaluates their efficiency, as well as any other units within that company. Their operational purpose is to assess the efficiency of these activities and the quality of information handling. Analysts are the vehicle for gathering and evaluating data regarding an organization's performance.

9.7 Does the systems analyst always work with computers?

The analyst's work covers a variety of areas and projects. The analyst may be involved with the evaluation of whether to buy or rent a new computer, the replacement of existing hardware with new terminals, the types of forms used to handle audits, customer responses or bank drafts, the preparation of new computer outputs using both softcopy and hardcopy formats, or the procedure used to handle employee personal data. The analyst's work can take him or her to literally every level of an organization to examine both manual and computerized procedures. Again, the analyst is concerned with improving the flow and quality of information through the organization, and an integral part of these activities is noncomputerized tasks. Thus analysts must concern themselves with both manual and computer-related activities.

9.8 Why then are analysts associated with computers?

Since much of today's work is computer-oriented, the analyst must focus on the computer's activities within an organization. The analyst cannot overlook the procedures that precede or follow the computer's processing of data. If input procedures introduce erroneous data, then all processing activities are of little value. Tardily distributed computer outputs equally negate the computer's impact. Manual procedures must be accurate and efficient to properly interface with the computer's handling of data and to complement data processing activities.

9.9 In performing systems studies, does the analyst work alone?

Though analysts may individually undertake small studies, the majority of systems analysis projects involve a team of people. The team-like structure permits the widest exchange of ideas and is the proper approach to systems analysis.

9.10 What does the word *system* mean?

The term *system* expresses a way of achieving a stated goal. Analysts may concern themselves with many aspects of a system, but generally a team is the best way to evaluate the performance of an entire system.

9.11 What are some examples of the projects that are individual and team-oriented?

A project individually undertaken by an analyst might include the redesign of an input form used to record payments received or an output that documents the number of salespeople attaining a special commission status. A team-oriented project might involve the analysis of a company's entire payroll processing or the bidding procedures used when purchasing and paying for new equipment. The first two applications involve individual items that may be handled on a stand-alone basis. The second two projects entail a larger quantity of resources and involve a coordinated group of activities to accomplish their purposes.

9.12 Why is the team structure suitable to systems analysis?

In analyzing a large system's activities, many factors come into play. Often analysts encounter special situations that are foreign to their knowledge and thwart analysis. By discussing these difficulties with the team, other analysts can offer advice based on their past experience as to how to overcome the problem. If they do not know an answer, they can suggest a potential source of data or someone who has encountered a similar systems problem. The systems team is really a crucible of ideas that permits analysts to test concepts and potential ideas and to offer advice.

9.13 What educational and professional backgrounds do most analysts have?

Most analysts have a minimum of five to eight years DP experience, in addition to a college degree. They generally have software development experience but prefer to apply their expertise on a broader basis. Analyzing systems provides a wider latitude within which to work. Disciplines common to analysts include accounting, engineering, philosophy, math, management science, and varied computer fields.

9.14 How long do systems projects last?

The length of time consumed by a systems project varies in proportion to its complexity. Generally, systems projects may extend from 2 to 24 months. A short project might involve the redesign of an I/O form, its testing and implementation. A far more time-consuming project might involve the replacement of an existing computer system—where time is needed to prepare for and implement the new hardware, train employees slated to work with it, and develop the procedures necessary to facilitate its use.

9.15 Do analysts rely heavily on their practical experience?

Yes. Practical experience is a key element in the analyst's education. This practical exposure provides the analyst with an internal yardstick against which to judge the viability of implemented solutions. Past experience enables the analyst to evaluate proposed solutions and modify them to maximize their effectiveness.

BUSINESS SYSTEMS

9.16 What is a business system?

A business system is an organized means of achieving a stated business goal. Naturally, the physical configuration of a system and the constraints applied to it reflect the organization in which it is used. These differences are reflected within the actual reports used, data handling procedures unique to each organization, deadlines applied to specific processing activities, and the employees involved.

9.17 Are there fundamental business systems from which most other systems are derived?

Yes. The five fundamental business systems from which most systems derive their structure are:
(1) Payroll system
(2) Personnel system
(3) Accounts receivable
(4) Accounts payable
(5) Inventory

These systems were the first to be developed to handle principal business activities deemed important by a consensus of management. Their development provided management with their initial exposure to computers. Using these five systems as prototypes, management was able to direct the preparation of subsequent business systems more suited to the unique requirements of their organizations.

9.18 What constitutes a payroll system?

A payroll system consists of all forms, procedures, files, equipment, personnel, and computer support necessary to completely process the payment of employees. A payroll system fully handles all tax deductions, personal deductions, and the update of payroll data related to each employee. It provides for the actual payment of employees, a record of that payment, the modification of all payroll records, and the preparation of payroll reports. The payroll system must also generate all tax documents to include paychecks, W-2 statements, 941 quarterly reports, and a wide range of federal, state, and municipal employment tax filings. Another payroll responsibility is the accurate reporting of all personal deductions to include bonds, medical and life insurance, profit-sharing plans, stock options, credit union deductions, and the garnishing of an employee's salary by a creditor. These accumulated totals must be reported accurately to both the recipient of these monies and the individuals from whose salaries these amounts were deducted. The computer's support makes it possible to accurately and promptly process a payroll, providing the input data are properly handled on a timely basis.

9.19 Do the other systems encourage such detail?

Yes. All the other business systems mandate an equal level of detail within their processing activities. Each system must be able to create the required files, update those files to maintain the most current level of data, and report the results of processing on a timely basis. All documentation used by a system must be clearly prepared and must detail every operational aspect of the system. It is the analyst's responsibility to ensure that a system is functioning properly and that it contains all the required elements and that each aspect of the system's operation is documented.

9.20 What does a personnel system monitor?

In a large organization there exists a need to monitor the employees working for it. Employees represent a valuable company resource, and access to information on what is known about their talents should be immediate and informative. A personnel system serves management in this capacity since it maintains up-to-date records on all employees. It should be noted that a personnel system is of greatest benefit to large corporations, where the size of the work force prohibits manual handling of such data.

9.21 How are the outputs of a personnel system used?

At one time the outputs of a personnel system were strictly an internal reporting vehicle. These outputs provided information on the size and personnel makeup of departments, the management existing at each level, departmental job openings, special job skills held by individual employees, and projected personnel needs for upcoming projects. In other words, the information concerning the people working for the organization and their skills. Recently, however, federal laborpower reporting requirements have made personnel systems more complex. Federal legislation now mandates that corporations report on their hiring and placement of women and minorities in their work force, as well as prepare a wealth of other affirmative action reports. In addition, internal organizational needs have necessitated the refinement of personnel systems. These systems must now produce lists of restricted work programs, candidates eligible for promotion and entry into critical management positions, and special assignments in emergency situations.

9.22 How might the features of a personnel system be used?

Consider a case in which an emergency situation calls for a group of corporate specialists to be brought together to handle a specific problem. An online personnel system could provide an immediate list of candidates in each category of specialization, ranking each individual by experience, skill, and cross-specializations. Within seconds of the data's entry, the computer could commence its outputs of information drawn from the supporting personnel system.

9.23 To what extent is immediate response a factor in accounts receivable and accounts payable systems?

Accounts receivable and accounts payable systems are operational opposites of each other; however, they do possess many similar features. Each monitors a flow of money, but in different directions. An accounts receivable system oversees monies that are owed to a company, whereas an accounts payable system oversees monies that are owed by the organization. Generally, an accounts receivable system incorporates a faster response vehicle because of an organization's need to collect cash from many individuals within a relatively short timespan. The timing factor is not as critical in accounts payable systems because the organization makes its payments on a periodic basis, within a weekly or biweekly time frame.

9.24 Where are accounts receivable systems commonly encountered?

Accounts receivable systems are the mainstay of credit card systems used by retail organizations. The monthly statement output by credit card organizations provides a summary of the monies owed to them for purchases made since the last reporting period. Use of this form of computerized accounts receivable system is widespread. Regional and national organizations like Sears and American Express are fully operative accounts receivable systems utilizing credit cards as a primary means generating inputs to their systems.

9.25 Do these types of accounts receivable systems exhibit the operational characteristics associated with other systems?

Accounts receivable systems are comparably configured with the other business systems. They too must provide for the creation and update of files and the prompt reporting of information, and be capable of adapting to changing conditions. These similarities apply to both accounts receivable and accounts payable systems.

9.26 Where are accounts payable systems found?

Any organization that pays bills, including households, is a potential user of an accounts payable system. This system's purpose is to advise the user of the amount that should be paid out and the payment due date and to generate the correct payment. Organizations that use large amounts of raw materials or possess vast inventories of goods are highly dependent on accounts payable systems.

9.27 Is time a critical factor with accounts payable?

Most accounts payable systems are configured to handle data within a periodic cycle. The period is based on the organization's needs, usually conforming to a 7-, 15-, 30-, 60-, or 90-day cycle, with payments issued accordingly. An integral factor in most accounts payable systems is the ability to adjust the required payment to a billing cycle, thus issuing the payment only when it is truly needed, that is, not prematurely. Consequently, a company can conserve its cash outlays and thus improve its cash flow since payments are made only in relation to their due dates. Another operational feature of accounts payable systems is the capacity to take advantage of discounts offered to organizations that make prompt payment. Often, vendors offer a discount if their bills are paid prior to a specific date. The vendors get their money early, and the buyer gets a reduced price. Again the system should adjust payments to required due dates, obtaining those discounts deemed essential by management.

9.28 Which of the two accounting systems is better suited to online processing activities?

The accounts receivable system is much more suited to online processing because of the frequency of transactions. Many retail organizations use online processing to support their credit card systems, verifying all transactions as they are handled. This type of online control has been instrumental in reducing the amount of bogus and fraudulent credit card sales. Using an online accounts receivable system, the clerk can quickly ascertain whether a customer account is valid and whether to complete the transaction. Questionable sales are automatically flagged by the system, which alerts the inquiring clerk to the credit refusal and directs him or her to request assistance from the floor manager. An online accounts receivable system enables any organization to respond to readily changing operational needs and to tightly control the issuance of goods on credit. In contrast, accounts payable systems do not have as critical a time constraint. If a discrepancy in billing arises or if the organization is not pleased with the goods or services received, payments may be delayed indefinitely until satisfaction is achieved.

9.29 How are accounts receivable transactions handled in an online system?

From our discussions in Chap. 4, recall the use of a point-of-sale (POS) terminal, which doubles as a computer terminal and cash register. The POS terminal (Fig. 9-2, page 193) enables users to interact directly with the computer, which rapidly verifies every charge account transaction. Within seconds a customer's account is assessed from the accounts receivable file and checked as to payments made, current balance, and status. If the account is valid the entire charge transaction is accepted. Modern accounts receivable systems make it possible to track the use of credit cards by time and place used, as well as by amount of purchase, current account balance, and credit limit.

9.30 How do the inventory systems compare to the other business systems?

Inventory systems parallel all fundamental business systems in both structure and operation. An inventory system is designed to monitor the number of items held within any type of inventory and to provide a current status report on any item. Often these systems are closely linked with accounts receivable systems in retail organizations because incoming sales data are used to update the files of both systems.

9.31 Must inventory systems be online?

Not always. The manner in which inventory systems are updated and their outputs generated relates directly to the organization's use of that information and to the turnover of inventory items. The greater the frequency of change, the greater the need for an immediate response. An online system is probably not needed for an inventory of 50 or fewer items that have a monthly turnover. This level of activity would probably not warrant the expenditure for online hardware. However, a 1000-item inventory with only a few days turnover would need the support of an online inventory system. This computerized system would provide one of the few ways of monitoring and controlling that rapidly changing inventory. With a small inventory an online computer system of any size may prove to be an efficient means of inventory management. With a large inventory an online system would prove to be a necessity.

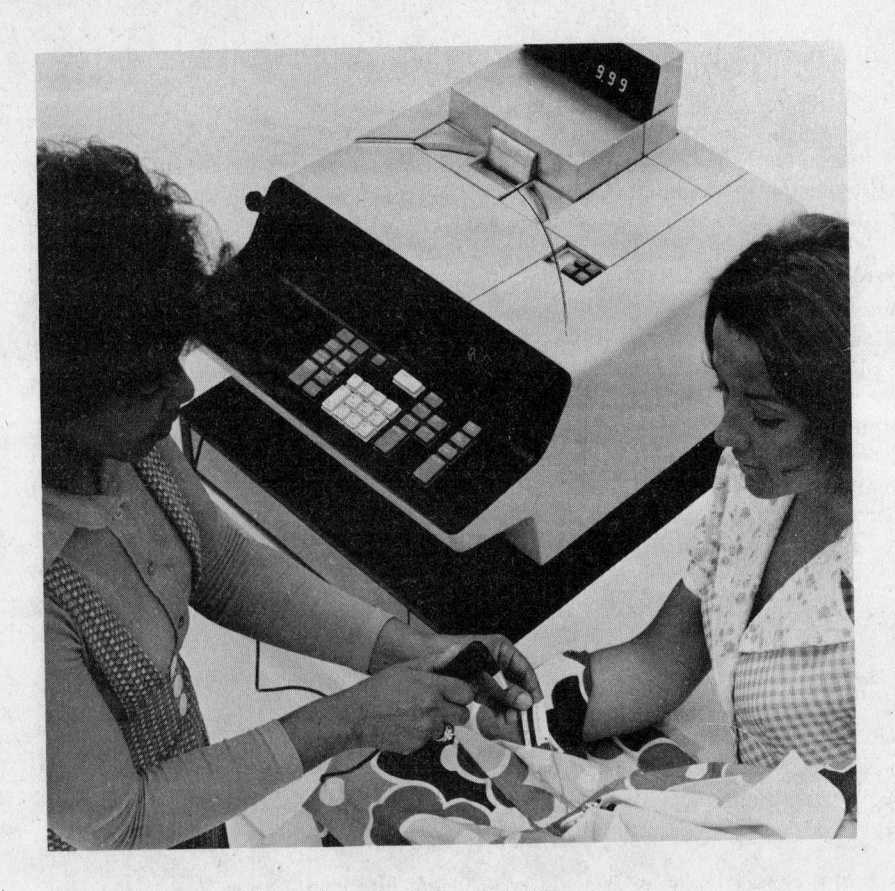

Fig. 9-2 A point-of-sale terminal. (*IBM*)

9.32 When discussing business systems, are only hardware devices considered, or are other factors involved?

Business systems encompass more than just computer hardware; in addition, they coordinate a variety of other resources. Business systems fully integrate people, equipment, procedures, and computers to accomplish the proper management and distribution of information. This fact is true whether the system is simple or complex or batch- or online-processing-oriented, or supports a large or small organization. To some degree all these factors are integrated to produce information that is useful to management.

SYSTEMS ANALYSIS

9.33 When is systems analysis applied to business systems?

When a business system no longer meets its intended goals, the modification of that system is considered. Systems analysis becomes the means for evaluating the existing system and detailing the problem areas within it.

9.34 What follows the detailing of problem areas?

With a complete analysis of the existing system and the detailing of its problems, the analyst may proceed to the design of the new system. Systems design identifies those efforts necessary to design a new (or replacement) system based on the problems uncovered and future considerations. In designing the new system, emphasis is placed on correcting problem areas and incorporating new techniques to handle both current and upcoming informational requirements.

9.35 What three major elements compose a systems project?

Using traditional problem-solving logic, a systems project is composed of the following three major components:
(1) Analysis of the existing systems
(2) Problem definition
(3) Design of the new system

The analysis of the existing system is an investigatory effort in which the efficiency of that system is evaluated and problems inherent in its operation are identified. The severity of each problem is assessed and examined in terms of its impact on the system's function. Obviously, some problems are more critical than others, having a more severe effect on a system's ability to handle data. After extensive analysis and evaluation, problems affecting the system's operation are detailed within the problem definition. This document is a narrative of each problem, citing its source, areas affected, and the severity of the problem. It does not suggest a solution since that is the purpose of the systems design effort. Many problem-solving approaches are considered in the design phase of a systems project. All potential solutions are coordinated within alternative systems designs from which management will choose. It is management's prerogative to select a design approach from those suggested and to direct its eventual implementation.

9.36 What factors bring about the need for systems analysis?

The need to begin systems analysis may result from one or more of the following:

(1) Management's desire to alter the organization and gain new markets
(2) New legislation or consumer protection rules
(3) Competition within the marketplace
(4) Changing operational demands
(5) Obsolescence of existing equipment

Any of the preceding reasons could be sufficient justification to analyze a system's operation.

9.37 How would new managerial objectives affect a system's performance?

Management directs a company's operation and how its resources are distributed. If management directs that a particular company operation will be dropped or expanded into a new market, the resources necessary to accomplish that change will be accordingly affected. These changes will impact computer services. If new information is required, systems analysis will reveal the best source of that data and the best way to process and distribute it. Analysis of the existing system reveals the most efficient means of implementing management's directives. Basically, a change in the information a business needs to function mandates an analysis of the potential sources of the necessary data.

9.38 How do new laws or regulations create a need for systems analysis?

The passing of new legislation, such as consumer protection laws, at any level of government can have a major effect on a company's computerized handling of data. If a law states that a consumer must possess a certain amount of data, then the organization must produce it by the required deadline. Systems analysis will reveal the most efficient means of generating that data. Again, as with changes induced by managerial objectives, new legislation will result in systems modifications that must be implemented. It's essential to produce the new consumer information; otherwise, the organization will be prohibited from doing business in that area.

9.39 What are some examples of systems analysis based on the prior two problems?

In relation to the implementation of managerial objectives, management may decide to introduce a new customer service or product. All informational handling features of the existing system would have to be modified to support this new product or service. As an example, consider a car rental agency that decides to rent out trucks. Although a computerized system would already exist, it would have to be modified to allow for truck rentals.

CHAP. 9]   SYSTEMS ANALYSIS AND DESIGN   195

Newly passed consumer debit protection rules have had an ongoing effect on sales organizations. The new rules mandate that specific data be presented to advise the consumer on the interest rate applied, the principal amount, and the loan time period. The enforcement of these rules affected every customer statement prepared as a result of installment or credit card purchases. Retail sales organizations had no choice but to comply. Systems analysis was essential in implementing both changes.

9.40 How can competition within the marketplace create a need for systems analysis?

The necessity to offer services comparable to an organization's competitors may generate the need for systems analysis. If new equipment is installed, if there is a new procedure for handling customer service complaints, or if new computer hardware is needed to remain competitive, systems analysis is a critical prerequisite. The analysis will focus on the best way to implement the change, the time at which it should be introduced, and where it will have the maximum impact. A good example is the stock market, where informational services are continually introduced. Brokerage houses must offer similar new services in order to remain competitive, be able to respond to changing market conditions, and highlight the superiority of their management.

9.41 Is the analysis necessitated by changing operational conditions similar to that of new managerial objectives?

Yes. However, the basis of analysis results from changes within the system, not from external influences. For example, if a system is equipped to handle a maximum of 500 customers, an increase to 750 customers will force an examination of existing business methods. Systems analysis will focus on areas where changes could be made to either keep the existing system with minor modifications or scrap the whole system and install an entirely new computerized configuration. This type of situation occurs in rapidly growing companies in which growth exceeds the organization's ability to function efficiently.

9.42 Does inadequate hardware support cause systems problems?

Yes. One common rationale for systems studies is the necessity to replace obsolete computer hardware. Generally, when upgrading hardware, most organizations improve all related procedures to streamline the data flow through the various levels. Very rarely will analysts uncover a situation in which changes are required in hardware but not in supporting procedures. The need to change hardware is usually signaled by a gradual decline in the system's performance. One could easily parallel these inefficiencies to the type of problems associated with a late-model car, when the age of the car often signals the onset of mechanical problems. Even a well-maintained system begins to falter when the supporting computer hardware proves insufficient for the existing workload. A systems study can provide valuable information on current operational conditions, projected needs, and problem areas that should be dealt with when new hardware is installed.

9.43 How does a request for systems analysis evolve?

The request for a systems study may result from a(n)
(1) Formal managerial directive
(2) Scheduled systems review
(3) Informal systems investigation by an analyst

9.44 How is a formal management request generated?

Management's desire to initiate a systems study may result from an operational objective or recognition of a problem. Management may desire to embark on a new business venture and, recognizing the need for adequate computer support, will direct the systems group to commence their analysis of what support is required. In doing so, top management has effectively chosen a course of action and is trying to pave the way for the proper support in preparation for it. In other instances management (of any level) may recognize the existence of a problem and consequently request assistance to solve it. The actual request may be handled in a memo or letter, addressed to the systems group manager, identifying the problem or asking for a meeting to discuss it. Formal management directives will normally be part of a coordinated and well-planned effort to launch a successful product.

9.45 How are scheduled reviews systems-study-oriented?

Every system should be examined periodically to ensure that it is functioning effectively. A *scheduled review* is a means of initiating the periodic review of a system and the effective distribution of its resources. Reviews are normally scheduled on a twelve-month cycle, but, of course, they may be rescheduled to fit any organization's particular needs. Scheduled reviews are written into a system's documentation once the system is implemented and in full operation. A review schedule is established for all systems, and individual systems are slotted into it. Analysts assigned to study different systems are required to acquaint themselves with the system to be reviewed, and the time, place, and point at which the review should begin.

9.46 How does an individual analyst's actions contribute to a system's study?

Often, when studying the interaction of two systems, an analyst becomes intrigued by the system's poor performance level. Though the system under study is functioning properly, the secondary system reveals major inefficiencies that should be immediately corrected. In his or her report the investigating analyst will document these problems, as well as draft a memo to the systems group manager identifying the problem found in the secondary system and the need to study it. After subsequent discussions a decision will be made as to when the review of the secondary system will actually commence.

COLLECTING DATA

9.47 What term is applied to the gathering of materials related to systems analysis?

The accumulation of the materials needed to perform the analysis of a business system is referred to as the *collection of data*. This data gathering effort is designed to amass information, in a raw or processed state, that can be analyzed to ascertain whether the system under study is operating properly.

9.48 Why is the collection of data critical in systems studies?

Without proper data the systems analysis effort is of questionable value and so is the analyst's reputation. Sufficient data must be gathered to substantiate any claims of a system's inefficiencies and justify the changes proposed to correct such problems. Though people are willing to accept verbal assessments, it is far better to have the facts speak for themselves. Often, when the personnel of a department under study feel maligned, they will question the accuracy and completeness of the study performed. Having irrefutable evidence at hand minimizes the impact of the employees' doubts and strengthens the recommendations in the study.

9.49 Where does the analyst start looking for materials to study?

Basically, the investigation of data begins everywhere, as analysts collect every fact, form, or scrap of information available. One must recognize that the collection of data phase is not a quick once-through but can last for a month or more, depending on the project's scope. Data will be initially gathered and analyzed, and then more data will be collected in the areas needing greater clarification. The collection of data will continue until the majority of the data necessary to substantiate the study's claim is gathered.

9.50 What means can analysts use to collect data?

Analysts can gather information regarding their systems studies from the following sources:
(1) Existing I/O documents
(2) Personal observations
(3) Personnel interviews
(4) Previous systems studies
(5) Procedure manuals

9.51 How are existing I/O documents helpful?

Existing I/O documents specify the data entering the system and the information output by it. With these I/O documents analysts can catalog every data item and bit of information used by the system. They provide a means of evaluating what items are correctly used and what information is really necessary to support the system's operation. Every I/O document should be identified as to its specific use, distribution, and frequency of preparation.

9.52 When analyzing a system, which are considered more critical: outputs or inputs?

Though both sets of documents are deemed important, the outputs of a system are far more critical to the analyst's work. This is true because it is the outputs of a system that prescribe the data used within it and their manipulations, as well as indicate the level of efficiency attained by the system. If a system's outputs are marginal, the organization it supports will probably demonstrate a high degree of operational inefficiency, sometimes leading it to completely ignore the system and rely on an alternative informational setup. No matter how good the inputs are, if the outputs are minimally effective, the quality of input data is invalidated. Thus much emphasis is placed on the evaluation of a system's outputs during the collection of data and their analysis.

9.53 What means are used to record I/O documents?

For the most part analysts will collect actual copies of I/O documents since they illustrate both the operational format and the actual data items composing each document. Whenever the actual document is not available, a graphic representation may be used. Using drawings has its drawbacks, but they do provide a useful means of representing I/O formats.

9.54 When, for example, would a graphic approach be necessary?

Two examples of situations in which a graphic display often proves helpful in recording an I/O format are the representation of softcopy on a CRT and the defining of fields composing a tape or disk file. In both instances it is not possible to physically capture the actual display of data or directly read the magnetic codes stored on the tape's or disk's surface. Thus some form of drawing is needed to record the information involved.

9.55 What graphic means is used when recording softcopy outputs or the contents of a file?

Two forms prominently used in recording I/O formats are the printer spacing chart and storage layout form. The printer spacing chart (Fig. 9-3, page 198) enables analysts to record the contents of both softcopy and hardcopy outputs. It is particularly effective when planning both types of outputs or recording the fields that compose them. The storage layout form (Fig. 9-4, page 198) documents all fields composing the record format used in computer files.

9.56 How are these two forms used?

Within the printer spacing chart, each field in the output is defined on a character-by-character basis for each type of line the output employs. Column headings, labels, individual lines of data, and summary totals are clearly defined as to their length, position in the output, and type of data to be used. Figure 9-3 shows a softcopy output of student personnel data. The contents of a file on employee benefits is recorded in Fig. 9-4. Here every field is consecutively classified by size, type, and name. The consecutive listing of fields gives the length of that record as it will appear when written onto disk.

9.57 How do personal observations assist systems analysts?

An analyst can read about a particular procedure, but until he or she actually observes that procedure, it is difficult to assess its effectiveness. First-hand observations are vital because they provide the analyst with a feeling for a system's operation. If a system is evaluated as being inefficient, a personal observation will help determine whether the potential fault lies with sloppy data handling, untrained personnel, an illogical sequence of steps, or a change in operating conditions.

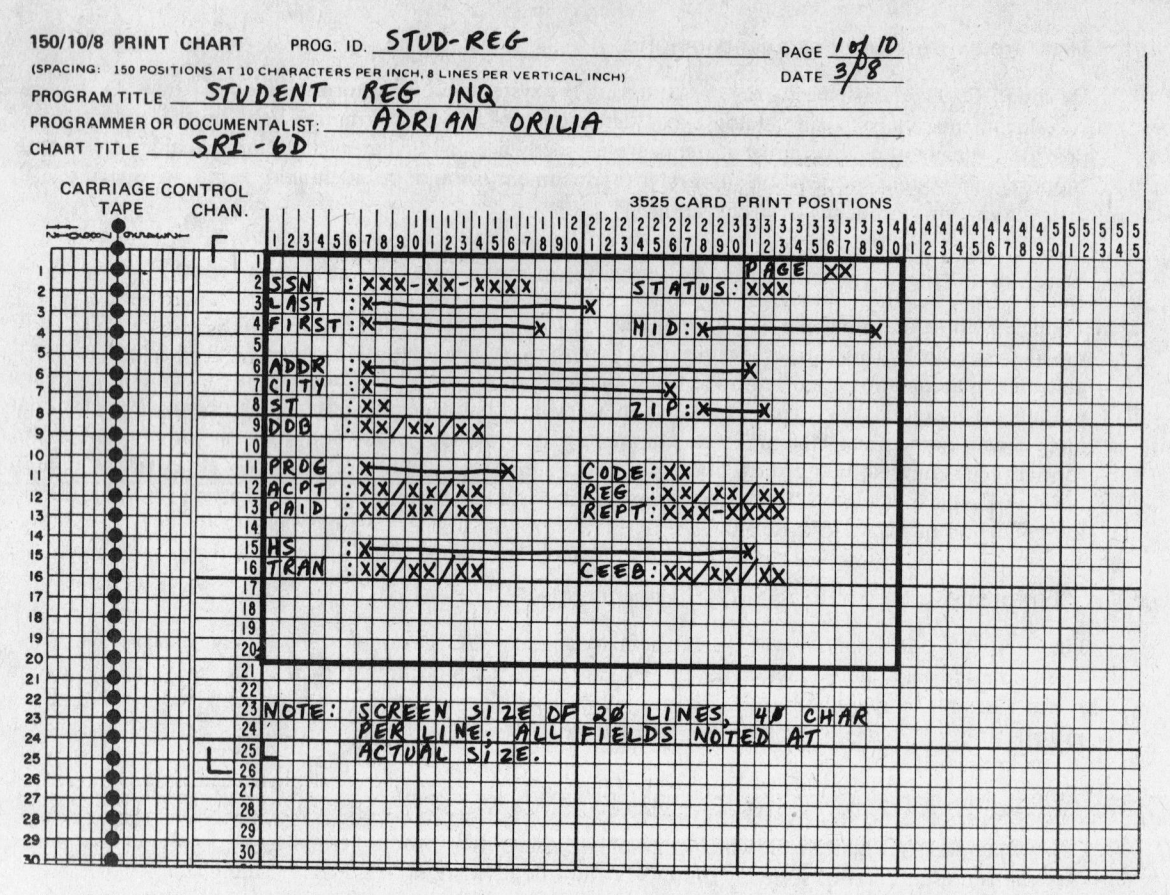

Fig. 9-3 This printer spacing chart shows the fields composing a softcopy display of student data. (*IBM*)

Fig. 9-4 A record layout form.

9.58 How are these observations recorded?

Analysts utilize many forms of documentation to record the results of a personal observation. Generally, a notepad identifying the time, place, and date of the observation and any salient points derived will prove sufficient. These notes will be continually reviewed when evaluating any aspect of a system.

9.59 Do personnel interviews serve the same purpose?

The interviewing of personnel directly involved with the system undergoing analysis provides first-hand insight to that system through a user's eyes and provides a basis of comparison for the analyst's own opinions. Analysts can compare what is said during interviews against what they have observed and draw conclusions on the validity of the data gathered.

9.60 Why are personnel interviews helpful to the study?

If the analyst can extract facts from the people who have worked with the system directly and know its strengths and weaknesses, these interviews can provide a rich source of information about a system's performance. The recommendations offered by many staff members during interviews provide invaluable assistance and often form the basis of sound systems solutions.

9.61 Are staff recommendations always followed?

No. The analyst must always beware of individuals who, when interviewed, attempt to deliberately or innocently mislead the interviewer. For some staff members, a proposed systems change may be an opportunity for a power play to grab more computer resources. The analyst should therefore use his or her practical work experience in evaluating the opinions offered in interviews.

9.62 How does the analyst use the data gathered from interviews?

The facts, opinions, observations, and hunches drawn from interviews are combined with all other data collected. These results tend to confirm the analyst's ideas or to serve as catalysts to other avenues of investigation. Frequently a previously overlooked problem is identified from an interviewer's comments, and suggestions garnered from interviews often serve as starting points for subsequent investigations.

9.63 Does the analyst place any importance on previous systems studies?

Reading reports from earlier systems studies can provide valuable insights into the areas being analyzed, and they can be the basis of comparison for current operations. The analyst can compare current operating conditions and procedures against the designs documented in the systems study documentation. Deviations from documented procedures may result from planned changes or convenience, but either signals an area for investigation. Previous studies also give insights into previous operating conditions and into methods for diagnosing and handling problem areas.

9.64 Where is earlier systems studies documentation kept?

In most systems groups a library consisting of current technical manuals, previous systems project documentation, and reference texts from all areas of business and science is provided for the analysts' use. During the analysis phase, analysts are encouraged to use these resources and develop a sound background knowledge of the area under study. In small companies a formal library may not exist, but an area is usually set aside for the cataloging of earlier systems documentation.

9.65 Are company manuals also stored in this library?

Generally, all manuals related to how an organization handles its data are cataloged in the systems group's library. These manuals are kept up to date since they detail all forms of organizational procedures. Every step within each data handling procedure is documented, providing a reference for employees throughout the company.

9.66 What types of procedures are outlined in these manuals?

Procedures for completing vacation request forms, bidding new job assignments, handling returned merchandise, or cataloging materials shipped under warranty work are some of the sets of instructions in the manuals retained by the systems group. As these books generally detail all procedures utilized by an organization, they are commonly referred to as *procedures manuals*. Generally, the larger the organization, the greater the need for a procedures manual and the thicker it is.

9.67 Is there another type of manual for analysts to refer to?

Yes. Another manual concurrently prepared with procedures manual is the *organization manual*. This book details every employment position in the organization and its job description, including the experience required to do that job. When used concurrently with procedures manuals, the organization manual helps the analyst identify each employee, the task assigned to that employee, and the procedures used by that employee.

9.68 How are both manuals used by the analyst?

The analyst will review both the organization and procedures manuals prior to a personnel interview, to reviewing any prior systems studies, and to making personal observations. This review provides a basis for evaluating any data collected from those analysis activities.

9.69 Once data are collected, what does the analyst do?

The analyst will carefully review all the materials collected, evaluate each aspect of the system, and determine which components of the system require modification. These results are recorded in a systems documentation packet carefully outlining each feature of the systems operation.

9.70 How is this documentation packet divided?

The entire systems documentation is composed of:

(1) An analysis of the existing system
(2) A problem definition
(3) The design of the new system

The section on the analysis of the existing system describes all aspects of the existing system to include procedures, I/O forms, files in use, the costs associated with the system, and the positions involved in data handling. This section essentially details the results of the systems analysis effort. The problem definition serves only to document each problem area uncovered by the analysis and to describe its specific position within the system. Whereas these two sections may be written subsequent to the systems analysis effort, the design of the new system cannot be documented until later in the project's course. This section is usually written well after the new system is implemented, when the new system's structure is solidified.

9.71 Why does the problem definition define only the problem areas uncovered?

The specific purpose of the problem definition is to pinpoint problem areas, not to offer solutions. Analysts will expend a great deal of time considering alternative solutions when the problem definition has been accepted as valid.

9.72 Why are alternative solutions considered?

Alternative solutions to existing problems form the basis of designing the new system's features. The alternative solutions are developed for management's consideration, offering them several approaches, each carrying a different price tag. The varied cost proposals permit management to select a system whose solution matches its budget. Analysts must consider the cost factor in the design of all proposed systems.

SYSTEMS FLOWCHARTS

9.73 What are systems flowcharts?

A *systems flowchart* is a diagram representing the flow of information through an organization. Systems flowcharts are used to describe how all data are handled within an organization. Unlike program flowcharts (see Chaps. 7 and 8), systems flowcharts document both manual and computerized activities.

9.74 How are systems flowcharts used within systems studies?

Systems flowcharts are used to document the steps taken throughout a system in the handling of data. Thus systems flowcharts can depict the steps involved in the handling of credit memos, the updating of a disk file of customer accounts, or the online entry of inventory data to determine the active status of critical production parts. Each of the steps constituting these representative activities is documented in the flowchart such that the analyst has a pictorial representation of the logic used.

CHAP. 9] SYSTEMS ANALYSIS AND DESIGN

9.75 What documentation is frequently associated with systems flowcharts?

A *systems narrative*, describing a processing sequence, is frequently appended to the systems flowchart. The narrative is a written, step-by-step description of every procedure, with each step symbolically represented in the supporting flowchart.

9.76 Is the systems narrative the duplicate of the written procedure used in normal processing activities?

The systems narrative associated with a systems flowchart prepared by the analyst may or may not parallel previously written procedures. The amount of similarity depends on how much the procedures have changed since it was written. If little change has occurred, the narrative and existing procedure will be similar. If radical changes have occurred, the systems narrative and flowchart will reflect that also.

9.77 Why are systems flowcharts helpful in the analysis of the existing system?

They enable the analyst to document the existing methods of data handling based on the analyst's personal observations and investigation. The flowcharts drawn detail the most current state of the system.

9.78 Can systems flowcharts be advantageously used in the planning of a new system?

Systems flowcharts are creative tools in the hands of analysts planning changes in the existing system. The flowchart permits the analyst to design proposed modifications (on paper) and have other team members evaluate their potential. System flowcharts are effective planning tools and provide a means of documenting the procedures and processing steps implemented in the new system.

9.79 What symbols are used in the preparation of systems flowcharts?

The symbols used in the preparation of systems flowcharts are shown in Fig. 9-5. A large set of symbols is required for systems flowcharts since they document so many diverse tasks.

SYSTEM FLOWCHART SYMBOLS

Punched card symbol notes the use of a punched card.

Document symbol identifies any printed document used in processing or output.

Processing symbol notes a processing operation or program used in processing.

Magnetic tape symbol defines the use of magnetic tape.

Offline storage symbol details the noncomputerized, offline storage of data on all types of storage media; including the storage of tapes, printed materials, etc., in file cabinets, libraries, or trays.

Online storage symbol indicates use of online storage device (such as a magnetic disk), whose data is directly accessible to the computer.

Online keyboard symbol notes use of online keyboard to input data directly into the computer (i.e., terminal or console typewriter/keyboard).

Display symbol defines use of a CRT plotter or visual display device in output operations where data is presented in a softcopy format.

Keying operation symbol denotes use of an offline keyboard device to prepare data.

Manual operation symbol describes an offline manual operation in which data is handled without mechanical assistance.

Transmittal tape symbol notes adding machine or batch total tapes employed to verify amounts prepared during processing.

Auxiliary operation symbol defines an offline mechanical operation that supplements the handling of data; often by use of office machines and EAM equipment.

Merge symbol defines an offline operation in which two sets of data are merged into one; often used to note EAM operations.

Punched tape symbol represents the use of a punched paper or plastic tape; not to be confused with magnetic tapes.

Sorting indicates an offline operation for ordering data; often used to define an operation performed on the EAM sorter.

Flow symbol indicates direction of processing or data flow.

Collate symbol describes an offline collating operation in which data from one or more files is manipulated and rearranged into one or more files, often associated with the use of EAM equipment.

Communication link symbol denotes the online transmission of data via telecommunication.

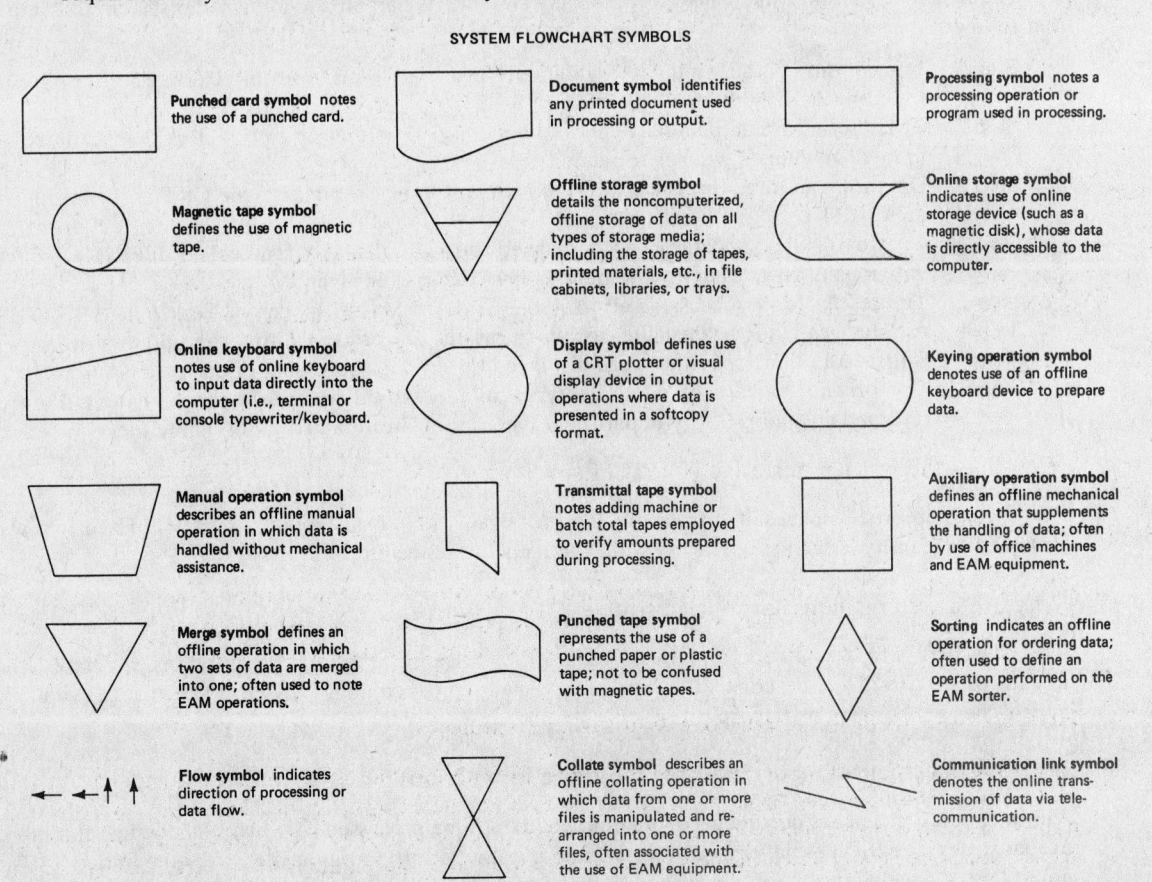

Fig. 9-5 A wide variety of symbols available for the preparation of systems flowcharts.

9.80 Which systems flowchart symbols are most commonly encountered?

Some of the more frequently used systems symbols are the:

(1) Document symbol, which represents printed documents of all types, including computer printed outputs, input forms, and typed reports
(2) Manual operation symbol, which denotes the manual preparation or handling of data in any form
(3) Offline storage symbol, which identifies the use of noncomputerized storage areas, such as file cabinets or desk-top bins
(4) Online keyboard symbol, which notes the online entry of data from the keyboard of a terminal
(5) Processing symbol, which identifies computerized processing operations performed on data, usually in the form of program software
(6) Online storage symbol, which denotes the storage of data via online storage devices, such as magnetic disk
(7) Auxiliary operation symbol, which indicates use of a variety of office and business machines to process data on an offline basis

The other symbols shown in Fig. 9-5 are also used in systems flowcharts but to a lesser degree. Most of the remaining symbols relate to card-oriented devices that operate on an offline basis, and they are not commonly employed.

9.81 How do these symbols represent a series of processing tasks?

A representative systems flowchart and supporting systems narrative are depicted in Fig. 9-6 (page 203). This flowchart depicts the major steps taken in a procedure to update an inventory file. As shown, three types of input forms are used to update that file. The three types of input documents are manually checked and corrected by an inventory clerk in one manual operation. This information is then keyed, via an online CRT, into an update program named UPINV4 (short for UPdate INVentory 4). This program processes each item entered and updates the master inventory file. The outputs related to this update are a printed list of all changes (UPDATE INV LIST), a visual display of the items as keyed, and the return of all input documents to an inventory file. The preceding statements paraphrase the written systems narrative that follows:

Step 1. Input forms containing inventory data are provided to an inventory clerk. The three forms used are the New Items Invoices, Dropped Items List, and Adjusted Items Listing.
Step 2. These forms are all manually checked and verified by that inventory clerk. Corrections are immediately made whenever needed.
Step 3. Data from all three forms are keyed directly into the system using the CRT in the inventory area (CRT 6).
Step 4. Control of this update is accomplished through the program called UPINV4, which individually posts each update item against the master inventory file.
Step 5. The result of this processing effort is the Updated Master Inventory Disk.
Step 6. All changes made against the inventory master are printed within the updated inventory listing. All online activities were displayed during the processing of each transaction.
Step 7. The original batches of all three types of input used to update the inventory file are returned to the inventory department where they are retained in an offline file.

9.82 Why does the written narrative consist of seven steps?

The seven-step procedure resulted from the analyst's evaluation of this update operation. Each step was designed to identify a distinct operation within this update procedure.

9.83 Why are a systems flowchart and narrative used concurrently?

The flowchart and narrative complement each other because they add descriptions to clarify the update procedure. They describe the steps both visually and verbally, providing the analyst with two approaches to the same procedure.

9.84 Why are document symbols used for the three input forms?

All three inputs are paper documents containing the data to be processed. As such, the document symbol properly identifies them as paper input forms. Note that the report output at the end of the update is also noted by the document symbol. Since the report is printed on paper, the symbol is correctly used.

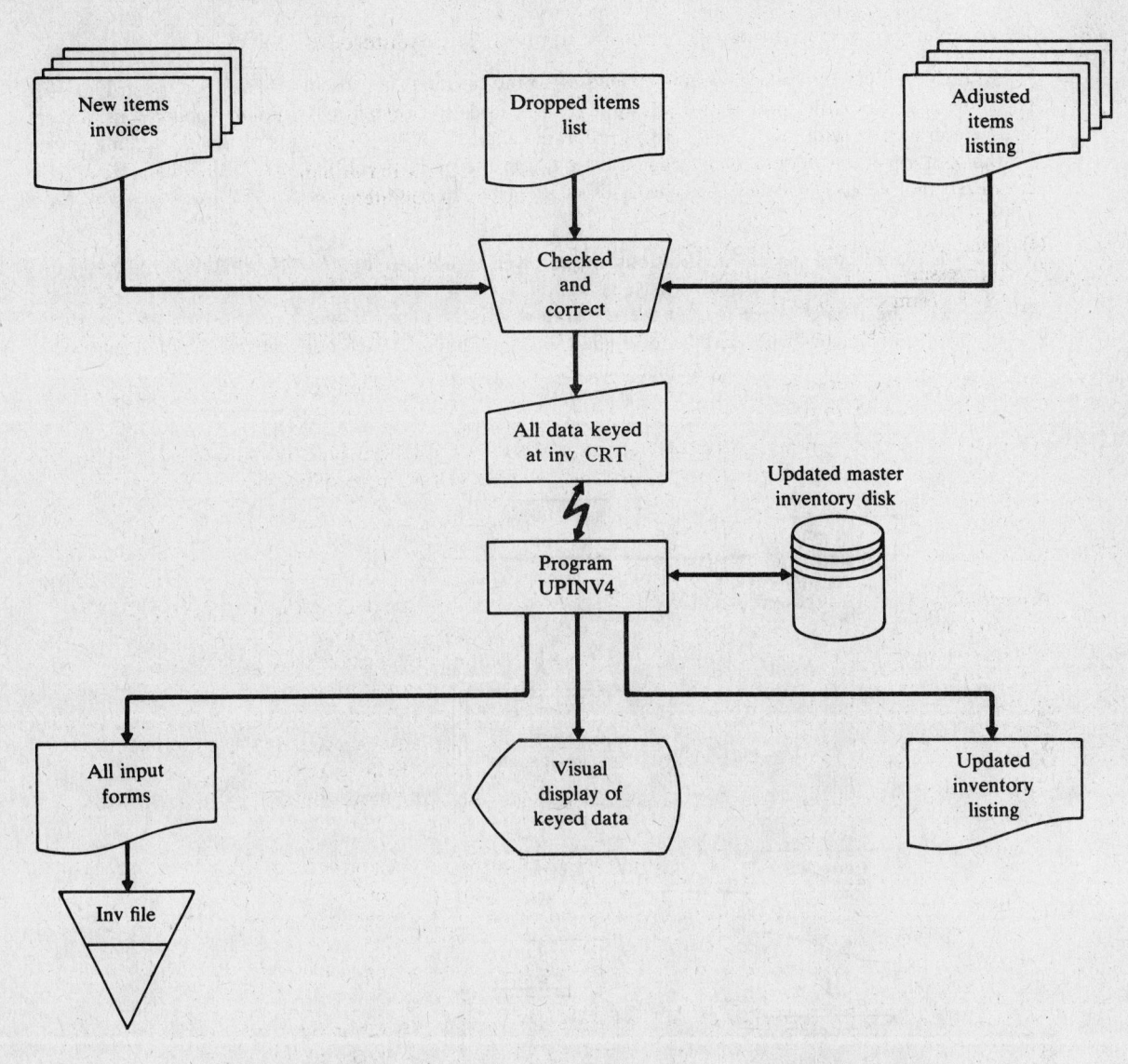

Fig. 9-6 The update of an inventory file is depicted using a systems flowchart.

9.85 What purpose does the zig-zag line between the online keyboard and the processing symbol serve?

The zig-zag line is called a *communication link* and is the flowchart symbol denoting the online hookup between a terminal and a supporting computer. It shows that the user is interacting with the computer on an online basis, utilizing the resources of the UPINV4 program.

9.86 What symbol relates to the updated disk?

The symbol used for magnetic disk is a special version of the online storage symbol, specifically used to denote magnetic disk files. The label used with it, UPDATED MASTER INVENTORY DISK, denotes that the master file of all inventory data exists in its most current form at the end of this processing effort.

204   SYSTEMS ANALYSIS AND DESIGN   [CHAP. 9

9.87 How might a card processing operation be depicted in a systems flowchart?

An example of a card processing sequence leading to the creation of a student file is depicted in Fig. 9-7. This flowchart shows the preparation of student data cards from corrected student applications. These cards are processed with the assistance of a program called STUCR. The results of this processing effort are the creation of a student file on magnetic tape, a printed report entitled STUDENT LISTING, and the disposition of the punched cards to a DP card file. The narrative associated with this flowchart follows.

Step 1. Corrected student applications are received in the DP student offline file and batched into groups of twenty-five for ease of handling.

Step 2. These batches are sent to the DP area where the data contained on those applications are keypunched onto cards and verified. The original corrected applications are then sent back to the admissions department where they are placed in an offline file.

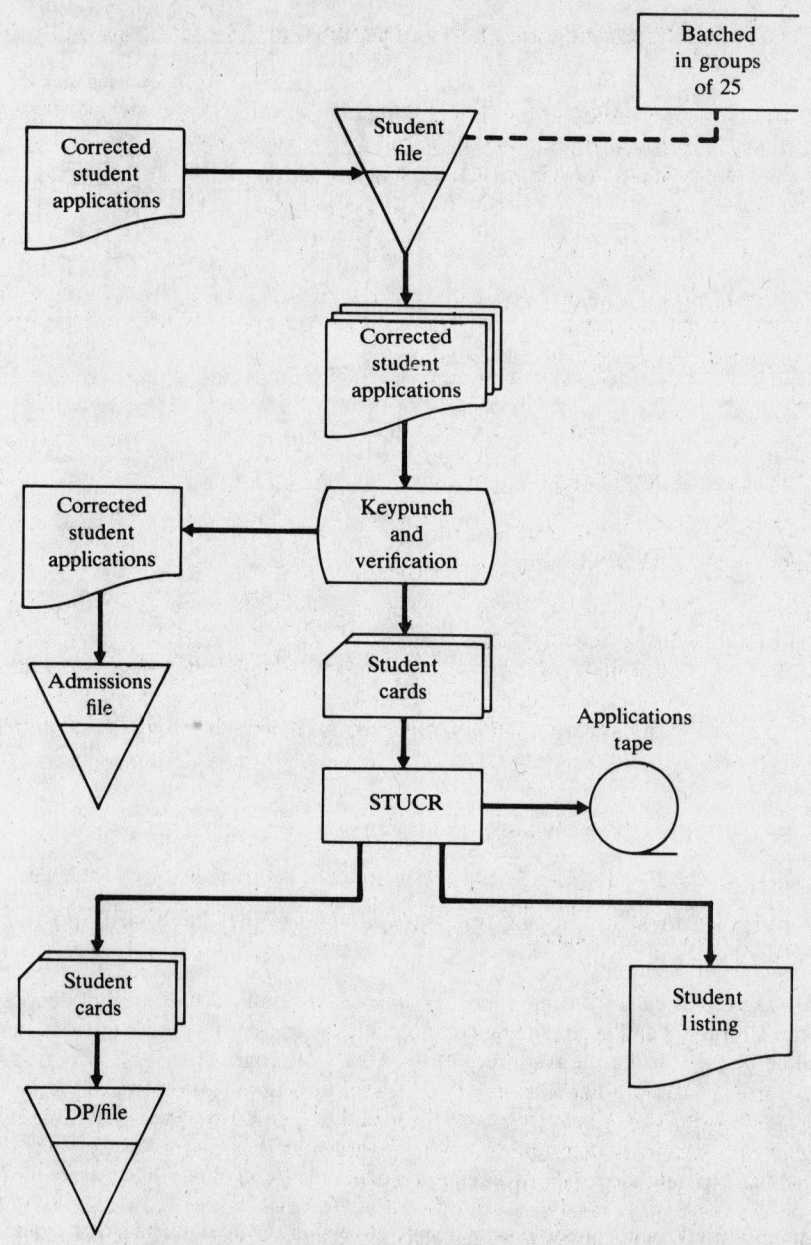

Fig. 9-7 Card processing operations related to the handling of student data are depicted within a systems flowchart.

CHAP. 9] SYSTEMS ANALYSIS AND DESIGN 205

Step 3. The cards produced from this keypunching effort are processed using a program called STUCR (short for STUdent CReate).
Step 4. The result of processing student cards is the creation of a new applications file on magnetic tape.
Step 5. The report output from this programming effort is the STUDENT LISTING, which lists all applicants composing that file.
Step 6. All applicant cards used in processing are returned to the DP area where they are kept in card storage trays for future processing.

9.88 What purpose does the annotation symbol serve?

The annotation symbol is used to add descriptive comments to flowcharts, advising analysts of special conditions.

9.89 What tasks result from the keypunch and verification operation shown in the flowchart in Fig. 9-7?

The keying operation results in the preparation of the punched cards and the issuance of the applicant forms to the admissions office. The applicant cards are slated for processing, whereas the original applications are retained in each student's personal file.

9.90 Are systems flowcharts a critical component within systems documentation?

Systems flowcharts and their supporting narratives are a vital part of any systems documentation package. They are important in detailing the existing system, as well as documenting processing procedures in the newly designed system.

DESIGN OF THE NEW SYSTEM

9.91 After completion of the analysis of the existing system and preparation of the problem definition, what task next faces the analyst?

With management's acceptance of the problem definition, the analyst is ready to proceed to the design of the new system to replace the existing system. Initially, however, the team of analysts will not work on one project but will attack a group of alternative replacement systems. Each alternative system will incorporate solutions to the existing problem areas, as well as any projected ones. Each alternative will present a different processing mode, ranging from low-level processing activities to a fully online, real-time system.

9.92 Why the divergent group of alternative systems approaches?

The variety of systems designs are for management's selection process. Each alternative carries with it specific advantages and limitations, which include a detailed cost estimate and description of its processing activities. Management may then select an alternative that satisfies their financial and processing requirements.

9.93 How detailed are the alternative systems designs?

The design for each alternative systems solution is prepared on an overview basis. The various solutions are assigned within the systems team, with a group of analysts working on a separate design. Each design addresses the problems determined from the previous analysis phase, solving them in terms of that alternative approach. General processing procedures are suggested, thus establishing the structure of that design's approach. A general list of hardware is prepared, as is a cost estimate related to that system's implementation. Systems flowcharts and narratives, as well as critical I/O and file formats, are prepared to illustrate that system's approach toward data handling and its solutions to problems found in the existing system.

9.94 In what way, for example, are alternative solutions configured?

As stated, alternative designs for the new system are deliberately distinct so that analysts can offer diverse processing options to management. Thus it is possible to have a processing approach that incorporates the use of computer cards and that has a relatively low cost or an approach that distributes the data processing workload among a large number of terminals and supporting databases. The latter system's alternative could conceivably carry a large price but could provide an exotic level of DP support. Essentially, both alternatives could support a retail inventory system with the level and degree of processing directly related to its design.

9.95 In addition to specifying a system's costs, do analysts consider the savings accrued from a new system?

In addition to the estimate of costs for an alternative system, analysts are expected to estimate the savings that may accrue from its use. The savings gained from a new system can be considerable and can help defray the cost of that system's implementation.

9.96 Why is an estimate of savings an important consideration?

Though management may not possess a high level of EDP expertise, they are keenly aware of budget matters and the finances associated with paying for a new system. They will critically scrutinize each cost estimate to determine its viability in terms of needed expenses and savings potential. Savings estimates must be realistic in terms of their projected amounts and their impact on the system. Unrealistic savings estimates can jeopardize the integrity of the project.

9.97 What type of savings are often incorporated into a system's report?

Savings may be gained from elimination of employee positions that were necessary because the system was operating inefficiently or from reduction of inventory maintained at levels higher than necessary due to poor inventory control. Savings might also result from reduced employee pilferage, due to better inventory control. Resource distribution may be improved such that the proper resource is made available to the right person, or procedures may be improved to remove unnecessary steps and speed the flow of information.

9.98 Where are the alternative systems detailed?

The designs of the alternative systems are presented in the systems documentation package following the analysis of the existing system and the problem definition. Whereas these two preliminary sections should not vary, the design portion of the systems package will change as the designs are proposed and modified.

9.99 When will documentation relating to the design of the new system be finalized?

The documentation of the new system becomes final after that design is selected from all other alternatives, it is implemented and in full operation, and it is certified for use by the systems staff. Only after these steps have been taken can documentation related to the analysis and design of a system be completed.

9.100 What procedure does management follow when presented with the alternative solutions for the new system?

With the finalization of the existing systems analysis and problem definition, alternative systems approaches are prepared by the systems staff. These solutions are evaluated by management, whereupon one is selected for implementation. The feasibility of the alternative solution is carefully examined, and its design is fully completed to include all aspects of the system. The fully developed design is then resubmitted to management for final approval. Once approved and fully implemented, the design is certified as operational and turned over to the company for full use. The last phase of the systems documentation packet relating to the new system's design is prepared and joined with materials already completed regarding analysis of the existing system and problem definition.

THE FEASIBILITY COMMITTEE

9.101 At what point are feasibility studies conducted?

Once management selects the alternative on which the design of the new system is based, they wish to know whether that design is feasible before committing vast sums of money to it. The feasibility study is an evaluation of all aspects of the design alternative chosen and a written report on the merits of that design. The study acts as a check on the proposed system, performed before it is fully implemented.

9.102 Why is the feasibility study necessary?

Though alternative solutions for the new system's design are generally explained, they lack the detail that a fully implemented systems design would exhibit. Since management wants to ensure that its decision is sound and that the systems alternative selected will work, they use a feasibility study as an intermediary safety check before committing all funds to the project.

9.103 How long does a feasibility study last?

Feasibility studies are generally completed within one to two months, depending on the project's scope. The cost of the study generally ranges from $15,000 to $150,000. The cost estimates vary greatly between organizations, systems staff resources, and budget allocations. The feasibility study is designed not as a long-term project but as a short-term project from which an immediate assessment of feasibility is derived.

9.104 What group actually performs the feasibility study?

The feasibility study is performed by a team of people called the *feasibility committee*. This committee is composed of a select group of individuals of varied backgrounds and experience who will interact with the proposed system if the design is accepted. Each has a personal interest in the project's future and wants the best available system.

9.105 Who usually serves on the feasibility committee?

The feasibility committee normally consists of the following people:

(1) A member of top management
(2) A senior systems analyst
(3) Representatives from the affected departments
(4) An outside consultant or specialist

9.106 What information does the top executive supply?

The feasibility committee member representing top management provides first-hand information on management's view of the project's potential, direction, and purpose; the budgetary constraints under which the committee must operate; and the organization's short- and long-term developmental plans. Decisions related to whether management might approve certain operational plans are rendered immediately since the top executive is normally granted authority to speak for management. Normally, the top executive also serves as chairperson of the committee.

9.107 Why is it important to know top management's position on the feasibility committee's work?

The knowledge provided by the top executive supplies the committee with immediate guidelines on which to base their work. If they know that an idea or approach will not receive management's sanction, then they will not waste time developing it. It is far better to pursue an idea that accomplishes the same goal and has a higher probability of acceptance. The top executive usually possesses a firm set of guidelines within which the feasibility committee may operate.

9.108 Why is the senior systems analyst included on the feasibility committee?

The senior systems analyst serves two vital roles on the feasibility committee. First, he or she has intimate knowledge of the organization's operating procedures and will ensure that these guidelines are followed during the committee's work. Second, he or she serves as a resource to the preceding systems study. Normally, the senior analyst in charge of supervising the initial systems study is automatically assigned to the feasibility committee. The inclusion of this senior analyst ensures a continuity in the design process.

9.109 What information does the senior analyst supply?

The senior analyst contributes his or her knowledge of the operating procedures used by the systems group during the analysis and design of the new system and ensures that only approved conventions are incorporated into the new systems design. Also, the senior analyst acts as a resource to information derived from the analysis of the existing system.

9.110 How do departmental representatives assist the feasibility committee's work?

The departmental representatives act as informational pipelines to their respective areas and as informational sources to activities in their departments. These representatives can advise the committee on the impact of proposed changes, evaluate their viability, and indicate how they may be implemented to maximize their effectiveness. They will also carry messages back to their departments, keeping them informed on how the new system will affect them and how to implement all newly designed procedures.

9.112 How does knowledge of a department's inner workings help the feasibility committee?

The departmental representatives should have in-depth knowledge of their area's function and be able to provide detailed data on each of the activities undertaken within it. First-hand knowledge of this type is immediately useful in designing the new system since the representative will indicate whether a newly planned activity has a chance of success. Also, the departmental representatives can provide a historical perspective on the success of procedures tried earlier, thereby preventing the resurrection of ideas that proved unsuccessful.

9.113 Why is it necessary for the departmental representatives to bring information back to their respective departments?

Nothing can defeat a properly designed system faster than uncooperative or threatened employees. The departmental representatives advise coworkers of how each newly instituted procedure may affect them. In so doing, the departmental representatives keep their coworkers abreast of the system's development, which prevents unnecessary surprises from occurring that might adversely affect working conditions.

9.114 How many departmental representatives are included on the feasibility committee?

The number of departmental representatives included depends on the number of organizational units affected by the proposed systems design. Generally, one representative is assigned to the committee from each major department, which results in approximately three to seven people being added. By contrast, only one top executive and one senior analyst, with an assistant, are asked to be on the feasibility committee.

9.115 Why is it necessary to have an outside consultant on the feasibility committee?

An outside consultant provides an independent voice to the committee's deliberations. Often other committee members will not express ideas that they feel will conflict with top management's position or jeopardize their employment. Since the consultant is hired on a short-term, contractual basis, he or she may render opinions or evaluations without fearing reprisal.

9.116 Can the consultant serve in a technical capacity?

Yes. Because of the nature of their business, consultants must maintain a state-of-the-art knowledge on almost all aspects of the computer field. Thus they have knowledge of trends developing in hardware and software that may be successfully incorporated into the proposed system, improving its performance. Consultants serve as a ready source of information on current computer technology.

9.117 What specifically will the feasibility committee do?

The feasibility committee will provide an in-depth evaluation of the systems solution selected by management. It will examine, expand, and evaluate all aspects of that design and determine whether the design offers a viable solution to the existing system's problem areas. The committee evaluates the proposed system in regard to its financial structure, the computer requirements, and the support it will provide.

9.118 Where is this information summarized?

The committee documents its work in the feasibility report. Every characteristic of the system being examined is listed with its evaluation, supporting procedures, and hardware criteria, together with explanatory remarks.

9.119 How are these results used?

The recommendations in the feasibility report are presented to management for their formal approval. They must approve these recommendations for the system to be fully implemented and for the funds to be authorized to complete the project. The report serves as a jumping-off point for the systems team that will fully implement the design, which may take anywhere from 2 to 24 months, depending on the project's scope.

9.120 Where is the feasibility report kept?

This document is prepared only after the committee's work is complete. Once presented, it is stored within the systems group's library along with all materials related to that project. These materials act as references for future studies. Much of the materials contained in the feasibility report will reappear in the final documentation of the proposed system.

Review Questions

9.121 There are no operational differences between the tasks assumed by the programming group and those of the systems group. (*a*) True, (*b*) false.

9.122 Analysts always perform their work in relation to computers and rarely study manual systems. (*a*) True, (*b*) false.

9.123 A *system* is defined as a way of achieving a stated goal. (*a*) True, (*b*) false.

9.124 Most systems studies are performed on a team basis, as they are normally more than one analyst can handle. (*a*) True, (*b*) false.

9.125 Payroll systems are responsible for the payment of employees, but they do not prepare federal tax documentation. (*a*) True, (*b*) false.

9.126 The problem definition describes problems within the existing system and offers tentative solutions. (*a*) True, (*b*) false.

9.127 Management's desire to reach new markets does not warrant a systems study. (*a*) True, (*b*) false.

9.128 An analyst's informal investigation of an existing system can result in a formal study of that system. (*a*) True, (*b*) false.

9.129 When collecting systems data, copies of all I/O documents or displays are gathered to enable the examination of the inputs and outputs used by the system. (*a*) True, (*b*) false.

9.130 In a systems analysis, personal observations of a system's performance are of little value since they do not provide a sound basis for evaluating the system. (*a*) True, (*b*) false.

9.131 Previous systems studies are of little value to the analyst since they describe earlier versions of the existing system. (*a*) True, (*b*) false.

9.132 Generally, only one systems design is prepared for management's evaluation since there is usually only one way to attack a systems solution. (*a*) True, (*b*) false.

9.133 Estimated costs and savings are part of any system's documentation because they are critical to management's evaluation of that system. (*a*) True, (*b*) false.

9.134 An independent voice on the feasibility committee comes from the outside consultant. (*a*) True, (*b*) false.

9.135 The analysis of how efficiently an organization handles its information is defined by the term (*a*) systems design; (*b*) collection of data; (*c*) systems analysis; (*d*) scheduled review.

9.136 The business system used to monitor monies owed by an organization is referred to as a(n) (*a*) accounts payable system; (*b*) accounts receivable system; (*c*) accounts payroll system; (*d*) customer credit system.

9.137 Difficulties within an existing system are detailed in a system's documentation within the (*a*) analysis of the existing system; (*b*) problem definition; (*c*) design of the new system; (*d*) systems narrative.

9.138 The need for systems analysis may result from (*a*) new legislation affecting the manner in which business is conducted; (*b*) new competition in the marketplace; (*c*) the inefficiencies of existing equipment or computer hardware; (*d*) all of the above.

9.139 The gathering of data on which to base a systems analysis is called the (*a*) systems study; (*b*) formal review; (*c*) data analysis; (*d*) collection of data.

9.140 A manual containing both job descriptions and procedures used in data handling is the (*a*) procedures manual; (*b*) organization manual; (*c*) forms manual; (*d*) systems manual.

9.141 A form used in the detailing of softcopy displays is the (*a*) storage layout form; (*b*) graphic display chart; (*c*) printer spacing chart; (*d*) visual layout form.

9.142 Documentation normally associated with a systems flowchart is the (*a*) systems design; (*b*) systems spacing chart; (*c*) systems narrative; (*d*) systems interview.

9.143 Paperwork used in a system is symbolically represented within a systems flowchart using the (*a*) document symbol; (*b*) processing symbol; (*c*) online storage symbol; (*d*) keyboard symbol.

9.144 The feasibility committee member that provides organizational budgetary data is the (*a*) top-level executive; (*b*) senior systems analyst; (*c*) departmental representative; (*d*) outside consultant.

CHAP. 9] SYSTEMS ANALYSIS AND DESIGN

9.145 Within the DP department, analysts are found within the _____ group.

9.146 Systems projects may require from _____ to _____ months to complete.

9.147 Organizations may monitor the people in their employ through use of _____ systems.

9.148 A practical example of an _____ system is the use of credit cards by a retail organization.

9.149 The effort to develop a new system to replace an existing system is identified as systems _____.

9.150 The periodic review of an existing system is referred to as its _____ review.

9.151 First-hand, user knowledge of a system's operation may be obtained when conducting _____ interviews.

9.152 The contents of a file may be detailed using a _____ form.

9.153 The steps composing a data handling procedure may be shown in a _____.

9.154 The documentation of a system study is completed only after the _____ system is fully implemented.

9.155 The evaluation of the alternative design solution selected by management is the object of the _____ study.

9.156 In the feasibility committee, _____ act as information sources on how data is handled within their respective areas.

Answers: 9.121 (*b*); 9.122 (*b*); 9.123 (*a*); 9.124 (*a*); 9.125 (*b*); 9.126 (*b*); 9.127 (*b*); 9.128 (*a*); 9.129 (*a*); 9.130 (*b*); 9.131 (*b*); 9.132 (*b*); 9.133 (*a*); 9.134 (*a*); 9.135 (*c*); 9.136 (*a*); 9.137 (*b*); 9.138 (*d*); 9.139 (*d*); 9.140 (*b*); 9.141 (*c*); 9.142 (*c*); 9.143 (*a*); 9.144 (*a*); 9.145 systems; 9.146 two, twenty-four; 9.147 personnel; 9.148 accounts receivable; 9.149 design; 9.150 scheduled; 9.151 personal; 9.152 storage layout; 9.153 systems flowchart; 9.154 final; 9.155 feasibility; 9.156 departmental representatives.

Supplementary Problems

9.157 What is the organizational structure of the data processing (DP) department? What are the responsibilities assigned to each of the groups composing the DP department?

9.158 What advantages accrue from using a team of analysts to perform the systems study? Explain.

9.159 Describe the five fundamental business systems and give examples of each from your daily environment.

9.160 Cite five circumstances that could result in a systems study and give an example of each.

9.161 What are the three ways in which a request for a systems study may evolve?

9.162 What is the significance of the collection of data for a systems project? List and explain the five methods of obtaining systems data.

9.163 Explain the purpose of systems flowcharts. Why are they valid ways of detailing the data handling procedures used within a system?

9.164 Prepare the systems flowchart that parallels the following systems narrative.

Step 1. Applications for leisure passes for municipal activities are received at the county clerk's office and grouped in batches of 100. The applications are kept in a bin until a group of 100 is collected.

Step 2. Each group of 100 is immediately sent to the DP department where a DP clerk receives them and immediately checks them for errors.

Step 3. Once checked, the batch of applications is given to another clerk who, using an online terminal, keys them onto the master disk file of applicants.

Step 4. The program LPUPDK is used to support the online update of the master disk, which results in an updated master disk when the keying process is complete.

Step 5. The other results of this processing are:
(a) The LP applicant report, which is sent to the county clerk's office
(b) A second copy of the LP applicant report, which is retained in the DP department for security
(c) The return of the original applications to the county clerk's office for record-keeping purposes

9.165 Why are alternative solutions prepared for management's approval when only one solution will be selected? Does this approach have any advantages for the systems staff?

9.166 What is the function of the feasibility committee? Who are its members and how do they contribute to the committee's work?

Glossary

Accounts payable system. The business system that details data related to monies owed by the organization.

Accounts receivable system. The business system that details data related to monies owed to the organization.

Collection of data. The initial phase of a systems study where information related to the existing system is gathered for analysis.

Data processing (DP) department. A data processing configuration, which in most organizations normally consists of three operational groups.

Feasibility committee. The committee assigned to perform the feasibility study.

Feasibility study. The study performed to determine whether the alternative chosen by management will suffice as the basis for the new system's design.

Inventory system. The business system that monitors the status of the goods maintained in an inventory.

Operations group. The DP department group that readies the computer hardware and directly implements the processing of data.

Organization manual. The manual detailing the structure of an organization and the job description of each employee position.

Payroll system. The business system that handles all tasks related to the payment of employees.

Personnel system. The business system that monitors the status of all employees working for an organization.

Point-of-sale (POS) terminal. The hardware device, employed in online retail systems, that combines the features of a cash register and a terminal.

Problem definition. Part of the systems analysis documentation that details the problem areas of the existing system.

Procedures manual. A manual detailing the procedures used by an organization in its handling of data.

Programming group. That unit of the DP department assigned the task of preparing and certifying all software written for the organization.

Scheduled review. The periodic review of existing systems to evaluate the overall efficiency and data handling capabilities.

System. An organized approach to achieving a stated goal.

Systems analysis. The evaluation of an existing system's ability to handle and distribute the information generated by an organization.

Systems analyst. The individual assigned the responsibility of performing systems studies.

Systems design. The steps composing the design of a new system to replace those systems deemed inefficient.

Systems flowchart. Diagrams describing the flow of information through an organization or the procedures used in data handling.

Systems group. That unit of the DP department assigned to systems studies and systems-related activities.

Systems narrative. The step-by-step narrative, accompanying a systems flowchart, that details the steps involved in data handling procedures.

Chapter 10

The Role of Secondary Storage

10.1 INTRODUCTION

Secondary storage is an online storage capacity directly attached to the CPU's primary storage unit. The purpose of secondary storage is to hold data that cannot be retained in primary storage during processing or data that must be retained on a long-term basis. Two general requirements of secondary storage are that it be online to primary storage and that all data be stored in a computer-acceptable format. Data can be retained in secondary storage indefinitely; in contrast, data in primary storage are destroyed when electric power is cut off from the CPU. The two most widely used secondary storage media are magnetic disk and tape.

10.2 MAGNETIC DISK

Magnetic disk offers a storage medium in which data items are randomly retrieved. The independent retrieval of data means that individual records can be accessed without affecting other data. This feature makes magnetic disk an ideal support vehicle for online processing activities.

The disk medium is composed of several flat disks, and data are retained on recording surfaces on both sides of the disk. *Read/write (R/W) heads* are assigned to each surface and jointly connected on the *access arm*. When one R/W head moves, all heads move. Both *removable* and *nonremovable disks* are available, with each affording distinct advantages. A *disk pack* is a removable disk of two or more surfaces.

Data are organized on a disk via track, sector, and cylinder. *Tracks* are concentric storage areas on each of the disk's recording surfaces. *Sectors* are subdivisions of each track where the storage of each record must commence. A *cylinder* consists of the same numbered track on all surfaces of a disk. The computer must have knowledge of all three factors in order to *randomly access* a record stored on disk. *Fixed-block addressing* is a concept related to fixing the size of sectors on disk. *Access time* refers to the time required to access a specific record on disk.

10.3 MAGNETIC TAPE

Magnetic tape is a secondary storage medium that records data on a *sequential* basis, that is, one record at a time, beginning with the first record stored. Data are recorded on tape or read from it sequentially. When the tape concept was introduced, data were recorded on tape and separated by *interrecord gaps* (*IRGs*). IRGs separated data and provided a means of accelerating to and from tape reading speeds. Modern tape storage utilizes *interblock gaps* (*IBGs*) instead of IRGs. IBGs separate *blocks* of data consisting of multiple records. *Blocking factors* detail the number of records in a block of data.

Tape was a major storage medium and has been replaced by disk only because of its random-access capabilities. Tape is still used to record permanent data items and to create backup storage to safeguard data retained on disk or other storage media.

10.4 HARDWARE CONSIDERATIONS

Additional secondary storage devices exist to facilitate long-term recording of processed data. Tape cassettes offer a limited and portable tape storage capacity. The computer codes currently used with tape storage include EBCDIC and ASCII.

Magnetic disks fall into a category of devices referred to as *direct-access storage devices*, or *DASDs*. A direct-access storage facility is a disk device consisting of multiple disks that are accessed as a single unit. A *mass storage system* is a cartridge storage that offers the random retrieval of data and has a capacity of 472 billion characters of data. *Magnetic drum* was a popular DASD device years ago because of its high transfer rate. Recent disk devices have exceeded the drum's capacities and have rendered it obsolete.

The offline preparation of tapes and disks is possible through *key-to-tape* and *key-to-disk devices*. A network of key-to-disk devices forms the basis of *distributed data entry system* (*DDES*). *Diskettes*, or *floppy disks*, provide a limited disk storage capacity for small and home computers. *Dual-density diskettes* permit data to be stored on both sides of diskettes.

10.5 FILE TYPES

The three major file structures used include a sequential file, direct-access file, and indexed sequential file. Each file type has its own operational characteristics. *Sequential files* are constructed one record after another, and data are accessed in exactly the same way. *Direct-access files* permit the random access of data from within its structure. The *indexed sequential file* utilizes an index of key storage locations to help access data. All three file types use a *key field* on which to base their file organizations. Indexed sequential files offer some advantages over direct-access files to include faster access time and fewer computational errors.

10.6 RELATED FILE SOFTWARE

File maintenance activities require the use of programs that perform similar activities despite their file structures. The general term applied to these programs is *utility software*. This software includes disk-to-disk, tape-to-tape, and disk-to-printer programs. Other utility software include sort programs and merge programs. *Sort programs* enable the ordering of file data, whereas *merge programs* enable the merging of two files of data in similar formats.

Compatible file formats are essential to the successful use of sort and merge programs. This constraint applies to the use of computer codes and storage densities on files. This is especially critical for tape files that use several *bytes per inch* (*BPI*) rates. Only files of like density and codes may be sorted, merged, and used in parallel. Files of like storage densities are usable on systems possessing the same operational characteristics.

Canned programs are prewritten programs used for specific applications. *Program packages* represent a group of prewritten programs used in major business systems.

Solved Problems

INTRODUCTION

10.1 What is secondary storage?

The term *secondary storage* defines the online storage areas attached to the central processing unit (CPU) to retain data used in processing. *Secondary storage* is the general term applied to the group of devices that perform that function in a computer system.

10.2 Why is secondary storage needed?

Secondary storage was developed to facilitate the handling of large amounts of data that could not be retained in primary storage. This necessity arose from the computer's being used to process large quantities of data in primary storage units that were extremely limited in size. In modern systems, data slated for processing are stored in secondary storage until they are needed.

10.3 Why is secondary storage related to the CPU?

Data retained in secondary storage had to be directly accessible to primary storage. Therefore, these two units had to be online and capable of transferring data between each other.

10.4 What two general requirements apply to secondary storage units?

Two characteristics of secondary storage are that it be online to primary storage and that it be stored in a computer-acceptable format. Retaining data in an online device means that it can be transmitted directly to the CPU whenever it is requested during processing. Being in a computer-acceptable format means that no conversion of the data is necessary, and thus they may be used directly in processing.

10.5 Why isn't the data retained in primary storage?

The primary storage units of most computer systems are limited to a fixed amount of storage. Even though great strides have been made in constructing bigger CPUs, they are still too small to store all the data used in most commercial applications. Thus secondary storage is an operational necessity. Another reason for primary storage's limited use relates to the fact that when the computer's power is down, all data kept in primary storage are destroyed. This is not the case with secondary storage since data recorded there are retained indefinitely, until they are deliberately erased or destroyed. Thus it is physically impossible to retain data in primary storage whenever the computer is shut off.

10.6 Do these restrictions affect the use of primary and secondary storage?

No. These restrictions do not affect the system negatively because each unit is designed to perform its particular function. Primary storage is needed during processing activities. Secondary storage retains data on a long-term basis, holding that data in a computer-acceptable format that is online to permit its immediate use.

10.7 What are the two most widely used secondary storage devices?

The two most reliable and widely used forms of secondary storage are magnetic tape and magnetic disk. Each has its operational advantages and will be reviewed in the following sections.

10.8 Are magnetic tape and disk the only means of secondary storage?

No. Other means of secondary storage exist that serve different operational functions. These devices are highly specialized, and they will be reviewed later in this chapter.

MAGNETIC DISK

10.9 What makes magnetic disk so critical to current data processing activities?

Magnetic disk is a secondary storage medium capable of retrieving data on a random-access basis. In other words, a data item retained anywhere in a file can be independently accessed without having to read through all the data items preceding it. Thus data regarding individual transactions, people, or events are independently available for processing.

10.10 Why is the random-access feature important to current users?

The random-access feature is important to users because it permits online processing activities to occur. For example, interactive processing sequences involving file inquiries are possible only because of magnetic disk support. Without it, immediate access to files and the individual records they contain would not be possible.

10.11 What type of processing is associated with online inquiries?

Online inquiries supported by the use of magnetic disk include determining what items are in an inventory, the amount of credit left available to a consumer, the status of a patient in a hospital, or the status of a license plate registration. Prior to disk inquiries these activities were not possible on a timely basis.

10.12 When were magnetic disk concepts introduced?

The operational concepts related to disk, enabling the random access of data from files, were introduced in the early 1960s. The introduction of these concepts permitted a radical change in how DP activities were conducted. Many activities previously not possible were now permitted, which forever changed the manner in which business is conducted. A fine example of this is found within the airlines industry. The introduction of magnetic disk permitted the development of online passenger reservation systems.

10.13 What features of magnetic disk permit the direct access of data?

The direct, or random, access of data is possible due to the physical construction of magnetic disk. Magnetic disk consists of a series of recording surfaces on disks that rotate on a center spindle, as shown in Fig. 10-1 (page 218). Figure 10-1a illustrates 6 disks stacked on a single spindle rotating at a high constant speed. The number of actual recording surfaces is computed at 10, as diagramed in Fig. 10-1b.

10.14 If there are 12 surfaces on 6 disks, why are there only 10 actual recording surfaces?

Though there are 12 surfaces, the top and bottom surfaces of the disk are not used (Fig. 10-1b). These surfaces are touched and handled by operations personnel and thus cannot be used for storing data.

10.15 Do all disks use 10 recording surfaces?

No. This discussion utilizes a 6-disk unit, consisting of 10 recording surfaces. However, these same principles apply to disks consisting of any number of recording surfaces.

10.16 What disk component moves between recording surfaces?

The units passing between recording surfaces, shown in Fig. 10-1b, are read/write (R/W) heads. Read/write heads provide the means of writing data onto each recording surface or reading data off of those same surfaces. For each recording surface, there is one read/write head that is used to access data.

10.17 How do the read/write heads work?

All read/write heads servicing a disk are tied together as one unit, called the *access arm*. The access arm moves the read/write heads between the recording surfaces. If one R/W head is moved, all of them move. The access arm aligns all R/W heads in a vertical column, one above the other. This fact is important in the actual organization and retrieval of data onto a disk.

10.18 Is the speed of data retrieval affected by the access arm?

Yes. The rule of thumb is that the more the access arm has to move, the slower the retrieval of data. This results from the fact that the access arm's movement is mechanical, whereas the actual transfer of data is electronic. Mechanical operations are generally slower than most electronic operations.

10.19 Are all disks physically the same?

No. Disks are divided into the two general categories: removable and nonremovable. Removable disks are portable and may be mounted into a disk drive for use. Once used, it is possible to remove that disk and exchange it for another disk that is mounted into the same disk drive. Nonremovable disks are permanently fixed into the supporting disk drive. The *disk drive* is the unit that holds either type of disk during operation.

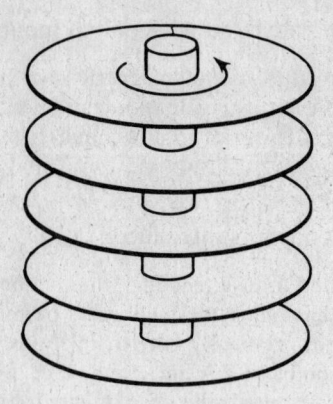

(a) All disks rotate on a center spindle at a constant speed.

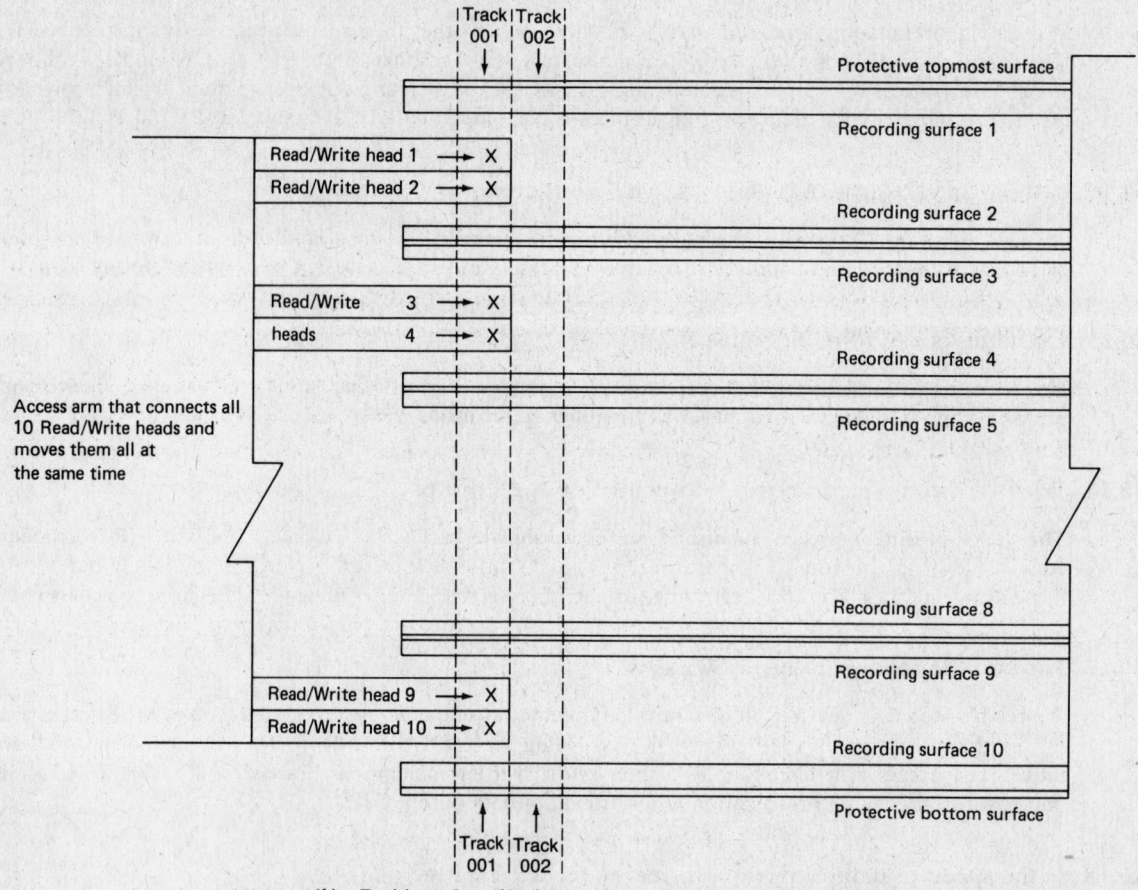

(b) Position of read/write heads in relation to disks' surfaces.

Fig. 10-1 Magnetic disk devices access data on a direct access basis. The structure of a disk unit supports this retrieval activity.

10.20 What does the term *disk pack* refer to?

The term *disk pack* refers to a removable disk consisting of two or more recording surfaces. Figure 10-1 illustrates a disk pack of 6 disks and 12 surfaces. Disk pack configurations vary considerably among computer manufacturers, and one example is shown in Fig. 10-2.

Fig. 10-2 Many types of disk pack are available to support disk handling activities. One of these is the disk cartridge shown here. This device has its read/write heads built into the disk module and comes as a fully contained unit.

10.21 What are the general advantages of either type of disk?

Removable disks offer flexibility in that they may be replaced as operational conditions dictate. However, because of their removability, some speed is lost in their ability to retrieve data. Nonremovable disks cannot be removed from their disk drive units and thus possess higher access speeds in retrieving data. Naturally, nonremovable disks are fixed and cannot be exchanged. Therefore, data must be read onto them, used, and then replaced by new data for the next application. The manner in which all disks are used varies according to the design and operational use of a specific computer system. No attempt will be made here to generalize on disk use since that differs widely as to type, size, and configuration of the system.

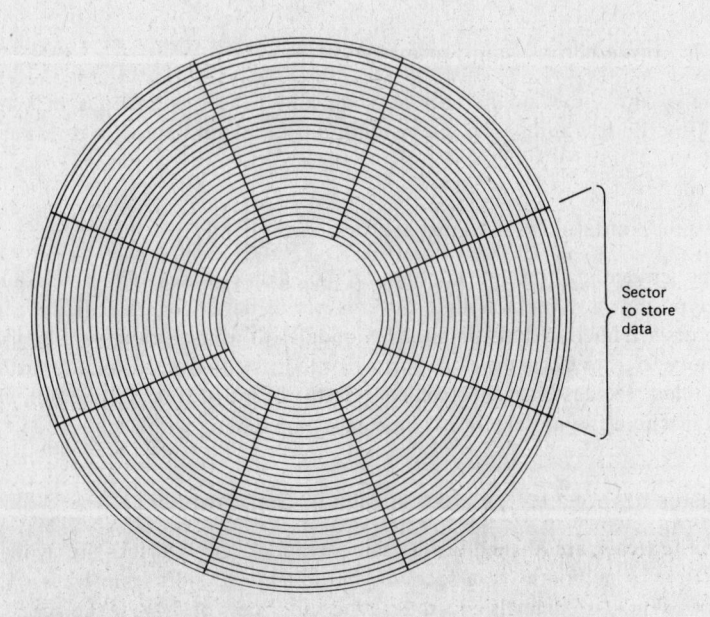

Fig. 10-3 Disks are divided into tracks which are divided into sectors.

10.22 How are data physically organized on a disk?

To answer that question, the structure of each recording surface on which all data are stored must be examined. Each recording surface is composed of a series of concentric storage areas called *tracks* (Fig. 10-3). Tracks are situated one inside the other, the tracks getting smaller as they approach the middle of the disk. Each track is further subdivided into *sectors*, which define the starting points for each record stored.

10.23 How is the sector boundary used?

The boundary of each sector reflects the point at which each new record begins. Each sector has the capacity to store a specific number of characters of data, depending on the manufacturer. Common sector sizes consist of 256, 512, or 1024 bytes of storage. Assuming a 512-byte sector, it is possible to store up to that amount in each sector. A record consisting of 460 bytes would commence at the start of a sector and utilize exactly 460 bytes of storage. The remaining 52 bytes of storage would remain unused. The next record would not begin at the end of the previous record but would commence at the start of the next sector boundary. Computer designers have found that although some space is lost, this operational configuration offers faster retrieval speeds and better internal data organization.

10.24 What does the term *fixed-block addressing* refer to?

Fixed-block addressing refers to the use of a fixed sector size within all magnetic disks produced by a specific computer manufacturer. It essentially forces the use of a common sector size by programmers designing files for that hardware. Fixed-block addressing simplifies the programming effort since only one size is used, it ensures that programs written for disk-oriented files will run in relation to any disk device. This compatibility eliminates the need to modify a program each time it is used with a slightly different disk drive.

10.25 What operationally follows the recording of data on each sector?

To observe how data are organized on a disk, one must now examine how tracks are organized on all surfaces of a disk. Reexamining Fig. 10-1b, it is possible to see that surfaces are stacked one above the other, aligning each track on each surface. Thus all tracks numbered 01 are aligned above each other, 02 are atop each other, and so on until the last inner track is reached.

10.26 What term is applied to all same numbered tracks?

The grouping of the same numbered tracks on all surfaces is called a *cylinder*. Thus there is an 01 cylinder, an 02 cylinder, and so on. Depending on its manufacturer, a disk may have from 100 to 400 cylinders.

10.27 How then are cylinders, tracks, and sectors configured?

The trick to understanding how data are organized on a disk relates to how cylinders, tracks, and sectors are integrated. Hypothetically, let us assume a user is storing data onto track 01, starting with sector 1. Once all available sectors are filled, a decision must be made as to what track should be used next. The question is whether to move to track 02 on the same surface or to move to track 01 on the surface immediately beneath the one just filled. Because it is electronically faster to move to the same numbered track on the lower surface, that is where the next record is written, commencing with sector 1.

10.28 Why is it faster to move to the next surface in that cylinder?

As all read/write heads are aligned on the same cylinder, all 01 tracks are available without moving the access arm. Thus in millionths of a second it is possible to shift from track 01, surface 1, to track 01, surface 2. Thus almost no delay is encountered in the access of data. If the access arm were to be moved, there would be a delay. Within disk storage all data are recorded on a cylinder-by-cylinder basis, moving toward the disk's center.

10.29 What hierarchy is used then in accessing data stored on a disk?

When identifying a record stored on disk, it is necessary to detail the cylinder, track, and sector of that record. Note that although these are the technical terms used, they are really misnomers. It would be more accurate to read them as indicating the cylinder, recording surface, and sector. The cylinder identifies the track used; the recording surface, the surface on which that track is specifically located; and the sector, the starting point at which the record is written. The difficulty arises from the misuse of the term *track*, which really implies surface in that hierarchy. However, once that terminology was adopted, designers were reluctant to change it.

10.30 Is the cylinder, track, and sector notation acceptable?

Yes. This notation is correct and is in fact required when identifying specific records. However, the user must remember that it really represents cylinder, surface, and sector.

10.31 When are these terms properly used?

The terms *cylinder*, *track*, and *sector* are primarily used by programming and systems personnel when discussing file structures and the data stored within them. It is not normally part of the average user's DP function. However, they should know what these terms mean since they relate to how data are stored on disk.

10.32 Are these terms used during input or output operations?

The cylinder, track, and sector notation is used whenever data are accessed from a file stored on disk. Whether data are written onto the disk (output) or read from data already stored on disk (input), these factors must be specified within the program supporting that activity. If one of the three is missing, locating a record on disk is not possible.

10.33 What term is used to define the speed at which data are retrieved from disk?

The term *access time* is used to define the time required to access a record stored on disk. The use of the word *access* is deliberate because it implies input as well as output operations.

10.34 What is the average access time for disk?

The average access time for disk may range from 15 to 75 milliseconds (thousandths of a second). This average represents a variety of manufacturers and devices.

10.35 Do the preceding considerations relate to the flexible floppy disks used with home computers?

Yes. The preceding concepts relate to disks used with conventional computer systems. Floppy disks will be reviewed in a later section.

MAGNETIC TAPE

10.36 Is magnetic tape another secondary storage medium?

Yes. Magnetic tape is the second most widely used secondary storage medium, after magnetic disk. This was not always the case, as the tape medium was first introduced in the mid-1950s. It was the first secondary storage medium to permit the online storage of data.

10.37 Why was tape replaced by disk?

Magnetic disk was introduced in the early 1960s, and it replaced magnetic tape because of its improved operational capabilities. Tape was a sequential storage medium, whereas disk is a random-access medium. It was not possible to jump out of order from one record to another with magnetic tape, because the tape had to be read through record by record, in order from the beginning. Disk offered more alternatives to the user and faster access to data in files.

222   THE ROLE OF SECONDARY STORAGE   [CHAP. 10

10.38 What is meant by sequential access via magnetic tape?

Magnetic tape is a sequential storage medium in which records are read one after another from record 1. This type of access is called *sequential access*. Magnetic disk permits the independent access of data, without passing through other records. This independent access is referred to as *random*, or *direct*, *access*. Sequential access requires reading from record 1 until the desired record is reached. Random, or direct, access enables the computer to go directly to the desired record.

10.39 Are records sequentially written and read from tape?

Yes. Data are written and read from magnetic tape sequentially under all conditions. When creating a tape file, data are written onto the tape from record 1. This same sequence is involved when reading data already written onto tape. The reading operation begins at record 1 and continues until the desired record is found. All data written onto tape or read from a tape are sequentially accessed as the tape passes over the tape's read/write head. Only one read/write head is incorporated into a tape unit in contrast to the multiple R/W heads used with magnetic disk.

10.40 How are data organized on tape?

To understand how data are currently stored on tape, the reader must first look at the origin of its storage concept. Originally, data were stored as shown in Fig. 10-4. From this figure, note that records were smaller than the blank spaces that separated them. Thus the original tape files were mostly blank.

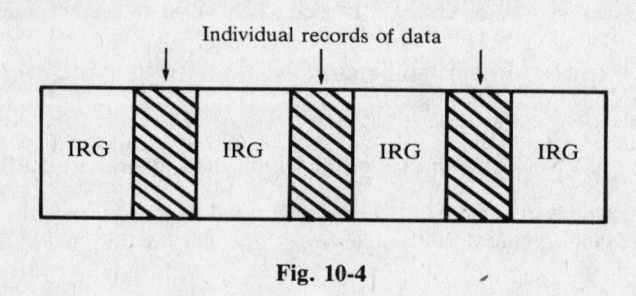

Fig. 10-4

10.41 What are the blank spaces between the records called?

The blank spaces between the records depicted in Fig. 10-4 are called *interrecord gaps*, or simply *IRGs*. The IRG was used to separate individual records and permit the tape to accelerate to and decelerate from reading speeds.

10.42 What was wrong with IRGs?

The IRG used the tape inefficiently because it represented blanks on the tape. A better alternative was to group the data being written onto tape. This grouping reduced the amount of blank space on the tape and the number of stops the tape unit had to make while reading individual records; it also lessened the wear and tear on the tape devices and improved their performance. The resulting storage configuration is shown in Fig. 10-5.

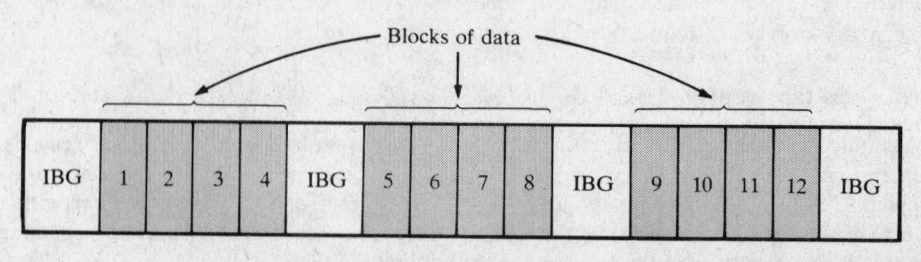

Fig. 10-5

10.43 What purpose does the IBG serve?

The *interblock gap* (*IBG*) serves the same purpose as the IRG except that it separates groups of records instead of individual records. Each grouping is referred to as a *block*. Figure 10-5 shows how 12 consecutive records may be written on tape; each block of data contains 4 records. The number of records written into a block is defined by its *blocking factor*. In Fig. 10-5, the blocking factor is 4.

10.44 Are data written sequentially when blocks are used?

Yes. Tape files are written sequentially, using blocks of data. Instead of writing individual records, blocking permits the recording of many records as one unit. Blocking efficiently uses the tape medium and is less taxing on tape hardware.

10.45 If tape was replaced by disk, what are the current uses of magnetic tape?

Disk replaced tape because it permitted the random access of data and supported online processing activities. However, tapes are used as storage mediums and as backup.

10.46 How is tape used as a conventional storage medium?

Magnetic tape is used to hold data that are infrequently handled, processed with a low level of change, or processed on a sequential basis. Tape can be used efficiently in these instances. However, because of disk's widespread use and processing speed, tape and disk are used in conjunction. For example, when a tape must be updated, it is dumped onto a disk, and the update is performed. When the update is complete, the contents of the updated disk are rewritten onto another tape, and that tape file is stored away. Switching from tape to disk and vice versa speeded up the processing of those data. What many users have learned is that it is faster to perform the tape update with disk than it is to perform the same update solely on tape. The data are retained on tape because it is economical to do so, and they cannot be retained on disk because sufficient space does not exist for the long-term storage of those infrequently handled files.

10.47 How are tapes used as backup?

Because of the expense related to data processing, it is necessary to avoid the repeated processing of the same material. This is especially true in updating files when the updated file is used as the basis for current processing activities. Thus a current copy of a file should be maintained to avoid having to reprocess and update that file. Under these conditions magnetic tape offers real advantages. After updating a file, an immediate copy of that file is transferred to magnetic tape and that copy stored away. Should something happen to the original disk, the tape copy is brought forward, a duplicate made for use in processing, and the original copy put back into storage. Tape is an inexpensive means of protecting the contents of a file and ensuring the continuous flow of data through an organization. Using tape as a backup storage medium overcomes the necessity of having to reprocess the update and incurring those related expenses.

10.48 How many copies of a backup tape are retained by an organization?

The number of copies of a backup tape retained depends on the organization. In some DP centers, only the latest version of a file's contents is retained. In others the last three or four versions of that updated file are kept to provide a means of going back to rebuild that file. Some companies that perform extensive data analysis may choose to retain copies of all files, after updating them, for a calendar year. Though this latter approach is expensive, it proves beneficial to those organizations and is part of their DP operation.

10.49 What type of application is best-suited for tape?

Tape operations are ideally suited for applications that are sequential by nature. That is, the computer must sequentially read through the entire tape file, processing the majority of records on that file. Some good examples are the update of a weekly payroll file, the monthly update of a personnel report, or the daily update of an inventory parts report. In most cases these examples represent some form of batch processing operation that is well-suited for using tape files. Generally, tape files cannot support online processing activities since they cannot efficiently and randomly access individual records.

HARDWARE CONSIDERATIONS

10.50 What are the major vehicles for providing secondary storage support?

The primary means of secondary storage are magnetic tape and disk. Figure 10-6 illustrates a disk drive unit and tape drive unit in which disk packs and tapes are used.

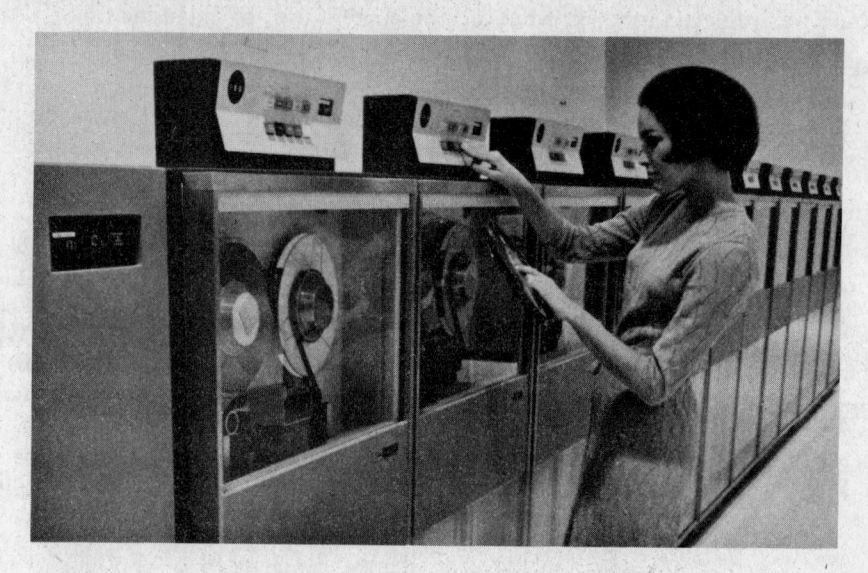

(*a*) A magnetic tape unit.

(*b*) A disk pack is placed in a disk storage drive.

Fig. 10-6 Magnetic tape and disk are the primary means of secondary storage. (*IBM*)

10.51 Have additional similar means been developed to provide secondary storage?

Yes. In addition to tape and disk, other secondary storage devices have been developed. These devices have provided additional storage means to diversify the storing and the entry of data.

10.52 How do tape cassettes serve this function?

A tape cassette, as shown in Fig. 10-7, is a small tape reel, which serves as a means of temporarily storing data and subsequently transferring it to conventional storage devices. The tape cassette is not designed as a major means of secondary storage; it has the capacity to retain a few million characters, but this capacity does not equal that of a conventional tape reel, which may contain upwards of 200 million characters of data.

Fig. 10-7 Magnetic tape cassette unit. (*NCR*)

10.53 What codes are used with the tape cassettes?

The ASCII code is used with tape cassettes, as opposed to the EBCDIC and ASCII codes that are used with conventional tape units. Initially, the BCD code was used when storing data, but this code was eventually changed to EBCDIC when BCD proved insufficient for the number of codes required for processing. Currently, the two major codes used when writing data onto magnetic tape are EBCDIC and ASCII. These codes were reviewed in Chap. 3.

10.54 Have additional disk devices been introduced?

Yes. Additional magnetic disk devices have been developed to aid secondary storage activities. These devices are referred to as *direct-access storage devices* (*DASD*) because they possess the ability to independently access data from a file. Two such DASD devices are the direct-access storage facility and the mass storage system, as shown in Fig. 10-8.

(a) A direct access storage facility. (*IBM*)

(b) The reading mechanism of the mass storage system. (*IBM*)

Fig. 10-8

10.55 How is the direct-access storage facility used?

The direct-access storage facility, as shown in Fig. 10-8a, is really a combined grouping of disks, dealt with as a single entity. This DASD device groups the collective resources of many disks into one operational unit. Direct-access storage facilities are configured to contain several disks, depending on the manufacturer. They provide a capacity for storing many billions of characters of data. Single disks currently available may provide anywhere from 800 million to 2.5 billion characters of storage per disk, depending again on the manufacturer and type of disk. Direct-access storage devices may incorporate removable and nonremovable disks in their construction, grouping their storage capacities.

10.56 Is the mass storage system a similar device?

The mass storage system, as shown in Fig. 10-8b, is a mass storage device capable of storing 472 billion characters of data. This DASD utilizes a honeycomb of cartridges in which data are stored and retrieved by a special cartridge selection mechanism. This device requires from 1 to 3 seconds to retrieve an item of data, compared to 15 milliseconds for a conventional disk drive.

10.57 Where would these devices be primarily used?

Direct-access storage facilities are used in computer systems in which access to a large volume of data in an organized form is necessary. This operational condition may exist within any good-sized DP center. Mass storage systems are used by insurance companies or large corporations that need access to a vast sum of data but can tolerate a slight delay in its online retrieval.

10.58 Where was the magnetic drum used?

Magnetic drum was a DASD that had the ability to rapidly access data at speeds that were superior to the then-existing disk devices. However, with the arrival of technically superior disk devices, which exceeded the capacities of the magnetic drum, it became obsolete. Current disk units exceed the capacity of the largest drum, which was 20 million bytes of storage and a transfer speed of 1 million characters per second (CPS). Because of the disk's technical superiority, the drum has been dropped from most computer configurations.

10.59 Have offline devices been developed to help secondary storage operations?

Yes. Two offline devices have been developed to speed and assist secondary storage operations. These devices, called *key-to-tape devices* and *key-to-disk devices*, as shown in Figs. 10-9 and 10-10 (page 228), enable the offline preparation of both tapes and disks.

10.60 How is the key-to-tape device used?

The key-to-tape device is used to key data, slated for storage on magnetic tape, onto small tape reels. These reels are then collected and compiled onto one large tape that is entered into processing.

10.61 Why was the key-to-tape device used?

DP professionals realized that conventional methods of creating tapes were indeed inefficient, tying up the computer for the entry of data. By using the key-to-tape device, the input of data occurs offline to the main computer and does not tie up its resources. The tapes entered for processing, produced by the key-to-tape unit, are ready for updating or creating other files.

10.62 Is the key-to-disk unit similarly used?

Yes. The key-to-disk device performs a parallel operational function, creating disks with data slated for processing. These disks may be used directly in normal processing activities.

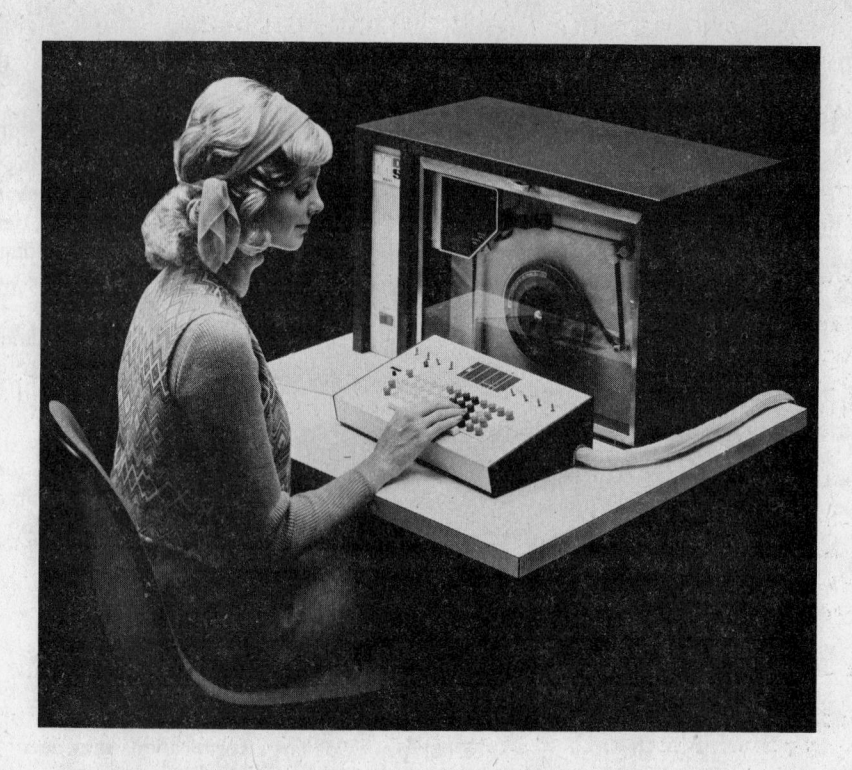

Fig. 10-9 A key-to-tape device. (*Mohawk Data Systems*)

Fig. 10-10 Key-to-disk devices are utilized for quick entry of data that will eventually be used to update files. (*Mohawk Data Systems*)

CHAP. 10] THE ROLE OF SECONDARY STORAGE 229

10.63 Have key-to-disk devices been incorporated into distributed networks?

Yes. Key-to-disk devices are essentially small computer systems whose sole outputs are magnetic disks. They speed the input of data onto disk in preparation for processing. These devices have been incorporated into distributed data entry systems (DDES).

10.64 How does a DDES function?

A distributed data entry system is a network of key-to-disk devices that are connected to a main computer. Data keyed onto disks at each device are telecommunicated to the main computer at regular intervals, eliminating the need to physically move the prepared disks onto the main system. These online networks speed the flow of input data to the main computer for immediate processing.

10.65 What type of organization uses a DDES configuration?

DDES networks are used by large corporations like General Motors and United Airlines that possess widely distributed service centers where large and varied quantities of materials are used. Using DDES networks, it is possible to quickly update their inventory and manufacturing records and avoid unwarranted delays and shortages.

10.66 Where do floppy disks come into play?

The floppy disk, or diskette, is a 5- or 8-inch-diameter disk recording medium, contained within a plastic envelope to cover its surface. It offers a limited direct-access capacity, which may exceed 1 million characters of data for a given disk. Diskettes are an integral part of most home computers and many of the smaller computer systems currently available. They provide a random-access capability, for limited quantities of data, at a reasonable price. Figure 10-11 illustrates a floppy disk in use.

Fig. 10-11 Floppy disks are used by many small computer systems to retain data on disk. (*Wang*)

10.67 Are diskettes designed to replace disk packs?

No. Floppy disks are not designed to replace the use of magnetic disks in conventional systems. They do not have the same storage capacities as conventional disks. Floppy disks are designed to add a direct-access storage capacity to systems that previously did not have it.

10.68 What is a dual-density diskette?

A dual-density diskette is a floppy disk that enables data to be stored on both sides of the disk's surface. This feature essentially doubles the storage capacity of a single diskette. Diskettes are a prime feature of home computers and really add to their operational capabilities.

10.69 With the variety of disk devices, what codes are used to record data within them?

Floppy disks are generally associated with the newer and smaller systems and utilize the ASCII computer code to record data. Conventional disks and disk storage devices will use either the EBCDIC or ASCII codes, depending on the computer system involved. As a rule of thumb, IBM equipment will utilize the EBCDIC code, and most other manufacturers, the ASCII code.

FILE TYPES

10.70 How many types of file structures are used in computerized file operations?

Three types of file structures are used in the majority of file manipulations. These file structures represent the major ways of organizing data when creating and updating the contents of those files.

10.71 How are file structures related to the handling of file data?

File structures dictate how a file is handled and how the data recorded within that file is accessed. The structure of a file and the device upon which that file is maintained require that the programmer follow certain conventions when writing software related to that file.

10.72 What are the three conventional file structures?

The three file structures encountered are:

(1) Sequential files
(2) Direct-access files
(3) Indexed sequential files

Each of these file structures organize their data in a specific way, unique to that format.

10.73 How is the sequential file configured?

A sequential file is organized as its name implies, one record after another, using some hierarchical sequence. Sequential files, like almost all files, must be ordered using a key field. The key field is a field upon which the file is ordered and which is found within every record stored on that file. Two good examples of a key field are an employee's social security number or a patient's name. A payroll file could be ordered numerically (in ascending order) using a social security number, whereas a medical patient file could be alphabetically sequenced by patient name.

10.74 Sequential files are then built up one record at a time?

Sequential files are created one record at a time, in order. They are also read one record at a time, commencing with record 1.

10.75 What secondary storage device is usually associated with sequential files?

Magnetic tape devices are normally operationally associated with sequential file structures since they ideally complement that storage medium. Tape files are sequentially read by individual records, and data are accessed as ordered in the file.

10.76 How does a direct-access file relate to sequential files?

Though some operational similarities exist, these two file structures vary considerably. Whereas sequential files require that data records be sequentially accessed, a direct-access file permits records to be randomly accessed. Individual records in a direct-access file are independently accessed, without having to pass through other records.

10.77 Which file type was developed first?

Sequential file structures were initially developed and reflected the existing technology. Direct-access files became a reality after the introduction of magnetic disk. Direct-access file structures are perfectly suited to use with magnetic disk since they offer the random-access processing of file data.

10.78 How is a direct-access file created?

Direct-access files, despite their random-access capability, must be created by sequentially writing each individual record. After the file is initially created and the file actually exists within some form of DASD, data within that file are independently accessible. However, the file is initially created as a sequential file.

10.79 Can a direct-access file be sequentially read after its creation?

Yes. Once a direct-access file is created, it is possible to read data records sequentially. However, doing so negates the advantages associated with using a direct-access file and a supporting disk device.

10.80 What disadvantages are associated with direct access?

Though direct-access files offer many advantages over sequential files, they possess some drawbacks. Direct-access files require that the programmer prepare a formula to compute the actual storage location of each record on file, based on the key field or characteristic input for the record desired. The programmer's task was not an easy one because the formula derived might provide duplicate, nonexistent storage locations for the same record or the same location for two or more records. Also the computational time needed to convert the input data to the storage location of the file was so great that it proved inefficient.

10.81 What file structure was developed to overcome these difficulties?

The indexed sequential file was developed to replace the direct-access file structure. It provides random access to all records in the file, but it simplifies the means of doing so. The programmer is not required to prepare a formula for determining storage locations, nor must he or she handle any of the technical details related to creating the file. These features are covered by current language structures, eliminating the need to write out these instructions. In addition, the time needed to determine the desired record's location is drastically reduced. Thus the vehicle for creating a random-access file structure was simplified, and access to the desired record was speeded.

10.82 Does the indexed sequential structure have a random-access capability?

Yes. Both direct-access and indexed sequential files offer a random-access capability, permitting independent access to records within each type of file. Both files are initially sequentially written and, once created, permit records within that file to be individually accessed. In effect, they provide the same operational features, but the indexed sequential file is faster.

10.83 How does the indexed sequential file differ?

The indexed sequential file accesses data records in a different manner. Instead of using a formula, the indexed sequential structure creates a table of key values and uses them as an index in searching data records. When a specific record is sought, the computer takes the key field and searches the index for the key storage location closest to that record. It then moves to that location and subsequentially moves to the desired record's location. Unbelievable as it may seem, this series of operations is faster (with all its comparisons and moves) than the computational sequence used with direct-access files.

10.84 Is it more difficult to prepare an indexed sequential structure?

No. Programmers prefer to create indexed sequential files because the operational software related to most current computer languages simplifies the task tremendously. These files are as easily updated when records are added or deleted from their contents.

10.85 How are indexed sequential files used?

Indexed sequential files are supported by DASD devices. Indexed sequential files must be created sequentially and then may be updated using their special random-access capabilities.

10.86 What type of applications lend themselves to each file type?

Sequential file structures lend themselves to batch processing operations, in which the entire file is processed at regular intervals. A weekly payroll, monthly update of an inventory, or the annual preparation of retirement benefit statements lend themselves to sequential file structures. Indexed sequential files, and before that direct-access files, are designed for online update of customer charge accounts, reservation systems, and any file requiring the use of random-access file capabilities.

RELATED FILE SOFTWARE

10.87 Do most file handling operations involve file updates?

No. Although many of today's file activities relate to updating their contents, they do not represent the totality of these program activities. Other file maintenance operations are required to keep them current and ready for updating activities.

10.88 What file maintenance activities might be performed to keep a file current?

File maintenance activities vary between DP centers but could include the transfer of files between storage media, the preparation of backup file copies, the ordering of data prior to inputting them to a file, or the output of an entire file for the verification of a file's contents. Each of these activities is usually performed as a part of file maintenance. File maintenance is considered as those steps taken to keep a file in its most current and correct status.

10.89 Is most of the software used in file maintenance specially written?

No. Though many file maintenance programs are specially written, there exists a group of manufacturer-supplied programs that are specifically used in performing these tasks. These manufacturer-supplied programs are called *utility software* and may perform a variety of file handling tasks. Utility software varies considerably among manufacturers, depending on the complexity of file handling activities required by larger computer systems. The larger the system, the higher the probability that file operations will involve large amounts of data, online processing of some form, and complex manipulations.

10.90 What are the basic types of utility software?

The basic types of file utilities involve I/O operations and the transfer of data between storage media. These utilities could transfer data between disk drives, from a disk-to-tape and vice versa, between two tapes, and from either device to a printer. Each of these activities involves the movement of the entire file or portions of a file as dictated by the programmer or computer operator.

10.91 How might these utilities be used?

It is sometimes necessary to duplicate the contents of a file, in its entirety, for security reasons. If this transfer involves the same storage media, then a tape-to-tape or disk-to-disk utility could be used. When making a backup copy of a file, a disk-to-tape utility is employed. The subsequent redumping of the backup file, should something happen to the original, would involve a tape-to-disk utility. When it is necessary to manually verify the contents of a file, a tape- or disk-to-printer utility is used to produce the listing of that file data.

10.92 Do other more specialized utilities exist?

Yes. Two more-specialized utility programs exist to order and combine file data. These programs, referred to as *sort programs* and *merge programs*, perform those functions.

10.93 How is the sort program used?

The sort utility program is used to order a file in numerical or alphabetical sequence. The numeric sequence may be in either ascending or descending order, depending on existing operational needs. The program must specify the ordering sequence desired and the key field upon which the file should be sorted.

10.94 May subsequent sort fields be specified if one key field is insufficient?

Yes. It is possible to specify more than one key field, if necessary, to accommodate the sorting sequence. This is often the case when common or similar data items appear in a single key field. This situation occurs when sorting a file by a person's last name. A last name is not enough. The sort hierarchy must include the first name, middle name, and social security number. Without these additional facts, how would two John Paul Joneses be distinguished?

10.95 Is the merge program similarly used?

Yes. The merge program is used in the same fashion. The programmer must specify the key field upon which the file is ordered. This key field becomes the basis of the merge operation since it will always be checked before a new record is added to the file.

10.96 What initial conditions must be satisfied before a merge utility can be used?

First, the merge utility requires that the key field be clearly defined. Second, all incoming data records have the same format as that of the file in which they are to be merged. Third, the incoming records must be sorted in exactly the same sequence as the file they will enter. If these conditions are not met, the merge program will not run and produce the desired blending of data.

10.97 Why the sensitivity of properly preparing for file handling?

There exists a common misunderstanding that the computer will overcome all obstacles and allow for errors. This is totally false. The computer has a specific set of conditions under which utilities will work. If these conditions are not met, they simply will not execute. Undefined conditions, erroneous data, improper file formats, and generally sloppy data handling render all utilities unusable.

10.98 Where might these compatibilities not be met?

Quite often organizations will purchase data regarding their business activities and have these data delivered to them on either tape or disk. For obvious reasons, it is imperative that the data purchased be in a format that is compatible with their own computer system. Many business managers have embarrassed themselves by overlooking this detail.

10.99 Aren't all tapes and disks similar?

No. As discussed previously, tapes and disks may record data using either the EBCDIC or ASCII codes. As long as a parallel code is used, magnetic disks are fairly compatible. The same is not true for magnetic tapes with which different storage densities may be used.

10.100 How are tape storage densities defined?

Two terms applied to the storage densities used when recording coded data on tape are *bytes per inch* (*BPI*) and *characters per inch*. These terms are interchangeable since they define the number of characters stored per inch of tape in either the EBCDIC or ASCII codes. The BPI term is most widely accepted.

10.101 What are the most commonly used BPI rates?

The BPI rates used when recording data on tape include the 800, 1200, 1600, 3200, and 6250 BPI. The last two rates were introduced within the past 5 years to add to the storage capacity of a magnetic tape. Most commercially available tapes are 2400 feet and can record upwards of 200 million characters of data.

10.102 Is it possible to use utility programs on tapes with different BPI rates?

No. It is not possible to do anything with tapes that have different BPI rates. Utilities must have compatible file formats, with like BPI rates, in order to be successfully used. For example, a 1200-BPI rate file cannot be merged with a 3200-BPI rate file. This constraint also applies to hardware. It is not possible to read a 1200-BPI written tape in a computer system that records its data at a rate of 1600 BPI.

10.103 Why was utility software written?

Utility programs were written to save programmers some work and to offer marketing angles to manufacturers. Systems manufacturers realized that these file handling activities were repeatedly being performed and that standardized programs could be written to perform these tasks. These utilities save programmers from having to write them each time they are needed.

10.104 Is prewritten software available for other computer-related tasks?

Yes. Prewritten programs are available from a variety of sources to include private software organizations and computer manufacturers. Two terms commonly used to represent these software are *canned programs* and *program packages*.

10.105 What is a canned program?

A canned program is a prewritten program that is applied to one specific type of problem. It is fully operational (within a specific set of conditions) and sold commercially to anyone who has need of its services. Canned programs are available to perform statistical analysis, analyze stock market trends, evaluate and audit business organizations, and determine optimum business strategies according to mathematical theories.

10.106 How is the canned program used?

The canned program is purchased and used as directed in its set of instructions. The user must learn how to use that software, prepare its inputs, and evaluate the outputs derived from it. The advantage of canned software is that it provides the user with an immediately usable program. Often canned software provides users with a starting point from which to develop their own software.

10.107 How does a program package differ?

Whereas canned programs usually relate to a single program related to a specific problem, program packages represent a group of programs related to an entire system or service. Essentially, the program package completely handles the application and no further software need be developed.

10.108 Why are program packages used?

Often an organization does not have the resources or time to write the software it needs to function. Thus the organization purchases program packages because they are usually immediately usable and represent the most current state-of-the-art technology available. The trade-off is between the cost of the program package and the immediacy of the organization's needs. Recent developments in the DP industry have tended to bring down the cost of program packages.

10.109 What types of program packages can be purchased?

Program packages are available for virtually any type of business activity. A program package frequently opted for is the payroll package. This set of programs fully handles the processing of a payroll, accounting for all employee payments, file manipulations, payroll reports, federal tax documentation, and any local paperwork. The program package comes fully documented, illustrating all inputs, outputs, and file formats. Other program packages are available for accounts receivable and payable systems, customer credit systems, audit and accounting systems, management evaluation systems, and business activities ranging from marketing to inventory control.

Review Questions

10.110 The term *secondary storage* refers to offline storage devices, incorporated into the CPU, to increase the storage capacity of the system. (*a*) True, (*b*) false.

10.111 Magnetic tape and disk are the only means of providing secondary storage. (*a*) True, (*b*) false.

10.112 Magnetic disk provides for the random, or independent, access of data from within a secondary storage field. (*a*) True, (*b*) false.

10.113 All disks are permanently fixed within the disk drive unit in which they are used. (*a*) True, (*b*) false.

10.114 When accessing a record on disk, it is necessary that the computer identify its cylinder, track, and sector. (*a*) True, (*b*) false.

10.115 Both magnetic tape and disk easily provide for the direct access of data during online processing applications. (*a*) True, (*b*) false.

10.116 Magnetic tape serves as an excellent backup medium because of its high storage capacity and relative low cost. (*a*) True, (*b*) false.

10.117 A mass storage system has a larger storage capacity than any existing disk drive. (*a*) True, (*b*) false.

10.118 Magnetic drum devices were used extensively years ago because of the high access speeds possible to limited amounts of data. (*a*) True, (*b*) false.

10.119 Floppy disks offer a limited direct-access storage capability in home computers and many small computer systems. (*a*) True, (*b*) false.

10.120 Direct-access files are sequentially constructed prior to random accessing of data from their contents. (*a*) True, (*b*) false.

10.121 In accessing data from an indexed sequential file structure, a formula is used to determine the actual storage location of a desired record. (*a*) True, (*b*) false.

10.122 The combining of two similar files is accomplished using a merge program. (*a*) True, (*b*) false.

10.123 When using sort and merge programs, it is not critical that similar file structures be involved since the computer will adjust for major differences in their respective formats. (*a*) True, (*b*) false.

10.124 It is possible to directly utilize a tape recorded at 1600 BPI in a computer system whose tape drives are rated at 3200 BPI. (*a*) True, (*b*) false.

10.125 The sole consideration when purchasing a program package is the expense involved. (*a*) True, (*b*) false.

10.126 A characteristic associated with secondary storage is (*a*) the use of input data on punched cards; (*b*) the use of offline devices to retain data; (*c*) the storage of data in a computer-acceptable format; (*d*) all of the above.

10.127 The subdivisions of tracks on a recording surface are called (*a*) bytes; (*b*) cylinders; (*c*) sectors; (*d*) blocks.

10.128 The term applied to all of the same numbered tracks on a disk is (*a*) blocks; (*b*) cylinders; (*c*) sectors; (*d*) *a* or *b*.

10.129 The blank space placed between groups of multiple records on tape is called a(n) (*a*) IBG; (*b*) IRG; (*c*) IBM; (*d*) IRC.

10.130 A computer code used in the storage of data on tape is (*a*) BCD; (*b*) EBCDIC; (*c*) ASCII; (*d*) all of the above.

10.131 Codes currently used in the storage of data records on disk are (*a*) Hollerith and ASCII; (*b*) EBCDIC and ASCII; (*c*) EBCDIC and BCD; (*d*) BCD and Hollerith.

10.132 The DASD device composed of a series of integrated disks is the (*a*) disk pack; (*b*) mass storage disk system; (*c*) direct-access disk drive; (*d*) direct-access storage facility.

10.133 DDES networks are constructed using (*a*) key-to-disk devices; (*b*) key-to-tape devices; (*c*) disk storage facility units; (*d*) mass storage systems.

10.134 The file structure most suited to magnetic tape storage activities is the (*a*) direct-access file; (*b*) indexed sequential file; (*c*) sequential file; (*d*) data structure file.

10.135 The file structure associated with independent retrieval of data records is the (*a*) direct-access file; (*b*) indexed sequential file; (*c*) sequential file; (*d*) *a* or *b*.

10.136 Sort programs make it possible to order file data (*a*) alphabetically; (*b*) ascending numerically; (*c*) descending numerically; (*d*) all of the above.

CHAP. 10] THE ROLE OF SECONDARY STORAGE 237

10.137 A group of programs designed to completely handle an entire customer credit system is referred to as a(n) (a) A/P system; (b) program package; (c) canned program; (d) utility program.

10.138 Data used in processing but not held in primary storage may be retained within _____ storage.

10.139 The random access of data from secondary storage is possible using magnetic _____.

10.140 All R/W heads on a disk are attached to the _____, ensuring that all of them move jointly.

10.141 The use of a standardized sector size is the basis of the technique called fixed-_____.

10.142 The time needed to access a record on disk is referred to as _____.

10.143 Magnetic tape is ideally suited for _____ processing applications.

10.144 The number of records in a block of data on tape is specified by the _____.

10.145 A limited amount of tape storage is provided via a _____ device.

10.146 The acronym _____ refers to secondary storage devices capable of the direct access of data.

10.147 The terms *floppy disk* and _____ are interchangeable.

10.148 The field upon which a file is ordered is the _____.

10.149 File maintenance activities can involve the use of _____ software.

10.150 Storage densities in tape storage operations are defined according to a file's _____ rate.

10.151 A prewritten program used to generate one type of business data may be called a _____ program.

Answers: 10.110 (b); 10.111 (b); 10.112 (a); 10.113 (b); 10.114 (a); 10.115 (b); 10.116 (a); 10.117 (a); 10.118 (a); 10.119 (a); 10.120 (a); 10.121 (b); 10.122 (a); 10.123 (b); 10.124 (b); 10.125 (b); 10.126 (c); 10.127 (c); 10.128 (b); 10.129 (a); 10.130 (d); 10.131 (b); 10.132 (d); 10.133 (a); 10.134 (c); 10.135 (d); 10.136 (d); 10.137 (b); 10.138 secondary; 10.139 disk; 10.140 access arm; 10.141 block addressing; 10.142 access time; 10.143 sequential; 10.144 blocking factor; 10.145 tape cassette; 10.146 DASD; 10.147 diskette; 10.148 key field; 10.149 utility; 10.150 BPI; 10.151 canned.

Supplementary Problems

10.152 Why would you prefer to store data in a direct-access storage mode rather than on a sequential-access basis?

10.153 Describe the three file structures used in recording file data. Why is the indexed sequential file structure so popular today?

10.154 In your own words and with supporting diagrams, explain the relationship between cylinders, tracks, and sectors when defining the location of a record on magnetic disk.

10.155 What is the difference between an IRG and IBG? Why is the IBG more efficient to use?

10.156 How can the key-to-disk device be used to speed the offline preparation of magnetic disks? Why is its use critical to the DDES network?

10.157 How does the distributed data entry system help a widely dispersed organization handle input data? Could a DDES network be of assistance to a small organization as well as to a large one?

10.158 What is the function of utility software? Cite some examples of this software and where it could be effectively used.

10.159 Explain why magnetic tape is an excellent backup storage medium.

10.160 As a business manager, what factors might lead you to purchase a program package? Which factor would be most significant in your evaluation?

Glossary

Access arm. The disk drive component that affects movement of all read/write heads.

Access time. The time required to access and transfer data from a disk device.

Block. The physical grouping of multiple records on tape.

Blocking factor. The factor that defines the number of records composing a block of data on magnetic tape.

Bytes per inch (BPI). The factor that specifies the storage density used to record data on tape (that is, 800 BPI, 1600 BPI).

Canned program. A prewritten program that is commercially available for use in a specific application.

Characters per inch. Serves the same purpose as BPI.

Cylinder. The term used to identify all of the same numbered tracks on each of the recording surfaces of a disk.

Direct access. The independent access of data from a DASD.

Direct-access file. The file type that permits the random access of data from a disk-oriented device.

Direct-access storage device (DASD). The general categorization applied to all devices capable of randomly accessing data from a file.

Direct-access storage facility. A DASD composed of multiple disks that are treated as a single entity.

Disk drive. The hardware unit in which a magnetic disk is used.

Diskette. The small circular flexible disks used for direct-access files on small and home computers.

Disk pack. Removable disks of two or more surfaces.

Distributed data entry system (DDES). The network of key-to-disk devices used to enter data on an online basis to a central computer.

Dual-density diskette. A diskette that permits data to be recorded on both of its sides.

Fixed-block addressing. A technical concept related to fixing the size of storage sectors within a track.

Floppy disk. Another term for a diskette.

Indexed sequential file. A file structure containing an index of key values that is used when accessing data records.

Interblock gap (IBG). The blank space separating blocks of data on magnetic tape.

Interrecord gap (IRG). The blank space once used to separate individual records on magnetic tape.

Key field. A field within a record that is used to order a file and to access a record.

Key-to-disk device. A device used to create magnetic disks on an offline basis; the prime component in a DDES network.

Key-to-tape device. A device used to create magnetic tapes on an offline basis.

Magnetic disk. The secondary storage medium used for the random access of file data.

Magnetic drum. A DASD that possessed a fast access time to limited amounts of data; it has been effectively replaced by newer disk devices.

Magnetic tape. The secondary storage medium used for the sequential storage of data.

Mass storage system. A DASD using a cartridge-like storage component capable of storing 472 billion characters of data.

Merge program. Utility software used to combine the contents of like files.

Nonremovable disks. Magnetic disks that are permanently fixed within their disk drives.

Program package. A group of prewritten programs that can fully handle the processing related to a business system.

Random access. The independent access of file data.

Read/write (R/W) head. The mechanism in secondary storage devices that is used to read or write data for that medium.

Removable disks. Disks that are interchangeably removed between disk drive units.

Secondary storage. The storage unit, directly attached to the CPU, that holds data not retained in primary storage.

Sector. The subdivision of tracks on a disk's recording surface in which individual data records are stored.

Sequential access. The sequential retrieval of data recorded in a file, commencing with the first record stored.

Sequential file. The file structure that enables the sequential access of data from within that file.

Sort program. The utility software used to order the contents of a file.

Tape cassette. The small, tape-like storage device used to record limited amounts of data on tape.

Track. The concentric storage areas on each disk's recording surface.

Utility software. Prewritten manufacturer-supplied programs that are used to perform many file handling activities.

Chapter 11

Management Information Systems (MIS)

11.1 INTRODUCTION

The initials MIS denote the computer configuration called a *management information system*, which represents a comprehensive system producing information for decision making by management. A major objective of an MIS is to provide management with the information necessary on which to base their decisions when managing an organization. Though everyone agrees on the MIS function, no consensus exists on a common configuration.

An MIS is designed to maximize the effect of management, providing them with the most current information available. These systems should fully integrate personnel, procedures, equipment, and the computer in providing their informational data. MIS projects can be quite lengthy due to their complexity, ranging from 6 to 36 months to complete. MIS structures may be developed in relation to any corporate size and informational needs.

MIS-generated data are distributed throughout all levels of management in an organization. Low-level management will use MIS data in managing day-to-day operations and handling the organization's immediate needs. Middle management administers the organization's interim plans, handling activities that relate from 3 to 12 months in the future. Top management must consider the organization's long-term goals, planning projects more than 1 year in the future. MIS data help administer the company's activities and equitably distribute the resources available to the organization.

Files supporting an MIS are fully integrated, permitting maximum access to all data retained in those files. Other characteristics of an MIS are that all outputs are decision-oriented, the information made available is user-oriented, and the overall system has sufficient growth potential.

11.2 REPORTING INFORMATION TO MANAGEMENT

Four report formats used with MIS-generated outputs are the regularly scheduled listing, exception listing, on-demand report, and forecasting report. *Regularly scheduled listings* are generally comprehensive reports that appear on a defined, periodic basis. *Exception listings* appear regularly but highlight data related to abnormal conditions. *On-demand reports* are made available by the specific request of the user. *Forecasting reports* are used to project future business activities and are used as planning tools.

11.3 MIS CONFIGURATIONS

MIS structures may assume many formats in relation to an organization and its informational needs. Four common MIS configurations are centralized, distributed, hierarchical, and decentralized. The *centralized MIS structure* is constructed around one centrally located computer that is the focal point of all processing activities. This configuration is different from the *distributed MIS structure* in which computer systems of comparable size create a network to share the workload. The *hierarchical MIS structure* parallels the structure of the organization it supports, providing gradually increasing computer services at each managerial level. The *decentralized MIS structure* offers the maximum in divisional security, restricting MIS services to each division of the organization.

11.4 DATABASE STRUCTURES

A *database* represents a fully integrated group of files that compose a single operational entity. Using a database, it is possible to provide access to data within each file, update the contents of those files, and cross-reference common data held within multiple files. Databases evolved to provide an organized access to a collective group of files and to avoid the waste of duplicate files, repeated data handling, and unplanned growth.

Special operational software is needed to construct and maintain a database. Using this software, it is possible to access data from many files, update files from a single input of data, and accommodate online inquiries. A *point-of-sale* (*POS*) *system* is a retail system that updates its database in such a fashion. *POS terminals* serve as the I/O medium in such retail systems.

The software used to support database operations are called *database management systems* (*DBMS*). These prewritten programs are available for data management in both large and small computer systems. The use of DBMS software saves organizations the time, effort, and cost of developing their own database programs, but it restricts them to those features available with that prewritten software.

Two data structures commonly used with ordering files in databases are the simple structure and the inverted structure. The *simple structure* organizes its file using a single common key such as storage location. The *inverted structure* uses a group of keys to organize its files, thus permitting the computer to access file data using multiple keys. The latter method is more difficult to conceive but offers more rapid access to data. A technique used with the inverted structure is *chaining*, whereby relationships are established to provide rapid access to related items of data.

11.5 ADMINISTRATION OF THE DATABASE

Database administration may be divided into the areas of software and personnel management. *Software management* relates to the planning, development, and maintenance of DBMS software. *Personnel management* relates to the handling of personnel composing the database group of the DP department.

Supervision of the database grouping is performed by the *database administrator*, who coordinates and supervises the work of all analysts, programmers, and technicians servicing the database. Although the number of people is not fixed, the database group may consist of four people. The key functions of the database administrator are the coordination of all database maintenance, supervision of the design and implementation of all database files, liaison with management and preparation of a *user's handbook*, coordination of all database documentation and the monitoring of all database security measures.

11.6 INFORMATION MANAGEMENT SYSTEMS (IMS)

Where MIS configurations are designed to generate information for management's use, *information management systems* (*IMS*) were created to efficiently manage the information made available by computer services. An IMS is a software package commonly found within an MIS structure. It is useful because of its ability to organize and manage information in preparation for its distribution within the MIS network.

Two examples of IMS techniques are CICS and DC/DB systems. *CICS* represents the *customer information control system*, originally developed to handle customer inquiries for Con Edison. CICS was developed to satisfy the need for an efficient method of accessing customer data from the Con Ed database and handling the data communications tasks associated with related customer inquiries.

Data Language/1 (*DL/1*) is a special IBM language used to prepare database-related software. This language overcame some of the difficulty associated with programs written to interface with CICS.

The *data communications/database (DC/DB) system* is a multiprocessing configuration whereby three computers share the workload. The first computer is assigned the responsibility of handling and coordinating all data communications requests. The latter two parallel systems share the processing workload and control access to the database. This twin-computer setup offers a measure of security to the large corporations that are usually totally reliant on the processing capacity of their DC/DB system.

Solved Problems

11.1 What do the initials MIS represent?

The initials MIS denote *management information system*, which is a comprehensive system designed to supply an organization's management with the information needed to administer the organization. An MIS is not normally a small system configuration; rather, it is composed of many operational aspects both computerized and manual. It is usually tailored to the specific needs of the organization it supports.

11.2 Is there a consensus on the MIS configuration?

No. Data processors will agree on the need to possess MIS support, but the concurrence stops there. Very few systems people agree on what constitutes an MIS. An MIS can be defined as a computer system that integrates equipment, procedures, and personnel to produce managerial information for decision making. The basis of this definition is the successful integration of people, equipment, operational procedures, and supporting computer to produce the information needed by management to guide the organization through the decisions that must be made.

11.3 Where does the controversy arise if everyone agrees on the structure of an MIS?

Everyone agrees on what must be integrated; the disagreement arises on how these components interface and the information that is produced. The lack of concurrence results from the fact that each organization utilizes different quantities of data, in different ways, to arrive at the decisions necessary to manage the company. Each organization functions differently and develops the information it needs to work with. Naturally, the MIS constructed for each company incorporates these differences and becomes unique to that organization. The MIS must reflect the specific procedures used in arriving at decisions and handling the required data, the guidelines applied by management, the equipment supporting the organization's work, and the software used to integrate these factors to provide the information for management's use.

11.4 Why are these factors so difficult to uniformly integrate?

Because no two organizations function similarly, their decision-making policies will vary. A decision to charge 0.5 percent more on an interest rate can have considerable impact on an organization's loan policy and future lending policies. When this type of decision is multiplied by the hundreds of similar operational choices an organization must make and plan for, one can begin to assess the complexity of an MIS and how unique it becomes to that organization.

11.5 Why is it necessary for an MIS to integrate personnel, procedures, equipment, and the computer?

Each of these factors, if improperly utilized, can wreck the effectiveness of an MIS. For example, the best procedures are defeated if the employees applying them are careless or improperly trained. Similarly, the best-trained and most-conscientious employees will be ineffective if the procedures used to run the business are poorly constructed, overly complex, or possess a large number of steps making them cumbersome to use. No amount of equipment will overcome the ineffectiveness of both people and procedures. Conversely, the best plans are defeated, if essential equipment is not available when the user thought it was. The computer supporting an MIS is equally vital. The computer utilizing faulty data is rendered as useless as the malfunctioning system whose software continually produces a stream of bad information from correct input data. All four factors must be properly integrated for the MIS to function efficiently and benefit the organization and its management.

11.6 What people help construct the MIS?

Systems analysts, working in project teams, are principally responsible for designing and implementing a management information system. They design and prepare all specifications regarding I/O documents, displays, supporting software, hardware, and procedures governing the handling of all data within the MIS.

11.7 What type of time frame exists for implementing an MIS?

An MIS project can take from 6 months to almost 36 months to fully implement. The length of the project depends on its complexity and scope.

11.8 Do these systems vary in relation to size of the organization?

Yes. Small companies, as well as large corporations, can profit from the implementation of an MIS. As small companies are generally not as complex, the scope of a supporting MIS will be less intricate. Again, however, the MIS used must relate to what the company is doing. A large corporation could conceivably handle data fairly straightforwardly, on a cash basis, and avoid the many complexities of a credit-oriented organization. Conversely, a small company could perform intricate analysis on small amounts of business data and project business activities into the millions of dollars. The scope of an MIS relates directly to the organization's function, size, and the information needed by its management.

11.9 Is MIS-generated information useful at all managerial levels?

Yes. All levels of management can benefit from MIS-generated data since the MIS is designed to provide the information on which a business is run. MIS structures are not designed solely for top management's use; rather, they must generate data for all management levels. It should be obvious that if two levels of data are available, one less current than the other, the organization will suffer. Imagine providing half of a stock brokerage firm current data and leaving the remaining half with two-day-old data! An organization's MIS should provide the entire organization with the most current data and distribute this information on a timely basis to all levels of management.

11.10 How do the lower levels of management use MIS data?

Lower levels of management are concerned with day-to-day operational matters. Thus they require information on what is currently happening and what will happen within the immediate future. In contrast, mid-level managers need a combination of control and projectionary data in order to administer their respective areas of responsibility. Their operational domain is the near future, from 3 months to 1 year away, whereas lower-level management is concerned with events no more than 3 months away. Middle management controls the organization, ensures that it is remaining within budgetary allotments, and implements policies to achieve the stated goals of the company. Low-level management controls all resources at the point of issuance and ensures that workers are carrying out these activities properly and efficiently.

11.11 How does top management differ?

Top management plans the organization's future, projecting the organization's activities more than 1 year into the future. Their informational needs are based on estimates of currently prevailing business conditions and plans regarding the company's growth. They synthesize existing data, future plans, company growth, business conditions, competition, and any other factors deemed important into a comprehensive plan governing the organization's future. The MIS is a vital part of this planning function because it provides the vehicle for coordinating all these factors and assessing their impact.

11.12 Why are these activities not handled by conventional business systems?

Conventional business systems are designed to focus on one major activity and its supporting I/O and file formats. They do not accomplish the integration of data nor the synthesizing of a group of facts from two or more diverse systems. Normal business systems may combine data drawn from within its resources, but it takes an MIS to integrate data from many systems and synthesize that data into intelligible and useful managerial information.

11.13 Then are business systems not useful?

No. The purpose of a business system is different from that of an MIS. Business systems can handle personnel or accounts receivable data within their respective systems, but an MIS is designed to integrate two or more systems into a single informational entity. Business systems often provide the basis for an MIS, providing the fundamental systems activities that must be integrated to produce managerial decision-making data.

11.14 How might different systems be integrated within an MIS-oriented inventory system?

A conventional inventory system would handle only inventory data and provide information solely on those items. An MIS-oriented inventory system could accommodate inventory data, as well as purchasing, accounts payable, and shipping and receiving data. For example, all inventory data would be updated on an online basis, advising inventory control personnel of the status of every item held in inventory. The system would indicate those items having an adequate inventory level, items requiring replenishment, items on order, and items having a zero balance. For items needing to be ordered, the MIS system would prepare the purchase order with specifications and alert the purchasing agent. When the order is actually made, computerized entries are posted against the purchasing and accounts payable files, respectively, noting finalization of that purchase and subsequent payment. In a conventional group of systems, each of these actions would be independently handled within each separate system. In an MIS a low inventory level triggers the entire series of transactions, leaving personnel to focus on their main functions and providing them with sufficient data on which to act.

11.15 Are MIS structures more complex than conventional systems?

Yes. Management information systems are more complex since they must do more than conventional systems. Their operational requirements require the interface of data drawn from many systems and the timely distribution of information to the proper people.

11.16 Are MIS files fully integrated?

Yes. Files supporting the MIS structure are, by design, fully integrated. They have the ability to transfer data between files, under the direction of programs supporting the MIS. This software clearly defines under what conditions the data will be passed and what specifically will be done with the transferred data. All informational relationships are clearly established between files and the activities performing their update.

11.17 Why are there no hard and fast rules regarding an MIS?

No such rules exist because each MIS assumes a different form in each organization and because it operates under slightly different conditions. One cannot dictate a specific set of reports because the informational needs vary enough to change who receives what reports and what facts those people need to function as decision makers. It is at this point that the controversy involving MIS configurations surfaces and that estimates of what constitutes an MIS are drawn into conflict.

11.18 In general, what is the overall objective of an MIS?

A management information system is designed to provide managerial personnel with the data necessary to perform their jobs. This principle is applied across all levels of management to include the top, middle, and lower levels. The MIS must accommodate the differences related to each level and the types of operational information needed by each manager. It is the concurrent preparation of data for all types of managerial positions that creates the complexities related to MIS structures.

11.19 What characteristics are generally associated with an MIS?

Three operational characteristics normally associated with MIS configurations responsive to user needs are:

(1) Decision-oriented outputs
(2) User-oriented information
(3) Sufficient MIS growth potential

11.20 Why are all outputs decision-oriented?

The requirement that outputs resulting from an MIS be decision-oriented reflects the totality of the MIS structure. Users should be able to make decisions based on the information provided, without having to perform additional data conversions. If this is not the case, the MIS is not functioning properly. It is senseless to perform computations manually that are readily performed by the computer.

11.21 Why is user-oriented information necessary?

Data that are not directly related to a user's needs are totally useless. All information developed must be approved by its user for it to have impact. The resources of an MIS should not be wasted on reports that are neither needed nor used. When this type of condition arises, it usually signals a system that is in need of review and change.

11.22 Why is sufficient growth potential needed?

An MIS project is a significant undertaking and may take upwards of 3 years to complete. It is the type of project undertaken to improve the efficiency of a growing organization to provide that organization with the information necessary to sustain its growth. It would not be logical to design an MIS to service existing needs if a larger operational load is projected. To overcome the possibility of outgrowing an MIS before it is fully implemented, additional growth potential is deliberately designed into the system. This permits the MIS to handle a larger load, without having to scrap the existing system. Also, if the MIS is sufficiently large, it can efficiently accommodate a period of growth and reconciliation. Ordinarily, an organization grows and consolidates prior to expanding again. A properly sized MIS can handle such expansion and service the start of the next expansion without a major overhaul.

REPORTING INFORMATION TO MANAGEMENT

11.23 How critical are the outputs derived from an MIS?

The outputs of an MIS are the lifeblood of the overall system. Evaluation of those outputs defines whether the MIS structure is performing properly and providing its users with adequate information. To accommodate its users, the MIS will utilize many types of output to present its information.

11.24 What report formats will an MIS utilize?

The four report formats associated with the MIS structure are:
(1) Regularly scheduled listings
(2) Exception listings
(3) On-demand reports
(4) Forecasting reports

11.25 When is the regularly scheduled listing used?

As its name implies, the regularly scheduled listing appears on a regular basis and represents one of the most widely used report formats. These periodic reports provide users with routinely used information, basically cataloging data regarding anything that occurs within the overall system. Examples representative of this report format include weekly payroll listings, monthly mortgage payment summaries, quarterly bank-interest-due reports, or the annual summary of taxes paid to all employees.

11.26 Who uses regularly scheduled reports?

Generally, the lower levels of management use regularly scheduled listings because they contain a volume of daily transactional data. It is these data that are used to verify customer accounts data, to uncover errors in inventory levels, and to answer inquiries regarding purchases made.

11.27 Are exception listings used differently?

Exception listings serve an entirely different purpose when compared to regularly scheduled listings. Exception listings selectively display data regarding conditions that reflect abnormal results. For example, instead of printing all people that have paid real estate taxes, an exception listing will document only those people that have failed to pay their assessed taxes. This type of report enables supervisory personnel to focus their attention on conditions that require immediate rectification.

11.28 Who normally utilizes the exception listing format?

Exception listings transcend all levels of management because they provide data on abnormal conditions occurring at all managerial levels. Normally, the data presented via exception listings are immediately incorporated in some form of decision-making cycle.

11.29 Are on-demand reports similar to regularly scheduled listings?

No. On-demand reports are prepared only when requested. They are produced on demand, that is, only when needed. Generally, on-demand reports assume a softcopy format because this form is visually informative and readily provided on a CRT. On-demand reports are designed to quickly provide data items in response to inquiries made on a terminal. These outputs are quite specific, relating usually to one form of output.

11.30 What management levels rely heavily on on-demand reports?

Both top and middle management are heavy users of on-demand reports because they are frequently responding to rapidly changing business conditions. Using an online inquiry, the president of a company can quickly check the level of current sales and how this sales activity relates to past years, future projections, and expected sales activity. Using this data, the president could authorize an increase in sales activity and direct that it be carried out by the lower levels of management. On-demand reports are also used by low-level management in replying to customer inquiries regarding the payment of credit card bills, adjustments to utility bills, and clearances of drivers' licenses and registrations.

11.31 How helpful are forecasting reports?

When planning activities are undertaken by top management, forecasting reports are the principal vehicle used. This report format permits them to develop planning strategies and to estimate the time, cost, and laborpower levels involved. Forecasting reports are strictly projectionary and may be developed for any desired time frame. As planning vehicles, forecasting reports may be used to map out many strategies, some of which are actually implemented and others which serve as only instructional models. Despite the final disposition of each plan, this report provides the means of estimating the results possible.

11.32 Are forecasting reports a major planning tool for top management?

Yes. Because of the planning nature of their work, the top levels of management frequently use forecasting reports. This report type enables middle and top management to plan strategies and verify the effect of currently developing trends. Thus a manager can assess a current sales trend, project its volume for up to 6 months ahead, and determine the impact that it will have on budgeted resources for the next two years.

11.33 Are each of these four formats used throughout an MIS?

Yes. Each format lends itself to particular situations. As an MIS services all levels of management in a variety of operational conditions, the probability exists that each format will be repeatedly used at many levels of an organization to accommodate a user's needs. The analyst will assess who needs what type of output format, and under what conditions.

MIS CONFIGURATIONS

11.34 Are the differences between management information systems reflected in their hardware?

Yes. The differences related to management information systems are carried throughout their design and actual structure. As such, the actual hardware and related configurations reflect these differences. The result of these alternatives is to produce certain configurations that parallel each other yet match the uniqueness of their organization's needs.

11.35 What MIS structures are most frequently encountered?

The four MIS configurations most often used by organizations are the:

(1) Centralized MIS structure
(2) Distributed MIS structure
(3) Hierarchical MIS structure
(4) Decentralized MIS structure

Each MIS configuration reflects a difference in how that system handles its data and how the resultant information is distributed throughout the organization.

11.36 How is the centralized MIS structure configured?

The centralized MIS structure (Fig. 11-1a) has at its heart a large computer that acts as the focal point of all processing activities. All processing must pass through this centrally located computer because it controls the flow of all data throughout the MIS and the information that is subsequently distributed.

(a) Centralized MIS structure   (b) Distributed MIS structure

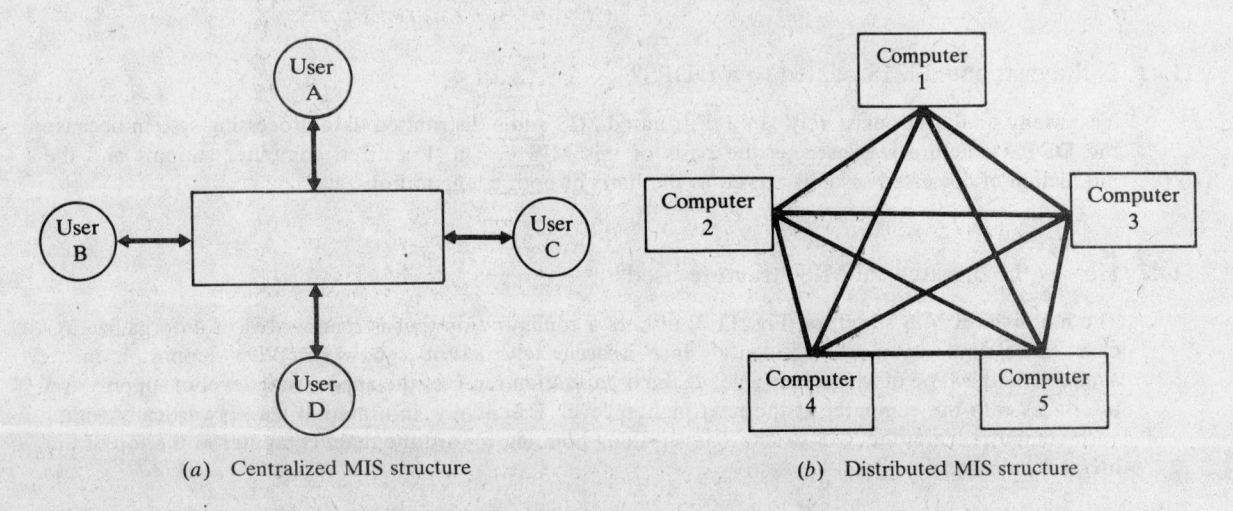

Fig. 11-1 The centralized MIS structure and the distributed MIS structure position their computer hardware differently. The computer is at the heart of the centralized MIS structure. In the distributed MIS structure, computers at local offices share the workload.

11.37 What are the merits of a centralized structure?

The advantages of a centralized MIS structure are its simplicity, relative low cost, minimal necessity to install duplicate hardware, and efficient use of hardware. As only one computer is required, hardware expenses are kept to a minimum. Supporting hardware costs are also controlled since hardware at the local levels primarily serves an I/O function or low-level computation function. The disadvantage of this structure is its vulnerability to a malfunctioning main computer. If the centralized system goes down, so does the MIS—leaving the organization without computer support. Processing activities to overcome this drawback must be incorporated into this MIS structure.

11.38 Does the distributed MIS structure overcome the drawback of the centralized structure?

Yes. The distributed MIS structure has an entirely different physical makeup and is not bothered by an inoperable main computer. As seen in Fig. 11-1b, the distributed MIS structure does not possess a main computer; rather, it utilizes a ring of computers to handle its processing load. This multiprocessing system[1] places equivalent-sized computer systems at each local office to share this workload and provide each local office with its own processing center.

11.39 How does this structure help the MIS concept?

The distributed MIS structure places the computing power where it is needed—at the location where processing activities occur. This structure enables each office to independently handle its own processing load and service its informational needs, as well as transfer the information generated to other systems in the system. A plus in this system's structure is that the failure of one computer does not close the entire system since processing is carried on by the other computer systems. Thus information is available from the other computers that are still online in the MIS.

11.40 What are the merits of the distributed MIS?

The relative independence of local computer centers is expensive because duplicate hardware and software must be developed. This aspect of a distributed MIS increases its cost and implementation time. However, to many organizations the operational freedom derived from having a continuous online system is well worth the additional expense. A real plus is the support provided to the local offices by this MIS configuration. On-site managerial decision making is truly possible, without invoking main management's approval. The distributed MIS structure is well-suited to widely dispersed organizations, whose local offices are free to operate independently while sharing pertinent data among themselves.

11.41 Is the distributed MIS related to a DDPS?

Yes. Many similarities exist between a distributed MIS and a distributed data processing system because the DDPS structure was used as the basis of this MIS design. Localized computer support and the interaction of dispersed systems served as the basis of both configurations.

11.42 How is the hierarchical MIS structure used?

The hierarchical MIS structure (Fig. 11-2) utilizes a configuration that is reminiscent of an organization chart. This similarity is not accidental since it accurately describes how computer support is made available in this type of MIS. Each level of the organization receives the appropriate level of support and interfaces with the computer at the next highest level. Essentially, information travels vertically within each computer leg of the MIS structure, everything pointing toward the main computer at the top of the hierarchical structure.

---

[1]Concepts related to multiprocessing and distributed data processing systems were introduced in Chap. 5.

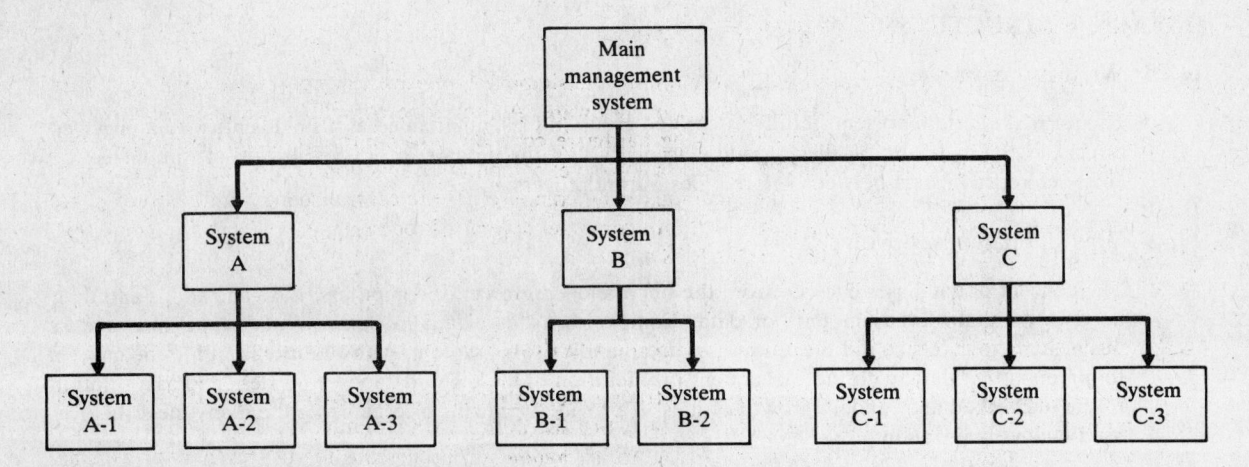

```
                    ┌─────────────┐
                    │    Main     │
                    │ management  │
                    │   system    │
                    └─────────────┘
           ┌───────────────┼───────────────┐
           ▼               ▼               ▼
       ┌────────┐      ┌────────┐      ┌────────┐
       │ System │      │ System │      │ System │
       │   A    │      │   B    │      │   C    │
       └────────┘      └────────┘      └────────┘
       ┌───┼───┐        ┌───┴───┐     ┌───┼───┐
       ▼   ▼   ▼        ▼       ▼     ▼   ▼   ▼
     ┌───┐┌───┐┌───┐ ┌───┐   ┌───┐ ┌───┐┌───┐┌───┐
     │A-1││A-2││A-3│ │B-1│   │B-2│ │C-1││C-2││C-3│
     └───┘└───┘└───┘ └───┘   └───┘ └───┘└───┘└───┘
```

Fig. 11-2 The hierarchical MIS structure chart is similar to an organization chart. Computers are positioned at each level of the system.

11.43 Is information easily transferred within this organized MIS?

Yes. The hierarchical MIS structure is primarily used where a corporation is broken into main divisions, with each division handling its own information and reporting to the corporate MIS center. The need to transfer data between organizational legs is kept to a minimum since the bulk of MIS-related information is developed within that organizational branch. However, communication links to all parts of the organization exist and enable the rapid transfer of information.

11.44 Is construction of the hierarchical network expensive?

Yes. As a result of the duplication of hardware in each organizational leg and the increase in the size of systems at successive levels of that branch, the hardware costs of the hierarchical MIS structure are quite high. It does provide each branch with excellent DP support and services that are well-suited to their needs. The sharing of data is not a major characteristic of this system because data are normally self-contained. However, the transfer of information upward to the corporate MIS system is readily accomplished. The hierarchical MIS is ideally suited for managerial control over a diverse group of projects and permits local control within each of the separate groups and at all levels of the organization.

11.45 Is the decentralized MIS structure similar to a hierarchical MIS?

Yes. The decentralized MIS structure also assumes a divisional structure, but it is totally isolated in that branch. Basically, each branch of the organization has its own MIS operation that is independent of all other MIS units. It gathers its own data, does not interact with any other organizational unit, does not share its resources, and reports only to the management of its division. In reality, the decentralized MIS structure is an isolated system, independent of a main computer, which handles its own informational needs.

11.46 What type of organization would use a decentralized MIS structure?

The decentralized MIS is best-suited to organizations that must remain independent of all other agencies. As such, the decentralized structure is used by governmental agencies, research institutions, and private foundations which need to maintain the strictest control over their informational resources.

11.47 Is the decentralized MIS expensive to set up?

Yes. The decentralized MIS structure is extremely expensive because it must develop and support all information gathering, processing, and distribution activities. For security reasons, it cannot draw on other sources, nor does it share its resources. Thus all aspects of this MIS system are specially and uniquely developed, often duplicating existing, but less secure, resources and communication lines.

DATABASE STRUCTURES

11.48 What is a database?

The term *database* represents a fully integrated group of files, maintained as a single entity, that provides direct access to a set of files, readily accomplishes the update of these files, and simplifies the cross-reference of data between related files during processing.

11.49 Why did databases evolve?

The concept of databases evolved from the unparallelled growth of computers in organizations and their need to maintain large amounts of data. Companies needed data to perform their functions, and as businesses expanded, so did the amount of data handled. This rapid growth required that files be created to maintain that data, with the subsequent proliferation of files. The database was designed as a solution to the unchecked and random growth of files. It provided a means of organizing the many file structures used by an organization.

11.50 What was wrong with conventional file organization techniques?

Existing file organization techniques were not designed for a group of related files. Those approaches, in effect, treated each file independently and did not provide the software to link file structures. As a result, files were constructed to support specific applications, even though the same required data existed on some other files. Thus a great deal of duplication occurred and resulted in the inefficient use of computer storage.

11.51 How does the database overcome these difficulties?

The first thing to remember is that a database is created by special software, and all of its processing activities are supported by the same specially written software. This software accommodates the construction of files but also permits the identification of common data items in multiple files. This feature is important when updating files within the database.

11.52 Why is the link between files important?

The relationship of files is important to their efficient update. The idea is to update the files without repeatedly entering the same input data, which is very inefficient. Inputs should be entered once into the database, permitting the database's supporting software to apply this data to the update of the required files. Thus the single entry of a data item triggers its update against as many files as directed.

11.53 Would a retail database utilize this form of update?

Yes. The idea of an online update is the operating concept of a point-of-sale (POS) system, which uses online inputs to update all files within its database. These updates are reflected in inventory, accounts receivable files for customer charge transactions, accounts payable files for corporate payments and credit payments, and salesperson commission payment files. Each of these files can be immediately updated in a POS system.

11.54 What device performs these retail updates?

The peripheral device permitting the online update of retail database files is the POS terminal, which is a combination online terminal and cash register. All transactions entered via the POS terminal, whether cash or credit, are immediately posted to the retail database. All files related to that transaction are updated from that single input, eliminating the need for repeated entries of the same data items.

11.55 What other efficiencies are attributed to the use of a database?

In addition to efficiently updating its files, databases avoid the duplication of files and the overhandling of both input and output records; they also improve the efficiency with which data is made available in the entire system. These advantages are attributed to any database system, retail or corporate, large or small.

11.56 What disadvantages are associated with databases?

The disadvantages associated with the use of database structures are the size, cost, and time to design and implement this feature. A database is scaled to the system in which it is implemented. Sufficient CPU size must be incorporated into the supporting system to accommodate the additional software needed to support the processing related to use of a database. The database is usually retained on a DASD device, but the supporting software must reside in primary storage for execution. Though hardware costs related to databases have declined considerably in the past few years, increased software developmental costs have added to the expense of database structures. Sufficient time is required to design, to prepare the software, and to implement a fully operative database. It is the type of project that requires a group of analysts and programmers to work on it, incurring the expense related to their salaries.

11.57 Can database software be purchased?

Yes. Program packages for defining database structures and their updates are commercially available from computer manufacturers or private software concerns. These software packages are called *database management systems* (*DBMS*). These prewritten DBMS programs are written for both large and small computer systems and are designed for specific conditions in which they may be used and the type of computers with which they are usable.

11.58 What restrictions are associated with DBMS software?

The restrictions associated with DBMS software are similar to those of any prewritten software. The programs are written for a specific range of computers, using selected peripheral devices and providing a limited range of processing activities. If the database activities do not closely match the DBMS software being evaluated, then the advantage of purchasing that software is negligible. The alternatives are for the user to write his or her own DBMS software, if time permits, or to modify his or her operating procedures to match the software commercially available.

11.59 Why do users purchase DMBS software?

In some circumstances it is cheaper and faster to purchase DBMS software than to write needed programs from scratch. This is especially true for organizations that are implementing a database for the first time or are totally replacing their database facility. As a rule of thumb, the longer the database has been in existence or the more specialized the activities performed, the more difficult it is to replace the database with commercially written DBMS software.

11.60 How does one become acquainted with the availability of DBMS software?

Two sources of DBMS software currently available are the computer manufacturer servicing a DP installation and the software periodicals that populate the marketplace. Each can provide insight into what is available and what the operational restrictions of the software are. It is advisable to exercise care in researching DBMS software and to visit a DP center using it.

11.61 Do differences exist in the way data are organized in a database?

Yes. Differences do exist in the ways data are organized, and often each organization devises its own order of reference. The two most widely used methods of ordering data within a database are the simple structure and the inverted structure.

11.62 How do these two methods differ?

The simple structure considers all records to be of equal importance and orders them using a common logical sequence, as a conventional file might order its data. The data presented in Table 11-1 presents data as they would be defined using a simple structure.

Table 11-1 Data Organized Using a Simple Structure

Storage Location	Part Description	Project ID	Bin Area
00618	Clamp	S123	B
00674	Tiedown	JP6	C
00726	Aligner	JP6	B
00768	Gasket	S123	A
00796	Screen	F108	C

11.63 What is the key to this data sequence?

In this simple sequence, all data records are sequenced by their storage location in ascending numerical order. Thus reference to an individual record is made solely by the storage location since that is how all data are ordered. The storage location is the only way that data are ordered and ignores the sequence of data in any other column of data.

11.64 Is this the case for the inverted structure?

No. In the inverted structure, multiple keys are used to access data because each item composing a record is ordered within its own column. Thus it is possible to access a specific data item using any one of the data fields composing that record. This restructuring of data is shown in Table 11-2, where the data items of Table 11-1 are ordered using an inverted structure.

Table 11-2 An Inverted Structure

Part Description		Project ID		Bin Area	
Item	Location	Item	Location	Item	Location
Clamp	00618	F108	00796	A	00768
Tiedown	00674	JP6	00674	B	00618
Aligner	00726	JP6	00724	B	00726
Gasket	00768	S123	00618	C	00674
Screen	00796	S123	00768	C	00796

11.65 How does this structure help access data?

The user now has three vehicles for accessing data based on part description, project ID, and bin area. With the simple structure, data could be accessed only by storage location. With an inverted structure, it is possible to access a record by any of the three columns because each is separately sequenced. Thus the record for a gasket, at location 00768, is accessible in three ways. It is fourth in the parts column, last in the project ID, and first in the bin area. Each of these three categories is identified in Table 11-2 by the encircling of each item. The inverted structure offers a more efficient and rapid means of data retrieval.

11.66 How does this structure assist in efficiently accessing data?

With the inverted structure, data can be accessed from a database file by more than one key. Data is retained in those three formats, reducing the time used to search through a database. Essentially, it is possible to access a data item by its part description, the project on which it is used, and the bin area in which it is located.

11.67 In what capacity is the term *chaining* related to database inquiries?

The term *chaining* represents the relationships developed via the inverted structure when ordering data within a database. As already noted, the advantage of the inverted structure is its ability to rapidly access data using any number of varied reference points. Chaining provides a linkage to these other values. Thus if a user specifies a data item, all possible records that may be accessed from that reference are readied. Chaining describes the process by which those relationships are established and access to related records is defined. In relation to Table 11-2, the specification of the location 00768 leads to three possible data items—the part description of gasket, the project ID of S123, or the bin area A. Chaining establishes the link from 00768 to those three items, enabling the user to select one or all three of them, as desired.

ADMINISTRATION OF THE DATABASE

11.68 What are the two general areas of database administration?

The two areas of data administration relate to supervising the organization supporting the database function and the software used in that effort. Supervising the organization relates to the handling of people and hardware, whereas software specifically relates to the programming effort involved.

11.69 How is the programming effort handled?

As already noted, control over the database is accomplished using DBMS software in conjunction with the system's operational software. The DBMS software operationally controls the database's activities, with many programs written to perform secondary tasks. With a functioning set of DBMS software, a few programmers experienced with its features are needed to maintain its efficient function. Maintenance programming efforts will continue until the condition of the database is reevaluated and a recommendation to modify its structure is rendered.

11.70 Are the programmers performing the maintenance work also under the umbrella of personnel management?

Yes. The programmers are in the second category of database administration. Generally, within large DP organizations, the team of programmers working with the database are segregated into their own special group. This database grouping simplifies the organizational responsibilities since its purpose is clearly outlined—to keep the database functioning efficiently.

11.71 Which individual is assigned supervision over the database group?

Supervision over this organizational group is assigned to a database administrator. This individual coordinates and schedules all activities of the programmers, analysts, and technicians that operate the database. The database administrator must possess both the technical expertise and administrative qualities necessary to lead this operationally complex and economically demanding group.

11.72 How many people does the database administrator supervise?

The database administrator will oversee a staff that is structured in relation to the operational demands of the database. That is, the number of analysts, programmers, etc., will depend on the scope of activities performed. Thus the larger the database, the greater the number of people involved and the greater the scope of activities undertaken. No firm guidelines exist for the database grouping since it is solely a function of the DP organization in which it is involved.

11.73 What are the key responsibilities of the database administrator?

The major responsibilities of the database administrator are:

(1) Coordination of all database maintenance activities
(2) Supervision, design, and implementation of all database files
(3) Liaison with management and all users and the development of a user's handbook
(4) Coordination and preparation of all database-related documentation
(5) Coordination of all security measures used to ensure proper access to the database

11.74 What activities constitute maintenance of the database?

Database maintenance encompasses a great deal of activity. A principal activity is to ensure that all DBMS software is fully operational and functioning. Maintenance of that software is part of that activity. Also included in database maintenance are activities to ensure the prompt and accurate systems response to user inquiries. The database administrator must monitor the speed with which responses are made to all inquiries because a delayed response normally indicates a level of inefficiency and a reduced level of performance. This condition may signal the need to examine the supporting DBMS software or the hardware involved, or it may signal that the database is approaching its maximum storage capacity and can no longer respond quickly to the inquiries made.

11.75 Where does the database administrator fit into database design activities?

The database administrator is responsible for coordinating the design, testing, and implementation of any database files. On the basis of the information provided, the database administrator must assess whether a file is needed or whether alternative methods of obtaining the same data exist. The database administrator coordinates the formulation, design, and implementation of all database files, assigning personnel to these tasks as required.

11.76 Why is liaison to management important to database operation?

The database administrator must be able to interact with all levels of management and assess their informational needs. Using this information, it is possible to determine whether the database is adequately serving the organization, and, if it is not, what modifications are required.

11.77 Why is it necessary to service all levels of management?

Each level of management has its own informational needs that shape the contents of the database. One cannot satisfy one managerial level at the sacrifice of the informational needs of another. Also, one must consider the relative importance of the data maintained within a file. All too often the placement of critical data is offset by the political needs of an organization, with subsequent negative effects. The database administrator must have sufficient guile to assess these types of difficulties and resolve them before they dissipate the DP organization's resources.

11.78 Why is a user's handbook critical?

The user's handbook is a guide to working with a database. It is not possible to personally introduce everyone to using a database, or to be there to answer every question. The user's handbook is designed as a reference containing answers to the most common questions; it also anticipates troublespots and documents the most commonly used procedures. If properly prepared, the user's handbook offers an operational guideline to all procedures used when interacting with a database. Questions not answered by the handbook should be transmitted to the database administration group for resolution.

11.79 Is the user's handbook part of the database's documentation?

Yes. Any paperwork prepared in relation to the database is deemed part of its documentation. Though many people perceive this paperwork as being of secondary importance, sound database documentation is essential. Without it, the database staff will operationally stumble, because no record of their work will exist, and users will be defeated in their efforts to extract data from the database's files. In such cases, the database staff is thwarted in its normal work effort by the number of user questions that are answered and the amount of duplicate work they must perform. It is the database administrator's responsibility to ensure that an appropriate level of documentation exists and that the staff workers adhere to its format and promptly document all actions taken.

11.80 Why are security measures necessary within a database?

It is essential that all unauthorized users be restricted from gaining access to records held within a database. It would be self-defeating to permit open access to corporate files. A competitor or an employee with a criminal intent could wreck the files and use the data gained from them to cause financial harm. A great deal of time is expended in developing and testing security measures that will restrict access to database information to only qualified users. The security issue is a matter of grave concern for today's database administrators, considering the nature of sensitive corporate data being retained.

11.81 What size staff does the database administrator supervise?

The database group usually has a minimum of four members to include the administrator, two programmers (one with a systems analysis background), and a secretary (who also serves as a librarian for the group). The actual size will reflect the amount of activity performed by the group, with the database accordingly sized. Generally, the larger the corporation, the more formal the structure of the database group. In smaller organizations database operations are not as clearly discharged or defined. Usually the critical and costly nature of database activities forces management to administer these resources judiciously.

INFORMATION MANAGEMENT SYSTEMS (IMS)

11.82 Are the initials IMS another way of describing an MIS?

No. *IMS* stands for *information management system*, which is a software technique used to manage the information generated by an organization's computer system.

11.83 How is an IMS different from an MIS?

Though the abbreviations are similar, the systems are designed to meet entirely different operational objectives. The MIS represents a system of activities that generates the information needed by management in its decision making, whereas IMS activities focus on the efficient management of the data being generated by a computer system. The IMS seeks efficient information management, whereas the MIS provides information to management. In other words, the IMS provides a means of managing the volume of information generated by a computer system.

11.84 Can an IMS be constructed within an MIS or vice versa?

In today's computing activities, a strong likelihood exists that an IMS would be present within an MIS. The opposite condition is not likely to occur. The reason is that to improve the impact of an MIS, the efficient management of data via IMS is essential—but the reverse is not true. An IMS makes it possible to manage and improve the ability of a management information system to generate the data used by management in its decision making. The MIS is more end-product-oriented, with the IMS focusing on the midlevel operations helping to develop the information subsequently used.

11.85 Are databases part of the IMS structure?

Databases are an integral part of the IMS since they hold the data managed by the IMS software. It is important to clarify one point—the IMS is in reality a complex group of operational software that enables the computer to efficiently handle large amounts of data. IMS software is invoked to simplify the access of data from a database, which facilitates a prompt response to data inquiries made against files.

11.86 Why was IMS software developed?

The increase in online processing activities created the necessity for the computer's operational software to handle both data communications and the retrieval of data from the database. The then-existing software was adequate for a moderate volume of inquiries but was insufficient for the high volume of inquiries in some applications. The computer's software performed its database-access function properly but did not adequately handle the data communications workload. Essentially, the computer's efficiency decreased as the volume of inquiries increased. IMS software was developed to efficiently handle data communications activities, the access of data from database files, and the transmission of data back to the user.

11.87 What was one of the initial successful examples of IMS software?

A successful version of IMS software is the customer information control system, or simply *CICS*. CICS software was developed for Con Edison, a public utility in New York City. Its volume of customers and the frequency of inquiries made against its customer database made it an ideal candidate for some form of IMS software. CICS was developed for Con Edison to enable them to rapidly respond to the thousands of information requests made by its customers.

11.88 What were the two specific tasks assigned to CICS?

The CICS software was written to perform two essential tasks, namely, the efficient access of data from within its corporate database and to supervise all data communications activities undertaken by the computer. CICS performed admirably and became the yardstick by which other forms of IMS software were judged.

11.89 Could CICS software be used to modify the contents of a database?

Yes. CICS was fully operational, permitting users to access data from a database and, when needed, permitting the modification of the contents of any customer record.

11.90 What was an initial drawback to CICS?

Though CICS was fully operational for data inquiries, processing operations subsequent to those activities had to be written in other languages. For some data processors the inconvenience of having to use an additional language was a disadvantage because of the interface between CICS and the subsequently written programs. In newer versions of CICS, this interface of CICS and supporting software is smoother and represents no major difficulties.

11.91 What was done to improve CICS?

To improve the software used to complement CICS activities, a new language was developed. A specialized language called *Data Language/1* (*DL/1*) was developed by IBM to support data manipulation activities and to smoothly interface with CICS software.

11.92 What was the operational function of DL/1?

CICS was designed to handle data access within the database and data communications. DL/1 was created to handle any of the processing activities subsequent to those inquiries to include the modifications of data within the database. The use of DL/1 permitted users to add or delete a record from a database file, modify the contents of a record, scan the contents of multiple records, and accomplish the output of those data in various forms of output media. It was those activities that were undertaken using other languages in the initial versions of CICS. DL/1 made it possible to use only one language in the performance of those tasks.

11.93 Have other hardware configurations been developed to improve IMS activities?

Yes. Many manufacturers have created multiprocessing systems to improve the access to and management of the data maintained within the files of a database. One such configuration to achieve recognition is the data communications/database (DC/DB) system. The DC/DB system is a multiprocessing configuration that is designed to improve the access to a database's files.

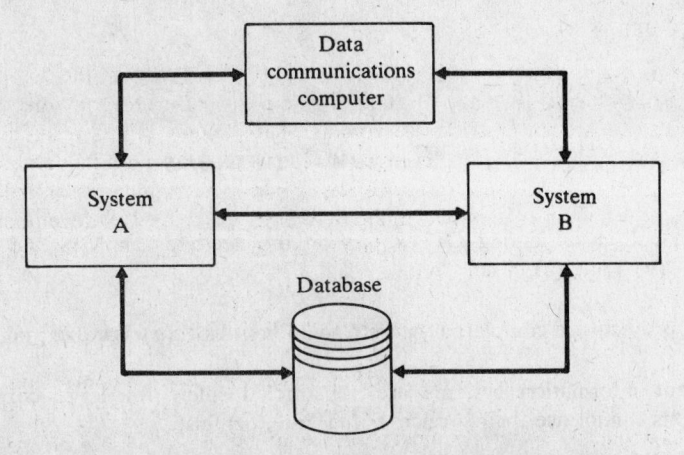

Fig. 11-3 The database/data communications system is a multiprocessing system in which three computers process data. The lead computer handles the data communications function, while the other two systems control all processing activities and govern access to the corporate database.

11.94 What configuration is adopted by a DC/DB system?

The hardware configuration associated with the DC/DB system is illustrated in Fig. 11-3. This multiprocessing system uses three computers to accomplish the aim of rapid data communications and prompt database response.

11.95 What tasks are assigned to the initial computer system?

The initial system is assigned the data communications function, dealing with any aspects related to the handling of data transmission to and from the database. The use of a computer for data communications increased the speed with which these activities were performed and speeded the scheduling and coordination of I/O transmissions. The volume of inquiries handled by the DC/DB system is considerable, as is the level of processing to be handled by this complex system.

11.96 What functions do the two parallel systems accomplish?

The two side-by-side systems follow the data communications computer, share the workload, and interface with the database. Their purpose is to share the processing performed by the entire DC/DB configuration and to access information from the supporting database in response to inquiries handled by the data communications computer. Using two parallel systems ensures that one computer is always available for processing. If the workload is at a low level, one system is sufficient for processing. If the workload exceeds the capacity of one system, the second computer can kick in and help handle the excess processing. Should one computer fail, the second system functions as a backup to continue processing.

11.97 Why is the backup feature of the DC/DB system important?

The ability to switch to a backup system is essential to the large systems supported by DC/DB configurations. The organizations requiring a DC/DB system are sufficiently large to accommodate its cost, but they also require its processing potential because of the workload. The DC/DB system is not built unless it is really needed. The corporations that use the DC/DB system cannot afford a break in their processing support, and the DC/DB affords them that luxury. It provides a high level of support and ensures that one computer is always available for processing. Rarely will both systems be inoperative, ensuring a continuous processing potential.

11.98 Which systems interact with the database?

The two parallel systems may individually or jointly access the supporting database, in either case providing prompt access to data. The interaction of the data communications computer and the parallel systems provides processing speeds that were previously not attainable with smaller systems. In DC/DB systems, both data communications and database access are handled rapidly by computer.

Review Questions

11.99 There is a consensus among DP experts on the need for an MIS and what constitutes the MIS structure. (a) True, (b) false.

11.100 Most MIS projects are completed within 6 to 36 months. (a) True, (b) false.

11.101 Management information systems are constructed solely for large corporations because smaller organizations cannot use their services. (a) True, (b) false.

11.102 Most business systems provide exactly the same operational information as MIS configurations. (a) True, (b) false.

11.103 A monthly listing of all accounts offers an example of a regularly scheduled listing. (a) True, (b) false.

11.104 Forecasting reports are a principal management tool, enabling the projection of future expenses and budgets. (a) True, (b) false.

11.105 The decentralized MIS structure has at its center a main computer system that provides local support to each division. (a) True, (b) false.

11.106 The linking of files within a database is critical to the efficient access of data. (a) True, (b) false.

11.107 Within a database, ideally one input should trigger a series of updates in related files. (a) True, (b) false.

11.108 The size and cost of constructing a database are disadvantages with the time factor not considered critical. (a) True, (b) false.

11.109 No restrictions are applied to the use of commercially prepared DBMS software. (a) True, (b) false.

11.110 Generally, the simple structure provides faster access to database files because of its simplified organizational approach. (a) True, (b) false.

11.111 The *database administrator* is another term applied to DBMS software. (a) True, (b) false.

11.112 Databases are designed to hold file data to service all levels of management. (a) True, (b) false.

11.113 Security measures are of minimal importance with a database since the data held within its files are made available to all users. (a) True, (b) false.

11.114 The terms IMS and MIS are used interchangeably. (a) True, (b) false.

11.115 Databases are an integral component in IMS structures, retaining the data to be efficiently distributed. (a) True, (b) false.

11.116 IMS structures represent sets of operational software used to efficiently manage the information generated by complex processing operations. (a) True, (b) false.

11.117 The DC/DB system is a multiprocessing system in which three computers are assigned only data communications activities. (a) True, (b) false.

11.118 Parallel systems within the DC/DB configuration can share the workload and provide access to the database. (a) True, (b) false.

11.119 Which of the following factors are integrated within an MIS? (a) supporting equipment; (b) operating procedures; (c) personnel; (d) all of the above.

11.120 Daily operational information is most often used by (a) low-level management; (b) middle management; (c) top management; (d) b and c.

11.121 A characteristic of an MIS is that (a) all information developed is input-oriented; (b) all activities are supported by offline processing activities; (c) all outputs are decision-oriented; (d) all of the above.

11.122 The visual display of a customer's current charges is an example of a(n) (a) forecasting report; (b) exception listing; (c) regularly scheduled listing; (d) on-demand report.

11.123 The MIS structure that gradually upgrades computer support up through each level of management is the (a) centralized MIS structure; (b) distributed MIS structure; (c) hierarchical MIS structure; (d) decentralized MIS structure.

11.124 A reason for the development of databases is (a) the introduction of direct-access file structure; (b) the phenomenal growth of duplicate files; (c) the reliability of offline processing activities in linking files; (d) all of the above.

11.125 An advantage associated with the use of a database is (a) the minimum handling of input data; (b) the efficient update of file data; (c) the lack of duplicate file structure; (d) all of the above.

11.126 The database file organization in which multiple keys are available for accessing data is the (a) simple structure; (b) direct structure; (c) inverted structure; (d) indexed structure.

11.127 A function not performed by the database administrator is (a) the actual running of database-related software; (b) liaison with all levels of management; (c) coordination of database security; (d) preparation of documentation related to database activities.

11.128 The efficient management of the data generated by a large computer system, in relation to a database, is accomplished via a(n) (a) DL/1; (b) BIS; (c) IMS; (d) MIS.

11.129 MISs are designed to generate information for management's _____ purposes.

11.130 Planning activities within an MIS are conducted by _____ for 1 to 3 years in the future.

11.131 Files supporting MIS activities are fully _____ to provide maximum support in the preparation of managerial data.

11.132 A report listing only those people that have not paid their taxes illustrates a MIS report format called the _____ listing.

11.133 In the _____ MIS structure, a network of computers at local levels is used to share the processing workload.

11.134 A fully integrated group of files, referenced as a single entity, is called a(n) _____.

11.135 A _____ system permits a retail organization to update its database files as sales transactions occur.

11.136 Commercially available operational software used to construct a database and monitor its use is referred to as _____ software.

11.137 The _____ structure technique organizes files within a database using a single common key.

11.138 The cross-referencing of common data items between files in a database is referred to as _____.

11.139 The _____ administrator is responsible for the design, supervision, and implementation of all database files.

11.140 A pamphlet developed to advise users on how to interact with a corporate database is the _____.

11.141 The development of decision-making information for management's use is the primary function of a(n) _____.

11.142 A primary example of IMS software used to service customer inquiries for utility companies is _____.

11.143 The specialized language developed by IBM to improve database manipulation activities is _____.

Answers: 11.99 (b); 11.100 (a); 11.101 (b); 11.102 (b); 11.103 (a); 11.104 (a); 11.105 (b); 11.106 (a); 11.107 (a); 11.108 (b); 11.109 (b); 11.110 (b); 11.111 (b); 11.112 (a); 11.113 (b); 11.114 (b); 11.115 (a); 11.116 (a); 11.117 (b); 11.118 (a); 11.119 (d); 11.120 (a); 11.121 (c); 11.122 (d); 11.123 (c); 11.124 (b); 11.125 (d); 11.126 (c); 11.127 (a); 11.128 (c); 11.129 decision-making; 11.130 top management; 11.131 integrated; 11.132 exception; 11.133 distributed; 11.134 database; 11.135 point-of-sale (POS); 11.136 DBMS; 11.137 simple; 11.138 chaining; 11.139 database; 11.140 user's handbook; 11.141 MIS; 11.142 CICS; 11.143 Data Language/1 (DL/1).

Supplementary Problems

11.144 Why would a large corporation desire the support of a management information system? What advantages do you feel would accrue from the use of an MIS?

11.145 Describe, both verbally and pictorially, four common MIS structures. Cite from your own experience examples of computer configurations that utilize each of these MIS configurations.

11.146 What are the differences between an MIS and an IMS? Why are IMS services potentially found within MIS configurations?

11.147 Describe the report formats used within MIS-generated outputs. If possible, record actual examples of each type of report format and detail why the format is used with that output.

11.148 Why does the inverted database structure offer better access than the simple structure? Create a series of data items and organize them according to either approach.

11.149 Briefly describe the responsibilities associated with the position of database administrator.

11.150 Describe in your own words the CICS and DC/DB configurations.

Glossary

Centralized MIS structure. The MIS structure that has at its center a centrally located computer that supports all processing activities undertaken by that system.

Chaining. The software technique incorporated into database operations that permits the cross-referencing of key data items using a common key or index.

Customer information control system (CICS). The set of operation programs that handles the data communications and access of data in response to the inquiries made against a database.

Database. An organized array of files where data files are fully integrated and the online access of data from those files is possible.

Database administrator. The administrator responsible for supervision of the database group in the DP department that handles maintenance of the database facility.

Database management system (DBMS). The package of operational software used to support database activities.

Data communications/database (DC/DB) system. A multiprocessing system whereby separate computers handle the data communications and database handling activities.

Data Language/1 (DL/1). The specialized language, developed by IBM, used to support database-related processing activities.

Decentralized MIS structure. The MIS structure in which processing activities are independently handled within each division of the organization.

Distributed MIS structure. The MIS structure in which a network of locally positioned computers shares the processing workload of the organization.

Exception listing. The MIS report format that highlights abnormal conditions, reporting them to management.

Forecasting report. The MIS report format used to output the processing results related to projecting future developments.

Hierarchical MIS structure. The MIS structure that organizes computer support at the various levels of management, building upward.

Information management system (IMS). The operational software system used to efficiently manage the data generated by today's complex computer systems.

Inverted structure. The database organizational technique by which data files are ordered by multiple indexes or keys.

Management information system (MIS). A computer system that integrates procedures, people, equipment, and computer services to provide management with the information upon which to make decisions.

On-demand report. The MIS report format that permits the rapid display of data when requested by a user.

Point-of-sale (POS) system. A retail system that uses online register terminals to update its database and provide immediate access to data retained in those files.

POS terminal. The terminal device that combines the operational features of a computer terminal and cash register.

Regularly scheduled listing. The MIS report format that is prepared on a periodic basis.

Simple structure. The database organization technique that orders its data files on a single, common key.

User's handbook. The documentation packet prepared to assist users in accessing data from their supporting database.

Chapter 12

A Survey of Computer Systems

12.1 TYPES OF COMPUTERS

Computers are classified according to their data handling capabilities and the applications in which they are used. *Analog computers* convert their measurement of physical properties into data used in processing. *Digital computers* use data solely in numeric formats. *Hybrid computers* combine the features of both analog and digital computers.

Computers are tailored to the applications in which they are used. *General-purpose computers* handle the widest range of data processing problems. *Special-purpose computers* are designed for unique applications not handled by conventional systems. Most businesses use general-purpose systems, with special-purpose computers reserved for truly unique applications. An example of a special-purpose computer is a *simulator*, a device used in the training programs for highly skilled professions. Two applications of special-purpose computers are computer-assisted design and manufacturing. *Computer-assisted design* (*CAD*) is used in design applications, with the automated production of those items accomplished using *computer-assisted manufacturing* (*CAM*) facilities.

12.2 MICROCOMPUTERS

The smallest computers produced are *microcomputers*, systems constructed using *silicon chips*. These chips duplicate the ability to perform I/O operations and processing. Four types of chips are utilized in the construction of microcomputers and larger systems too.

Random-access memory (*RAM*) chips are used for primary storage since data can be written into or read from RAM storage. *Read-only memory* (*ROM*) permits data to be read from its contents, but data may not be added to the ROM by the user. In other words, the alteration of ROM storage is not possible. PROM and EPROM chips are ROM chips with special features. *Programmable read-only memory* (*PROM*) chips are initially blank and subsequently filled with data only once. *Erasable programmable read-only memory* (*EPROM*) chips are initially blank and may be filled, erased, and refilled any number of times.

Microcomputers use peripheral devices scaled to their capacities. Tape cassettes and floppy disks provide a sequential and direct-access file capability. Color CRTs provide a graphic capability with plotting devices available also. Voice I/O devices permit verbal interaction with microcomputer users. Both operational and application software are used with microcomputers. BASIC and PASCAL are popular microcomputer languages. Online processing is an important feature of microcomputer systems.

12.3 MINICOMPUTERS

Minicomputers are task-oriented systems, providing the processing capabilities of much larger and more expensive systems. Minicomputers are designed to support specific data processing activities, excluding other applications. This limitation permits drastic cost savings since the computer is uniquely designed. Online processing activities are a hallmark of minicomputers, enabling the rapid update of files.

Minicomputers can support multiple terminal devices and online storage of billions of characters. Disks and floppy disks are utilized, as are magnetic tapes and tape cassettes. A wide range of printers, plotters, and terminals may be incorporated into minicomputers, as well as card devices and audio response devices. Terminals are used for file interrogation activities.

At one time minicomputers were classified into three categories according to their operational capabilities. Minicomputer systems offered online access to a limited number of files. Midi-minicomputers offered a batch and online processing capability, with each type of task being separately performed. Maxi-minicomputers enabled concurrent online and batch processing activities, offering the widest range of operational capabilities to their users.

12.4 FOUR COMPUTER CATEGORIES

Four categories of computers are established to assist users in comparing the resources of comparable computer hardware. *Small-scale computers* have CPU sizes of 1K to 64K, offering many operational capabilities but to a limited degree. Many microcomputers and minicomputers fall into this category.

Medium-scale computers have CPUs of 64K to 512K and represent the largest percentage of systems used today. These systems perform the bulk of DP activities performed, using a full range of I/O devices and supporting all levels of processing.

Large-scale computers have CPUs of 512K to 5 megabytes of storage and support the online storage of billions of characters. Real-time processing, file interrogations, and online updates are characteristic of large-scale systems.

The largest computers are *supercomputers*, exhibiting CPUs of larger than 5 million bytes and costing more than $10 million. These systems are two to five times faster than large-scale systems, attaining speeds of 70–100 millions of instructions executed per second. A measure used in evaluating computer speeds is the *MIPS rating*.

12.5 MANAGERIAL CONSIDERATIONS IN PURCHASING NEW COMPUTER HARDWARE

Management will critically examine requests for new hardware, asking for justification. Questions asked relate to the DP services required by the organization, the type of computer hardware needed to support the level of processing selected, the options of renting or leasing the hardware, the peripherals necessary for processing, the type and cost of vendor maintenance, the type of software necessary to support the system's processing activities, and the level of training anticipated for employees.

Extensive studies are performed to obtain this data to provide management with sufficient information on which to base their decisions. All aspects of the system are evaluated when researching that data. *Scheduled* and *unscheduled maintenance* are considered when assessing the costs related to servicing the system. Adequate time must be afforded for the proper training of employees who will interface with the new system.

Solved Problems

TYPES OF COMPUTERS

12.1 Aren't all computers constructed to handle the processing in similar ways?

No. Computers are constructed to respond to a variety of different operational conditions. To assist in recognizing these differences, three broad categories of computers have been established. The three classifications are:

(1) Analog and digital computers
(2) Hybrid computers
(3) General-purpose and special-purpose computers

Each category defines operational characteristics unique to that type of computer.

12.2 How do analog and digital computers differ?

Analog and digital computers differ in how they derive their data. An analog computer is said to measure toward its data, whereas a digital computer counts toward its data. Analog computers do not arrive at their input data by ingesting a number. These computers must measure some physical property via sensors, convert that measurement into an equivalent numeric quantity, and then use that data in processing. Digital computers are provided with numeric data initially to commence processing, thus bypassing the necessity to measure and derive input data.

12.3 What type of properties does an analog computer measure?

The sensors associated with analog systems may measure many properties and convert those measurements to numeric equivalents. For example, an analog computer can measure the voltage passing through a particular point in a circuit, assess its strength, and assign it a numeric value. A sensing device could measure the quantity of light striking a photoelectric cell, determine its intensity, and assign a value that is used in processing. Similarly, a sensor could measure the time span between emitting and receiving two images, in much the same way that radar operates. The essential analog characteristic is that a numeric quantity results from the measurement of some physical property, and that number is subsequently used in processing.

12.4 Are analog computers, then, less reliable?

Not necessarily. A critical factor in assessing analog computers is the accuracy of their sensing devices. Obviously, if the sensing units are not properly calibrated, the resulting measurements will be incorrect and erroneous input data will be entered into processing.

12.5 Considering this drawback, why are analog devices favored?

Analog devices are much faster than digital devices in relation to deriving input data. Since the analog device is designed for the direct conversion of input data, it does not have to wait for the manual conversion of that data. The analog gains its speed advantage in that its direct input capabilities avoid the delays inherent in the manual preparation and subsequent input of that data.

12.6 How do digital computers operate?

One may draw an analogy between digital computers and pocket calculators because both are digital devices. Both are provided with data directly in a digital form, with no conversion or other internal preparatory work necessary. Once the data are input, normal processing begins. The important fact here is that the digital computer commences its processing with the data's adopting a numeric format.

12.7 Do both systems react similarly when provided with input data?

Yes. Once provided with input data using a numeric format, both the analog and digital systems function similarly. The advantage gained by analog devices is that they may generate a continuous stream of input data that is made immediately available for processing. A digital system would have to wait until similar results were computed and provided to it. The disadvantage associated with this processing approach is that if the sensing devices are malfunctioning, a great quantity of invalid data could enter the system before being detected. Corrective measures, which increase the total cost, must be built into analog computers to overcome this type of difficulty.

12.8 Where are analog and digital systems used?

Analog computers are used in manufacturing facilities where production is totally automated. An analog computer controls the entire manufacturing process, measuring temperatures, calibrating metal thicknesses, varying machine speeds, determining when a unit is complete, and registering that unit into inventory. Full-scale automated computer systems exist in the areas of marine navigation, aircraft landing systems, space explorations, pollution control, and sewage treatment. Digital systems are primarily used in the business sector, where most data are derived in a numeric format. The vast majority of all computers supporting large and small businesses are digital systems.

12.9 How does the hybrid system relate to the other systems?

The hybrid computer combines the features of analog and digital devices. Hybrid computers can accept manually entered online inputs, as well as the automated input of data derived from sensing devices. They in effect permit users to employ a computing device that can serve in two capacities. When needed, the hybrid system can monitor a production facility, automatically controlling sensory devices. The same hybrid system can process production data, as well as other business-related data, assuming a digital format. Thus the business may process payrolls, accounts receivable and payable transactions, production invoices, inventory control schedules, and managerial budget data with which to physically run the business.

12.10 Who uses hybrid computers?

Any organization requiring the combined services offered by a hybrid system will avail itself of this type of system. Organizations using hybrid computers include manufacturing or production facilities, naval or aviation operations, medical and engineering laboratories, and educational institutions. These organizations need to be able to input data from both sensory devices and online terminals.

12.11 What other designations are attributed to computer systems?

Two other classifications assigned to current computer hardware are general-purpose and special-purpose computers. The general-purpose-computer designation is assigned to computer systems capable of handling the widest array of applications. This designation implies that the system will readily process complex scientific and mathematical formulas, as well as fundamental business information. General-purpose computers represent the most versatile systems available, and thus they are currently found in most business DP-related centers.

12.12 Where are the more specialized computers found?

Highly specialized data processing activities require more than conventional general-purpose units because the supporting computer must be built to satisfy the special needs of that organization. Systems designed for such unique applications are called *special-purpose computers* because they are specifically created for such tailor-made activities. Special-purpose computers are constructed to meet specific operational requirements not normally associated with conventional business applications.

12.13 Where might special- and general-purpose devices be encountered?

Any business establishment might use the resources provided by a general-purpose computer. These systems provide a range of services to support batch processing operations using magnetic tape and online processing involving the update of records within database files. Special-purpose computers are usually applied in situations where generalized systems are inappropriate and do not possess the operational characteristics necessary. Computers that are used to train NASA's astronauts in navigational procedures, using the lunar module or space shuttle, and to troubleshoot problems in the space capsule are special purpose. Also the computers included on all spacecraft, as well as those supporting NASA ground services, are specially built systems.

12.14 What designation is applied to most business computers?

The majority of the computer hardware used to service business/DP applications are designated general-purpose, digital computers. That is, these systems are applied to a wide range of services that involve the use of data directly derived in a numeric format.

12.15 What designations are applied to special-purpose computers?

Many specialized systems accommodate the designation special-purpose hybrid computer because they are specially constructed and combine the abilities of analog and digital systems. For those systems in which analog qualities are not present, the special-purpose digital tag is appropriate. The preceding designation might describe a computer that supports a manufacturing plant where both automated and conventional production facilities are used, requiring both analog and digitally produced data. A special-purpose digital machine might be constructed to handle large amounts of biological data for scientific and national-defense-planning purposes.

12.16 What type of special-purpose systems are used in education?

Many general-purpose machines are used to support conventional education activities, including teaching and administrative services. A special-purpose computer constructed to accommodate the training of people in highly skilled jobs is the simulator. The simulator is a controlled device that artificially creates the environment in which these employees will work. Simulators have been constructed to train aircraft pilots, merchant marine captains, astronauts, racing car drivers, and emergency medical personnel. Models were constructed of the consoles or equipment the individuals would use, with the computer then creating a series of tasks the trainees must react to. The computer then records the performance of each individual, rating his or her effectiveness in many categories. Figure 12-1 illustrates the simulated console used to train merchant marine officers.

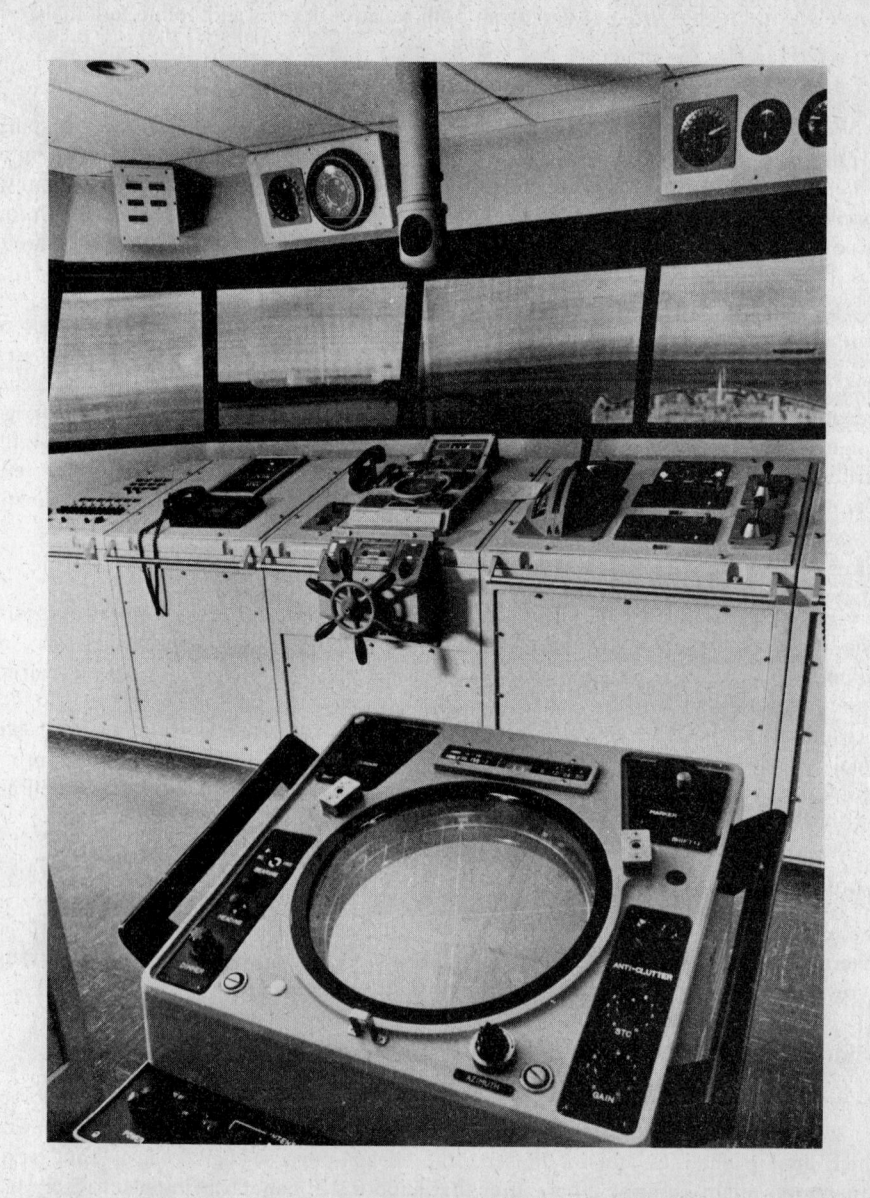

Fig. 12-1 Console of a merchant marine training simulator. (*Courtesy of Newsday*)

12.17 Why are simulators valuable training devices?

Simulators help cut training costs and save lives. A $1 million simulator can repeatedly train many pilots, freeing a $40 million jet that would have to be set aside for such service. Also, any set of operational conditions may be re-created, from the potential death of an accident victim to an aircraft's having serious airborne problems. These conditions can be created without actually endangering a person or aircraft, while requiring the trainee to react to them. The simulator can then assess and record the trainee's reactions, some of which might go undetected under human supervision.

12.18 Where else might special-purpose systems prove helpful?

Two additional areas for applying special-purpose systems relate to computer-assisted design (CAD) and computer-assisted manufacturing (CAM) services. Both CAD and CAM require special-purpose systems because of the specialized nature of the work they support. CAD activities require the design of machines based on a profile of factors input. Using specially prepared software, this array of values is analyzed against a database full of production data to produce the optimum design representing those values. CAM represents the other half of the CAD/CAM process, actually controlling the manufacture of the designed component. CAM makes the theoretical design a reality, handling all phases of production. It controls the entry of material resources, the machines producing the component, and the updating of resources associated with the production effort. CAM software also permits the online entry of data to fine-tune production or correct design elements not meeting quality-control standards.

12.19 Are CAD/CAM activities popular?

Yes. They represent one of the emerging production fields and an area where much managerial emphasis is being placed. Many corporations recognize CAD/CAM as a way of improving their production facilities and their operational efficiency.

MICROCOMPUTERS

12.20 What are microcomputers?

Microcomputers are the smallest computer systems available, represented by the group of home computers currently available. Figure 12-2 illustrates two of the more popular microcomputer systems commercially available.

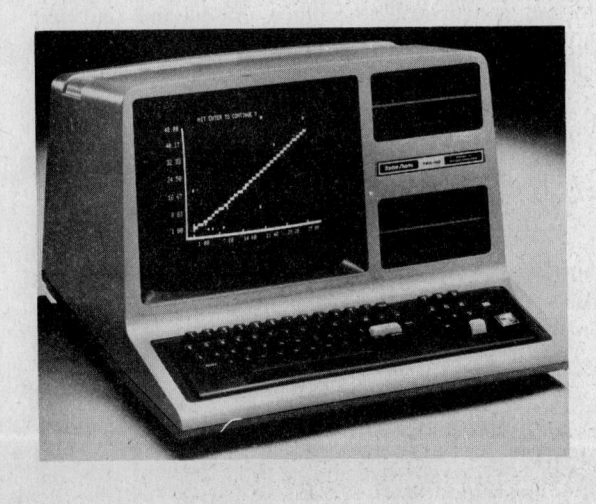

(*a*) The TRS-80 microcomputer. (*Radio Shack*)   (*b*) The Apple microcomputer. (*Apple*)

Fig. 12-2 Two popular microcomputer systems. (*Radio Shack and Apple Computing*)

12.21 How are microcomputers constructed?

Microcomputers are constructed using silicon chips which completely duplicate the conventional computer's ability to perform input, processing, and output operations. The silicon chips represent microminiaturized circuits that permit the construction of microcomputers and their small size.

12.22 Do microcomputers have a CPU capacity?

Yes. Microcomputers possess a CPU facility for primary storage and the other required control units. These facilities are totally contained within a single chip.

12.23 Does only one type of chip exist?

Essentially, four types of chips exist and are used in the construction of microcomputers. The four types are ROM, RAM, PROM, and EPROM chips, with the type and number of chips varying among microcomputers.

12.24 How are ROM and RAM chips used?

These two types of chips are regularly found within most microcomputers because they are used to define the operational characteristics of that device. Random-access memory (RAM) provides a storage capacity into which data may be stored or read from. This storage chip is equivalent to primary storage. Read-only memory (ROM) provides a protected storage area where data remain in an unaltered state, being read solely from within its contents. It is not possible to write anything into ROM storage once it is filled with its initial instructional set. ROM storage is used to record the operational software needed for the microcomputer to effectively function. The ratio of RAM to ROM storage varies extensively among models of microcomputers.

12.25 What purpose do PROM and EPROM chips serve?

Both of these chip types represent new technology. They provide the ability to alter the operational capacities of home computers, adding features desired by the user. Programmable read-only memory (PROM) chips are blank ROM chips that can be loaded with data or instructions once and then function as ROM chips. Once loaded, PROM chips are unalterable. Erasable programmable read-only memory (EPROM) chips are blank chips that can be loaded with instructions, then erased and reloaded. However, although they contain data, they function as ROM chips, protecting their contents. PROM and EPROM chips are primarily used by the sophisticated home hobbyist who wishes to radically alter the processing potential of his or her microcomputer.

11.26 Do microcomputers offer the capacity of conventional larger machines?

No. Microcomputers offer extraordinary processing features at remarkable cost advantages, but to a limited degree. They cannot offer the tremendous storage capacities or speed of much larger systems, but they do have many similar features. For example, where the CPU associated with a microcomputer may be 64K, it will not possess the execution speed nor support the same level of peripheral devices as a conventional computer of comparable size.

12.27 Do microcomputers have large CPUs?

In specially adapted microcomputers, CPUs possessing a million or more bytes of storage have been constructed. However, this is far from the norm. The average microcomputer possesses a CPU of 64K, which is sufficient for the average hobbyist or small business utilizing such a device.

12.28 What types of peripheral devices are available with microcomputers?

A wide range of peripheral devices are available to support microcomputers. Many of these devices have been covered in preceding chapters. These peripherals include the use of one or more floppy disks (5- or 8-inch diameter); printing devices that enable the output of from 20 to 133 characters on one line; color graphics on color CRTs; plotters specially scaled for small drawings and microcomputer applications; and the use of audio I/O units to provide for a spoken output and voice input. Virtually every day the microcomputer industry introduces new technological features that add more processing potential to the microcomputer.

11.29 In what applications are microcomputers used?

Microcomputers are applied to virtually any type of problem, with the exception of applications that obviously exceed their capacities. They have been successfully used in small businesses to prepare payroll, accounts payable/receivable data, control inventories, and a variety of other tasks. Homemakers are using microcomputers to retain personal data, recipes, and menus. Many people use their microcomputers for tax planning and preparing their annual tax statements. Laboratory test results, statistical testing, financial statements, and stock market analysis are all activities handled by microcomputers. These small systems have helped students, accountants, engineers, researchers, biologists, physicists, nurses, and many others perform needed functions.

12.30 Are microcomputers related to computer games?

Yes. Microcomputers are at the heart of the home computer game industry. Using microcomputers and their color-graphics capabilities, many people have entertained themselves for hours.

12.31 What type of software is supported by microcomputers?

Both applications and systems software are commercially available from manufacturers and private software houses. The systems software represents the operational and utility programs used in supporting all processing activities. Applications software is available for a wide range of activities from a variety of sources. In fact, magazines exist that describe software and its cost for the hobbyist and professional.

12.32 Is microcomputer software a growing industry?

Yes. The area of microcomputer software is one of the fastest growing fields, attracting many people who have the desire and creativity to prepare their own specialized programs. Many small software houses have prospered from their development of specialized microcomputer programs.

12.33 What are the principal languages used with microcomputers?

The major languages associated with microcomputers are BASIC and PASCAL. Microcomputers can support other languages, providing that the devices have been properly upgraded to support their use. For example, interactive versions of FORTRAN and COBOL, as well as other more specialized languages exist for larger microcomputer systems.

12.34 What type of file structure may be constructed using microcomputers?

It is possible to construct both sequential- and direct-access files on microcomputers, depending on the peripheral devices incorporated into the system. For example, tape files using a sequential format may be written using the tape cassette unit associated with many microcomputer units. Floppy disks may be used to construct direct-access files where individual data records are independently retrieved.

12.35 How are additional features added to microcomputers?

Through the addition of special RAM, ROM, PROM, and EPROM chips, it is possible to add operational features to a microcomputer and increase its processing potential. Some manufacturers encourage this growth and willingly help the home enthusiast, whereas others advise against such tampering (which may negate their device's warranty). Users should carefully examine whether it is possible to alter their microcomputers and what features may be added and at what cost.

12.36 What are the cost factors of microcomputers?

Current costs of microcomputers range anywhere from $100 to $12,000. The cost of each system relates directly to the size of the computer, its CPU, special features added, and supporting software.

12.37 What types of special features could add to these costs?

Current microcomputers provide the ability to add fixed disk devices and program packages to their operational features. The fixed disk can add almost $2000 to the cost of their systems, in addition to requiring the purchase of special operational software costing $500 or more. Program packages to handle payroll, accounts receivable or payable, general ledger, or inventory information are individually or jointly available starting at $400. Word processing software to provide for the preparation of office documentation, ranging from mailing labels to manuscripts, also can be purchased. The costs range from $99 to $1000, depending on the level of software sophistication. Users must carefully monitor the peripheral devices and software added to their system and the costs related to them. Also, users must research the features they wish to incorporate into their devices. As technology improves, the availability of special supporting devices and software increases at declining costs.

MINICOMPUTERS

12.38 What are minicomputer systems?

Minicomputers are task-oriented systems that possess operational features comparable to large conventional systems, but to a lesser degree. In general, minicomputers are larger than microcomputers.

12.39 When were minicomputers first introduced?

The first minicomputer systems were introduced in the early 1960s by the Digital Equipment Corporation. These initial minicomputers were designed to perform specific processing operations and prepare data for input to a larger computer system. What these initial, small systems showed was that minicomputers were capable of efficiently supporting a continuous workload for a specific set of operational tasks at a minimal cost. The concept of a small, task-oriented system was realistic, and the move toward minicomputers was on its way. In later years the successes of minicomputers lead researchers to conceive of smaller personal computers, which paved the way for microcomputers.

12.40 What was the operational concept of minicomputers?

The rationale used in constructing minicomputer systems was to provide users with a computing power uniquely suited to their needs. What many users realized was that in purchasing a conventional computer system, they overbought and were forced to buy components for which they had little use. These components were part of the system being purchased, added to its cost, but were not really to be used. Essentially, the marketing strategy was that a package deal was offered, and the user paid the same price for one or all components. The Digital Equipment corporation realized that many users required only one portion of that computer power and believed that they could produce a competitively priced small system designed for specific tasks.

12.41 How has this rationale been used?

Consider a user that operates a retail inventory organization consisting of 12 employees but possessing over 2500 different items in inventory. The user doesn't need a variety of business systems to handle payroll or accounts payable or receivable since the primary operational need lies in inventory control. What the user desires is online control over the inventory and the ability to update those files as required.

12.42 Why was that not possible with conventional computer systems?

The necessary file updates were possible with conventional systems, but the general-purpose systems available were designed for a wider range of activities. Thus these systems possessed features that would remain unused since they were not really needed for file handling. The minicomputer best-suited to the inventory user's needs specifically provided the online update capacity but sacrificed other processing capacities. Since these capacities were not needed, the user was not hurt. Because the minicomputer was tailored specifically for online activities, cost savings could be achieved at the expense of unwanted processing capabilities.

12.43 Were the savings truly that great?

Though the resources provided by minicomputers were somewhat limited, the cost savings were considerable. A conventional computer system to support the preceding online inventory illustration would have cost approximately $500,000. By comparison, the minicomputer designed for online inventory control would have cost only $100,000. Note that the actual benefit of this tremendous cost savings depended on the user truly understanding the limitations of the minicomputer and on the organization not dramatically increasing its operation.

12.44 What limitations applied to minicomputers?

The limited resources available with minicomputers were truly taxed as the upward limits on its storage capacity and number of terminals were reached. When these limits were confronted, the user was required to jump to a conventional computer system because the minicomputer could no longer support the workload.

12.45 Do these operational conditions still exist today?

No. The capacities of current minicomputer systems far exceed their primitive counterparts. Where many initial minicomputers were limited to 64K, current systems have exceeded CPU sizes of 2000K. Online disk storage capacities are now approaching 1 billion characters of storage, while making well over 30 terminals concurrently available for online processing activities. A wide range of peripherals may be incorporated into current minicomputer systems.

12.46 Do all minicomputers possess the same operational features?

No. A wide range of minicomputer systems exist, each possessing a specific set of operational features that define its processing capabilities. For example, some small minicomputers can support up to 3 CRTs, whereas some larger systems can support up to 33 terminal devices. Small minicomputers may be limited to 80 megabytes of disk storage (80 million), whereas larger systems have a capacity of 800 megabytes. The limitations of each minicomputer define its operational use and its cost.

12.47 Were designations applied to help distinguish between types of minicomputer systems?

Initially, three categories of minicomputer systems were created in an effort to distinguish each type and its operationsl capacities. The smallest minicomputer systems were referred to as mini-minicomputers; the middle range of systems, as midi-minicomputers; and the largest of these systems, as maxi-minicomputers. The categories were established in relation to CPU size, with the categories defined as 4–16K, 16–64K, and 64–256K, respectively.

12.48 What happened to these designations?

The definite limits associated with each minicomputer category became blurred as technology improved and the use of peripheral devices crossed over into each category. For example, mini-minicomputers may now be equipped with CPUs of 512K, which was normally within the maxi category. The classifications were no longer operable in terms of the limits they represented.

12.49 How are the three minicomputer classes currently used?

The three classes of minicomputers are used as guidelines to the operational limits of each category. Mini-minicomputers generally provide the lowest level of support, primarily designed for the single user with a restricted set of operational needs, which generally means online access to a small number of files that were personally constructed. The midi-minicomputer range supports either batch processing or online processing, but not at the same time. Thus if online inquiries are underway, the batch processing of data must wait until the system's resources are free to handle that workload. This midi-range of systems adequately supports either activity, but one task at a time. The maxi-minicomputer category approaches the operational capacities of much larger conventional systems, and it supports a full line of activities and devices. It is possible to concurrently support both batch processing and online processing activities without impeding either processing activity. The maxi systems offer a truly remarkable processing capacity.

12.50 How do prices compare within each category?

The prices for minicomputers may range from $6000 to $300,000, depending on the system's size, capacity, and peripherals. A user must carefully shop around to ensure that the manufacturer quotes received are truly competitive. Minicomputer systems may be purchased from many manufacturers, including IBM, Digital Equipment, Honeywell, Burroughs, NCR, and Hewlette-Packard.

12.51 What is the major feature associated with minicomputers?

The key operational feature of minicomputer systems is online processing. The minicomputer is designed to provide an online processing capability and to permit users online access to data retained in computerized files. Much of the operational software designed for minicomputers focuses on line processing, file interrogations, and updating files.

12.52 Do minicomputers use disk devices?

Yes. Minicomputers support the use of many secondary storage devices. It is possible to use fixed or removable disks, as well as floppy disks, to create an online storage capacity. Tape storage is also possible using conventional tapes or small tape cassettes when a limited portable tape medium is required. Card-related operations are also supported by minicomputers, with the extent of these activities defined by the organization purchasing the system. Generally, cards are used on a limited basis and for low-level tasks.

12.53 What storage codes do minicomputers use?

The code principally used with minicomputers is ASCII. It is used in recording data, on tape or disk, as well as within primary storage. The Hollerith code is used when handling 80-column cards. RAM and ROM storage chips are used to construct storage capacities within minicomputers. The ASCII code is used to retain data or instructions within those chips.

12.54 Do hardcopy printing devices exist?

Yes. Most minicomputer systems possess a hardcopy printing capability to record the results of processing. The type of printing device relates directly to the system's needs. Available printers can possess speeds of 30 characters per minute to 1200 lines per minute. Printers commonly used with minicomputers include band, wire-matrix, and daisy-wheel printers.[1] Plotters are also available for the output of curvilinear drawings and graphic displays.

---

[1] A full discussion of printing devices was presented in Chap. 4.

12.55 Do minicomputers support softcopy outputs?

Yes. A complete range of softcopy devices are available for use with minicomputers of all sizes. These include color CRTs, graphic terminals (black and white or color), and conventional CRTs. Minicomputers also support the use of voice input and audio response units, thus providing a verbal I/O capability to their operation.

12.56 In what fields are minicomputers used?

Minicomputers are used in fields requiring sound data processing support. These devices are used, for example, by accountants, dentists, doctors, farmers, economists, travel agents, and brokers in the areas of insurance, stocks, and commodities. Organizations related to any of these fields have successfully used minicomputers including the U.S. military, international credit card companies, airlines, publishing houses, and schools of all sizes. Minicomputers provide reliable DP support to a wide array of organizations.

Fig. 12-3 The Burroughs B 900 is a maxi-minicomputer which can support teleprocessing operations and the distributed handling of data in computer networks. (*Burroughs Corporation*)

12.57 Are minicomputers used in distributed networks?

Yes. Distributed data processing systems may be fully supported by minicomputer systems. Figure 12-3 illustrates a maxi-minicomputer incorporated into distributed data processing operations. DDPS networks composed of minicomputer systems have successfully supported widely dispersed retail, insurance, travel, and medical organizations. Distributed word processing operations, combining the resources of many dispersed offices, are also achieved using minicomputer systems.

FOUR COMPUTER CATEGORIES

12.58 What difficulties arise when an attempt is made to evaluate the operational capacity of a computer system?

Users find it difficult to assess what a specific computer system can do because the hardware and software composing a system can vary considerably. Minor variations in either the supporting hardware or operational software can alter a computer's processing potential. Also, considering the number of models of computers currently available, it is difficult to choose between various models of computers.

12.59 What steps have been taken to assist users?

In addition to publishing technical manuals on each model of computer, an industrywide classification scheme was established to help users. The classification scheme is based upon CPU sizes according to the following four categories:

(1) Small-scale computers
(2) Medium-scale computers
(3) Large-scale computers
(4) Supercomputers

These classifications segregate computers into categories ranging from the smallest to the largest systems.

12.60 Where are the smallest systems placed?

The smallest computer systems are positioned within the category of small-scale computers. Computers in this category possess CPU sizes from 4K to 64K and demonstrate operational features that parallel much larger systems. These systems may support teleprocessing operations and card-oriented batch processing.

12.61 What type of computers are in the small-scale category?

Many minicomputers and microcomputers are considered small-scale computers, as well as small conventional systems. Examples of small-scale computers are the IBM/38; Digital's PDP-11/24 (Fig. 12-4); Burroughs 90; Honeywell 60; and Data General Nova.

Fig. 12-4 The PDP-11/24 is a small-scale computer capable of time-sharing and teleprocessing activities. (*Digital Equipment*)

12.62 Which organizations use small-scale systems?

Many small businesses, manufacturing plants, schools, municipal governments, software development shops, banks, architectural and engineering firms, and consultants utilize small-scale systems to assist their project work and to administer their organizations.

CHAP. 12] A SURVEY OF COMPUTER SYSTEMS

12.63 What devices are used with these small systems?

Virtually any form of peripheral device can be attached to small-scale systems to include magnetic tapes, disks, floppy disks, printers, audio I/O devices, plotters, CRTs, and card-oriented devices. Essentially, these systems provide the same services as their larger counterparts, but they cannot accommodate as many types of peripherals and the same quantity.

12.64 What distinguishes the medium-scale systems?

Medium-scale computers possess CPUs of size 64K to 512K and constitute the category following small-scale computers. Computer systems in the medium-scale classification are the IBM Series 4300; UNIVAC 1100; Hewlett-Packard 3000 (Fig. 12-5); Honeywell Series 600; Burroughs 4900; and BASIC-4 730. Many of the larger minicomputer systems are in this category.

Fig. 12-5 The Hewlett-Packard 3000 is a medium-scale computer system. (*Hewlett-Packard*)

12.65 Are medium-scale systems popular?

Yes. Computers defined as medium-scale compose the largest single group of systems in use. The vast majority of business organizations are supported by computers in this category. Their size makes them adaptable to the data processing needs of the average user and affordable to most organizations.

12.66 What type of organizations use medium-scale systems to support their DP needs?

Almost any organization from a retail store to a brokerage house might use the services provided by medium-scale systems. Many municipal, defense, industrial, and commercial organizations place medium-scale computers at the heart of their DP operations.

12.67 Do medium-scale systems support a full range of peripheral devices?

Yes. Medium-scale systems perform a wide range of DP activities and, as such, require a full range of peripherals. These devices include a full array of card-oriented, disk, tape, printing, and terminal devices. Batch and online processing activities are supported by these systems, utilizing all forms of peripherals to complete I/O activities.

12.68 What are the cost differences related to small-scale and medium-scale systems?

On the average, small-scale systems will cost less than their medium-scale counterparts. Medium-scale systems with a normal complement of peripheral devices can typically rent for $2000 to $20,000 per month. Small-scale systems may be purchased for as little as $100. More realistically, the average business-related small-scale system will have a minimum purchase price of approximately $3000, with the price increasing as the system grows. The purchase price of the largest of these small-scale systems can exceed $200,000, with a typical rental cost averaging $2000 per month.

12.69 Is the jump to the large-scale category significant?

Yes. The category of large-scale computers represents a major jump in computer hardware. Large-scale systems are used by organizations that require their vast processing potential. Large international and domestic corporations supporting databases and distributed processing activities are likely users of large-scale systems.

12.70 What CPU sizes are involved?

Large-scale systems use CPUs ranging from 512K to 5 megabytes of storage. These systems support online storage capacities in the billions of characters, formulating databases to handle the array of files needed to hold operational data. The costs related to large-scale systems are quite high, due to the complexity of the processing involved. Typical rental costs range from $45,000 to $75,000 per month.

12.71 What processing activities are normally associated with these larger systems?

Online processing, signaled by satellite telecommunications and teleprocessing activities, are normally a hallmark of these systems. Online file inquiries, updates, and real-time processing are also characteristic of large-scale systems. Computers representative of these systems are the IBM 370/168; Burroughs 6900 (Fig. 12-6); Honeywell 66/80; Control Data Cyber 175; and Amdahl V5.

Fig. 12-6 Large-scale computer systems, such as this one, are used by organizations that require extensive processing potential. (*Burroughs Corporation*)

12.72 How do large-scale systems compare with supercomputers?

The designation supercomputer identifies the largest and most sophisticated commercially available computer systems. These systems possess CPU sizes in excess of 5 million bytes of primary storage and can support virtually any type of peripheral device. The costs associated with supercomputers will normally exceed $10 million. These costs reflect the level, size, and scope of processing associated with supercomputers. They offer processing capabilities not possible within the other computer classifications.

12.73 How fast are supercomputers?

The average speed associated with conventional computer systems is 3 million instructions per second. This rating reflects a computer's ability to execute a specific number of instructions a second and is called a *MIPS rating*. The acronym MIPS denotes *m*illions of *i*nstructions *p*er *s*econd. Large-scale systems can carry a MIPS rating of 20 to 40 million instructions per minute. Under ideal conditions supercomputers have attained internal processing speeds at which over 100,000,000 instructions were executed in one second. Generally, it is estimated that supercomputers operate at speeds that are two to five times faster than large-scale systems.

12.74 What type of organizations require the vast processing speeds of supercomputers?

Supercomputers support those organizations requiring real-time update capabilities, via satellites, concurrently, at widely dispersed locations, that receive a continuous series of updates from online locations into a database of billions of characters of data, where the frequency of inquiries is in the thousands of data requests per hour. The U.S. Weather Service, NASA, the U.S. Department of Defense, national intelligence, and international crime fighting agencies are organizations that rely on their supercomputer systems. The work attributed to these organizations reflects the online handling of millions of data items, online requests from dispersed locations, vast databases in which data items are continually cross-referenced, and a continuous stream of outputs. In comparison, the responsibility of solely handling data communications and updating the database require, at minimum, the support of a large-scale system. Only a supercomputer can handle those activities and all of the other processing required of such a complex system.

12.75 Are supercomputers as plentiful as other systems?

Only a few companies manufacture supercomputers because of the cost, complexity, and technical expertise required to construct them. Two examples of supercomputers are the Control Data Corp. Cyber 7600 and the CRAY/Models 1 and 2 systems.

12.76 How are the four classifications used?

The four computer classifications provide a means of comparing computer systems and identifying like systems. The classifications by themselves will not specify the processing capacities of a single system since these are discovered only by examining a particular system in detail. However, they do provide a means of examining systems that fall within the same category and thus should possess similar processing characteristics.

MANAGERIAL CONSIDERATIONS WHEN PURCHASING NEW COMPUTER HARDWARE

12.77 Why does management express grave concern over computer conversions?

Most managerial personnel do not have the knowledge of computerization to permit them to freely operate within that sphere of work. Also, the dollar figures can be staggering, often requiring the preparation of lengthy economic justifications prior to the purchase of hardware. The issue of what hardware to use requires extensive study. Essentially, most managers cite the costs associated with hardware and their unfamiliarity with the computer area as the major stumbling blocks in their decision-making process.

12.78 What questions should management attempt to answer during its deliberations?

Management should use the answers from the questions that follow as a basis for evaluating the scope of computer services needed.

(1) What form of DP services are suited for the organization?
(2) What computer system, with what CPU and speed, is required for that level of DP activity?
(3) Should the hardware be rented or purchased outright?
(4) What peripherals are needed to support the anticipated DP services?
(5) What type of vendor maintenance is available, and what are the related expenses?
(6) What types of operational and applications software are required?
(7) What personnel are required to function within the DP area, and what training will they need?

In answering these questions, management can derive the data to intelligently determine the type and scope of data processing suited to their organization.

12.79 How can management determine the DP services that are appropriate for the organization?

The systems study of the organization, if properly performed, should reveal the scope of DP support required for that organization and the inefficiencies of existing data handling operations. With these facts, management can readily adopt a processing mode to suit their financial condition and desired mode of processing. The fixing of the processing mode to be used focuses the direction of the DP activities and enables the analysts to prepare lists of required hardware, software, and personnel.

12.80 How does the fixing of the processing mode help?

If a batch processing mode is chosen, then the analysts may select a smaller computer system, with less complex software and design procedures that are less constrained by time. Batch processing operations are not as complex nor are they as demanding in terms of time. Online processing requires a higher level of activity, more sophisticated hardware and software, and procedures that complement the rapid handling of data. This processing approach is generally more expensive than batch processing and requires more planning and better-trained employees. Management's selection should reflect the resources that must be made available for the mode of processing chosen.

12.81 How is the selection of computer hardware made?

Once a processing mode is selected, the hardware to support that processing approach can be purchased. This purchase includes all I/O devices, lines, secondary storage units, and the main CPU. In acquiring this hardware, users must specify the system desired and the MIPS rating associated with that computer.

12.82 Why would the hardware be affected by the mode of processing?

The more sophisticated the processing mode, the more complex the hardware needed to support it. Batch processing operations using cards require less complex hardware than those devices used with online activities. Also the number of terminals to be used affects the CPU size. The greater the number of online terminals, the larger the system required and the larger the CPU.

12.83 Should the required hardware be purchased or rented?

A major consideration when obtaining computer hardware is the choice between renting or outright purchasing of the equipment. There are tax considerations that must be examined in relation to renting or buying hardware. Often the cash flow of a company determines whether sufficient funds are available for the purchase of hardware.

12.84 What advantages accrue through renting?

The rental of hardware enables users to retain those devices for a specific time period and then trade in the devices for newer ones. The manufacturer is responsible for disposing of the old equipment. When users purchase hardware outright, they are responsible for its ultimate disposal. Also, rental costs are normally assessed on a monthly basis and do not place a large initial financial burden on the user. The decision whether to rent or buy must be carefully scrutinized from all angles.

12.85 How are the number and type of peripherals arrived at?

Management's selection of a processing mode also dictates the type of hardware to be used. Included in this package are the peripheral devices integrated in that design. The analysts preparing the alternative systems from which management will select should detail the suggested peripherals to compose each alternative. Essentially, management is presented with all the information it needs to make a cogent decision.

12.86 Must all peripherals be obtained from the same manufacturer?

No. Users are free to mix and match the peripherals composing their systems. The only consideration relates to the compatibility of the hardware purchased. Any device acquired must interface with the CPU positioned at the heart of the computer system. Many DP professionals have been embarrassed by overlooking the compatibility of hardware devices obtained from different manufacturers.

12.87 Is the maintenance of new hardware really that important?

Yes. The maintenance of computer hardware is a major consideration of any system. It is often one of the factors that is frequently overlooked because of its extra cost or just through error.

12.88 What types of maintenance are required?

Generally, two types of maintenance are performed. Scheduled maintenance is performed on a regular basis, to ensure that the entire system is functioning within its calibrated limits. Unscheduled maintenance is performed as necessary, when a unit malfunctions or errors are detected. Scheduled maintenance is usually performed by the operations staff on a weekly or daily basis. Unscheduled maintenance is normally performed by the manufacturer when the computer or peripheral device malfunctions. Users are concerned with unscheduled maintenance because of the costs involved. Without an adequate service contract, maintenance costs can prove prohibitive.

12.89 How are service contracts paid for?

Maintenance contracts are paid on a flat-fee basis or included as part of the monthly rental cost. Flat fees are normally paid by people who purchase their hardware outright. Monthly maintenance costs are usually a percentage of the rental cost charged by the manufacturer. Either fee should be included in cost comparisons of the systems under consideration.

12.90 Must service be obtained from the manufacturer?

No. Maintenance contracts can be obtained from the manufacturer or private service organizations. The rates charged are usually competitive. Most organizations usually opt for service contracts from the manufacturer, believing that the best service is provided by the original manufacturer.

12.91 How is the operational software selected?

The operational software acquired relates directly to the processing mode chosen. The operating system must provide the software necessary to support the processing to be performed. Online inquiries do not occur by magic but are well-planned activities supported by the system's operational software. Each manufacturer has specific types of operational software that clearly define the processing modes they can support. Generally, lengthy discussions are conducted with manufacturer representatives to ensure the acquisition of the proper operating system.

12.92 Where is the application software obtained?

Application software can be purchased from private software houses or written by in-house programmers. The decision whether to buy or write software will usually relate to available time, personnel, and budget. Normally, during the delivery period for a new computer, sufficient time is provided to prepare the application software.

12.93 Can existing personnel interface efficiently with new systems without training?

No. It would be a major error to believe that employees could work with a new system without sufficient training. Except in emergencies, sufficient time should be set aside for adequately training all employees slated to interface with the new system. This time is needed to familiarize each employee with his or her new assignment and the new system. Any peculiarities related to the specific job should be highlighted during that training period.

12.94 When are staffing requirements developed?

Normally, the reports describing each alternative system will define both the hardware and the personnel needed to support that system. Management's selection of an alternative provides tacit approval for those staffing requirements. This again signals the importance of selecting the processing mode under which the new system will function.

12.95 When and where is training conducted?

The training of personnel can occur at any time but is usually scheduled as the new system approaches its final form. Doing so ensures that no major changes will be made in the new design and enables the personnel to train with the procedures most likely to be used. Training is usually performed on-site or in classes specially scheduled for these purposes. Depending on existing operating conditions, employees in training may be released for these classes or they may receive instruction after normal working hours. The release of some employees may not affect the organization, whereas other employees are so critical to the flow of data that they cannot be excused. Training requirements are normally established when the original systems package is documented and approved.

Review Questions

12.96 All computer systems are classified as either analog or digital computers. (*a*) True, (*b*) false.

12.97 Analog computers are generally faster than digital computers because of their rapid conversion of input data. (*a*) True, (*b*) false.

12.98 Most computers used in a business environment are referred to as *general-purpose, analog computers.* (*a*) True, (*b*) false.

12.99 CAD/CAM systems are used in computer-assisted production facilities. (*a*) True, (*b*) false.

12.100 Only one type of chip is used in the construction of minicomputers. (*a*) True, (*b*) false.

12.101 Minicomputers are task-oriented systems that offer processing features which parallel larger systems. (*a*) True, (*b*) false.

12.102 Many minicomputers offer processing features equivalent to those of larger minicomputer systems. (*a*) True, (*b*) false.

12.103 Minicomputer systems were initially subdivided into three categories depending on their operational capabilities. (*a*) True, (*b*) false.

12.104 Supercomputers are used by virtually every large corporation because they offer the utmost computerized services for management's use. (*a*) True, (*b*) false.

12.105 The selection of computer hardware by management usually reflects many months of deliberation. (*a*) True, (*b*) false.

CHAP. 12] A SURVEY OF COMPUTER SYSTEMS 281

12.106 A principal activity related to the selection of computer hardware is the determination of what DP services are best-suited for the organization. (a) True, (b) false.

12.107 Computer hardware should always be purchased outright because no tax advantage exists in renting those devices. (a) True, (b) false.

12.108 The operational software incorporated into a computer system relates directly to the processing activities to be performed by that system. (a) True, (b) false.

12.109 Normally all applications software is purchased when acquiring new hardware, as insufficient time exists to write the programs required. (a) True, (b) false.

12.110 When implementing a new system, sufficient time should be allocated for employee training. (a) True, (b) false.

12.111 The measurement of some physical property and its conversion to a numerical format is an integral part of a(n) (a) analog computer; (b) digital computer; (c) general-purpose computer; (d) all of the above.

12.112 A simulator used in the training of airline pilots could be considered a(n) (a) special-purpose computer; (b) analog computer; (c) hybrid computer; (d) all of the above.

12.113 The type of chip used to conduct primary storage activities is the (a) EPROM chip; (b) PROM chip; (c) RAM chip; (d) ROM chip.

12.114 A principal language of microcomputers is (a) BASIC; (b) COBOL; (c) PASCAL; (d) a, b, and c.

12.115 A characteristic associated with minicomputers is (a) CPU sizes limited to 64K; (b) online disk storage of up to 1 million characters of data; (c) concurrent use of over 30 terminals; (d) all of the above.

12.116 A characteristic associated with the midrange of minicomputers is (a) the sole use of cards; (b) the alternate performance of online and batch processing; (c) the concurrent performance of file inquiries and batch processing; (d) distributed processing from remote local offices.

12.117 Most microcomputers are classified as (a) small-scale systems; (b) medium-scale systems; (c) large-scale systems; (d) supercomputers.

12.118 The computer classification representing CPUs of 512K to 5000K is (a) small-scale computers; (b) medium-scale computers; (c) large-scale computers; (d) supercomputers.

12.119 A characteristic of supercomputer systems is (a) real-time processing; (b) vast database; (c) DDPS services; (d) all of the above.

12.120 Computer maintenance costs are (a) often included in monthly rental costs; (b) never considered until the system is more than 12 months old; (c) often contracted under a separate service contract; (d) a and c.

12.121 A computer system combining the best features of an analog computer and a digital computer is a _____ computer.

12.122 The computer assigned to the widest array of applications in both the business and scientific areas is the _____ computer.

12.123 The basic component used in the construction of microcomputers is the _____.

12.124 A ROM chip that is once loaded with data and remains unaltered is a(n) _____ chip.

12.125 The largest minicomputer systems may be referred to as _____ -minicomputers.

12.126 The _____ code is principally used to record data in minicomputer systems.

12.127 The bulk of business DP services are performed using _____ -scale computers.

12.128 The relative internal processing speeds of computer systems may be evaluated using the _____ rating.

12.129 When selecting a computer, it is critical that users specify the _____ size necessary to support their processing activities.

12.130 Maintenance activities performed on a regular basis are referred to as _____ maintenance.

Answers: 12.96 (*b*); 12.97 (*a*); 12.98 (*b*); 12.99 (*a*); 12.100 (*b*); 12.101 (*a*); 12.102 (*a*); 12.103 (*a*); 12.104 (*b*); 12.105 (*a*); 12.106 (*a*); 12.107 (*b*); 12.108 (*a*); 12.109 (*b*); 12.110 (*a*); 12.111 (*a*); 12.112 (*d*); 12.113 (*c*); 12.114 (*d*); 12.115 (*c*); 12.116 (*b*); 12.117 (*a*); 12.118 (*c*); 12.119 (*d*); 12.120 (*d*); 12.121 hybrid; 12.122 general-purpose; 12.123 silicon chip; 12.124 PROM; 12.125 maxi; 12.126 ASCII; 12.127 medium; 12.128 MIPS; 12.129 CPU; 12.130 scheduled.

Supplementary Problems

12.131 Would you consider the hardware supporting computerized games special-purpose or analog computers? Explain.

12.132 Examine the following list of applications, and determine whether a general- or special-purpose computer would be involved in that activity.

Offtrack betting activities
Surgery simulator for nurses' training
CAM plant where robots produce steel products
Computer scoreboards at sports arenas
Analyzing census data and outputting graphic displays
DDPS activities for a network of brokerage houses

12.133 In your own words describe the differences between microcomputers, minicomputers, and conventional computing systems. What devices are used in creating files in these systems?

12.134 Describe the three categories developed with minicomputers, and detail how each defines a different processing activity. Why do minicomputers offer cost savings to their users? Cite examples of systems from each classification.

12.135 Detail the four categories assigned to computer systems and the limits of CPU storage for each category. Cite examples of applications associated with computers from each category.

12.136 What are the operational differences between RAM, ROM, PROM, and EPROM chips?

12.137 If you were a manager, what information would you want in order to make a decision on the purchase of computer hardware? Prepare a list of questions you might ask to obtain that data. Where would you look to acquire that data, and what investigations would you conduct?

Glossary

Analog computer. A computer that derives its input data from the measurement of some physical property.

Computer-assisted design (CAD). The computerized technique that monitors and controls all aspects of a design with computer software and that adjusts to operating conditions as they are sensed.

Computer-assisted manufacturing (CAM). The companion technique to CAD whereby a computer controls the actual manufacture of computer-designed materials.

Digital computer. A computer that uses data input in a digital, or numeric, format.

Erasable programmable read-only memory (EPROM). An ROM chip that is initially blank but may be reprogrammed any number of times; protects its contents once filled.

General-purpose computer. The computer type that is capable of handling both business and scientific problems.

Hybrid computers. A computer that combines the features of analog and digital computers.

Large-scale computer. The third computer classification for complex systems having CPUs of 512K to 5000K.

Medium-scale computer. The second computer classification for systems having CPUs of 64K to 512K.

Microcomputer. The smallest computer system, constructed of silicon chips, represented by home and personal computing systems.

Minicomputer. Small task-oriented system possessing limited operational characteristics similar to conventional computers.

MIPS rating. A rating that reflects the computer's ability to execute a specific number of instructions per second (usually in the millions of instructions per second).

Programmable read-only memory (PROM). An ROM chip that is initially blank and then loaded with a desired set of instructions or data.

Random-access memory (RAM). A storage chip in which data may be written or read from.

Read-only memory (ROM). A storage chip from which data may be only read and not altered.

Scheduled maintenance. The periodic testing of a computer system to ensure that it is functioning within its calibrated limits.

Silicon chip. The technology used to construct today's computers; the principal component of microcomputers.

Simulator. A special-purpose computer specifically used in training for certain occupations.

Small-scale computer. The computer classification for systems having CPUs of 4K to 64K; the smallest system commercially available.

Special-purpose computer. A computer system constructed to support specific and specialized applications.

Supercomputers. The largest and most expensive computer, possessing a CPU in excess of 5 million bytes of storage; the fourth computer classification.

Unscheduled maintenance. Maintenance activities that result from malfunctions in the software or hardware supporting a system.

Index

Index

Abend, 100
Access arm, 214, 217
Access time, 214, 221
Accounts payable systems, 185, 191–192
Accounts receivable systems, 185, 191–192
Accumulator initialization, 123, 141–142
Accumulators, 123, 141–145
Accuracy, 1
Alphabetic card fields, 30
Alphabetic characters, 30
Alphameric card fields, 30
Alternative systems designs, 205–206
ALU (arithmetic-logic unit), 13
American Standard Code for Information Interchange (ASCII) code, 31, 46–48
Analog computers, 262–264
Analyst teams, 185
Analysts:
    senior systems, 208
    systems, 185, 188
    systems group and, 185, 187–189
Annotation symbols, 122, 127–128
Application software, 279
Applications:
    business, 107
    microcomputers, 269
    scientific, 100, 107
Applied Text Management System (ATMS), 96
Arithmetic-logic unit (ALU), 13
Arithmetic operations, 4, 17
ASCII (American Standard Code for Information Interchange) code, 31, 46–48
Assembly language, 100
Assembly language codes, 103
Asterisk, 128
ATMS (Applied Text Management System), 96
Audio response unit, 70
Automated looping sequences, 123, 139–140
Automatic typesetters, 54, 76
Auxiliary operation symbol, 201–203
Average unit cost example, 132–134
Average unit price example, 136–141

Backup storage, 214, 223
Band printer, 60
BASIC, 101, 110–111
Batch processing, 84
Batch processing mode, 278
Batches, 85
BCD (Binary-Coded Decimal), 30, 38–42
BCD equivalents:
    for Hollerith digit punches, 39
    for Hollerith zone punches, 39
Bidirectional printer, 62
Binary-Coded Decimal (*see entries beginning with the term*: BCD)

Binary notation, 31
Bit, 31
Blocking factors, 214, 223
Blocks of data, 214, 223
Bottom-up techniques, 154
BPI (bytes per inch), 215, 234
Branches:
    conditional, 122, 131
    unconditional, 122, 132, 133
Brush card readers, 53
Buffers, 13, 24
Business, data processing techniques for, 54, 76–79
Business applications, 107
Business systems, 185, 190–193
Buying versus renting equipment, 278
Byte, 13
Bytes per inch (BPI), 215, 234

CAD (computer-assisted design), 262, 267
CAM (computer-assisted manufacturing), 262, 267
Canned programs, 215, 234–235
Card, Hollerith, 30–33
Card fields, 30, 36–38
Card processing operations, 204–205
Card reader, 12, 53
Card reader/punch, 53, 58
Card-related devices, 53, 55–59
Cards per minute (CPM), 58
Cassettes, tape, 214, 225
Cathode ray tube (CRT), 12, 14–16, 53
Central processing unit (CPU), 12, 13, 16–18
Centralized data processing system, 95
Centralized MIS structure, 240, 247–248
Chain printer, 59
Chaining, 241, 253
Channels, 13
Character recognition, 54
Characters per inch, 234
Characters per minute (CPM), 62
Chief programmer team (CPT), 155, 178
Chips, silicon, 262, 268
CICS (customer information control system), 241, 256
COBOL, 101, 108
Collecting data, 1, 186, 196–200
Color display terminal, 68
Color printer, 62, 63
Columns, card, 30
COM (computer output microfilm), 54, 79
Commas, 127
Communication link, 203
Company manuals, 199
Compilation, 100
Compiler, 100, 105–106
Computer-assisted design (CAD), 262, 267
Computer-assisted manufacturing (CAM), 262, 267

Computer categories, 263, 273–277
Computer codes, 30–52
Computer factors, 1–3
Computer games, 269
Computer output microfilm (COM), 54, 79
Computer program, 4
Computer system components, 12–29
Computer system overview, 12–16
Computer system survey, 262–283
Computer types, 262–267
Concurrently, term, 92
Conditional branches, 122, 131
Conditional symbols, 147
Connector symbols, 123, 133
Consultants, outside, 208–209
Control block sequences, 155, 164–165
Control block structures, 155, 164–167
Control unit, 13
Controls, 1
Core, 18
Counter decisions, 123, 136
Counter initialization, 136
Counters, 123, 134
CPM (cards per minute), 58
CPM (characters per minute), 62
CPT (chief programmer team), 155, 178
CPU (central processing unit), 12, 13, 16–18
CRT (cathode ray tube), 12, 14–16, 53
Customer information control system (CICS), 241, 256
Cylinders, 214, 220–221

Daisy-wheel printer, 60, 61
DASD (direct-access storage devices), 215, 225–227
Data, 1, 122
 blocks of, 214, 223
 collecting, 1, 186, 196–200
 raw, 1, 4
Data collection terminals, 54, 70
Data communications/database (DC/DB) system, 242, 257–258
Data communications facilities, 84, 89–91
Data Language/1 (DL/1), 241, 256
Data processing concepts, 1–11
Data processing (DP) department, 185, 188
Data processing techniques for business, 54, 76–79
Database, term, 250
Database administration, 241, 253–255
Database administrator, 241, 253–255
Database management systems (DBMS), 241, 251
Database structures, 241, 250–253
Datanames, 122, 127
DBMS (database management systems), 241, 251
DC/DB (data communications/database) system, 242, 257–258
DDES (distributed data entry systems), 215, 229
DDPS (distributed data processing systems), 84–85, 93–95
Debugging, 100

Decentralized MIS structure, 240, 249
Decision symbols, 130
Decisions, 122
 counter, 123, 136
 multiple, 124, 145–147
Dedicated lines, 90
Dedicated systems, 13
Departmental representatives, 208
Design review:
 formal, 155, 179
 informal, 155, 178
Desk checking, 101, 112
Detail HIPO diagrams, 154, 163–164
Dialed services, 84
Digit bits, 46
Digit punches, 30
Digital computers, 262–264
Direct access, 222
Direct-access files, 215, 230–232
Direct-access medium, 20
Direct-access storage devices (DASD), 215, 225–227
Disk drive, 217
Disk pack, 214, 218, 219
Disk storage drive, 224
Diskettes, 215, 229–230
 dual-density, 215, 230
Disks:
 floppy, 215, 229–230
 magnetic, 13, 214, 216–221
Distributed data entry systems (DDES), 215, 229
Distributed data processing systems (DDPS), 84–85, 93–95
Distributed MIS structure, 240, 247, 248
Distributed word processing systems (DWPS), 85, 95–96
DL/1 (Data Language/1), 241, 256
DO/UNTIL looping sequence, 155, 169–175
DO/WHILE looping sequence, 155, 169–170
Document symbol, 201–203
Documentation, 101, 113, 116–117
 flowcharting, 122, 124–126
 HIPO, 154, 158–164
 self-, 106
 systems, 200
Documents:
 source, 1, 6
 turnaround, 57
Dot-matrix printer, 60
Downtime, 1
DP (data processing) department, 185, 188
Drum, magnetic, 215, 227
Dual-density diskettes, 215, 230
DWPS (distributed word processing systems), 85, 95–96

EBCDIC (Extended Binary-Coded Decimal Interchangeable Code), 31, 42–46
EBCDIC digit bits, Hollerith digit punches and, 43

EBCDIC zone bits, Hollerith zone punches and, 43
Editing, 54
EDP (electronic data processing) cycle, 1, 3–5
Eighty-column card, 30–33
Electronic data processing (EDP) cycle, 1, 3–5
Electronic mail, 54
Electrostatic printer, 62, 64, 65
Erasable programmable read-only memory (EPROM), 262, 268
Exception listings, 240, 246
Execution, program, 101, 112–113
Extended Binary-Coded Decimal Interchangeable Code (*see entries beginning with the term*: EBCDIC)

Face up and face down, terms, 33
Feasibility committee, 187, 207–209
Feasibility report, 209
Feasibility study, 187, 207
Fiber optics, 75
FICA (Federal Insurance Contributions Act) deductions, 134
Fields:
    card, 30, 36–38
    key, 215, 230, 233
File, term, 7
File software, 215, 232–235
File structures, conventional, 215, 230–232
File types, 215, 230–232
Fixed-block addressing, 214, 220
Floppy disks, 215, 229–230
Flowchart loops, program, 122–123, 126–134
Flowcharting, 117, 122–153
Flowcharting concepts, additional, 124, 145–149
Flowcharting documentation, 122, 124–126
Flowcharts, 122, 124–153
    program, 122, 124–153
    systems, 122, 124–153, 186, 200–205
FOR/NEXT looping sequence, 155, 168–169
Forecasting reports, 240, 246
Formal design review, 155, 179
Format, output, 4
FORTRAN, 100, 107–108
Frequency, 1

Games, computer, 269
General-purpose computers, 262, 265
GO TO, 122, 132
Gross pay example, 126–128

Hardcopy, 12
Hardcopy terminals, 53, 68
Hardware, 12
    considerations, 214–215, 224–230
    managerial considerations in purchasing new, 263, 277–280
Hierarchical MIS structure, 240, 248–249
Hierarchy plus input-process-output (*see entries beginning with the term*: HIPO)

HIPO (hierarchy plus input-process-output) documentation, 154, 158–164
HIPO package, 154, 162–164
Hollerith card, 30–33
Hollerith code, 30, 33–36, 41, 45
Hollerith code configurations, 36
Hollerith digit punches:
    BCD equivalents for, 39
    EBCDIC digit bits and, 43
Hollerith zone punches:
    BCD equivalents for, 39
    EBCDIC zone bits and, 43
Hybrid computers, 262, 265

IBGs (interblock gaps), 214, 223
IBM 3800 printing subsystem, 72–73
Identification number scheme, 160–162
IF/THEN/ELSE sequence, 155, 164–166
Image Printer, 75
Impact printers, 53
IMS (information management systems), 241, 255–258
IMS software, 256
IMS techniques, 241–242, 256–257
Increments, 123, 136
Indexed sequential files, 215, 230–232
Informal design review, 155, 178
Information, 4
    reporting, to management, 240, 245–247
Information management systems (*see entries beginning with the term*: IMS)
Information processing systems, 84–99
Initial conditions, 123, 136
Ink-jet printer, 62, 64, 65
Input, 1
Input device, 12
Input-output (*see entries beginning with the term*: I/O)
Intelligence, word, 54
Intelligent devices, 54, 70–73
Intelligent printers, 54, 72, 75
Intelligent terminals, 54, 71
Interactive language, 111
Interactive processing, 84
Interblock gaps (IBGs), 214, 223
Interrecord gaps (IRGs), 214, 222
Interviews, personnel, 198–199
Inventory application, 1, 5–7
Inventory file update example, 202–203
Inventory systems, 185, 192
Inverted structure, 241, 251–253
I/O bound, 13
I/O devices, 12, 53–83
I/O forms, existing, 186, 197
I/O symbols, 122, 123, 127
IRGs (interrecord gaps), 214, 222

Job control language (JCL), 101, 112–117
Jobstream, 101

K (symbol), 13
Key field, 215, 230, 233
Key-to-disk devices, 215, 227–229
Key-to-tape devices, 215, 227–228

Labels, special, 123, 139
Languages, programming (see Programming languages)
Large-scale computers, 263, 276–277
Laser printer, 62, 64, 65
Last record check (LRC), 122, 123, 131
Leased lines, 84
Left-justified fields, 30
Line printer, 14
Lines per minute (LPM), 61
Literals, 123, 138
Logical operation, 18
Looping sequences, 123, 134–140, 155, 164–166, 168–175
  automated, 123, 139–140
Loops, program flowchart, 122–123, 126–134
LPM (lines per minute), 61
LRC (last record check), 122, 123, 131

Machine independence, 105
Machine languages, 100
Macroinstruction (macro), 100
Magnetic disks, 13, 214, 216–221
Magnetic drum, 215, 227
Magnetic ink character recognition (MICR), 54, 77
Magnetic tape unit, 224
Magnetic tapes, 13, 214, 221–224
Mail, electronic, 54
Main control module, 154, 160
Main storage, 18
Maintenance requirements, 1
Maintenance types, 279
Management:
  personnel, 241, 253
  reporting information to, 240, 245–247
  software, 241, 253
Management information systems (see entries beginning with the term: MIS)
Managerial considerations in purchasing new computer hardware, 263, 277–280
Manual operation symbol, 201–203
Manuals:
  company, 199
  organization, 199
  procedures, 199
Mass storage system, 215, 226, 227
Master computer, 94–95
Master control program, 21
Maxi-minicomputers, 263, 271–272
Medium-scale computers, 263, 275–276
Megabyte, 18
Memory, 18
Merge programs, 215, 233
MICR (magnetic ink character recognition), 54, 77

Microcomputers, 262, 267–270
  applications of, 269
  peripheral devices with, 262, 269
Microfiche, 54
Micrographics, 54
Microimage terminals, 79
Midi-minicomputers, 263, 271–272
Millions of instructions per second (MIPS) rating, 3, 277
Minicomputers, 262–263, 270–273
Mini-minicomputers, 263, 271–272
Minus sign, 128
MIPS (millions of instructions per second) rating, 3, 277
MIS (management information systems), 240–261
MIS characteristics, 245
MIS configurations, 240, 247–249
MIS growth potential, 245
MIS initials, 240, 242
MIS objective, 244
MIS structure:
  centralized, 240, 247–248
  decentralized, 240, 249
  distributed, 240, 247, 248
  hierarchical, 240, 248–249
Mnemonic, 100
Modular construction, 157
Multiple card layout form, 101, 113–114
Multiple decisions, 124, 145–147
Multi-ply forms, 65
Multiprocessing, 84, 91–93
Multiprocessing system, 257
Multiprogramming, 84, 91–93

Nanoseconds, 22
Narrowband channels, 84, 91
Net pay accumulation example, 143–145
Net pay example, 134–136
Nine edge of card, 32
Ninety-six column card, 30
Nonimpact printers, 53
Nonremovable disks, 214, 217–219
Numeric card fields, 30
Numeric characters, 30

Object program, 100
OCR (optical character recognition), 54, 78
Offline, term, 6
Offline devices, 1
Offline storage symbol, 201–203
On-demand reports, 240, 246
Online, term, 6
Online batch processing, 84, 87–88
Online devices, 1
Online keyboard symbol, 201–203
Online processing mode, 278
Online processing systems, 84–89
Online storage symbol, 201–203
Operand, 100

INDEX

Operating system, 21
Operation (op) code, 100
Operational software, 13, 20–21
Operations group, 185, 188
Optical character recognition (OCR), 54, 78
Organization manuals, 199
Output, 1
Output device, 12
Output format, 4
Outside consultants, 208–209
Overlapped processing, 13, 21–24
Overview HIPO diagram, 154, 162–163

Pages, 14
Parallel card readers, 53
Parentheses, 128, 134
PASCAL, 101, 111–112
Payroll system, 185, 190
Percents, 124
Peripheral devices, 12, 16
   with microcomputers, 262, 269
Personnel, 155, 178–179
Personnel interviews, 198–199
Personnel management, 241, 253
Personnel systems, 185, 190–191
Personnel training, 280
Photoelectric-cell card readers, 53, 55
PL/1, 101, 108–109
Plotters, 53, 66, 67
Plus sign, 128
Point-of-sale (POS) system, 241, 250
Point-of-sale (POS) terminals, 78, 192, 193, 241, 250
Polling, 87
POS (point-of-sale) system, 241, 250
POS (point-of-sale) terminals, 78, 192, 193, 241, 250
Predefined process symbol, 155, 173–175
Predefined subroutines, 100
Primary storage, 13, 216
Priming read, 155, 170–172
PRINT symbols, 123
Printer spacing chart, 101, 114–116, 186, 197, 198
Printers, 12, 14, 53, 59–67
   intelligent, 54, 72, 75
Printing devices, 53, 59–67
Private lines, 90
Problem definition, 186, 194
Problem-oriented languages, 100
Procedure-oriented languages, 100
Procedures manuals, 199
Processing, 1
   overlapped, 13, 21–24
Processing and control modules, 154, 160
Processing modules, 154, 160
Processing sequence, 155, 164–166
Processing symbols, 122, 128, 201–203
Program execution, 101, 112–113
Program flowchart loops, 122–123, 126–134
Program flowchart symbols, 125
Program flowcharts, 122, 124–153

Program packages, 215, 234, 235
Program specifications, 101, 113–117
Programmable read-only memory (PROM), 262, 268
Programming, structured, 101, 155, 167
Programming group, 185, 188
Programming languages:
   current, 100–101, 107–112
   early, 100, 102–105
   high-level, 100, 105–107
   introduction to, 100–121
   modern, 100–101, 107–112
   symbolic, 103
Programs:
   canned, 215, 234–235
   computer, 4
   supervisory, 21
PROM (programmable read-only memory), 262, 268
Pseudocode, 155, 175–178
Punch card, standard, 30–33
Purchasing versus renting equipment, 278

Quotation marks, single, 123, 138

RAM (random-access memory), 262, 268
Random access, 214, 222
Random-access feature, 216
Random-access memory (RAM), 262, 268
Raw data, 1, 4
Read-only memory (ROM), 262, 268
READ symbols, 122, 123
Read/write (R/W) heads, 214, 217, 218
Reading wands, OCR, 78
Real-time systems, 84, 89
Record layout form, 101, 115, 116
Record of a unit, 53, 57
Register, 18
Regularly scheduled listings, 240, 245–246
Reliability, 1
Remote-job-entry (RJE) stations, 84, 88–89
Removable disks, 214, 217–219
Renting versus buying equipment, 278
Report Program Generator (RPG), 101, 109–110
Reporting information to management, 240, 245–247
Reports, 1
   forecasting, 240, 246
Representatives, departmental, 208
Request for systems analysis, 195
Retrieval, 4
Review, scheduled, 186, 196
Right-justified fields, 30
RJE (remote-job-entry) stations, 84, 88–89
ROM (read-only memory), 262, 268
Rows, card, 30
RPG (Report Program Generator), 101, 109–110
R/W (read/write) heads, 214, 217, 218

Sales commission accumulation example, 145–147
Sales commission computation example, 128–132
Sales commission totals example, 141–143
Scheduled maintenance, 1, 279
Scheduled review, 186, 196
Scientific applications, 100, 107
Secondary storage, 13, 19–20, 214–239
    term, 214, 215
Sectors, 214, 219–221
Security measures, 255
Select commissions example, 147–149
Self-documentation, 106
Senior systems analyst, 208
Sequential access, 214, 222
Sequential files, 215, 230–232
Serial card readers, 53
Service bureaus, 84
Service contracts, 279
Silicon chips, 262, 268
Simple structure, 241, 251–252
Simulators, 262, 267
Simultaneously, term, 92
Slash, 128
Slave computer, 94–95
Small-scale computers, 263, 274–275
Softcopy, 12
Software, 12
    application, 279
    file, 215, 232–235
    operational, 13, 20–21
    utility, 215, 232–234
Software management, 241, 253
Sort programs, 215, 233
Source deck, 100
Source documents, 1, 6
Source programs, 100, 106
Special characters, 30
Special labels, 123, 139
Special-purpose computers, 262, 265–266
Speed, 1
Staffing requirements, 280
Standard punch card, 30–33
START symbols, 122, 126–127
STOP symbols, 122, 126–127
Storage layout form, 186, 197, 198
Structure chart, 154, 158–160
Structured design, 154–184
Structured design techniques, 155, 167–175
Structured programming, 101, 155, 167
Structured walkthroughs, 155, 179
Subroutines, 155, 175
    predefined, 100
Supercomputers, 263, 277
Supervisor control program, 21
Supervisory program, 21
Symbolic programming languages, 103
Syntax, 100, 106
System:
    design of new, 187, 205–206
    term, 189

Systems analysis, 186–188, 193–196
    and design, 185–213
    request for, 195
Systems analysts, 185, 188
    senior, 208
Systems designs, 186, 193
    alternative, 205–206
Systems documentation, 200
Systems flowcharts, 122, 124–153, 186, 200–205
Systems group, 185, 188
    and analysts, 185, 187–189
Systems narratives, 186, 201
Systems software package, 21

Tape cassettes, 214, 225
Tapes, magnetic, 13, 214, 221–224
Team structure, 189
Telecommunications, 84, 86
Teleprocessing, 84
Terminal symbols, 122, 126–127
Terminals, 6, 53–54, 67–71
    (*See also specific terminals*)
Thermal printer, 62, 63, 65
Time-sharing systems, 84, 88
Top-down design concepts, 154, 156–158
Tracks, 214, 219–221
Training, personnel, 280
Turnaround documents, 57
Twelve edge of card, 32
Twin-head printer, 62
Typesetters, automatic, 54, 76

Unconditional branch, 122, 132, 133
Unit-record concept, 53, 57
Unscheduled maintenance, 1, 279
Updating, 1
    term, 7
Utility software, 215, 232–234

Video display terminals, 54, 69
Virtual storage (VS), 14, 24–25
Visual display terminal, 14
Visual table of contents, 154, 160–162
Voice-grade channels, 84, 91
Voice input device, 70
Volume, 1
VS (virtual storage), 14, 24–25

Walkthroughs, structured, 155, 179
Wide area telephone service (WATS) line, 90
Wideband channels, 84, 91
Wire-matrix printer, 60
Word processing (WP) systems, 54, 73–76

ZIP code field, 36
Zone configuration, 46
Zone punches, 30
Zone rows, 30

Catalog

If you are interested in a list of SCHAUM'S
OUTLINE SERIES send your name
and address, requesting your free catalog, to:

SCHAUM'S OUTLINE SERIES, Dept. C
McGRAW-HILL BOOK COMPANY
1221 Avenue of Americas
New York, N.Y. 10020